Luminos is the open access monograph publishing program from UC Press. Luminos provides a framework for preserving and reinvigorating monograph publishing for the future and increases the reach and visibility of important scholarly work. Titles published in the UC Press Luminos model are published with the same high standards for selection, peer review, production, and marketing as those in our traditional program. www.luminosoa.org

Christianity, Islam, and *Orișa* Religion

THE ANTHROPOLOGY OF CHRISTIANITY

Edited by Joel Robbins

1. *Christian Moderns: Freedom and Fetish in the Mission Encounter,* by Webb Keane
2. *A Problem of Presence: Beyond Scripture in an African Church,* by Matthew Engelke
3. *Reason to Believe: Cultural Agency in Latin American Evangelicalism,* by David Smilde
4. *Chanting Down the New Jerusalem: Calypso, Christianity, and Capitalism in the Caribbean,* by Francio Guadeloupe
5. *In God's Image: The Metaculture of Fijian Christianity,* by Matt Tomlinson
6. *Converting Words: Maya in the Age of the Cross,* by William F. Hanks
7. *City of God: Christian Citizenship in Postwar Guatemala,* by Kevin O'Neill
8. *Death in a Church of Life: Moral Passion during Botswana's Time of AIDS,* by Frederick Klaits
9. *Eastern Christians in Anthropological Perspective,* edited by Chris Hann and Hermann Goltz
10. *Studying Global Pentecostalism: Theories and Methods,* by Allan Anderson, Michael Bergunder, Andre Droogers, and Cornelis van der Laan
11. *Holy Hustlers, Schism, and Prophecy: Apostolic Reformation in Botswana,* by Richard Werbner
12. *Moral Ambition: Mobilization and Social Outreach in Evangelical Megachurches,* by Omri Elisha
13. *Spirits of Protestantism: Medicine, Healing, and Liberal Christianity,* by Pamela E. Klassen
14. *The Saint in the Banyan Tree: Christianity and Caste Society in India,* by David Mosse
15. *God's Agents: Biblical Publicity in Contemporary England,* by Matthew Engelke
16. *Critical Christianity: Translation and Denominational Conflict in Papua New Guinea,* by Courtney Handman
17. *Sensational Movies: Video, Vision, and Christianity in Ghana,* by Birgit Meyer
18. *Christianity, Islam, and* Orișa *Religion: Three Traditions in Comparison and Interaction,* by J. D. Y. Peel

Christianity, Islam, and *Orișa* Religion

Three Traditions in Comparison and Interaction

J. D. Y. Peel

UNIVERSITY OF CALIFORNIA PRESS

University of California Press, one of the most distinguished university presses in the United States, enriches lives around the world by advancing scholarship in the humanities, social sciences, and natural sciences. Its activities are supported by the UC Press Foundation and by philanthropic contributions from individuals and institutions. For more information, visit www.ucpress.edu.

University of California Press
Oakland, California

Suggested citation: Peel, J.D.Y. *Christianity, Islam, and* Orișa *Religion.* Oakland: University of California Press, 2016. DOI: http://dx.doi.org/10.1525/luminos.8

Cataloguing-in-Publication Data is on file at the Library of Congress.

ISBN 978-0-520-28585-9 (paper : alk. paper)

ISBN 978-0-520-96122-7 (electronic)

24 23 22 21 20 19 18 17 16 15
10 9 8 7 6 5 4 3 2 1

For Anne
and for my grandchildren,
Josie, James, Jonny, Lizzie, Hannah, Edith . . .

CONTENTS

LIST OF ABBREVIATIONS APPEARING IN THE TEXT AND NOTES

AC	Action Congress
ACN	Action Congress of Nigeria
AD	Alliance for Democracy
AG	Action Group
AIC	African independent church
APC	African Peoples Congress
AUD	Ansar-ud-Deen Society of Nigeria
C&S	Cherubim and Seraphim
CAC	Christ Apostolic Church
CMS	Church Missionary Society
COCIN	Church of Christ in Nigeria
DMR	divergent modes of religiosity
Ecomog	Economic Group of West Africa Monitoring Group
Festac	Black and African Festival of Arts and Culture
HGCA	Carl Christian Reindorf, *History of the Gold Coast and Asante*
HY	Samuel Johnson, *History of the Yorubas*
JNI	Jamaʿatu Nasril Islam (Society for the Victory of Islam)
LASU	Lagos State University
LIA	League of Imams and Alfas
MSS	Muslim Students Society
Muswen	Muslim Ummah of South-Western Nigeria
Nasfat	Nasrul-Lahi-il-Fathi
NCNC	National Council of Nigerian and the Cameroons (later National Congress of Nigerian Citizens)

NEPA	Nigerian Electric Power Authority
NNDP	Nigerian National Democratic party
NPN	National Party of Nigeria
NSCIA	Nigerian Supreme Council of Islamic Affairs
OPC	Oodua People's Congress
PDP	People's Democratic Party
RCCG	Redeemed Christian Church of God
SDP	Social Democratic Party
SIM	Sudan Interior Mission
SOAS	School of Oriental and African Studies (University of London)
UI	University of Ibadan
UNESCO	United Nations Educational, Scientific and Cultural Organization
UPN	Unity Party of Nigeria
YTR	Yoruba traditional religion

ACKNOWLEDGMENTS

The germ from which this book grew was the Birkbeck Lectures in Ecclesiastical History, which I was invited to give in 2009 by the University of Cambridge, in conjunction with Trinity College. I was later invited to give the Bapsybanoo Marchioness of Winchester Lecture in May 2011 at the University of Oxford, hosted by the Institute of Social and Cultural Anthropology (then headed by Professor David Gellner) and All Souls College. The last chapter grew from a lecture given at the Instituto de Antropología at the Cuban Academy of Sciences in Havana, organized under the auspices of the British Academy. A two-week sojourn at the Zentrum Moderner Orient in Berlin in 2010 gave me the opportunity to present an early overview of several chapters. I remember with pleasure and gratitude the generous hospitality of all these institutions.

While African Christianity had been a principal research interest of mine for over half a century, I was increasingly aware of just how skimpy was my knowledge of Yoruba Islam. So to prepare for the Birkbeck Lectures, I decided that I needed to undertake more field research specifically on Islam. This was funded by two awards from the admirable Small Grants Scheme of the British Academy, in 2008 and 2009. For this I was based at the University of Ibadan, where the Institut Français de Recherche en Afrique (IFRA) under successive directors, Dr. Ruth Marshall and Dr. Jean-Luc Martineau, provided me with accommodation and much good company during both visits.

As a neophyte in the study of Yoruba Islam, I have been very fortunate to come to know Imam Salahuddeen Busairi, through whose example and friendship I have learned so much, especially about Muslim life in Ibadan at the local level. Professor Amidu Sanni of Lagos State University helped me greatly with contacts in Lagos and through sharing the broad sweep of his knowledge of matters Islamic. At the University of Ibadan, members of the Department of Arabic and Islamic Studies, particularly Professor M. O. Abdul-Rahmon, Dr K. K. Oloso, and Dr. L. O. Abbas, were always helpful in responding to my inquiries. For the warm reception I received on a visit to Al-Hikmah University, Ilorin, I thank its vice-chancellor, Professor R. D. Abubakre. A two-week visit to Kaduna was greatly facilitated by Fr. Matthew Kukah (now Catholic bishop of Sokoto), who also kindly arranged for Mr. Samuel Aruwan to serve as a most knowledgeable guide round the city.

As over many years past, my time in Ibadan was greatly enhanced by the company of old friends: above all by Professor J. F. Ade Ajayi—may he rest in peace—his wife, Christie, and other members of his family; by Segun Oke, Tunji and Funmi Oloruntimehin, Bolanle Awe, Tunde Adegbola, and Chris Bankole. I cannot omit mention of the Ven. J. S. Adekoya and his parishioners of St Paul's Church, Yemetu, who extended the hand of fellowship to me on Sunday mornings.

I have gained more from the help of friends, colleagues, and former students, in discussing ideas, making suggestions, and commenting on the draft chapters of this book than I can readily acknowledge. Preeminent here is the long conversation I have had since the mid-1960s with Robin Horton, which has done so much to sharpen my own thinking. I am greatly indebted to Tom McCaskie for the countless exchanges we have enjoyed over the years, as well as to my long-term colleagues in the School of Oriental and African Studies (SOAS) Richard Fardon and Paul Gifford. Ruth Marshall, Hermione Harris, Michelle Gilbert, Caroline Ifeka, Murray Last, Karin Barber, Paulo Farias, Keith Hart, Louis Brenner, Birgit Meyer, David and Bernice Martin, David Maxwell, Joel Robbins, Michael Carrithers, David Gellner, Trevor Marchand, Gabi vom Bruck, Marloes Janson, Stephan Palmié, Matthews Ojo, Frank Ukah, Akin Oyetade, David Pratten, Kai Kresse, Amanda Villepastour, and Wale Adebanwi have all helped me more than they probably know. I am indebted to Duncan Clarke for providing me with the image for the book's front cover. It shows an *adire*-cloth design known as *Ibadan dun* (Ibadan is sweet), an evocation of the great Yoruba city where my research began and ended.

J.D.Y.P.
London
Easter 2015

Introduction

In May 2013 a young man called Michael Adebolajo, London-born and of Christian Yoruba background, hacked a soldier to death with a cleaver, in broad daylight, outside the military barracks in Woolwich, southeast London. He did this in the name of Islam, to which religion he had converted some years before. When he was charged in court a week later, he brandished a Koran and shouted *Allahu akbar!* to underscore the point, and likewise his accomplice, another young man of similar background. The incident was shocking enough in itself, to people of all religions and ethnicities, though it was not unthinkable, as it would have been a few years earlier. It led to a range of what are, by now, fairly predictable public responses, ranging from the criminal and disgraceful, such as retaliatory attacks on mosques, to the evasive and implausible, such as the insistence of Muslim leaders and some others that the attack "had nothing to do with Islam."

No doubt the backstories to this incident—the preconditions that we need to know to make it rightly intelligible in all its detail—ramify so widely in time and space as to pass beyond the bounds of any final understanding of what happened. In the main, they are stories of movement and change, and stories that serve to connect people and religion. If we start from the Yoruba background of the perpetrator, there has been for decades a large-scale migration of Yoruba to London. It goes back to the 1950s—a time bright with the prospect of Nigerian independence—when the migrants' main motive was to gain qualifications to enhance their life chances when they returned home. A good majority of them were already Christians when they came, and their migration was grounded in a process of social transformation that already went back for more than a century. A key element in this was the conversion of roughly half the Yoruba to Christianity, the other half becoming Muslim. "Conversion" was never a narrowly religious process, for it went with the adoption of a whole complex of values: education as a key to personal and communal advancement, progress and prosperity, modernity.

Over the years the Yoruba have grown to become the largest single African-heritage group in London. They have brought with them the whole spectrum of their rich associational life, including a great variety of churches, among which Pentecostalism now bulks large. At the same time, they have become socially differentiated in British terms, ranging from a substantial professional stratum to a mass of middle- and lower-income folk, mostly concentrated in a broad swath of south London stretching from Brixton to Thamesmead. Some of their children (to the anxiety of their parents) were drawn into the multicultural lifeworld of inner-city youth, with its linkages to delinquency, drugs, and gang violence. A measure of disaffection from mainstream society and its institutions was fueled by the experience of racism, especially at the hands of the police.

Among the various forms that disaffection may take, radical Islam has emerged as an option attracting young men from diverse cultural origins. Though Adebolajo came from a solid family background and was popular at school, he went through a period of teenage alienation in which he was involved in petty crime (dealing in marijuana, stealing mobile phones, etc.) before becoming a Muslim at the age of sixteen, to the dismay of his Christian family. The bitter irony of his having adopted a violently jihadist form of Islam is that Yoruba Islam is not at all like this. In Yorubaland, Islam and Christianity, although rivals, coexist peaceably within a framework of shared community values, in marked contrast to the situation in Northern Nigeria, where a jihadist tradition has contributed to a pattern of endemic religious violence whose most recent manifestation is the militant Islamist organization known as Boko Haram. Paradoxically, if Adebolajo's own background had been Muslim rather than Christian, he would probably have been *less* susceptible to jihadism, since he would have lacked the incentive to that self-proving extremism that is so commonly a mark of the convert. Yet in the end, his Yoruba or Nigerian background is less relevant to what he became—he might as easily have been Jamaican or Ghanaian—than certain conditions provided by the worlds of multicultural London and of global Islam.

The Islamist group that played the prime role in radicalizing Adebolajo was a later-banned organization called Al-Muhajiroun. Its name (The Emigrants) alludes to an epochal event in early Islamic history, the Prophet's withdrawal (*hijra*) with a group of companions from Mecca to Medina in 622. The contemporary sources of Muslim anger (colonialism, the Israeli occupation of the West Bank, the invasion of Afghanistan, etc.) were thus configured in terms of a long-span vision of Islam's history that also yields precedents for action. The most consequential *hijra* in West African history was surely that of Shaykh Usman dan Fodio in 1804, which led to the launching of the jihad that established the Sokoto Caliphate and that has deeply shaped the politicoreligious order of Northern Nigeria ever since. Though religious traditions (which include much more than what is in their scriptures) are capacious and multivocal, they still give a strong cultural steer to the actions and aspirations of their adherents. This occurs not automatically but through a complex, two-way exchange between the messages of the tradition and the pressures of the contexts in which believers turn to it for guidance. So debates among Muslims about the import of their faith are, from an anthropological perspective, directly constitutive of it. At the same time, where grievances arising in a specific context are articulated through the lens of a world religion, connections are necessarily made across large gulfs of time and space. The full explication of what happened on 22 May 2013 thus points toward an analysis that is both comparative and historical.

. . .

The story just told has touched on many of the general themes of this book: religious conversion, new movements in Islam and Christianity, relations between world religions, the conditions of religious violence or amity, the transnational flows of contemporary religion, the interplay between tradition and the demands of an ever-changing present. The people at the center of the story are the Yoruba of southwestern Nigeria, who are also the starting point for the various comparative forays, both internal and external, that are undertaken in the course of it. They are the second largest language group (over 35 million) in Nigeria and are concentrated in its most developed region, Lagos and its hinterland, reaching some two hundred miles into the interior. Before their incorporation into the colonial state, they formed a cluster of a few dozens of mostly small kingdoms or city-states, among which a few larger ones achieved periods of wider regional domination, notably Oyo (up to ca. 1830) and its principal successor state, Ibadan. The name Yoruba came into currency as a self-designation only in the late nineteenth century, but there is no reason to doubt a good measure of cultural continuity between today's Yoruba and the culture of classical Ife (fl. 11th–16th centuries), known for its magnificent bronzes. Ife (which Yoruba have also seen as the site of their cosmogony) is powerfully evoked in the myths of the *oriṣa* (deities), who are the centerpiece of their traditional religion.

For over four hundred years the Yoruba have straddled two geocultural spheres, one reaching north over the Sahara to the world of Islam, the other linking them via the Atlantic to the Euro-American world. Besides their trade networks, these two external spheres were the source of contrasting cultural influences, notably those emanating from the world religions (Islam probably going back at least to the seventeenth century, Christianity to the mid-nineteenth). Since it was only in the late 1930s that these religions, taken together, came to command the allegiance of a majority of Yoruba, there is the unusual theoretical bonus that we can compare *three* religions in one society. Moreover, the Yoruba have not only imported

Islam and Christianity but have also exported their own *orișa* religion to the New World. Besides the voluntary modern diaspora that has created Yoruba communities in London and elsewhere in Euro-America, there was an earlier involuntary diaspora, reaching its peak in the second quarter of the nineteenth century, which took tens of thousands of them as slaves to the New World, and with them *orișa* religion. Ironically, the internal disruption that fueled those wars of enslavement also contributed to the spread of Islam and Christianity among the Yoruba at home. The intertwined character of the three religions in Yorubaland and the dense imbrication of religion in all other aspects of its history are what this book sets out to explore.

. . .

The research on which this book is based goes back now over half a century, to when I first went to Nigeria, in 1964. The five chapters of Part I are revised versions of papers published between 1987 and 2009, while those of Part II all largely depend on research done since 2008, were written as a set, and appear here for the first time. Part II deals largely with Islam and the contemporary situation, but so much of the ground for it was laid in the earlier papers that it made for greater completeness and coherence in the collection as a whole for them to be included. All the chapters are strongly comparative in their approach. Their thematic sequence bears the traces of an interlinked double history, between how the religious scene in Yorubaland and Nigeria at large has evolved since the 1960s, and how its study has developed. Of course these two strands do not move in lockstep: apart from the inevitable time lag between social reality and its representation, or between history as lived and history as written, the study of Nigerian religion has been shaped by currents in African studies at large, as well as by intellectual trends grounded outside Africa altogether. It is almost normal that a research project of any duration—from its conception through research and writing to final publication—will be framed in one social and intellectual context and find itself concluded in another; and will so bear the traces of its own history.

Fifty years ago Nigeria was coming to the end of the first flush of its postcolonial existence, and my first book, *Aladura* (1968), being a study of independent churches that emerged in the midcolonial period, fitted in with the nationalist zeitgeist. Such churches were often placed within a larger literature on supposedly similar movements in other colonial settings—cargo cults, millennial and "revitalization" movements, and so forth—that saw them as "religions of the oppressed" or applied a Marxist schema that viewed them as the immature precursors of a political nationalism that would supersede them.[1] Closer analysis, however, led me to see the Aladura rather differently: "nationalist" in being a self-directed African initiative, but one addressed to practical and existential problems that arose from the encounter between two religions and cultures under specific colonial conditions.

What followed on from *Aladura* was strongly shaped by the review essay of it written by Robin Horton, which branched out from appreciation through critique to develop a general and influential theory of African conversion.[2] Horton's theory treated both colonialism and the world religions as merely catalysts of a process of cognitive adjustment grounded in indigenous terms. Its clarity and generalizability allowed the theory to be greatly taken up, applied, confirmed, rebutted, or qualified over the next twenty years. But religious change tends to be a very multidimensional process, and there were important aspects that his theory neglected or underplayed. To draw these out, comparison was an essential instrument. I had previously made use of internal Yoruba comparison to throw light on the spatial patterns of conversion within Yorubaland, and now I used an external comparison to test his theory.[3] This took two polities, the Ijebu-Yoruba and the better-known case of Buganda in East Africa, which both experienced mass conversion movements in the 1890s. What that comparison showed was that beneath considerable surface differences were linkages of conditions and outcomes similar to those that Horton had proposed. But a more searching comparison, one that would not just confirm the theory as far as it went but drive the analysis of religious change forward on a broader front, would need to be one where the conditions specified by the theory went with divergent outcomes. Such appeared to be the case when the Yoruba were compared with the Akan of southern Ghana.

That paper appears below as chapter 1: "History, Culture and the Comparative Method: A West African Puzzle." The puzzle was defined as such within the terms of Horton's theory. Since the relevant conditions, of increase in social scale, were equally present in both societies, why was the patterning of conversion over time so different, with the Yoruba being precocious and the Akan tardy? My answer was that this needed to be explained by a factor that lies quite outside the terms of the theory, namely the role of religion in a society's political integration. Now, there was produced in the 1960s and 1970s a substantial literature on the conditions of political centralization in precolonial West African kingdoms. This had its theoretical roots in a genre of regional comparative studies that had grown up in British social anthropology since the 1940s and had led to a revival of interest in the "comparative method" as a distinctive feature of anthropology. But there was inadequate recognition that comparison had been practiced in a number of very different modes and that hardly anyone (except Radcliffe-Brown) was still attached to the classic comparative method that nineteenth-century social theorists had advocated. The ahistorical character of most anthropological comparison became a problem when the work on West African kingdoms required a measure of convergence between anthropology and history. For there was still a strong penchant to discount cultural factors (including religion) and to look for social-structural or technoecological factors to explain variations between kingdoms. Since the former were seen as essentially a reflection of social structure, they could produce only circular explanations. But culture is the way that the past of a society reaches into its present, to continuously inform the choices and actions through which social forms are realized. Akan/Asante and Yoruba each derived from their pasts a view of what mattered to them, to which what we may call "religion" was integral; and this underlay their differential responses to the challenge presented by the world religions. What this perspective allows us to address is something neglected in Horton's very "cool" view of religious change—as a process of cognitive adjustment to change in the conditions of social life—namely as a "hot" process often attended by passion, conflict, and violence.

This argument, without doubt, was speculative, because our factual knowledge of West African religions as historical entities is so patchy and limited. So with the aim of developing it through a substantial comparative study of religion in the forest kingdoms of precolonial West Africa (Oyo, Asante, Dahomey, and Benin), I thought I had better begin by getting a better picture of Yoruba religion itself. So I embarked on an exhaustive reading of what is by far the richest documentary source, the archive of the Church Missionary Society (CMS), an evangelical Anglican body that started its Yoruba operations in the 1840s. Over several years this led to a displacement of my original objective, as I came to write a detailed account of the encounter between evangelical Christianity and the Yoruba when their indigenous *orịṣa* religion was still absolutely predominant.[4]

As historians tend to appreciate better than anthropologists, theoretical objectives have to be adjusted to what the source material makes possible. Yet a theoretical thrust can still make itself felt, even though it may entail brushing against the grain of the evidence. I wanted to tell as much as possible a Yoruba story, a story with a Yoruba starting point and the story of an African initiative in religion (as *Aladura* had been), even though the evidence was almost entirely derived from missionary reports. So it was a great help that so much of this material—as well as the greatest literary achievement of the mission, Samuel Johnson's *History of the Yorubas*—had been written by the African agents of the CMS. Even so, in the writing of *Religious Encounter and the Making of the Yoruba* the greatest challenge was not to give an adequate account of the encounter itself but to avoid anachronism in reconstructing what *orịṣa* religion had been at the first point of encounter and to be especially careful in doing what is very hard to avoid, namely filling the gaps in the evidence from what "traditional" religion had *subsequently* come to be. What we too readily forget is that "tradition" itself is subject to change. Chapters 2 and 3 deal with the two sides of the encounter.

Chapter 2 follows on directly from chapter 1 in that it involves a comparison between the pioneer local historians of the same two societies: Samuel Johnson of the Yoruba and C. C. Reindorf of Akan/Asante. As a comparison it is uneven, since it is much more a study of the making of Johnson as a historian, beside whom Reindorf stands mainly as a foil. So the play of resemblance and contrast, which is the essence of comparison, is used more for expository than explanatory purposes. Its aim is to bring out the singularity of Johnson's achievement, in transmuting his social experience so as to produce the extraordinary work that came to play such a large role in forming modern Yoruba identity.

Chapter 3 is complementary to chapter 2, since it is a sample analysis of the other side of the equation, namely what Johnson, as a Christian missionary, pitched himself *against*. Yet it would have been impossible to write without the evidence about nineteenth-century life, especially the worship of the deities (*orișa*), that Johnson and his colleagues provided in their journals. Its subject, Ogun, the god of iron, was arguably the most extensively worshipped of the quite small number of truly pan-Yoruban deities. The argument is built around two axes of comparison. The first contrasts different regions of Yorubaland, showing that the worship of particular *orișa* varied from one region to another; and the second compares Ogun and other *orișa*, showing that many of their functions and attributes were not stable but variable between one *orișa* and another. The paradox here is that, though Johnson and his fellow Yoruba clergy subscribed strongly to the idea of an essential Yoruba unity—evident in the standard form of the language that they actively promoted and the legend of common descent from Ife as "the cradle of the race," which they accepted as historical truth—their concrete observations, taken in the aggregate, tend to undermine it. We are left with a picture of "Yoruba traditional religion" as a dynamic entity, with fluid and malleable deities, less a single religion than a spectrum of local cult complexes.

With chapters 4 and 5 we come forward in time, both in the real time of the events and in the time of writing. They stand loosely together, for they both focus on Pentecostalism, but their approaches differ according to the logic of the comparison that they employ. Both were commissioned for conferences dealing with wider-than-African themes, so the consideration of Yoruba matters is subsumed within a wider theoretical or thematic framework. As in chapter 1, the argument of chapter 4 is driven by a theory-led contrast, this time Harvey Whitehouse's distinction between two modes of religiosity, which he terms "imagistic" and "doctrinal."[5] These depend on two contrasting forms of memory by which religions may perpetuate themselves but that are variably present in particular cases. Since this model is abstracted from the contrast between the indigenous religions of Papua New Guinea and mission Christianity, its relevance to the situation of West Africa is obvious. And since as a model it is abstract, it allows us in principle to make comparisons between religions in many other situations, such as between different indigenous cults or religions, or different forms of world religion. Chapter 4 applies it across the long span of Yoruba religious forms, from those of the *orișa* to Aladura and contemporary Pentecostalism, finding that the success of the latter can be seen in terms of how Pentecostalists are able to combine elements of both the imagistic and doctrinal modes.

Chapter 5, by contrast, takes off from an empirical comparison—between the post-Soviet and the postcolonial African worlds—and so follows a more open and exploratory path.[6] It opens with the unlikely story of an Ijebu-Yoruba founding the largest Pentecostal church in the Ukraine—which prompts us to ask: What it is about Pentecostalism and the present global conjuncture that makes such an outcome possible? The argument proceeds by a series of ad hoc but strategic comparisons: between the articulations of religion and polity in the two regions; between different former colonial regimes in Africa in terms of their propensity to adopt socialist solutions to their problems after independence; and among the three African regimes (Benin, Mozambique, and Ethiopia) that claimed to be Marxist-Leninist. It culminates in an analysis of how Pentecostalism gained massively after the fall of these regimes at the end of the 1980s and why it has such appeal in the neoliberal world order.

. . .

Part II, like Part I, opens with a chapter of much wider scope, which sets out the theoretical basis for the empirical studies that follow. Whereas the chapters of Part I mostly compare contexts (societies, regions, states, etc.) to clarify the conditions under which religions—chiefly forms of Christianity—gain support or take on a particular character, in Part II the main logic of comparison is reversed: Christianity and Islam are compared within a single setting, first Yorubaland and then Nigeria as a whole. And while in the papers of Part I comparison is mainly an analytical instrument of the observer, in Part II it also comes into the picture as part of what is observed, namely as a key aspect of the interaction between the two religions.

Islam got all too short shrift in the earlier papers. While this might be considered venial in an author whose main interest has been on Yoruba Christianity, it also reflects a serious weakness in the literature on modern Yoruba religion as a whole. There has never been a serious in-depth anthropological study of Yoruba Islam and virtually the only historical study appeared over thirty years ago.[7] References to Yoruba Muslims in writing on modern politics are quite frequent but brief, and the specific character of Yoruba Islam gets little detailed attention. For that, one has to turn to scholars grounded in religious or Islamic studies. As academic disciplines these tend to be very distinct, with the former mainly the province of non-Muslims, the latter of Muslims—a division unfortunately now solidified in the organization of Nigerian universities.[8] Much of the research produced in the latter has a strong literary or philological bent, though it also contains very useful material on Islamic movements, aspects of Muslim religious life, and the intellectual concerns of the *ulama*. There is much of value in Ph.D. theses, particularly from the Arabic and Islamic Studies Department at Ibadan, but these nearly all remain unpublished. In 2008 and 2009, I undertook six months' fieldwork, mainly collecting local documentary materials and conducting interviews with Yoruba Muslims. I found myself on a steep learning curve. In the comparative chapters that follow, I have tried to give particular attention to Islam in order to do something to even up the coverage that the two religions have received in the past.

Chapter 6 picks up from where the argument of chapter 1 ended, with its plea, against the dominant tendency in social anthropology, for a mode of comparison that takes seriously the fact that societies have histories, meaning that they are shaped by the reach of the past into the present that we call culture. Now, the world religions may be seen as an ideal terrain for exploring this, with their richly documented histories and their realization in so many culturally diverse settings. Yet anthropology was slow to study them and slower to attempt any theorization of them as objects of study. Eventually this got under way not at a generic level but rather as a series of religion-specific initiatives, hardly connected with one another: an anthropology of Islam started to emerge in the 1970s,[9] then Buddhism and Hinduism,[10] and last of all Christianity. Chapter 6 argues that these need to be brought together in a common comparative framework, not just because of their close coexistence in today's world but because they present common analytical problems. The main one is how to treat the characteristic features of religion *X* without defining it in terms of a single set of enduring attributes (an "essence") that is held to underlie all its manifestations. I argue that we can avoid this through a notion of tradition, which reciprocally interacts with the contexts through which it passes over time and by which it is simultaneously reproduced and transformed.

The extended comparison of Christianity and Islam as they have developed in the one Yoruba context, which follows in chapters 7–9, shows this in operation. These three chapters, all covering roughly the same time span, explore from different angles the complex patterns of convergence and divergence that have played out between Muslims and Christians over the long twentieth century. The Yoruba context was not, of course, historically static, but a large component of it, a nexus of values built round the notion of community, did serve to connect the Yoruba to a sense of their own past—and not least to certain aspects of their "traditional" *orișa* religion, which overall they were in the process of abandoning.

Chapter 7 thus begins by analyzing the process of conversion to the world religions. It goes on to examine how the new potential for religious conflict that they brought was checked by strongly held community values, and how each community of faith still drew on its inherited cultural template to realize itself institutionally in the Yoruba setting. Yet Yoruba religious amity is to be seen not as a timeless cultural absolute but as always needing to be worked at; and at times it has come under strain. This showed above all in the sphere of modern politics, which initially was dominated by Christians, because of their higher level of education. The significant measure of Muslim disaffection that had emerged by the 1980s has since receded, as the Yoruba default system was restored, and the Muslim/Christian divide was neutralized as a source of political cleavage.

Chapter 8 turns to a countertendency that arises from the cultural trajectories inherent in each religion's history. Staring from a baseline around 1870, when Islam was widely seen as much better adapted to Yoruba culture than Christianity was, I draw a systematic contrast between the Christian project of inculturation or Africanization, and the Muslim "Reformist" project, which tended toward the adoption of a more universalizing form of Islam. The outcome has been that Muslims are now more likely than Christians to set themselves off from previously shared Yoruba attributes by adopting marks of religious distinctiveness. The acme of this, Sharia law, adumbrates the possibility of further cultural divergence, but it remains unappealing to the great mass of Yoruba Muslims and an unrealizable objective in the foreseeable future.

At the same time, this divergent tendency is checked by a counterforce that fosters convergence, which paradoxically has its roots in the very fact of the competition between the two religions. Since the Yoruba religious field is like a marketplace with potential converts as consumers, local criteria of religious value will tend to prevail, giving the rival faiths a strong incentive to borrow effective elements from each other. Chapter 9 traces this process over time, noting shifts in the direction and content of the borrowing that has taken place. Since the rise of neo-Pentecostalism since the 1980s, influence has flowed mainly from Christianity to Islam, evoking a range of Muslim responses, of which the most notable has been NASFAT, the largest new movement in Yoruba Islam. Yet again there is a check: the market model, while illuminating, is itself limited by constraints arising from within the distinctive traditions of each faith.

In chapters 10 and 11, the geographical focus is expanded, first to Nigeria at large and then beyond Africa. Chapter 10 examines critically the claim that Pentecostalism has its mirror image in "fundamentalist" Islam, or Salafism. For comparative purposes the argument moves from Yorubaland, where Pentecostalism is strong, Salafism weak, and interfaith relations peaceable, to Northern Nigeria, where Salafism is strong and interfaith conflict has been acute and often violent. I argue that, despite some formal resemblances, their ethos and historical trajectories have little in common and have very different implications for the Nigerian public sphere. The argument is clinched by a comparative reading of two recent histories by Yoruba authors—a Pentecostal view of Nigerian Christianity and a Salafist one of Nigerian Islam—which brings out how radically divergent are the conceptions of state, nation, and culture promoted by the two traditions.

An irony of Yoruba religion today is that whereas the *orìṣa* cults in Nigeria itself (Circle 1, the historical baseline) are deep in decline, eclipsed by the two Abrahamic faiths that demonize them (Circle 2), *orìṣa* religion in the New World (Circle 3) is flourishing and spreading. Yet the two sets of phenomena, of interest to different bodies of scholars (and believers), have been studied largely in isolation from each other—which chapter 11, in a very preliminary way, attempts to rectify. I conclude with reflections on the cross-pressures of re-Africanization and universalization evident in Circle 3, as phenomena of religious globalization.

. . .

The essays are linked not just by their Yoruba point of reference but by their commitment to comparison as a tool of analysis. It is odd that comparativism has had such a faltering, on-and-off presence in the history of anthropology, granted that the "comparative method" was virtually its founding charter.[11] But it came to be widely seen as an embarrassment, whether because of its link with a discredited unilinear evolutionism, or because its generalizations failed the test of evidence, or because it seemed wedded to a scientific program too exclusively positivist. The well-worn antinomies of nomothetic (generalizing) vs. idiographic (particularizing) or of causalistic vs. hermeneutic analysis have given rise too readily to an overlimited view of the possibilities of comparison. If the blind trial of a newly developed drug in medical research may be taken as a kind of gold standard in the use of comparison to test causal relations, the social sciences can still go some way to emulate this within the limits of what is practicable for their subject matter, as with the statistical analysis of large data sets used in the study of social mobility. These are theory-led inquiries, which are made easier if the data can be "constructed" in a controlled way, as when informants are questioned. But even when these strict conditions cannot be met, the same logic underlies more informal and open-ended comparisons. Historians (and to a large extent anthropologists) have to work with the evidence as they find it, and their comparisons mostly arise from given circumstances, such as a historic path not taken, the contrast with a neighbor, the divergent actions of two groups within a nation or region, and so forth. Such comparisons are often ad hoc, made within the flow of a narrative and various in their aims: to bring to light new factors, to clarify or rule out causal hunches, to give a sharper definition to probable connections. And moving right away from positivistic or cause-seeking conceptions of the comparative method, what could be more essentially comparative than translation between languages, the very germ of hermeneutics?[12]

Comparison is in fact so basic to human beings' engagement with the world in which they live that it is as integral to mundane, practical reasoning as in its more formalized and systematic applications. It is at least implicitly present whenever there are choices to be faced. It belongs as much to *pensée sauvage* as to scientific inquiry, as much to the moral as to the cognitive options that human beings face. For wherever it is applied, comparison implies difference, and so opens up a range of possibilities for seeing the world and for living life differently. Few subjects take us more directly to comparison in social practice than those treated in this book, such as conversion from one faith to another and the interaction between religions. What the anthropologist or historian attempts, therefore, is both a meta-activity and a deeper and more systematic pursuit of the same activity, albeit from a more detached subject position, than those engaged in the practical comparison of religions can usually manage. It thus has the potential to flow across from the study of the social processes of religion in history to a real-life engagement with them.

In the five or so years that this book has been in the writing, violent Islamism has shot up the register of public attention, in Nigeria as in the rest of the world, and this is reflected in the content of its later chapters. It seems fair to say that much more discussion, at least in the West, has been given to how to control it than to understand what gives rise to it. As to the latter, there are diametrically opposed opinions, with *It's nothing to do with Islam* and *That's the way that Islam is* at the extremes. Comparison can release us from these hopeless polarities, because it opens up a wider range of possibilities and enables us to choose between them. And here there is a way for Nigeria not just to address its own agony over Boko Haram but to serve a wider purpose, since it furnishes two sharply contrasting cases—Yorubaland and the North—that suggest two broad conditions for the absence or presence of religious violence, which have their analogues in many other situations. The first is sociological: the crosscutting of communal and religious ties (universal in Yorubaland, much rarer in the North), which greatly raises the cost of religious violence and so reduces its incidence. The second is cultural: the virtual absence from Yorubaland of a jihadist tradition, such as had such has a strong presence within Northern Islam.[13]

In general, we are much more inhibited about probing the cultural than the social conditions of Islamist violence, whether because we feel it is politically inexpedient,[14] or because we wish to avoid essentializing Islam, or because we don't want to be accused of Islamophobia. That perhaps explains the very circumspect tone in which Michael Cook argues that the exceptional degree of Islam's engagement in modern politics, compared with other religions, has clear roots in its heritage, going right back to the teaching and example of its Prophet.[15] Violence as such, except implicitly under the headings of jihad and warfare, does not figure saliently in his analysis, though it is the inescapable concomitant of any attempt to turn a confessional community into a state, as the Prophet and his successors set out to do; and the Prophet was not squeamish in endorsing violence when he thought it justified.[16] Cook's compelling case for the capacity of Islam for political mobilization rests primarily on his mastery of the foundational texts of Islam and of works by later Muslim scholars, in relation to the course of Islamic history as informed by them; but it is strengthened by a systematic comparison with Hinduism in India and Catholicism in Latin America, where he finds this capacity lacking. His conclusion is carefully balanced: "no [religion's] heritage is a reliable predictor of the behaviour of those who inherit it, but just as surely heritages are not interchangeable."[17] The implication is that while a religion's tradition can be powerfully constrained by any fresh context in which it is realized, it still makes some responses to fresh contexts more or less likely than others; and that produces what we regard as the typical features of that religion in practice. But here a limitation arising from the broad scope of Cook's book shows itself. Because he has to compare the religions in the different regions of the world where they have been dominant, there can be little contextual overlap (except to a degree in South Asia) between the three cases. This means that the power of comparison cannot be fully brought to bear on the crucible where religions are at their most concrete, the social contexts where traditions prove themselves. The sparrow hawk coursing the hedgerows is closer to its quarry than the eagle scanning the ideological terrain from on high. So I offer a historical anthropology of a context where Islam and Christianity both coexist and interact with each other: the exemplary Yoruba, who have so much to tell us about how different religions can live together in peace.

PART I

1

History, Culture, and the Comparative Method

A West African Puzzle

At the most general level, comparison is not a special method or in any way unique to anthropology.[1] Comparison is implicit in any method of deriving understanding through *explanation*—that is, by determining the sufficient and necessary conditions for the existence or occurrence of any phenomenon or action. To say *why* a thing is so is to indicate particular obtaining conditions, and it follows that where these conditions obtain otherwise, so also must the object of explanation. If it does not, the adequacy of the alleged explanatory conditions, or the description of the *explanandum,* or both, are called into question. Comparison's key role, then, is as a test on explanations, in the manner classically set out in John Stuart Mill's *System of Logic,* the Method of Difference providing a more powerful test than the Method of Agreement.[2] This is as true in principle for explanations of occurrences in daily life as it is for those sought in science, as true for explanation of sociocultural as of natural phenomena. The more elaborate or systematic explanations that we call theories may be little invoked in fields like history or textual criticism, but the logic of explanation is still present in such seemingly idiographic exercises as the construction of a plausible chain of events in history or the determination of a most likely reading in a classical text.

But the West African puzzle of my chapter title does arise from a theory: namely the systematic explanation that Robin Horton has given for the widespread occurrence, timing, and distribution of conversion to the world religions in Africa over the past two centuries.[3] Briefly, it explains this as an adaptive response to changes in the scale of people's social experience. As traditional African religions make cogent sense of living in localized, small-scale communities, so when people move into a wider field of social relations—as through labor migration or more extensive trade networks—they are drawn to more general, transcendental forms of religion. This theory made much sense of the Yoruba data (see further chapter 7) but failed completely to explain why the trajectory of religious change of the seemingly comparable Akan should be so different. Since the Akan yield nothing to the Yoruba in terms of the kind of factors that Horton's theory specifies as relevant to conversion—they even had earlier direct relations with Europe, a richer export-oriented colonial economy, the earlier development of modern education, and so on—why should their religious development have been markedly so much slower and more uneven?

In 1960, according to the *Population Census of Ghana,* just over 60 percent of all the Akan were reported as being adherents of world religions, the great majority of them Christians. By contrast, already by 1952 well over 80 percent of Yoruba were Christians or Muslims, though the proportions varied considerably by region.[4] By 1960 the difference between the two peoples had grown to over 30 percent. Only after the mid-1960s did this gap start to close, with the further growth of Christianity among the Akan. Other divergent features of their religious histories appear to correlate with the difference. In fact, what first pointed me in this direction was puzzlement as to why the strains of high colonialism had produced a Christian-prophet movement known as Aladura among the Yoruba, whereas the main Akan response had been to turn to pagan antiwitchcraft shrines.[5]

So we have to look elsewhere than to the factors specified in Horton's microcosm-to-macrocosm theory in order to explain the Akan/Yoruba difference. The explanation I shall eventually propose—that it is to do with the contrasting relationship between religion and political authority in the two societies—will involve us in a critical reappraisal of the strong comparative literature produced by social anthropologists, mostly in the 1960s and 1970s, about the conditions of state formation in West Africa. But to get our intellectual bearings here, it is helpful to go further back and consider the tradition of comparative study from which it arose, and in which *the* comparative method occupied a central position. This was seen as a means toward developing a natural science of society, in opposition to history as the study of unique sequences of events. But it has been far from being a unified enterprise; and I shall argue that it has involved several distinct modes, which differ in how they handle history. This will bring us back to the Akan/Yoruba contrast, where I shall argue that they need to be compared in their histories, not (as with most anthropological comparison) as static social systems.

MODES OF THE COMPARATIVE METHOD

The comparative method, sometimes argued to be *the* method of social anthropology[6] or treated as if it were one, single thing,[7] exists in at least five distinct modes:

1. a single, universal, ideal history or natural history of society;

2. a branching, concrete history, on the model of comparative philology;
3. where history is denied or ignored, as comparison is used to derive sociological universals or general laws;
4. where a degree of common history is presumed, as in regional comparative studies;
5. where it is histories, not societies, that are compared.

These modes tend to be products of particular historical moments, but at the same time they have a perennial appeal, since they represent distinct logical options for the analysis of social phenomena.

Mode I: An Ideal, Universal History

Mode I began as a projected natural history of society or *histoire raisonnée;* and it involved the search for a single, logically appropriate (and hence also normative) sequence of stages. The comparative method was to provide the confirming evidence. This mode existed fully fledged by the 1760s and 1770s in the four-stages theory of Smith, Turgot, and Millar.[8] The presents of backward societies were the equivalent of the pasts of advanced societies, so that comparative evidence from contemporary non-European societies could be used to fill in or corroborate evidence for stages of Europe's past. "It is in [the American Indians'] present condition we are to behold, as in a mirror, the features of our own progenitors."[9] The nineteenth century produced much fresh data, more complicated stage models, and several special applications (e.g., to marriage types, forms of religion), as well as the authoritative paradigm of comparative anatomy and physiology, worked through most thoroughly in Herbert Spencer's theory of social evolution; but the basic components were the same.

Though social evolution had ceased to be the absolutely paramount form of social thought by 1914, this mode of the comparative method continued to be practiced in anthropology for some time. Indeed one could hardly find better instances of it than in such late works as those by L. T. Hobhouse, G. C. Wheeler, and Morris Ginsberg, or by A. M. Hocart.[10] Neoevolutionism apart, some of its devices continue to find valid heuristic employment within projects of a quite different overall character. For example, the device of using an undeveloped community as a model to reconstruct the baseline form from which a culturally related but developed community has grown has been used by M. G. Smith (contemporary Abuja = pre-Fulani Zaria) and Robin Horton (contemporary Niger Delta fishing villages = New Calabar before the Atlantic trade).[11]

Mode II: A Branching, Concrete History

Mode II emerged in the early nineteenth century, its paradigm being comparative philology. The achievement of William Jones and Franz Bopp was to explain the affinities between Greek, Sanskrit, and other languages in terms of their descent from a putative common ancestor, Indo-European, and to work out rules governing the phonological shifts that lay between them. The essential point of comparison here was to reconstruct a particular *ur*-form, the actual histories of the languages being paths of divergence from it. Compared with Mode I, Mode II dealt with several actual histories rather than with one ideal or normative history, and its focus was the point of origin or departure rather than the path of development from it. Moreover, whereas Mode I depended on a unity grounded *in nature* ("the psychic unity of mankind"), Mode II pointed to a limited and *cultural* unity, that of the Indo-European (or Ural-Altaic, or Semitic, . . .) stock. A linguistic version of Mode I was found in a theory like Alexander von Humboldt's, which held that *all* languages, by virtue of their common human nature, pass through the same sequence of developmental stages. Even in modern anthropology there are instances of Mode II, such as Luc de Heusch's study of Bantu mythologies.[12] Besides Claude Lévi-Strauss, the major influence on de Heusch was the work of Georges Dumézil on the transformations of mythical archetypes in Indo-European cultures.[13] Both Dumézil and de Heusch, characteristically, are more concerned to demonstrate the existence of an *ur*-form that serves to bring out the resemblances between diverse myths than to map the historical path of that model's transformations.

COMPARISON: FOR OR AGAINST HISTORY?

All use of the comparative method in the nineteenth century, and especially in its dominant Mode I, was informed by two profound inclinations. The first was to reduce a vast and perplexing variety by postulating an underlying unity of some kind: in the terms of Mill's *Logic* the Method of Agreement got vastly more attention than the Method of Difference. Consequently, the manifest variations or differences are less often explained than set aside or treated as superficial: comparative analysis thus pointed away from history.

Second, there was the impulse to make sense of things in terms of how they had come to be, in terms of origins, sources, or paths. That led Auguste Comte to regard the comparative method (Mode I) as a *méthode historique,* which for him also had the appeal of providing scientific grounds for divining the path into the future. But this is a historical approach only in a very particular sense: in the sense of dealing with time and change but not in the sense of dealing with the unique totalities or conjunctures, the action and the contingencies, out of which concrete instances of social change are formed. Spencer went further and expressly set the project for a science of society in opposition to any notion of a humanistic history, in terms of a series of antinomies: process vs. events, structure vs. individuals, necessity vs. contingency, and so forth.[14]

It was the legal historian Frederick Maitland who saw that such ahistoricism was self-defeating and succinctly stated comparative anthropology's dilemma:

"by and by anthropology will have the choice of being history or being nothing."[15] Rarely has a clear statement been so often misunderstood by being read out of context.[16] Maitland was *not* telling a functionalist anthropology that it should study social change. His essay "The Body Politic" was directed at the whole organicist metaphor in which the comparative method (Mode I) sought laws of development, taking Spencer as the great exemplar. His point was that processes of change must be seen in terms of contingencies and specific conditions, not as the working out of immanent laws of organic development. The great irony was that, whereas Maitland wanted the time perspective without organicism, what British anthropology eventually produced after the structural-functionalist revolution was a form of organicism without the time perspective.

The fundamental methodological issues here were posed most sharply in Germany, where a strong attraction to evolutionary and organicist models of society coexisted with the greatest contemporary school of historical scholarship and an antipathy to Anglo-French universalism and utilitarianism in such fields as law and economics. The famous *Methodenstreit* concerned the antithesis of history and science, of *Geist* and *Natur* as objects of study, and of the placement of any so-called social sciences in this academic scheme. Sociology was precisely what Max Weber called his attempt to transcend the distinction, to meet scientific standards in the definition and analysis of historical problems without denying the meaningful character of their subject matter.[17] But for all Weber's vast influence on the history of sociology, anthropology was shaped instead by the rather different response to this dilemma proposed by Franz Boas, the main conduit by which German historical idealism was transmitted to American anthropology. Boas polarized the historical method, concerned with the development of unique cultural wholes, and the comparative method.[18] The latter sought to establish synchronic links between discrete variables expressed in the terms of a general theory.

This distinction between history and comparison was already implicit in what has come to be called Galton's Problem.[19] At the first presentation of Edward Tylor's famous essay in Mode I comparative method on the evolution of systems of marriage and descent, Francis Galton drew attention to a major difficulty with its research design.[20] How could one tell whether the adhesions or correlations between variables were independent cases of the postulated causal relationships between traits, thus serving to confirm the theory, or were the result of societies' borrowing traits at some particular stage in their history? The problem indicates the tension that must exist between the search for a theory specifying causal relations that hold irrespective of time and place, and the evident fact that social variables may be rather loosely fitting and combine in unique configurations (cultures) under contingent circumstances (history). In that sense, as Boas saw, both culture and history presented refractory materials for the comparative method.

Mode III: History Ignored

Mode III applies when the comparative method is detached entirely from considerations of time and change. This was decisively achieved only after the structural-functionalist revolution, but some of the groundwork had already been laid. Even when, as with Mode I, the ultimate object of the comparative method was to construct a natural history of society, the temporal sequence was essentially something added to the correlations from outside. The sequence itself usually followed from some naturally ordered feature such as population size or density, degree of social differentiation, or level of technology. The comparative method was to determine the corresponding sequence of religious beliefs, kinship systems, ethical values, and so on; and obviously it could continue to be used apart from any social-evolutionary project.

Moreover, there is an ambiguity in the very notion of explaining a thing by reference to its source or origins. This may be interpreted phylogenetically, in which case an institutional history (as with a language's descent from an *ur*-form) is required; or ontogenetically, in which case the genesis in an individual of an instance of the thing is required. These two interpretations can be combined, as in Freud's theory of religion, where a historical myth about its supposed origins is taken up in an account of the origin of individual neuroses that reach out to religious solutions. We find the same thing in James Frazer. For besides the evolutionary progression from magic to science, he also seeks explanation by looking for a link between some need or habit of thought inherent in human individuals and some type of magicoreligious action. The intellectual tedium of *The Golden Bough* is largely due to the fact that the vast range of comparative materials is used to provide repeated illustration of such linkages between source and effect according to Mill's Method of Agreement.

We are here only a very short step from Mode III, which was described by Alfred Radcliffe-Brown as a means "to pass from the particular to the general . . . to arrive at the universal, at characteristics which can be found in different forms in many societies."[21] This is the Method of Agreement exclusively and *à l'outrance.* In the next generation this universalist ambition was sustained above all by Meyer Fortes. In *Oedipus and Job in West African Religion* Fortes acknowledged the lead of Frazer in the great project "to bring home to us the unity behind the diversity of human customs," and where he refers to the beliefs of other West African peoples it is only to point out the similarities, not to use the differences to get a better explanatory purchase on the specifics of the Tallensi situation.[22] Again, in "Pietas in Ancestor Worship" he gives far more attention to parallel cases that fit his theory of ancestor worship as a ritualization of lineage authority,[23] and even to extensions of it to such spheres as the "pietas" displayed by Russian cosmonauts and Cambridge college fellows, than to problematic countercases such as the Tiv that might sharpen up the explanation.[24]

The conditions for finding generalizations applying to "all human societies, past, present and future"[25] were better met when Lévi-Strauss displaced the subject matter of anthropology upward, from social relations to cultural forms such as myths, and explanation was sought in terms of laws of the mind, not of society. Rodney Needham's book *Exemplars,* written very consciously as comparativist, shows the clear outcome of Mode III. Though Needham considers a historical sequence of writers, neither their pastness, nor the temporal relations between them, nor their historically specific circumstances are of essential concern to him; for through comparison he is looking for "fundamental inclinations of the psyche" or "natural proclivities of thought and imagination."[26] Such things point to "cerebral vectors" as where explanation must ultimately lie; and at that point the natural science of society teeters on the edge of physiology.

Mode IV: Regional Comparative Studies

The trajectory of Mode III, from Radcliffe-Brown to Needham, was not, however, the most typical development of the comparative method in social anthropology from the 1950s onward. This was Mode IV, where more limited comparisons are essayed, usually dealing with particular social institutions and within a particular ethnographic area. For Africanist anthropology, it arrived in the classic volumes *African Political Systems* (ed. Fortes and Evans-Pritchard, 1940) and *African Systems of Kinship and Marriage* (ed. Radcliffe-Brown and Forde, 1950), albeit prefaced with Mode III manifestos from Radcliffe-Brown. This mode of the comparative method did not simply make use of ethnographies but, more than any of the preceding ones, really arose out of ethnography and remained close to it. Consequently much more use is made of Mill's Method of Difference, in two principal ways: explanation and exploration.

Two essays by S. F. Nadel—who had a better idea of what he was about theoretically than any of his contemporaries[27]—indicate the difference in emphasis. Explanation is predominant in the tightly organized argument of "Witchcraft in Four African Societies"[28] (1952): two pairs of closely related societies, a single definite question about each (presence or absence of witchcraft beliefs? female or male witches?), and a clear guiding hypothesis (that witchcraft beliefs answer to frustrations and anxieties arising from the pattern of social relations). His essay on Nuba religion, on the other hand, is more exploratory, seeking to clarify a rather diffuse difference between the religions of two further Nuba peoples, one of which has a more anxious, ritually obsessive outlook, and the other, a more serene and submissive attitude toward the gods.[29] No definite explanatory hypotheses are evident here, beyond an assumption that one should look for "more significant, because more far-reaching, causal relations connecting religion with acts of an altogether different order, that is with conditions which are functionally autonomous and hence represent 'independent' variables."[30] So Nadel proceeds to look at a number of variables, most of which are germane to his interest in social psychology: the regulation of adolescence, the jural status of wives, sexual morality, attitudes to homosexuality, and so forth. Thus ethnography reaches, through the comparative method, to further and better ethnography.

In the early 1950s, a time when the surge of new ethnography studies encouraged several reviews of the comparative method,[31] Isaac Schapera strongly urged its methodological advantages, in contrast with sweeping cross-cultural studies such as those based on the *Human Relations Area Files.* At the very least, where social-structural relations were being investigated, comparison within an ethnographic region enabled culture to be held much more securely constant. Its further potential was that it allowed variations genuinely to be analyzed as variants or transformations of locally given basic forms. This remained a productive seam, as was shown in such fine studies as those of Adam Kuper on Southern Bantu marriage systems,[32] or Richard Fardon on social organization in the Benue Valley region of Nigeria and Cameroon.[33] One original aim of Mode IV was to avoid being bothered by culture through setting up situations where it could be set aside as a constant, yet the regional focus eventually pointed the way back to historical questions, and hence reintroduced the problem of culture. Mode IV could also converge with Mode II, as with the work of de Heusch.

REGIONAL COMPARISON WITHIN BRITISH SOCIAL ANTHROPOLOGY

Before turning to issues that bear directly on my initial puzzle, it is necessary to examine two closely related features of British social anthropology as practiced in the 1940s and 1950s: holistic presentism and sociological reductionism. These infused most exercises in Mode IV comparative method without being strictly entailed by it, and together they utterly inhibited an adequate analysis of the role of culture in social transformation. Holistic presentism followed from the practical rejection of historical explanation by the founders of structural functionalism. Where the histories of preliterate societies were judged to be unknowable, conjectural history, using Mode I's comparative method, was worthless, and so apparent history or oral tradition made better sense when interpreted as a charter for present social arrangements. Thus, all social phenomena had to be explained in terms of other social phenomena with which they cohered in whole systems or else in terms of the external conditions of such systems. With this doctrine, social anthropology acquired a wonderful self-sufficiency as a discipline, since ethnographic fieldwork, if sufficiently thorough, could provide all the material needed for explanation.

What holistic presentism did *not* provide was guidance as to what explains things. In principle, it might be environment, race, technology, cultural values, . . .

But after Radcliffe-Brown, it was social structure: social anthropology for a while became more sociological than sociology. Now, while this still left open many questions about the relations between such social institutions as politics, law, kinship, the economic division of labor, and the like, it did propose a definite answer, or rather two somewhat inconsistent answers, to the interpretation of culture. The core message was: culture does not matter much in social analysis.

On the one hand, culture is a kind of clutter, which has a certain obscuring tendency and so needs to be cleared away if valid comparisons are to be made. Because there might be "the same kind of political structures . . . in societies of totally different culture," comparison should be "on an abstract plane where social processes are stripped of their cultural idiom and reduced to functional terms."[34] Over thirty years later I. M. Lewis, in *Ecstatic Religion*, was to propose just the same thing. He urged "the crucial importance of distinguishing between the unique cultural forms of particular institutions and their actual social significance in any society." Only if anthropologists did this would they be able to "develop useful typologies which cut across cultural *forms* and which facilitate meaningful comparison." Thus would anthropology be able to storm "the last bastion of the unique," religion.[35]

Alternatively, instead of varying randomly, culture was argued to covary exactly, as a dependent variable, with the forms of social structure. If the Tallensi have a cult of their ancestors, it is not (as Frazer would have argued) because of a fear of the dead, "but because their social structure demands it."[36] And it was precisely with those forms of religion—ancestor worship and witchcraft/sorcery beliefs—that seem *in fact* to reflect social structure most closely that the comparative analysis of religion was attempted to best effect.[37] As R. E. Bradbury put it in a fine study of the Edo cult of the dead, where "relations with the objects of worship derive very directly from the typical experiences of individuals in their relations with certain categories of deceased persons . . . severe limits are set upon the imaginative capacities of the religious thinker."[38]

Bradbury clearly recognized that this need not be true of all forms of religion, but any great exploration of cultural autonomy was long impeded by a strong methodological resistance from social anthropologists. John Middleton and E. H. Winter, for example, counterposed two ways to explain the content of witchcraft beliefs: cultural analysis and sociology. Only by sociological analysis, they argued, can we develop explanations that subsume the facts from more than one society; and cultural explanations are in any case untestable.[39] But why should cultural explanations be less testable in principle than sociological ones? The contention that phenomenon *A* in society *X* is due to its being Muslim (a cultural fact) can indeed be supported by showing that it is also present in other Muslim societies *Y* and *Z* (the Method of Agreement), especially if it is absent from otherwise comparable but non-Muslim societies *P*, *Q*, and *R* (the Method of Difference). But there has to be a theoretical interest in finding explanations of this kind; and mostly, in the comparative analysis of the 1950s and 1960s, this interest was excluded by satisfaction at the power of social-structural determinism to explain at least some of the empirical variation of African religions.

But what eventually became clear is that substantial amounts of variation were left unexplained by sociological facts, and that these often pointed to culture. Two examples suffice to make the point. Max Gluckman's extended comparison of domestic systems among two centralized Bantu societies, Zulu and Lozi, is a good example of synchronic, social-structural Mode IV comparative method.[40] He explained the presence or absence of the house-property complex and related phenomena in terms of the presence or absence of strong agnatic lineages. Compelled thus to extend the range of comparison, he found his explanation supported by the same correlations among a cluster of peoples in northeastern Africa. Things started to get untidy when a group of patrilineal peoples in West Africa (Tallensi, Fon, Igbo) provided a negative case—no house-property complex—but this he was able to handle in a theoretically plausible but also ad hoc way, by adducing an extra negative condition—their having brother-to-brother succession. But what is then the import of a case like the Yoruba, another patrilineal West African people, who manage to combine some major features of the house-property complex typical of the Zulu with other features more characteristic of the Lozi, who lack it? Clearly it does not simply invalidate Gluckman's detailed explanation of the Zulu/Lozi differences, but it does negate any idea of a necessary link between the two variables. There is just greater free play between social-structural variables than Radcliffe-Brown's program supposed, so that where variables do cohere, it is within a complex of other conditions that is the product of a particular local history. Any necessity of things is the rolling product of determinations accumulating over time—a subject matter that social anthropology, for a time, forswore to touch.

Mary Douglas's classic paper "Lele Economy Compared with the Bushong" brings us more expressly to a similar conclusion.[41] She asked why the Bushong of the Congo were so much more productive than their neighbors, the Lele, despite identical levels of technology and a similar natural environment. Her convincing answer was that it was due to different patterns of labor use, which in turn depended on contrasting evaluations of what activities were appropriate to particular age/sex categories. In other words, the key factor was specific cultural patterns, which existed in the present simply as a precipitate of the past and were themselves only to be explained historically. By the same stroke, we are forced to take culture/ideas/religion seriously and to open social explanation to history. Holistic presentism excludes historical explanations but not explanation by reference to culture, the form in which the past exists in the present. There were good grounds for this suspicion of historical explanations. But only its companion dogma, sociological reductionism, really closed the door, by refusing to acknowledge the effectiveness of any constituent of present reality besides the social relations themselves or, for those of an even harder turn of mind, their ecological and physical conditions of existence.

HISTORY REVIVED IN ANTHROPOLOGY?

For all that these were *idées maitresses* of British social anthropology at its acme, they never won universal assent. Opposition to them was most sharply expressed by E. E. Evans-Pritchard. Yet this opposition was both shifting and equivocal, and did not lead to a resolution of the problems of an ahistorical anthropology. This was because Evans-Pritchard was unable to transcend Radcliffe-Brown's terms of debate, which themselves had been set in the Montesquieu/Spencer/Durkheim tradition of science vs. history. He merely opted for the other alternative. Despite his own remarkable analysis of structural transformation (*The Sanusi of Cyrenaica*, 1949), Evans-Pritchard's case for anthropology as history had less to do with the treatment of time or change than with insistence on the uniqueness of what the anthropologist studies: individual cultures. History acknowledged this uniqueness, which a natural science of society would deny.[42] The kind of explanation he wanted had nothing to do with causes: it was "exact description which bears its own interpretation."[43] He was consequently unenthusiastic about the comparative method, that handmaid of science. Some comparative religion he was prepared to countenance, but insofar as it goes beyond hermeneutics, he allowed it only the very weak causal aspirations of relational study.[44]

For the anthropologists who most seriously reengaged with history did *not* take their cue from the later writings of Evans-Pritchard. The new concern arose among those who had done fieldwork in some of the larger-scale African societies, typically societies that had acquired some depth of literary tradition and whose ethnic traditions had the most direct relevance to the newly emergent states: peoples like the Yoruba, Akan, Tswana, Somali, Akan, Ganda, and Hausa-Fulani. Methodological essays[45] led on to monographs[46] and to collaborative volumes.[47] Though the forms of the anthropological engagement with history varied considerably, its typical position was in fact diametrically opposed to Evans-Pritchard's. Rather than adopt the supposed traits of history (idiographic, hermeneutic, etc.) in order to be adequate to its subject matter, anthropology should preserve its own disciplinary identity, which was as some sort of science, and bring it to bear on questions of change. Anthropologists might interact closely with historians, but they would do distinctive things with historical data.

A full account of the contrasting styles of history and anthropology is not needed here. Suffice it to note briefly three characteristic ways in which anthropologists tackled historical questions. First, potted histories or ethnographies were used to test general theories of social processes, or else theoretical models were used to shed light on historical questions, as with Lloyd's conflict model applied to Yoruba kingdoms.[48] Second, anthropologists opposed the supposed historian's interest in unique sequences of events to their own search for structural regularities or sociological time.[49] Here the most telling voice was M. G. Smith's, since few anthropologists of West Africa had collected more extensive oral-historical data or pursued such a consistent theoretical project. From *Zazzau* (1960) to *Daura* (1978) his (parahistorical, as he called it) objective had been to establish relations of logical necessity holding through time.[50] He did not shrink from the implication that the elements to be so temporally ordered required abstraction from the total historical process and that causal analysis, qua determination of the conditions of concrete historical reality, were not what he was about. Finally, of course, there was again the comparative method. Thus Mode IV, though still marked by some ahistorical tendencies that ran back a long way, was brought directly to bear on historical questions. How it fared in relation to substantive issues in the history of West African societies, I now turn to consider.

ANTHROPOLOGY AND STATE FORMATION IN WEST AFRICA

From the 1950s to the 1980s the dominant theme that brought anthropologists and historians together was state formation. In the age of African nationalism, it was of pressing interest to West Africans themselves, and the local schools of academic historiography made states and elites their central topic.[51] Social anthropology was able to respond effectively because it had, in its own tradition, already addressed some cognate issues. Fortes and Evans-Pritchard in *African Political Systems* provided the conceptual groundwork for later collections on precolonial states.[52] Behind the presentist ethnography of structural functionalism there still lurked the evolutionary schemes, based on Mode I comparative method, of Lewis Henry Morgan and Henry Maine. The dichotomy between segmentary lineage systems and states that was used as a static typology in *African Political Systems* was turned again into a description of process in the studies of political centralization. This was thus conceived as a process in which the decline of lineages was the essential condition of the state's advance.

Discussion about the factors making for political centralization in precolonial West Africa faces a considerable initial difficulty. How do we distinguish a state of greater from one of lesser centralization? The most appropriate sort of evidence would seem to be historically concrete actions indicative of the center's political capacity: a king able to tax his subjects heavily, to raise armies and use them to ends determined by himself, to effect his will in distant provinces and to maintain public works, to place his own nominees in influential positions and to remove them at will. By such criteria Asante and Dahomey are reasonably considered centralized kingdoms. Elsewhere, adequate historical evidence of *actions* being lacking, inferences are often made from *institutions,* typically observed in the twentieth century but presumed traditional, which are considered appropriate indicators or proxies of relative centralization. The typology contained within *African Political Systems* gives clear guidance as to what those institutions might be. The baseline for development would be a segmentary state, in which titled offices belong to lineages and the king is selected by nonroyal titleholders from the segments of a royal lineage.[53] Of the four forest kingdoms that were at the center of discussion—Asante, Benin, Dahomey, and Oyo (Yoruba)—the Yoruba approximate most closely to this model, and, in true Mode I fashion, their present condition was taken as analogous to the condition from which the others are presumed to have developed.[54]

There are several difficulties with this procedure. The first is logical. The argument becomes circular when the same thing—for example, the decline of descent groups—is *both* used to define centralization *and* treated as a factor of change itself.[55] In a diachronic analysis, of course, the same institution may at one moment be treated as a cause or condition, at another as an effect. But here the comparisons are essentially static, between one generalized societal description and another, as in the manner of Gluckman's Zulu/Lozi comparison, albeit with the aim of isolating historically significant variables; so circularity is hard to avoid. Hence the perennial appeal of technological determinism, which offers a way to break the circle. Thus the argument, first put forward by Peter Morton-Williams to explain Asante/Oyo differences, and elaborated by Jack Goody for West Africa more widely, that military technology (specifically the horse vs. the gun) was the main factor determining the allegedly greater centralization of the forest kingdoms.[56] Behind military technology lay geography (savannah vs. forest), since rulers near the coast would get the guns, which they could store and use to take power from lineage chiefs into their own hands. But empirically, as Robin Law showed,[57] Goody's hierarchy of causes—geography, technology, sociology—just doesn't work. To give just one example, the introduction of guns into nineteenth-century Yorubaland, one of the later areas to receive them, served to accentuate political fragmentation and conflict, both between states and within them, rather than to create a greater centralization of power.

But centralization cannot be *plausibly* defined in this question-begging way, with a theory of the process built into the definition. The case of Asante shows this most clearly. P. C. Lloyd expressed a once common view when he grouped the Asante *with* most of the Yoruba in one category (open representative government), while Benin and Dahomey were placed in another (government by political association). In the first of these, chiefs are selected as lineage representatives, an arrangement that expresses the coherence and importance of the lineages in society at large. The latter category, indicated by nonlineage titles, close succession in the royal house, and so forth, is more centralized. The same linking of Asante and

Yoruba occurs in Fortes's essay "Strangers," where he argues that in both societies, because lineages are the building blocks of the community, strangers can become members of the community only through assimilation to it.[58] Mostly by the 1970s, however, the Asante and the Yoruba were being placed in contrasting categories, the Asante alongside Dahomey and Benin as relatively centralized states (gun-using, with nonlineage titled offices), in contrast to less centralized states (cavalry-using, with lineage titles), such as Oyo, Gonja, or Mossi.[59] The shift in the classification of Asante resulted from Ivor Wilks's demonstration of the bureaucratic aspects of the Asante state in the late eighteenth and nineteenth centuries,[60] which had eluded the attention of an anthropology too rooted in the colonial period.

Wilks's work forced a reconsideration not just of Asante but of the whole comparative framework derived from *African Political Systems*. What had seemed to justify its model of centralization was that, linked to the declining significance of lineages, there should be a number of other socially significant features, including such commonsense criteria of centralization as royal executive capacity. All this now collapsed in the light of Wilks's account of Asante. Certainly the late eighteenth-century Kwadwoan revolution in government involved the establishment of new bureaucratic offices, which were detached from the matrilineages to which titles of general community leadership belonged.[61] But the matrilineages remained of great consequence in social life, access to land, and other local functions, and so continued to be represented in the colonial ethnographies after the structures of the expansionist Asante state had fallen away.[62] The advance of the state did *not* entail the withering away of the lineage.

Does the model fare better with the other kingdoms? Dahomey, like Asante, combined a powerful royal system of control with the continued existence of corporate, landholding (patri)lineages, which M. J. Herskovits called "the pivot of Dahomean social organization."[63] At first, the Yoruba would not have seemed to present much of a problem, since the ethnographic consensus represented their town structures as federations of lineages[64] that failed in diverse ways to become centralized; but this consensus came to be severely questioned.[65] Great difficulties arise from the regional variety of Yorubaland, but in general it can be said that the importance of lineage as *the* basis of social organization was much exaggerated. Yoruba title systems do not reflect lineage structure alone; in many instances residential groupings, such as quarters, are as important a principle of cooperation as descent; the ancestral cult known as *egungun* shows a much less decisive recognition of the importance of corporate descent than do the ancestor cults in Dahomey or Asante. It is curious that corporate lineage, this supposed token of the baseline of political development, should have been more strongly emphasized in accounts of the northwestern Yoruba, none of whose communities in its present form predates the wholesale upheavals of the last century, than in the centuries-old communities of the southeastern forests, such as Ondo and Ilesha. Indeed Lloyd ends by admitting of Ibadan—the new military master of Yorubaland in the nineteenth century, which chronically failed to create a stable political center—that its strongly corporate lineages were "a product of the development of the political structure in response to new opportunities in the sphere of trade and war."[66] It is true that at Ilesha the importance of nonlineage titles and nonlineal social units (such as the quarters) grew as an aspect of the town's successful expansion; but they did not bring (and cannot be used as an indicator of) any marked centralization.

The last case to be considered is Benin. Its contrast with the Yoruba now looks less sharp, though the evidence of its relative centralization is not to be denied: the periodically impressive executive outreach of its kings, the extraordinary role of the palace associations in the integration of the kingdom, the stem dynasty. But is there a plausible trajectory of development? Bradbury argued, from the evidence of the ritual opposition between the *Oba* (from a dynasty of Ife—i.e., Yoruba—descent) and the kingmaker *Uzama* chiefs (representing the elders of Benin), for a convergence of Yoruba and Edo (Benin) political cultures. Divergences from the Yoruba pattern were put down to *ur*-Edo cultural elements (e.g., primogeniture, lineages shallow, nonlandholding). But should we equate what seems distinctively Edo to a twentieth-century ethnographer with a putative *ur*-Edo baseline? Some things count against this: some less centralized peoples of the Edo-speaking periphery in fact have landholding patrilineages more like the Yoruba than Benin;[67] and the *Uzama* titles at Benin, those supposed tokens of *ur*-Edo culture, are widespread as very ancient titles among the forest Yoruba.[68] In sum, it strongly looks as if at least some of those institutions distinctive of Benin were the product of its political development rather than drawn from an *ur*-Edo baseline. If, moreover, the reduction in the significance of lineages in the heartland of the Benin kingdom was part of this process, it seems that Benin's development squares with the lineages-to-state model suggested by *African Political Systems* better than Asante or Dahomey do.

So what can we conclude from this debate about the conditions of political centralization in precolonial West Africa? First, the notion of centralization is thoroughly confused. In fact, at least three distinct criteria seem to be involved. (1) All forms of political development appear to have entailed some concentration, an essentially spatial process by which the population and disposable resources of a region come to be concentrated at a power center. Such concentration appears to be a necessary but not a sufficient condition of (2) the sort of power transfer between institutions within the emergent center that the lineages-to-state concept of centralization is mostly about. Then there is (3) a growth in the capacity of a state executive to extract and direct to its own ends the labor and resources of its subjects. Criteria (2) and (3) need not coincide. Take, for example, the nineteenth-century jihadist state of Masina, on the middle Niger.[69] This was a cavalry-based state with a mass dynasty, and so belongs to Goody's group of the less centralized, by criterion (2). But its Fulani Muslim ruling estate maintained their cavalry by extremely heavy taxation of the Bambara subject population; the land was expected to produce at least double the subsistence of its cultivators, a very high level of exploitation by West African standards. Masina was highly centralized, by criterion (3). Process (3) is surely the one that, from a general viewpoint, has the greatest historical significance. It refers to an increase in societal capacity, achieved through rulers' finding ways of controlling their subjects more, making more continuous calls on their labor and resources, and thus being able to take political and military initiatives not open to the rulers of less geared-up societies. The large armies they raised, the vast size of their palace establishments, the accumulation of resources at their annual Customs (as these ritual occasions are styled), the road networks they maintained—all indicate that states like Dahomey and Asante took a definite developmental step. The question then is: How did they manage to do it?

It is evident that neither anthropologists nor historians have produced very satisfactory answers. The leading anthropological idea, that the advance of the state is linked to the decline of the lineage, has proved to have very little in it; process (2) is only contingently connected to process (3). Technological determinism, military or otherwise, is hardly more helpful; and even the presence of trade routes (for there is plenty of trade without rulers in West Africa)[70] does not sufficiently explain why states come into being or, in a handful of cases, succeeded in gearing themselves up to higher levels of societal performance. Can we do no more than agree with Law when he writes, after a careful review of the comparative literature, that "ultimately, perhaps, explanations are to be sought in specific historical circumstances [for the failure of Oyo to become more centralized]"?[71] Law raises questions here about the specific factors of change and about the value of the comparative method in general.

RELIGION, IDEOLOGY, AND THE STATE

One large area of thought and activity has by and large been neglected by both historians and anthropologists in their attempts to explain the differences between these societies: religion. For the social anthropologists this neglect is hardly surprising in the light of the sociological reductionism that has been the main key to their interpretation of religion. Even Goody's essay "Polity and Ritual: The Opposition of Horse and Earth,"[72] which is almost the only treatment of religion in relation to the debate about political centralization, seems to assume that, while religion may have some real effect on the behavior of individuals, it has no significant role in the creation of social forms.[73] Historians too have tended in practice to deny significant historical effects to religion. The two major studies of the forest kingdoms, Wilks on Asante and Law on Oyo, have little to say about it. It is only with Islam that a role for religion as a force of social change seems readily conceded, as with Marion Johnson's argument that "Islam, military force and taxation are connected in a complex way" in Masina's development.[74]

Available evidence suggests that it was not utterly different for the pagan religions, that they too served as models for as well as models of social relations.[75] For all that they have been little investigated, it is clear that religious innovation and controversy were integral aspects of the growth of state power in eighteenth-century West Africa. In Asante, one king met effective resistance from his chiefs when he contemplated adopting Islam;[76] and in Dahomey, the great king Agaja (1708–32) introduced the Ifa cult of divination from the Yoruba[77]. The central occasion for the exercise of the state's mastery over the resources and activities of its subjects was the great annual religious celebration known as the Customs, preparation for which structured the activities of the entire population of the kingdom for a large portion of the year.[78] In Asante a further key role in this regulation of subjects' activities was the *Adaduanan*, or forty-two-day calendrical cycle, which T. C. McCaskie calls a veritable *Grundnorm* of Asante life, a rooting of social activity in a cosmic pattern.[79]

Here at last we can start to return to the initial puzzle: Akan resistance to adoption of the world religions, compared with Yoruba openness to them. For what that comparison of twentieth-century patterns of action showed is that even after the British had dismantled the structures of Asante state control, the Asante long retained a lively sense that the integrity of their society depended on the sanctions of the traditional religion. A most significant instance of this was the petition of Christian clergy, both missionary and local Akan, to the *Asantehene* (king of Asante) in 1944, arguing that Akan Christians were loyal subjects of their chiefs, even though their religious scruples prevented them from treating Thursdays, sacred to the Earth goddess, as rest days within the *Adaduanan* cycle.[80] It is utterly inconceivable that Yoruba Christians should have had to make such a protestation as late as the 1940s. The same Akan attitude was evident in other ways too: for example, in the much greater and longer-enduring sense that chiefship and church membership were flatly incompatible, or the much commoner practice of requiring Christian converts to withdraw from the town to live in a quarter outside it, usually known as Salem.[81]

So my argument about religious change in twentieth-century West Africa leads back to an argument about political change, and the role of religion in it, in eighteenth-century West African kingdoms. Common to both is an insistence on an aspect of religious change that finds little cognizance in Horton's theory of African conversion from which I began. That is essentially cognitive or cool: change is explained as occurring insofar as people's new experience renders their old explanatory frameworks inadequate. The present argument, however, is that religious change is a much more affective or hot process, because religion (in addition to having explanatory functions, as Horton says) also serves to define the membership of social groups and to underpin authority in them—and especially so in highly geared-up societies such as Asante. It is important, when we recognize that religion serves as an ideology, to stress that it *must* be more than that. There is a danger here of another form of sociological determinism, the quasi-Marxist functionalism that embodies a teleology: the ruling class needs an ideology to justify its position, and so religion must somehow be on hand to provide one. Such strategies often paper over crucial gaps in the explanation. So Wilks tells that in late eighteenth-century Asante, "government *had* to be extended in range . . . in scope . . . and in proficiency" (my italics).[82] He tells us *how* it was but not how it *could* be so. The need does not suffice to produce the effect; the crucial cultural conditions had to be met. If it *had* to be ideology to work the trick because purely material conditions fall short—and we must never forget that in West Africa the most segmentary peoples and the most centralized states share the same technological, ecological, and physical conditions of existence—there had to be some independent strength in the religious ideas drawn upon. Religion had this power because it was already the shared idiom in which both chiefs and people confronted the pains and anxieties of the human situation. *Asantehenes* really feared witchcraft; kings of Dahomey, two of whom died of smallpox, respected its cult for all that they disliked it.[83] If this was the bottom line of their reality, on what else could rulers better seek to build structures of higher obligation and control—and themselves remain constrained by its premises?

REINTRODUCING HISTORY

It is now clear that some of the failure of the comparative method to explain West African centralization is to be attributed to the neglect of culture or ideology as a causal agency. But the problem goes deeper. The comparative method, as employed by social anthropologists on these questions, is really a combination of two modes: it is Mode I in its view of the process of centralization and Mode IV in its views as to causes. Now, both these modes proceed by abstracting their data from history, even when their aim is an idealized, general history or the determination of real historical causes. For what they compare are either societies described in a detemporalized ethnographic present or a cross-section from a society in history, a frozen moment taken as some kind of whole; and they aim to establish relationships between variables that hold apart from historical time. But it is inconsistent with a realistic concept of what society is, and human experience within it, thus to base comparison on a procedure that eliminates change, incompleteness, and potentiality, memories, and intentions—in a word, historicity. It is small gain to rectify the omission of culture from explanations by introducing it as yet another factor in a *presentist* scheme of comparison. For it is then reified rather than viewed as the hinge between the past of which it is the precipitate and the future that it aims to prefigure.

Mode V: Histories Compared

What we need is a Mode V of the comparative method, where it is histories, or societies in change, rather than just societies that are compared, following the path blazed by the great historical sociologists or comparative historians such as Frederick Maitland, Max Weber, and Marc Bloch. Other modes of the comparative method (except Mode II) pose questions about general sociological categories, aggregates of things taken from their several historical contexts. Underlying this is the antithesis of science and history, and the assumption that if the data are to be treated scientifically, their historicity must be purged from them. Mode V differs in several related ways. Its aim is to explain historical particulars through applying to them general statements, which are theories or models, rather than to move from particulars to empirical generalizations or laws. This is to hold to the general logic of scientific explanation as to the use of comparison but to refuse to distort the data by dehistoricizing them, that is by taking them out of their placement in a time sequence. For their place in a time sequence is an *essential* feature of social facts, constituted as these all are by individual actions. Natural science, whose example has done so much to inspire the comparative method, need have no concern with historicity, since it deals with entities that have fixed properties and hence highly determinate relationships with one another. Social anthropology's attempts to develop such generalizations about the variables of its own subject matter have been extremely disappointing. Virtually all its generalizations turn out to be no more than tendencies, or true only by definition, or holding only under particular historical or cultural conditions, or able to state only the very minimal conditions under which social facts exist. Between its variables there is much more free play: we are forced to conclude that the linkage of variables in particular cases often results less from their inherent properties than from *how they have come to be combined,* through human action in a succession of contexts. By comparing histories or societies in change, Mode V offers a path to the explanation of social phenomena without misrepresenting the general way in which they are brought about.

A FINAL CONTRAST BETWEEN YORUBA AND AKAN

A final recourse to the Yoruba/Akan comparison illustrates the role of culture as the pivot of social change. I have argued that the relative reluctance of the Akan, especially Asante, to embrace the world religions had much to do with their sense that the integrity of their society depended on sanctions bound up with the old religion. Asante society was not religiously static; but the world religions could not be subjected to local chiefly control as other imported cults were. The Asante knew their political community as founded by human agreement, though also given spiritual sanction by the Golden Stool. McCaskie brilliantly conveys the Asante sense of the fragility of their achievement, speaking of their "abiding fear that without unremitting application and effort, the fragile defensible space called culture would simply be overwhelmed or reclaimed by an irruptive and anarchic nature."[84]

The Yoruba perception of themselves and their situation was rather different. Again it is instructive to look back from their response to the world religions. Though conversion brought both conflict and persecution, the fact remains that the Yoruba were much more open to religious change. It was, of course, a less highly geared-up society, which could allow more religious toleration—already within Yoruba paganism there was both cultic diversity and religious choice—and whose rulers were perhaps less able to stop religious novelty. Whereas, after *Asantehene* Osei Kwame's flirtation with Islam in the late eighteenth century, the Asante authorities quarantined Islam and effectively prevented its further spread, in the Oyo empire at the same time Islam made such strides that Muslims became a key component in its overthrow; and Islam grew steadily in Oyo's successor states in the nineteenth century. A highly distinctive feature of Yoruba traditional religion was its oracular cult called Ifa, whose priest-diviners (*babalawo*) had great prestige as religious professionals. Through consultation with Ifa an individual might be directed to the worship of a particular deity. But most remarkably, *babalawo* could, and on occasion did, advise clients to become Muslims or Christians.[85] Why could Ifa, a key element in the traditional religion, thus sponsor major religious change?

The many Yoruba kingdoms never enjoyed political unity or a common ethnic name till the twentieth century; but they recognized their affinity through the claim of all their kings to descent from Oduduwa, a god who had reigned at Ile-Ife. Ife had been the first great kingdom of the West African forest (*fl.* 1100–1450),[86] and even after it had declined to a town of modest political importance, the Yoruba always looked to it not only as a supreme cultic center but as the very site of the creation of the human race.[87] Ife's sacred prestige in later centuries was especially conveyed in the cult of Ifa. This was not just because Ife is especially prestigious as a center for the training of *babalawo* but because of the way that Ife is represented in Ifa.

Ifa comprises a vast number of poems (*ese*), organized under the 256 figures (*odu*) that the *babalawo* may cast with his apparatus.[88] The *babalawo* then recites the *ese* appropriate to the figure cast, one of which will give the key to the client's problem. Each *ese* takes the form of a mythical precedent, in which such-and-such a diviner or diviners (named by praise names that often encapsulate the problem) is consulted by some archetypal figure, who does or does not do what Ifa advises, usually to make a specified sacrifice; and the outcome is told, usually in the form of an extended myth, parable, or fable; finally the precedent is applied to the case in hand. Ifa is, therefore, a vast corpus of coded messages about the past.

More important than the fragments of specific historical information it may contain is its overall vision of the meaning of the past.

The forty-two-day calendrical cycle or *Adaduanan* of the Akan bears a certain comparison with Ifa—as central elements of their respective cultures and so, as we have seen, factors in the reception of the world religions. Both are to do with the ordering of social life through the assertion that things do, and should, repeat themselves. The *Adaduanan*, with its lucky and unlucky days, is much more to do with the mastery of time as such, structuring human activity in short cycles, well expressive of the perpetual anxiety of that hard-won and humanly constructed political order. Ifa, by contrast, is less concerned with time than with the past, specifically with the Glory that was Ife. For the mythical precedents that prefigure all possible later contingencies are stated or presumed to have taken place in Ife, "un état autrefois florissant, et dont la capitale fut une ville sainte . . . une patrie mystique," as a *babalawo* working in Dahomey in the 1930s put it.[89] Ifa presents to its adherents the highly refracted image of a past great civilization, and it is *here* that for the Yoruba the essential order lies, an ideal order. It is moreover a divinely given, not a humanly constructed order; for Ife (unlike Kumasi, Abomey, or Benin) was also the site of a cosmogony. While the *Adaduanan* actually creates definite patterns of activity, Ifa does not stipulate but rather sanctions, in the name of this past, those actions that the client is deeply disposed to take. The flexibility and openness to change of Yoruba society is thus conditioned by the belief that the ultimate order is eternally guaranteed by how things began. What our comparison most importantly teaches is that culture is less a reflection of society than a reflexion on history.

2

Two Pastors and Their Histories

Samuel Johnson and C. C. Reindorf

The last chapter ended with the assertion that culture is less a reflection of society than a reflexion on history.[1] The contrast between the two Latin forms *reflectio* and *reflexio* allows the expression of a distinction often concealed in English, between the thing made and the process of making it, as in the term "work." Yet that ambiguity may have its uses, in pointing us to the intimately reciprocal character of the making of culture and history. In so far as Yoruba ethnogenesis was a cultural work,[2] it was mainly achieved through the efforts of those who worked on Yoruba language, religion, and history. It is not surprising that these were the critical areas for such work or that so much pioneer work in all these fields was done by the native agents of the missionary societies, since establishing a standard written form of the language was crucial to Bible translation; understanding the character of "heathenism" was vital to combatting it; and writing local history was a means to incorporate Christianity into it. Here "history" shows a similar ambiguous duality of meaning, as given events or *res gestae* (things done) in the past and as narratives about them. Narrating or re-presenting that past is thus a central part of the self-realization of both culture and society.

The two historians I consider now come from the two West African societies whose cultures and histories were compared in the last chapter. They are the Rev. Samuel Johnson and the Rev. Carl Christian Reindorf, authors, respectively, of the *History of the Yorubas* (hereafter *HY*) and the *History of the Gold Coast and Asante* (hereafter *HGCA*). Both books were completed in the 1890s, and stand as two great monuments, towering over lesser literary efforts like the steeples of the Anglican and the Presbyterian churches in a small Ulster town. They invite comparison with each other, but they are much less alike than seems at first glance—and hardly anyone is equally familiar with the interior of both edifices. While my knowledge of Johnson and his background is perhaps as thorough as anyone's, what I know of Reindorf's work rests on little more than a good day's reading of *HGCA*. So this comparison is asymmetrical, with Reindorf mainly used as a foil to Johnson.

Now there are two ways in which we may want to evaluate or assess the work of past historians. The first comes readily to those who work on the same region and period as the historian in question: it focuses on the relationship between the historian and his sources, and examines where he got his information, how reliable it was, and what he did with it. The second is more external, and is less directly concerned with the quest for historical knowledge (at least according to a correspondence theory of truth). Indeed, it is likely to come with a reserve toward historical positivism, as with most literary approaches to historical texts. A supreme example of this is the work of the critic Hayden White, who gives precedence to form over content, to a history's emplotment or narrative structure over its treatment of source material, and to its related "ideological implications."[3] Though he comes to it from a different direction, the social anthropologist is likely to find this external approach more congenial, since, being inclined to skepticism about the objective truth value of any proposed version of the past, he characteristically seeks to make it intelligible in terms of its users' interests and its social function. The justification of this approach is that a historian's intention, formed from his experiences and his prior notions of what an account of the past might look like and be useful for, must always be prior to his use of the evidence, even though it will surely be modified by his working on it.

Here I take this second line and aim to shed light on the kind of work that Johnson produced by looking at how it was shaped by the concerns and assumptions he brought from his professional life as an African Protestant pastor. "Pastor of Oyo" is how he styles himself on the title page, just as Reindorf appears on his as "Native Pastor of the Basel Mission." The focus is on the peculiar interests of the native agent of a missionary society, a man to some extent alienated by his Christianity from the mass of his compatriots but identifying with them even as he wished to convert them; and on a mind shaped by the narrative resources of the Bible and of European historical writing as well as by the traditions and uses of the past current among his own people.

THE HISTORIES *COMPARED*

With its 650 pages of historical narrative (that is, excluding its preliminary essay on the Yoruba language and some appendixes), *HY* weighs in at nearly 290,000 words, over twice as long as *HGCA*. In one sense *HY* has to be regarded as a more original book than *HGCA*. The precedents for what Johnson set out to do were much more limited: apart from some short essays by various authors on Yoruba history, put together from oral materials, that appear in missionary journals, local newspapers, or as modest pamphlets,[4] he virtually created his own genre. His source material was almost entirely oral, whether it was consolidated traditions of the remoter past (some derived from professionals like the Oyo court bards or *arokin*), informants' memories and commonly circulating accounts of the more recent past, or Johnson's own memories and records for the last thirty or so years. He did not have available such published historical accounts by Europeans, going back to the seventeenth century, as provided Reindorf with both information and historiographical models for his own work.

The very existence of these published sources—arising from the long European presence on the Gold Coast—meant that Reindorf's *HGCA* both could and had to incorporate much more of the long-term interaction of Africans and Europeans than *HY*. The latter by contrast is a more purely native history, albeit one seen from that period when the European presence, which had been growing for over forty years, was eventuating in colonial annexation. At the same time, *HY* is much more immediate to the writer's present. Whereas *HGCA* comes to an end in 1856 with the consolidation of British rule on the Gold Coast after the cession of the Danish forts, a generation before Reindorf's writing, Johnson takes us right up to 1897, the year in which he laid down his pen; and in fact over a third of the entire massive book deals with the last great war among the Yoruba kingdoms (1878–93), in whose closing stages Johnson played an important political role as a mediator. While what he says about Yoruba history from its mythical origins up to the fall of Old Oyo in the 1830s is uniquely indispensable as source material,[5] the chief glory of his history lies in it how it treats the politics of Ibadan, where Johnson lived for most of his life, from midcentury onward. *HY* is at its greatest as contemporary history, and it is from this feature that we learn most about its general orientation, even in regard to earlier periods.

The point of greatest commonality between *HY* and *HGCA* arises from the authors' value commitments, as native pastors. I use this term pointedly, with its implicit reference to the two sides of their public identity, as Christian professionals and as patriots, members of their own African communities. The relevance of this dual allegiance is signalized in the notably parallel ways in which the two authors bring their narratives to a conclusion. Both abandon historian's prose for emotionally more charged forms of speech. Johnson expresses his fervent hopes in prayer (*HY*, 642):[6]

> But that peace should reign universally, with prosperity and advancement, and that the disjointed units should all be once more welded into one from the Niger to the coast as in the happy days of ABIODUN, . . . that clannish spirit disappear, and above all that Christianity should be the principal religion in the land—paganism

and Mohammedanism having had their full trial—should be the wish and prayer of every true son of Yoruba.

Reindorf, by contrast, breaks into a kind of free verse, invoking Britannia. After celebrating her victory over external enemies, he identifies the two "inner and dangerous" foes that still exist—ignorance and funeral custom—and concludes (*HGCA*, 341):

To exist, and then to rule, rule at ease,
Is never the spirit of Britannia.
By thee no nation ever was paralysed.
'Tis mission's duty the gospel to preach,
The government's, classical education.
One word, and the funeral custom will die,
And all will sing, "Rule, Britannia, Rule."
Superstition will then flee far way,
And Christianity will rule supreme!

Common to both is the expression of hope that Christianity will triumph and transform the nation. In fact the Christian *Bildung* of the two men is even closer than may appear, since though Johnson was Anglican, the missionaries who had the greatest impact on him were two of the many Württemberg Pietists (often Basel-trained) whom the Church Missionary Society employed in the nineteenth century. One was David Hinderer, who founded the Ibadan mission and led it between 1851 and 1869, to whom Johnson, "as a former pupil," dedicated *HY*. The other was Gottlob Friedrich Bühler, between 1858 and 1864 the principal of the CMS Training Institution at Abeokuta, which Johnson attended from 1862 to 1865. When they are compared with their English colleagues, the Germans stand out for two things: the strongly paternalist but spiritually intimate relationship that they cultivated with their African pupils and staff; and their commitment to a seriously liberal education for Africans. Bühler came into conflict with his senior colleague, the Englishman Henry Townsend, over the latter's disapproval of overly academic education for men intended as native agents.[7] Bühler's curriculum gave pride of place to religious subjects—Old and New Testaments, Scripture history, biblical geography, catechism, and the like—but also found room for general history and geography, natural history, and philosophy, along with some Greek and Latin.[8] Reindorf's view of the complementarity of "the gospel" and "classical education," even if he looked to the government to provide the latter, expresses very much the same cultural philosophy as Buhler's curriculum.

Of the differences, some are less significant than others: Reindorf's dominant note of the British bringing enlightenment can be readily paralleled from elsewhere in Johnson[9]—and in any case Reindorf was writing from within an established colonial order; Johnson, from the edge of one. A much more significant difference has to do with each man's relationship to his presumed ethnic and national constituencies. Just as Reindorf is proud of being a Ga and of his descent from the "national officiating high priests in Akra and Christiansborg,"[10] so is Johnson of his being an Oyo or Yoruba proper and descended from Abiodun (d. 1789), the last *Alafin* of Oyo before its decline. Reindorf also seems sensitive enough about his mulatto descent to insist that, at one point, it was those of mixed blood who "became the protectors and deliverers of their country from its enemies" (*HGCA*, 97)—an aspect of identity that did not affect Johnson. On the other hand, Johnson, like many of his colleagues, was a repatriate from Sierra Leone, with the burden of slavery and social deracination in his parents' recent past.

But the link between these received ethnic or communal identities and the wider emergent nations that both men envisaged was more complicated and problematic in Reindorf's case. The Ga people of Akra (Accra) were not numerous or central enough to be the core of a plausible modern nation; there was also "the principal and important portion of the Gold Coast, Fante, the land of history, the land of poetry and enlightenment and semi-civilization" (*HGCA*, v), whose early history Reindorf felt he had to leave on one side; and then again there was by far the most impressive indigenous state in the area, the still-independent Asante, which figures somewhat awkwardly in his account both as an ally of Akra and as an oppressor of the Fante. It was plainer for Johnson. The process by which a name applied by the Hausa to the Oyo ("Yoruba") got expanded to cover a mass of peoples with closely cognate dialects and cultures, dominant in the British colony of Lagos and its large hinterland, was begun by the CMS itself in the 1840s in Sierra Leone. And who could be more fitted than an Oyo pastor, resident for most of his life in Ibadan, the principal successor state to Old Oyo, to write the charter history of this emergent Yoruba nation? Things were as yet uncomplicated by the incorporation of Lagos and the Yoruba into an entity called Nigeria.

This relationship of the historians' primary ethnic roots (Ga and Oyo, respectively) to what they each saw as the potential nation (Gold Coast and Yoruba, respectively) profoundly shaped the emplotment of both *Histories*. Because Reindorf took as his collective subject a regional entity, defined originally by European activities and of much linguistic diversity, he plotted his as a universal history of enlightenment and progress working itself out in the Gold Coast. There are traces of other plots, such as the Rev. J. Zimmermann's scheme of Hamitic migration from the ancient seats of religion and civilization, followed by a "deathlike sleep of more than a thousand years," and finally the renewed call for Africa to rejoin "the history of the world" (*HGCA*, 1). And Middle Eastern, especially Jewish, origins had other, more specific uses: they could be used to back up such claims as that "no African nation or tribe [is] ever known to have so advanced in their religious views as the Akras" (*HGCA*, 6). But in the main, after an opening that gives us the *Bevölkerung* of the Gold Coast and early visitors from outside, *HGCA* presents a continuous history, with some ups and downs, but still with the overall impression of an upward movement. This effect is chiefly achieved by there being three (out of the 29) chapters that are thematic rather than segments of the chronological sequence that structures the work as a whole. The first (chapter 8) is a remarkable comparison of Tshi (Akan) and Akra (Ga) political forms, in terms partly of an antithesis between despotic and patriarchal government,[11] partly of a developmental sequence from prophet to priest to king (which surely derives from the Scripture history of mission training); and it urges on "the educated community [the need] to reorganize the whole structure of government on Christian principles, before we shall be acknowledged as a nation" (*HGCA*, 117). The second (chapter 19), interpolated in the main narrative sequence at the 1820s, covers the whole history of education and the missions from 1720 to 1890. The third (chapter 22), interpolated at the 1830s, deals with agriculture and runs the whole historical span from the time of Adam, through early farming on the Gold Coast, the new crops introduced by Europeans, problems of agricultural production, and finally "What the Government Should Do to Get the Colony Prosperous." It looks as if Reindorf found it impossible to work up most of his material in his preferred mode, as a story of progressive development, so he left it in a relatively unplotted chronicle form; but he provided the three chapters that, by each treating an aspect of long-term cultural change, could serve as hermeneutic keys to the whole, an invitation to the reader to discern steady progress even through the vicissitudes of wars and political history.

If the emplotment of Johnson's *HY* is more finely integrated, this fundamentally depends on his having a more amenable collective subject, the Oyo-to-Yoruba nation. Johnson was as committed to progress and Christian enlightenment as Reindorf, but he was able to combine it with the contrasting theme of restoration. This theme, entirely absent from the exordium of Reindorf's *History*, is given great prominence in Johnson's: British rule will bring not only modern advancement but also the welding together of the "disjointed units . . . as in the happy days of ABIODUN." This combination of recursion with progression is deeply set into the narrative structure of *HY*. The thirty-five chapters of *HY* are divided into two parts: part I, which presents an ethnographic introduction (140 pages, with another 55 mostly on the language), and part II, which is the history itself. Such an extensive ethnography gives a very strong definition to the Yoruba collective subject of the narrative to come. Part II is divided into four periods: of these the first (a mere 12 pages) and the second (a further 32 pages) may be taken together as covering the history of Old Oyo up to its culmination with the peaceful and prosperous reign of *Alafin* Abiodun; the third period (95 pages) covers the decline, disintegration, and eventual collapse of Oyo (ca. 1789–1836) through the joint agency of weak and incompetent rulers, disloyal subjects within, and ruthless enemies without, notably the Fulani jihadists; and the fourth (374 pages) presents the turbulent history of the mid- to late nineteenth century as a restoration, which Johnson saw as beginning with the growth of Ibadan (which stopped the Fulani tide) and hoped to see continued under British rule. So although *HY* is very unevenly weighted toward the fourth period, its narrative is clearly plotted in three stages, as the growth, decline, and recovery of a single nation.

Johnson's ideological coup was the persuasive alignment of Yoruba and Christian destinies, by means of a great romance of national redemption.[12] Since the notion of a redemptive history is a profoundly Christian one, we may say that *HY* offers a content of Yoruba experience organized within a Christian form. It is worth noting that, in contrast to Reindorf's devoting one of his thematic chapters to them, Johnson makes relatively few and passing references to the establishment and activities of the missions themselves. His Christianity makes itself felt in the more diffuse and profound way of how *HY* is emplotted. Michel Doortmont has made a case for Johnson's classicism, even suggesting that we should view *HY* as a Greek history, consciously modeled on the work of Xenophon in particular, who was in the Bühler curriculum.[13] This is not very persuasive. The few explicit references to the Greeks strike me as being essentially decorative in nature, classical grace notes like such baptismal names as Claudius, Pythagoras, and Zenobia, which were popular at the time with the Christian elite.[14] The similarities that Doortmont sees between Johnson's *HY* and Xenophon's *Hellenica* are either commonplace or likely to be fortuitous (e.g., both men wrote about their people's internecine wars, were participant observers of them, accepted the reality of divine intervention in human affairs, were interested in the portrayal of character, etc.). But however much of the *Hellenica* Johnson may have read with Bühler—and actually there is no *direct* evidence that he read any—it would have been of minimal importance compared to the Scripture history and Bible study that was the staple of his education. We know that Bühler had his pupils learning New Testament stories by heart; and at the end of a course on the Old Testament he wrote of his uplift at "their attention, their interest and their astonishment about the wonderful ways and dealings of God with Israel and the nations who came into contact with them and the whole plan of God for the redemption of the world."[15] The Bible in the King James Version, in which Johnson was saturated, and which he must have read virtually every day of his adult life, was incomparably the most important external literary influence on his historical thought.

THE EVANGELIST BECOMES A HISTORIAN

To appreciate the experiential ground of Johnson's historical work, we need to turn to the invaluable record of his and his fellows' daily thoughts and activities, and through them of so much of the life of the community at large, that is provided in the journal extracts that CMS agents were required to send back to the mission's headquarters in London. Johnson's first journal is dated 1870, when he was a young schoolmaster, 24 years old. In hesitant, immature prose he records his weekly sorties in Ibadan, after taking Sunday school, to preach under an *ọdan* tree. His superior, Daniel Olubi, reported of him that "often he came home with almost the words of the disciple, 'And the Seventy returned with joy saying, Lord, even the devils are subject to us through thy name.'"[16] On the evidence of his own journals, Johnson was highly combative in these encounters, showing little tenderness toward the pieties of his pagan auditors. At the same time, he early shows an interest in their history and an awareness of the importance of history to them: in his first journal he tells us of the settlers in Ibadan from the destroyed town of Ikoyi—though he gets the date of its destruction much too early—with the ex-king they had honored in their locality.[17]

We cannot but read Johnson's early journals for signs of the great *History* to come. At the outset they are far from unique, since the journals of several other African agents contain references to history, both in the past and in the current life of Yoruba towns, and to manifestations of local culture. Of course, because Johnson *did* write his history, we can sometimes identify in his journals passages that were later drawn on directly in *HY*, among the most remarkable of them one that tells of a man's near-death experience in which he had a revelation of the gods.[18] In fact we get the first real foretaste of Johnson's destiny as a historian not in his occasional references to past events but in the detail and zest of his narratives of political conflict in contemporary Ibadan, where we can compare him directly with his colleagues Olubi, Allen, and Okuseinde. Already in 1874 he gives us the most detailed blow-by-blow account, some of it eyewitness, of the downfall and murder of Efunsetan (the *Iyalode* or senior female chief), and by 1877 his handling of the civil disturbances round the downfalls of two other chiefs, Aiyejenku and Iyapo, is even more fluent, expansive, and assured.[19]

From the late 1870s too, Johnson's journals start to offer more historical amplification of his experiences, as if he was now continuously aware of the traces of the past in his routines of the present:[20]

> In July 1879 while out and about in Ibadan, he meets a middle-aged man, who greets him cordially. The man says he is an Agberi, and to Johnson's account of himself, replies: "I hold my communion directly with the invisible beings and I am too enlightened to be taught by you. . . . I am a diviner and can show you Sango, Oya, the maker [Obatala] and your own guardian angel [Ori]. . . ." Johnson emphasizes the uniqueness of Jesus, and how we cannot know the future, but only how to live and the future state after this life. He preaches a whole account of "Jesus and Him crucified." The man prostrates and says he'll come to hear more.

While there are dozens of reports of evangelistic encounters in the CMS journals that are rounded off something like this, Johnson goes on to tell us something about the Agberi:[21]

> "a tribe living to the east of Oyo, and . . . regarded as great doctors and charmers. Before the destruction of Oyo, they were the King's doctors and instruments of evil. . . ." He would use them if he wanted to kill a powerful chief, and for their skills they were held "in slavish veneration."

About this time Johnson starts to travel more widely, especially to the east of Yorubaland, which was never under Oyo rule, and he acquires a sharper sense of regional variety and local history. He does not lack confidence in his judgments, made against a cultural standard provided by the Oyo: Yoruba civility required that people lived in towns (*ìlú*) and had a king (*ọba*). So in 1880 he describes the Ikale, a Yoruba subgroup who lived toward the creeks in the far southeast, as:[22]

> a set of people still inferior to the Ondos [a kingdom of the southeast] in intellect and mode of life. They are a half naked, greasy bodied, dirty and covetous people, occupying a vast portion of land, but living in thickets without any regular town. Each village consists of a family or families and the headman is their chief. . . . No sign of royalty to distinguish them, they are all in their primitive state.

By 1882 he had started occasional diplomatic service with the governor of Lagos to end the war. As he passes through Modakeke on his way northeast to the war camp of Kiriji, where the armies of Ibadan and the Ekitiparapo faced each other, he gives a potted history of the origins of the Ife-Modakeke quarrel, though again his dating is loose ("about the commencement of the 18th century [surely he meant the 19th] when the Yoruba kingdom was destroyed").[23] I suspect that the great project of the history may have crystallized in his mind about now—he must have been stimulated by what he learned of the antecedents of the bitter interstate rivalries expressed at Kiriji. In November 1882, news of an insurrection against the reigning *Alafin* Adeyemi at Oyo led him to comment that "in this country as in [a] civilised country the person of the king . . . [is] sacred," so if a king is rejected, it is a message from the people that he must kill himself; and he mentions the precedent of the death of Abiodun's successor Aole, the *Alafin* at Old Oyo under whom the decline began.[24] A week later he has an argument with some Muslims in Ibadan about the religious authority of the Koran. When one of the Muslims says Mohammed proved he was a prophet by giving an account of five generations before his birth, Johnson ripostes: "I can now tell you the names and histories of the kings of Yoruba since it was kingdom, generations before King Abiodun, am I therefore a prophet?"[25] It is from this point that we can be pretty sure that Johnson was working on the *History.*

YORUBA EXPERIENCES, BIBLICAL INTERPRETATION

Johnson's maturation as a historian took place against the background of near-continuous evangelistic and pastoral practice (except for the periods in 1882–84 and 1886–87 when he was on diplomatic business). So how was doing history relevant to *that?* History among the Yoruba may be seen as grounded in two contrasting forms (which, however, also touched and sometimes merged with each other): tradition and memory. By "tradition" I mean those socially consolidated versions of the past, and particularly accounts of the origins of institutions, that served to define communities and underwrite authority in them. By "memory" I mean those traces of past experience present in the consciousness of every human being that provided the essential but problematic basis for the sense of personal identity, as well as the constraining or enabling basis for future action. Tradition is social and hierarchical; memory is individual and open-access. In mid- to late nineteenth-century Yorubaland the break point between the two was largely associated with the collapse of Old Oyo and its knock-on effects. Hence references to the two key figures of this transition—Abiodun, the *Alafin* of Oyo at its apogee, and Afonja, the ruler of Ilorin whose alliance with the Fulani led to Oyo's final destruction in the 1830s—were commonplace in popular historical discourse and thence taken up by Johnson.[26] In 1876, he mentions a female baptismal candidate over seventy years old, allegedly born about 1800 in the reign of Abiodun, "whom Mungo Park knew."[27] As late as 1883 there died a parishioner of Olubi's, an old lady so full of years that she had seen eleven kings of Yoruba crowned.[28] Tradition and personal memory thus took on another contrast: the former was idealized as past order whereas the latter was full of the experiences of warfare, dislocation, enslavement, loss of kin, and so forth. David Hinderer commented, in a report of a journey through the region of the old Egba towns, destroyed in the wars of the 1820s, that a book of touching interest might be written from the tales that his Yoruba companions told of them.[29] The recent past, the past of memory, was characterized by Yoruba as an "Age of Confusion," a time under the sway of Esu, the trickster deity.

The aim of any mission is to insert itself into the ongoing history of the evangelized people and so to transform it. With successful missions a complex mutual adaptation nearly always occurs, in which Christianity is seen as fulfilling or conforming with key elements of local culture even as it challenges or rejects others. To appropriate and rework local versions of the past so as to legitimate the new religion is a critical aspect of this process. It is also a highly assertive act, for it insists both that the Christians *belong* to local society and that their leaders have authority. The clash of rival authority claims was very evident in Johnson's encounters with the Agberi diviner and the argumentative Muslim that I have already noted. But the very real epistemological issues were never more clearly expressed than in an exchange with a Sango devotee, who responded to Johnson's preaching by demanding to know "How could you know God's mind?" Johnson continues his account:[30]

> I replied it was revealed in Christ His blessed son 1800 years ago. He interrupted me by saying, "What a liar! Were you then born? How do you want to believe on Him whom you have not seen?" I replied, "Let me answer your question by another. Was Abiodun really a king of Yoruba?" "Why, decidedly," he replied, "Who knows not that?" "But were you then born?" I asked again. "No," he replied. I then said, "How then do you want me to believe him to have lived and reigned whom you have not seen?" He replied, "Eyewitnesses over whom he reigned are living testimonies who

> testified the same to us." "Even so," I rejoined, "Eye and ear witnesses have handed it down in writing of all that Jesus did and taught on earth." He dropped the conversation and asked for rum.

Here speaks someone who placed the verification of Yoruba and of Christian history within a single cognitive framework, with the figure of Abiodun providing a critical point of common reference between him and his interlocutor.

In the battle against heathenism, Johnson was quite prepared to use his acquired knowledge of history (qua tradition) against those who owned it. In particular, he argued that the histories of *oriṣa* (deities) showed that they were *merely* deified men, unscrupulously elevated to the status of gods by their priests—a strategy especially useful in the case of the Christians' worst bugbear, Sango, the thunder god, who was reputedly an early *Alafin* of Oyo. The great occasion when this argument was deployed was when the mission house was itself struck by lightning in 1883—Johnson himself narrowly missed being killed—and a large crowd of Sango worshippers surrounded the house to demand the usual heavy fines and to carry out the appropriate rituals of appeasement. The Christians refused to comply, and an angry confrontation ensued, but the Sango people were repulsed. In the next few days, as many visitors flocked to the mission house, Johnson challenged the cult by explaining the nature of electricity and divulging Sango's history: "The history of Sango are [*sic*] only known to the Priests and this the common people were also made to know, and the cruel deceits of the Priests exposed by us to their shame."[31]

In contrast to this polemical euhemerism, the Christians also sought to associate themselves with the best of Yoruba tradition. In 1898 the elderly Daniel Olubi gave a remarkable sermon at the ordination of Johnson's long-term friend and colleague, F. L. Akiele, taking as his text II Timothy 2:1, "Then therefore, my child, be strong in the grace of Christ Jesus":[32]

> Olubi gave the *Ẹṣọ*, the elite of military chiefs at Old Oyo, sometimes called the *Alafin*'s bodyguard, as the exemplar of the virtues commended to the ordinand. Renowned for their courage, loyalty, endurance and obedience to their royal master, the *Ẹṣọ* had ever to be braced and ready, always prepared to suffer for the cause, and their dying words to their king must be "I am coming to meet you." . . . "Your devotion, your obedience, your love must be unquestioning, you cannot prostrate yourself to the world, you cannot suffer yourself to be turned aside from the path of duty, you cannot allow yourself to grow slack, even in your death you will still be your master's servant."

This sermon had an electrifying effect on the congregation, whose members perfectly understood the symbolic meaning of the *Ẹṣọ*. Johnson's *History* (completed the previous year) shows us why: it quotes sayings still current that celebrated the honor and staunchness of the *Ẹṣọ* and emphasizes the pride people still felt in being descended from one (*HY*, 73–74). Olubi's sermon and Johnson's *History* may well be taken together as documents that mark a certain moment in the inculturation of Christianity by the Yoruba. The Christians in Ibadan had long been regarded as "a quiet people, averse to fame and worldly honour,"[33] and their young men had sometimes been accused of being cowards for their reluctance to enroll as warriors, so this conspicuous endorsement of a military elite indicates a major rhetorical shift. It is significant that the model was a historical one, set back in *Old* Oyo, while the context of its use was an Ibadan newly under the *Pax Britannica*. Olubi's sermon expresses a new confidence in the Christian body, as it felt itself able to move from the margins of society closer to its center and able at last to appropriate something of the values of a past that it once deemed deeply inimical to it.

In contrast to this appropriation of tradition in order to place Christianity within Yoruba history was the appeal to memory, or the personal experience of recent events, in order to give a providential Christian shaping to that history. What Johnson does in *HY* has its roots in the mundane theodicies through which people sought meaning in the sufferings and successes of their lives. Though only Christianity had the theology for a transcendence of suffering through acceptance ("Thy grace is sufficient"), Yoruba pagans and Christians also shared much common ground: success was read as a sign of divine favor and suffering as a punishment to bring man back again to a proper relationship with God. In 1884 Johnson read a paper at the annual prayer joint meeting of the three Ibadan churches, "enumerating some of the special merits vouchsafed to us as a church during the past year."[34] The main items were the delivery of the houses of several leading Christians from pillage by the agents of the war chiefs, and the happy outcome of the lightning strike on the mission house, which had ended in the confusion of the Sango people.[35] The converse of this divine favor for God's people was the retributive justice that Johnson saw in the downfall of Iyapo, one of the ringleaders of the movement against Aiyejenku (*HY*, 410).

The politics of Ibadan were such as virtually to preclude a consistent moral response to them by Christian leaders. In his journal entries for 1874 describing the murder of Efunsetan by her own slaves at the instigation of the head chief, Latosisa the *Arẹ-Ọna-Kakamfo* (leading general of the Oyo army), Johnson leaves the reader in no doubt as to Latosisa's full involvement.[36] When charged, Latosisa denied it with oaths, "was acquitted to prevent civil war"—and then, with matchless hypocrisy, presided over the assembly that condemned the slaves to death for murder. In an act of necessary diplomacy, the Christian agents (including Johnson) then paid a formal visit to the *Arẹ-Ọna-Kakamfo* to congratulate him for being acquitted and also "to express our feelings of sympathy for the present state of the town." Johnson records that he "really was shaken" at the instant and ruthless execution of the slaves; and he concludes his narrative by exclaiming, "'Whoso sheddeth man's blood, by man shall his blood be shed' Oh! the consequences of sin." Yet a year or two later he describes Latosisa as "this good chief" and as a "good chief" of "kindly" actions on account of support he had given to members of the Christian body.[37] There was realpolitik on both sides to this friendship: Ibadan needed to keep the goodwill of the British in Lagos, and the African agents of the mission counted as *oyinbo* (Europeans). In the *History,* with benefit of distance and hindsight, Johnson is able to make a more measured judgment of Latosisa. The moral condemnation of many of his actions is still strongly present, but it is offset, not by facile plaudits for his favors to the Christians but by an understanding of his actions in Yoruba historical terms. Johnson opens his mature account of Latosisa's move in 1877 to pull down old Chief Aiyejenku by observing (*HY,* 407):

> The *Arẹ* [Latosisa] now began to evince more and more the characteristics of a Kakanfo. Experience has shown us that a Kakanfo always caused trouble at home and abroad. Their paths were always marked with blood. We have only to recall the history of Afonja of Ilorin, Edun of Gbogun and Ojo Amepo who were rivals, of Kurumi of Ijaye among others; and now Latosisa of Ibadan was on the same track.

So while Johnson judges Latosisa as a Christian, he explains his actions as a Yoruba.

Latosisa encapsulated the whole problem of Ibadan—and by implication of Yoruba culture generally—for the Christians. On the one hand Ibadan was dominated by values and practices deeply antithetical to those of the Christian missions: idolatry, slavery and slave raiding, polygamy, a militaristic ethos fostered by constant warfare, notions of personal worth and achievement diametrically opposed to those of the bourgeois individualism promoted by the missions. Yet at the same time, Johnson felt, there was an objective and overarching sense in which Ibadan was on the same side as Christianity in God's providential plan for his country. He makes his perspective plain at the close of the chapter dealing with the foundation of Ibadan, where he does not mince words in describing the violence and cruelty of its politics. But he concludes (*HY,* 245–46):

> The moral and social atmosphere of such a place as has been described could easily be imagined. Yet they were destined by God to play a most important part in the history of the Yorubas, to break the Fulani yoke and to save the rest of the country from foreign domination; in short to be a protector as well as scourge in the land. . . . A nation born under such strenuous circumstances cannot but leave the impress of its hardihood and warlike spirit on succeeding generations, and so we find it in Ibadan to this day. It being the Divine prerogative to use whomsoever He will to effect His Divine purpose, God uses a certain nation or individual as the scourge of another nation and when His purposes are fulfilled He casts the scourge away.

Johnson did not initiate this rationalization of Ibadan as a God's scourge of the Yoruba, for it was a regular part of the moral discourse of the CMS missionaries in

Ibadan. An African catechist, James Barber, had written in 1856 that the Ibadans "are proud of the conquering power which the Lord has lent them for a time [but] . . . they do not know themselves to be nothing but a whip in the hand of God to chastise their fellow sinners."[38] Over twenty years later, Daniel Olubi, travelling through Ondo, quotes a view that the Ibadans were "made as rods by God to correct these nations, and when he pleases to finish with them, there will be an end."[39]

The passage quoted above is Johnson's most central and solemn statement as to the purpose of his *History:* an attempt to discern the purposes of God operating through the turbulent history of his times and his people, and (as a corollary) to give a secure place to Christianity in that history. He achieves this by plotting his *History* as a romance, the story of a people's redemption through its suffering, a story whose outcome would bring both a restoration of the nation and its renewal through the enlightenment of the Gospel. Ibadan and the Christian mission, though mutually opposed in so many ways, by God's providence combined to offer salvation to the Yoruba nation. The comparison of Johnson with Reindorf from which I began seems to point more clearly to the differences than to the similarity between them. Their contrasting circumstances, which indicated historical problems unique to each of them, meant that this had to be so. But they were both native pastors of their respective churches; and if there is any indication from Johnson as to how we should read Reindorf, it is that we should not overlook how the life of the mission agent engendered the historian[40]—or, as the Yoruba might put it: *Alufa baba ọpitan,* "The pastor is the begetter of the historian."

3

Ogun in Precolonial Yorubaland

A Comparative Analysis

Clerical intellectuals like Samuel Johnson prided themselves on being the constructors of a more nearly unified concept of Yoruba society and culture,[1] including something that they called "Yoruba heathenism."[2] Yet they were well aware of the variety that stood in the way of this task, since their very activity as evangelists introduced them to religious practices in dozens of communities across a large swath of Yorubaland, and their detailed reports necessarily document it. In this chapter my aim is to use this evidence in a deconstructionist spirit, suggesting that the sheer extent of regional diversity in Yoruba religious practice calls into question whether we should be speaking of Yoruba religion as a single entity at all. We have to deconstruct Yoruba religion if we are to see it as an entity with a history rather than (as most of the literature presents it) as a pantheon of deities with unchanging, even eternal attributes, as first manifest in the archetypal setting of primordial Ile-Ife.

Ogun, the Yoruba god of iron and war, makes an excellent subject for this purpose, since his cult is spread all over Yorubaland, placing him clearly in the quite small number of truly pan-Yoruba *orișa*. In this task, comparison will play a key role, in two dimensions: between the manifestation of Ogun in different areas/locations and between the functional attributes of Ogun and other *orișa*. What will emerge is a view of Yoruba traditional religion as less a single pantheon of deities with fixed attributes in relation to one another, spread evenly across the whole country, than a spectrum of varying cult complexes, each one the product of a unique set of local and historical circumstances.

EVIDENCE FROM THE CMS JOURNALS

The great bulk of the evidence will be drawn from the journals and reports of missionary agents—in the great majority, Yoruba ones—of the Church Missionary Society, active since 1845 and the richest contemporary source for almost any aspect of Yoruba life These men were hardly disinterested observers of what they considered to be "idolatry," and only rarely can their observations be called ethnographic, in the sense of attempting to portray "heathen" religious practices in some detail as being significant in their own right. There is, for example, little detailed description of the rituals of *orịṣa* worship or record of myths or prayers. What we have is hundreds of mostly brief references to the *orịṣa* and their devotees as they came to the attention of CMS agents proceeding about their pastoral and evangelistic duties. These fall into several main categories: observations of *orịṣa* worship by individuals encountered in streets or houses; references to public festivals, sacrifices, or oracular consultations; conversations and arguments with devotees or priests about their *orịṣa* or about *orịṣa* worship in general; itemizations of which idols have been given up by new converts; and, very occasionally, general characterizations of particular *orịṣa* or of the cults of a particular community. In contrast to much of the large existing literature on *orịṣa,* which is strong on general characterizations of the *orịṣa* drawn from oral sources such as myths, Ifa divination literature and other kinds of religious poetry, and on analyses of their rituals, particularly the great annual festivals, as observed in the present, the CMS data focus our attention on the more prosaic, day-to-day character of *orịṣa* worship. Where modern studies of traditional religion commonly present it as detached from the main preoccupations of daily life, the CMS journal writers, even if their accounts do not often penetrate very deeply, cannot but forcefully convey the omnipresence of the *orịṣa* in the lives of ordinary Yoruba in the nineteenth century. Their evidence, taken as a whole, tells us a great deal about both the settings wherein and the occasions when Yoruba people entered into relations with the *orịṣa.*

So this body of source material has weaknesses of which we must be aware, as well as strengths that we should try to exploit. The most significant strength is the sheer number of references to *orịṣa* cults—in my reading of the entire archive, I have noted 778 of them and have doubtless missed some—made under broadly similar assumptions over a large swath of Yorubaland. This makes possible systematic comparison between different towns and regions in terms of their cult profiles and between the manifestations of particular *orịṣa* in different places. Through comparison, and particularly through the use of appropriate contrast cases (e.g., Sango vs. Ogun, Ogun in eastern vs. in western Yorubaland), we can make much more out of what are often rather passing observations. And just as a determined historicism is the best antidote to the tendency to essentialize Yoruba religion

TABLE 3.1 *Oriṣa* Reported in Church Missionary Society Journals, 1845–1912

Oriṣa	Abeokuta		Coastal Southwest		Ibadan		Other Oyo		East		TOTAL (n)
	n	%	n	%	n	%	n	%	n	%	
Ogun	11	4	6	4	10	7	5	6	21	14	53
Sango	41	16	23	16	41	27	29	38	12	8	146
Oya	3	1	1	1	9	6	7	9	1	1	21
Orisa Oko	14	6	1	1	12	8	5	6	0	—	32
Obatala	30	12	4	3	11	7	2	3	8	5	55
Other white *oriṣa*	13	5	8	6	4	3	3	3	1	1	29
Ifa	40	16	31	22	25	17	15	19	29	19	140
Esu/Elegbara	19	8	14	10	9	6	2	3	27	17	71
Osun	15	6	6	4	8	5	0	—	13	8	42
Yemoja	12	5	6	4	1	1	1	1	0	—	20
Other water *oriṣa*	5	2	5	3	2	1	1	1	4	3	17
Osanyin	3	1	8	6	1	1	0	—	1	1	13
Sopona	9	4	3	2	2	1	0	—	6	4	20
Buruku	6	2	1	1	2	1	0	—	0	—	9
Ori	6	2	4	3	3	2	3	4	0	—	16
Ibeji	5	2	3	2	2	1	0	—	0	—	10
Other	21	8	20	14	8	5	4	5	31	20	84
TOTAL	**253**	**100**	**144**	**102**	**150**	**99**	**77**	**98**	**154**	**101**	**778**

NOTE: Percentage totals may exceed or fall short of 100 percent on account of rounding. *Abeokuta* includes all Egba and Egbado towns and villages, but more than 90 percent of references relate to Abeokuta itself. *Coastal Southwest* means Lagos, Badagry and vicinity, Awori towns (Ota, Igbesa, Ado Odo). *Ibadan* is just Ibadan and its farm villages. *Other Oyo* means (in order of importance) Ijaye, Iseyin, New Oyo, Oke Ogun settlements, Ogbomosho, and observations made on journeys through the Oyo towns to the east of Ibadan. *East* means (in order of importance) Ondo, settlements on the Eastern Lagoon (Leki, Itebu, Ikale), Ilesha, and a small part of western Ekiti.

across time, so is regional comparison to the too easy assumption of pan-Yoruba uniformity. It is not that pronounced continuities do not exist in Yoruba religion across both time and space but that they need to be seen as existing in the face of historical vicissitudes and variable local circumstances.

Table 3.1 presents references to the main *oriṣa* in the journals and letters of CMS agents organized according to five distinct regions, each of which has its own cultural character. Because of the uncertainties attaching to the figures, they are better used comparatively with one another—because the effects of the uncertainties will then tend to cancel one another out—rather than treated individually as indicators of an objective state of affairs. Moreover, because they are biased by where the CMS was active, as well as by the number of mission agents and the length of time they served—nearly a third of the references relate to Abeokuta, and just over half to the southwestern corner of Yorubaland, while Ijebu and large parts of the farther north and east are missing—cross-regional comparisons need to be made on the basis of the proportion of references that each *orișa* receives in a particular region. Thus we can compare the 4 percent of references to *orișa* that Ogun receives in Abeokuta with Obatala's 12 percent in the same town or the 14 percent that Ogun reaches in the East. The table needs to be read down (comparison within a region) before it is read across (comparison between regions).

Of course, these kinds of data present certain problems in their use. Most important, the aggregate references to *orișa* in the CMS agents' reports can be at best only an approximate measure of their actual significance in the lives of communities, since strictly speaking they record not the real frequency of cult observance among the Yoruba but rather what struck missionary observers most frequently as worthy of report. Religious prejudice, as such, seems less of a problem than less obvious forms of bias, such as a tendency to give more space to what caught the eye or to neglect those aspects of religion that were private or implicit in other activities. Doubts about arguments that proceed largely from silences or thinnesses in the sources are well recognized in principle in historical methodology but are less easy to quell in practice. I simply say that I am very aware of them, and I will address them as they become pertinent at particular points in the argument.

TWO QUESTIONS ABOUT OGUN

So what do the figures tell of Ogun? To begin with, they clearly confirm what is often remarked on in the literature, that the cult of Ogun is especially strong in eastern Yorubaland. From the Eastern Lagoon up through Ondo to Ilesha and the edges of Ekiti, Ogun accounts for 14 percent of *orișa* reported, third after Ifa (19%) and Esu (17%). Ogun's important cult center at Ire[3] is unfortunately unreported—most of Ekiti was not visited by evangelists until the twentieth century—and so is the famous Olojo festival of Ogun at Ife.[4] But Ogun's importance at Ondo and Ilesha is strongly attested. At Ondo, unlike Abeokuta or Ibadan, the annual festival of Ogun is referred to as a major event in the public life of the town.[5] Though references to Ilesha are relatively sparse compared with the rich documentation available for Ondo from 1875 onward, the CMS agent there wrote in June 1889 of "the annual festivity of Ifa . . . which with Ogun, wh[ose] festivity is always kept about six [months] after this, make the two great idols worshipped in common by the whole town from the king to the poorest man."[6] Ifa and Ogun still structure the Ijesha year in this fashion, and the dominance of precolonial religion by these two *orișa* is strongly confirmed by the responses to a question put to household heads in a sample survey that I conducted in Ilesha in 1974: Ifa and Ogun each made up 26 percent of all *orișa* named as those worshipped traditionally in the household, followed by Osun at 8 percent and Orisa Onifon (the local equivalent of Obatala) at 7 percent.[7] It so happens that the agents who provide us with information about the cults of these eastern Yoruba towns were themselves mostly Egba, and they clearly understood that the cult profiles of this area were significantly different from what they knew at home in Abeokuta. So the first question is: Why is Ogun more prominent in the religious systems of eastern Yorubaland?

The second question concerns the nature of Ogun's presence in western Yorubaland. My initial reaction on collating the evidence of the CMS reports was one of surprise that in the whole southwestern area Ogun accounted for only 4 percent of references and was outstripped by Sango in the ratio 4:1, even though Sango was a deity associated with the Oyo enemies of the Egba.[8] In Abeokuta itself, Ogun also came behind such *oriṣa* as Ifa, Obatala, Esu, Osun, Orisa Oko, and Yemoja. In Ibadan and the Oyo areas, Ogun came up somewhat more often but at 7 percent still did not reach more than half the level reported for the east. This was the more surprising since Ogun appears to occur far more often as the main element in personal names than any other *oriṣa* (with the possible exception of Ifa). Notable examples include Ogunbona and Ogundipe, the two *balogun* (war chiefs) who successively between the 1840s and the 1880s were the chief patrons and protectors of the CMS at Abeokuta; Ogunmola, the *Baṣọrun* of Ibadan; Ogunkoroju, the *Balogun* of Ijaye who gave quiet support to the mission there; and Ogunbiyi, the first Lagosian chief to become a Christian. The explanation I shall propose will be partly a matter of religious *realities,* that Ogun was part of a more complex cultic division of labor in the Center and the West, and partly one of religious *appearances,* that Ogun was of a particularly immanent character, which reduced his saliency to the missionary gaze.

OGUN AND IRON

Ogun is most commonly glossed by the CMS journal writers as the god of iron and war, and the relations between these aspects have provided a primary focus for discussing Ogun's place in the cultural and political development of forest-belt West Africa. Ogun appears as god of iron in a more direct and unmediated sense than as god of war, since he is not merely *of* iron, in the sense of being the force or principle behind iron technology, but virtually iron itself, worshipped as a personal force. The epithet god of iron sounds analogous to such expressions as god of brass or god of palm nut, applied to Osun and Ifa, respectively, which missionaries sometimes used to make their point that the *oriṣa* were *merely* idols: inanimate material objects or artifacts taken to represent imaginary beings. Ogun is sometimes described in this way as god of stone,[9] which refers to the blacksmith's anvil stone, taken as one of his symbols. But with iron, it seems less fitting to say that Ogun was represented by iron than that Ogun *was* iron. Perhaps this would explain why Ogun, despite the very personalized way in which he appears in myth, is never portrayed in carved human form, as such a representation could only be inferior to iron itself.[10] Such thoughts appear to have been in the mind of the Ibadan catechist

James Barber when, in his report of a deep discussion with a diviner or *babalawo,* he first wrote "Ogun (the god of iron, which is of hunting and war)," and then crossed out the first "of," so that it reads simply "Ogun (the god iron)."[11]

This is consistent with the common practice of Ogun's cult as CMS evangelists observed it. At Erinla, near Ondo, a man worships Ogun in the form of some iron implements with a piece of skin from an elephant's tail,[12] and at Leki, on the Eastern Lagoon, a pastor encounters six men in an enclosure next to a house worshipping Ogun as "twelve guns arranged horizontally in a row, an animal having been sacrificed to worship them."[13] But what particularly underscores how much Ogun is identified with iron is that clear instances of Ogun worship are often described without Ogun being named as such—something that happens with no other deity. A Lagos pastor sees a dead fowl hanging over the anvil and bits of kola lying around in a blacksmith's shop. Asked why he doesn't eat them instead, the blacksmith replies that he must be "paying religious homage to his tools as such acts make him to be always lucky."[14] The German missionary J. A. Maser gives a more detailed account of a rather similar ritual at Abeokuta:

> Abroad in the town, he encounters a family group gathered in a blacksmith's shop for an oracular consultation. Seven "country hammers," the blacksmith's tools, are set up erect, and he addresses each in turn, breaking kola as he does so. As the pieces fall, the answers are lucky or not. The sacrificial fowl is held up in front of the hammers. As Maser retires, not wanting to disturb the ceremony, the blacksmith calls him back to partake of the kola, which he declines.

Maser does not say that the ritual here is addressed to Ogun, but this is confirmed when he calls back ten days later to find the blacksmith in the "house of Ogun" close by, "making *odun* [festival]" with his fellow worshippers.[15] Elsewhere, in the absence of the clinching presence of the blacksmith, iron objects of worship can be only presumptively attributed to Ogun, though I think the presumption must usually be very strong, as with the calabash with a plate, an old rusty sword, a mug, and half of a pair of scissors that made up the idol of a man at Palma,[16] or the "new god of iron" that Chief Olikosi of Ota set up in the center of his house.[17] A case that is less certain is a reference to people rescuing their "gods of iron" from their houses during a fire at Abeokuta, for the plural may have indicated other deities, such as Orisa Oko or Osanyin, whose cult objects were also made of iron.[18]

The links between Ogun and iron appear more directly in connection with blacksmiths, who are engaged in the mysterious transformations of ore and metal, than with other occupational groups, such as hunters, warriors, and farmers, who merely use iron tools. Here there is a very marked and curious bias in the CMS references. Although Ogun was more widely worshipped (both by individuals and as the major deity of the community) in the east, nearly all the references to blacksmiths, whether or not they also refer to Ogun, occur in documents relating to central or western Yorubaland. This does not seem likely to have occurred randomly, and yet obviously there were many blacksmiths in the east, so it is a real puzzle that they are virtually missing from the detailed and continuous reportage that we have over more than thirty years from Ondo, for example.[19]

The most likely immediate reason has to do with the public saliency of blacksmiths, which would affect the frequency of missionary allusion to them. In central and western Yoruba, blacksmiths' shops are often mentioned in reports of public preaching about the town, for they were places where people liked to congregate, like markets, thus providing the evangelist with a ready-made audience. The processes of ironworking were also a rich source of useful metaphors. In one case the evangelist affects to accuse the blacksmith of cruelty for putting the iron in the fire and inflicting blows on it—"iron being worshipped by the people as the god of iron," he adds—and goes on to ask them: "To whom then . . . should we give thanks—He who makes the iron for our use or the iron which is made?"[20] In another case, a catechist chances on workers separating the dross from the pure iron and likens it to sin. "As this iron was useless before you smelted it, so is our body," he tells them. "We are to be purified before we are made fit for the kingdom of heaven and there is no furnace that would make us pure, but the blood of Christ which cleanseth from all sins."[21]

These two cases come from Ota and Ibadan, and apparently blacksmiths' shops were not the same kind of public place as this in Ondo. Weavers' sheds—again a venue suitable for the evangelist to make contacts[22]—present something of a parallel case, being present in Ibadan and Abeokuta, but absent in Ondo. Here there is an obvious reason: the East lacked the tradition of men's weaving that existed among the Oyo and Egba.[23] Though this does not help us directly, it still suggests that regional comparison may clarify things. For as well as the contrasts between eastern and central/western Yorubaland in the prominence of the Ogun cult and in the frequency of reference to blacksmiths in missionary reportage, there is a third: the scale of ironworking activity itself. As map 1 shows, whereas the great civic festivals of Ogun are to be found in the East, especially in its forest regions, the centers of iron mining and smelting—the real seat of iron technology—are located in an arc running from the Awori country west of Lagos up into Egbado, to a large area of north-central Yorubaland between Ibadan, Iseyin, and Ogbomosho, possibly to Ilorin.[24]

That blacksmiths' shops in the Center/West appear more prominently as public venues may be related to the practice here of a wider and more elaborate range of ironworking techniques, which included smelting. Though Eugenia Herbert in her comparative study of African ironworking has underscored the contrast between smelting and smithing, the correlations we have found for Yorubaland rather undermine her linkage of smithing with the public and smelting with the secret and isolated.[25] It was in the Yoruba East, which lacked a strong tradition of smelting, that blacksmiths appear to have worked inside their compounds, just as women did their weaving. Yet it was also here, where iron was most scarce

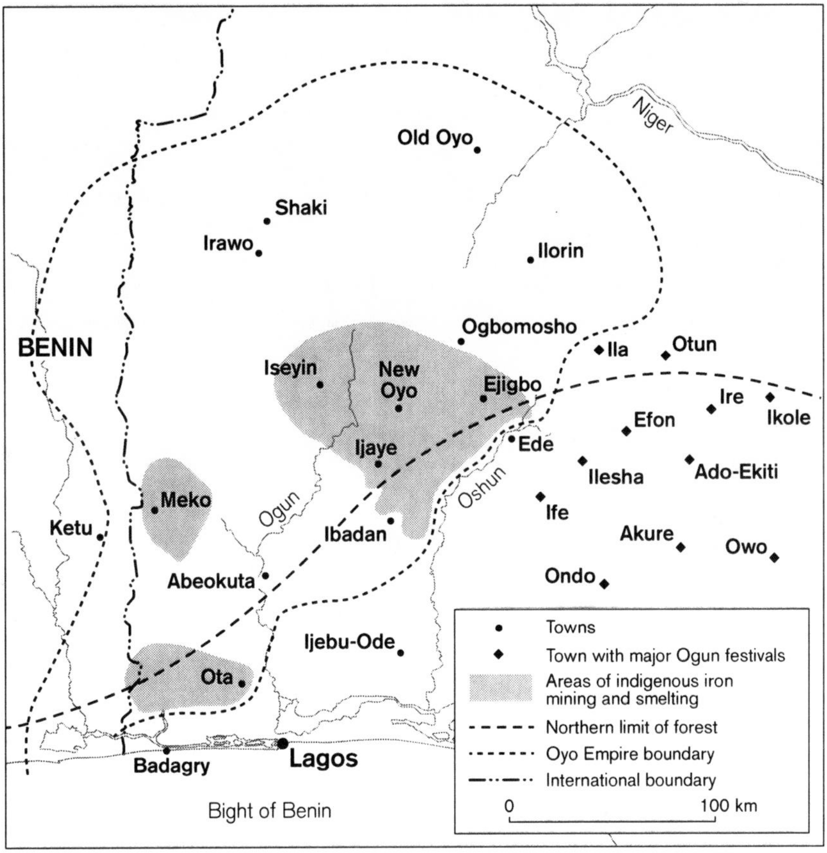

MAP 1. Yorubaland: Iron and Ogun.

because it was not locally produced and was imported from the smelting areas of the West and North,[26] that Ogun was held in the greatest honor.[27] For iron must have been particularly crucial in enabling agriculture and human settlement to take place in the formidable environment of the southeastern forests. *Ẹni pe Ilaje l'oko, ko ni irin ajo Ogun ye* (Whoever calls Ilaje a farm will not have Ogun to clear his journey's path) goes an Ijesha proverb, referring to a small village that was once the kingdom's capital before the foundation of Ilesha.[28] What this proverb declares, like the festivals of Ogun in towns such as Ilesha and Ondo, is how much the overall viability of the community depends on the use of iron. The festivals do this most emphatically through the parades of the male citizenry through the town, marshaled by their *ẹgbẹ* or quarter-based bands of militia under their *ẹlẹgbẹ* chiefs, which are such a prominent feature of their title systems.[29] This tendency to associate Ogun with the generality of the townsfolk rather than just with those whose work brings them into close contact with iron is perhaps the keynote of the cult of Ogun in eastern Yorubaland.

OGUN AS SNAKE: A LOST CULT?

Nothing that has been said so far—whether about the individual devotions of blacksmiths and others who worked with iron or about the communal importance of Ogun in eastern Yorubaland—challenges the notion, widespread in the literature, that (as R.C. Abraham's *Dictionary of Modern Yoruba* puts it) "Ogun is worshipped only by men, not by women." This may seem to make symbolic sense for a deity of iron and war, yet it is not true. Pierre Verger has given a detailed account of women's participation as "femmes dediées à l'Oriṣa et qui chantent pour lui" in a festival of Ogun Igbo in the Nago villages of Ilodo and Isede, and Margaret Drewal has described women possessed by Ogun not far away at Igbogila in Egbado.[30] For a more prosaic instance of female devotion to Ogun, there was the female butcher noted by E.M. Lijadu far away at Ondo in 1892.[31] As she went into her stall in the market, she gathered up her iron implements, split kola and threw the pieces several times over them, and offered some incantations. To Lijadu's question, she said she was "consulting Aje the goddess of money through Ogun the god of iron [and that] Aje promises to send me many customers with much money to carry home after the market." This Ogun-Aje linkage is attested from elsewhere;[32] and as a woman's ritual directed at personal wealth, it may perhaps be seen as practically analogous to the cult of Ori, which was popular among wealthy women in central and southwestern Yorubaland but apparently absent from the East.[33] As described here by Lijadu, such elements of the ritual as breaking kola over iron tools seem identical to those practiced by male workers with iron.

But the main way in which Ogun appears in the CMS journals as an object of women's worship is quite different: not as iron but as a snake. It was not exclusively a women's cult, though women were most active in it (as indeed in most forms of *oriṣa* worship). The most dramatic account of the cult of Ogun as snake comes from Ijaye in 1855:[34]

> It was the annual Ifa festival of the *Arẹ* Kurunmi, despotic ruler of the town, and large crowds had gathered before the gate of his compound. Most of them were said to be "worshippers of the orisa called Ogun or snake," for Kurunmi's late mother had been one of its principal devotees, and this was in remembrance of her. Lots of snakes of different sizes from different parts of the town were brought to "play" with Kurunmi, but he wouldn't allow them inside his house since (says the African catechist Charles Phillips) he was afraid of them. So they were displayed on a platform set up in front of it. The worshippers took them up and carried them in their arms: mild unless irritated, some were up to six feet long and as thick as a man's thigh. The people looked upon them with curiosity and praise.

Kurunmi's own premier *orişa* was Sango, and a rather similar (though reversed) family linkage of Sango and Ogun came up during a pastoral visit at Ota in 1855: a female devotee of Sango has a child dedicated to Ogun, whose snake is kept in a calabash, where it is fed with rats.[35]

The cult was most publicly manifest when its members went about the town with their Ogun snakes, offering blessings in the god's name and receiving gifts (in essence, sacrifices) of cowries in return.[36] An African pastor in Abeokuta in 1852 met two women, "one of whom had a large snake curled round her neck, while the other as a crier went before singing and extolling Ogun the god of blacksmith [*sic*]."[37] Many years later another pastor, on the road to the Ibadan camp at Ikirun, met a "snake charmer" who had once even attended church at Ibadan with a Christian friend, and reproached him for "directing [people] to worship Ogun through the snake to earn his livelihood."[38] Back in Ibadan, a catechist told a woman sitting by the roadside with her snake and getting a few cowries from passersby that Ogun was not the true God to worship.[39] A traveling Methodist missionary was visited by a female "snake charmer" at Oyo in the early 1890s.[40] Our last glimpse of the cult is again in lbadan, when a European woman missionary encounters "sitting by the roadside an old woman, an Ogun worshipper with a huge snake coiled round the body, and she asking alms of the people."[41]

This form of the cult of Ogun has gone almost unremarked in the secondary literature, save for the briefest passing reference in P. Amaury Talbot's *Peoples of Southern Nigeria* (1926) to "snake charmers, . . . who adore [Ogun] in the guise of a smallish snake called Mana-mana."[42] This does not sound as if it derives from any very close acquaintance with the cult, since *mọna-mọna* means "python," which better fits the descriptions of the sometimes large snakes that occur in eyewitness reports from the nineteenth century. Evidently erased from the memory of Abraham's educated informants in Ibadan in the early 1950s (along with the memory that women also worshipped Ogun), it seems likely that it died out rather rapidly in the early twentieth century. The old woman whom Mrs. Fry met with her snake near Kudeti church in 1911 must have been one of a dwindling band. It looks likely that it died out sooner among the Egba than among the Oyo Yoruba: the sole Abeokuta reference is from the 1850s, whereas those for the Oyo areas continue into the 1880s and later. This seems supported by the confused reference to the cult in Rev. Tom Harding's summary account of Egba religion in 1888: he emphasizes the importance of Ogun in a listing of *orişa* that goes on to mention Orisa Oko and Yemoja, and right at the end notes that worship is also given "to a snake called Manumanu."[43] Harding's failure to link "Manumanu" explicitly with Ogun, if it is not due to misunderstanding or ignorance, suggests that this form of Ogun's cult was by then rare if not extinct at Abeokuta.

It is not easy, in the absence of evidence of other kinds from outside the CMS papers, to explain why Ogun's cult should take this form. But one final negative clue gives us a little help. There is only one reference to Ogun as snake from outside the central and western areas, but it is an exception that seems to prove the rule that this cult was exotic to the east:[44]

> At Ondo in 1878 a man and a woman were seen to have brought from Ile-Ife several snakes which they publicly exhibited "as the god Ogun, blessing the people in its name . . . [and getting] large amounts of cowries in return." But next day one of the quarter chiefs took against them when they started their display in his street, and threatened to cut the snakes to pieces. This triggered a popular clamor against them, and the *Lisa* [Ondo's most powerful chief of the day] advised them to get out of town.

Since the site of Ile-Ife was all but deserted at this time, it seems quite likely that these two religious entrepreneurs were not themselves Ifes but Oyos from the adjacent settlement of Modakeke, where the cult must have been as prevalent as it was in Ibadan or Ijaye. However that may be, the Ondos clearly took it greatly amiss that strangers should come and present one of their most important deities in such an outlandish form.

So we need to seek an explanation in terms that apply specifically to the situation in central and western Yorubaland. Dahomey may seem a possible source, since it had two notable snake deities. There was the *vodun* Dangbe, represented by a large python at its major cult center at Whydah, and also worshipped along the lagoon eastward as far as Badagry;[45] and there was also the rainbow serpent Dan, otherwise known as Aido-Hwedo or (by the Yoruba) Osumare, whose origins were traced to the Mahi country north of Abomey.[46] But neither of these seems to have any affinity with Ogun (or with Gu, his Dahomean form). In any case, an explanation of a cult in terms of external origins is less helpful than one that deals with its intrinsic meaning.

Unfortunately, the lack of external evidence to supplement the thin accounts in the CMS journals prevents anything more than the most hesitant speculation. Snake symbolism in general can carry a number of different connotations, but one of the most widespread is of earth-rooted or chthonic power, and this would fit with the technologies of iron *production,* mining, and smelting, long practiced in central and western Yorubaland. Ogun as snake evidently had its heartland in the Oyo towns where Ogun, while not attaining the degree of civic recognition that it got in the iron-hungry East, was nevertheless an ancient cult, probably more so than Sango.[47] It was at Oyo in the 1950s that Peter Morton-Williams came across the *orișa* Alajogun, a refraction of Ogun known as the deity of fighting.[48] Alajogun, unlike Ogun himself, *was* represented in human form, and in one instance was accompanied by his wife Oke Ijemori, she standing with a snake around her neck (for she was said to play with them). Their children were hills (*oke*), and one wonders if iron-bearing hills were particularly intended. For what more appropriate as a symbol of this great power drawn from the earth than *mọna-mọna,* the python?

OGUN AND ORISA OKO

The prominence of any one of Ogun's potential meanings or functions in a particular place depends partly on local circumstances (such as the mining and smelting operations of the Center/West or the acute iron hunger of the East), but it is also affected by what other deities are present in any local complex of cults. By "local cult complex" I mean the ensemble of cults found in a particular place, which is likely to include both several *orịṣa* found more widely and others of more local currency, perhaps even locally unique. These complexes are the practical, concrete reality of Yoruba religion, rather than the pan-Yoruba pantheons—models or idealizations that give the *orịṣa* their particular characters, temporally and spatially standardized, and set them in a system of complementary relations with one another—that dominate the literature.[49]

What is generally held to be distinctive of an *orịṣa* is also qualified by the fact that all *orịṣa* are required by their devotees to provide much the same range of general benefits: protection, health, guidance, children, wealth, and so on. This means that female *orịṣa* (such as the gentle and fecund river goddesses Osun and Yemoja) sometimes take on traditionally male qualities like fierceness, while *orịṣa* with predominantly male functions (such as Ogun or Sango) can also reward their female devotees with fertility.[50] The mobility of *orịṣa,* whether as a consequence of the migration of their ordinary adherents or through the promotional zeal of their priests, also promotes shifts in the character of *orịṣa.* An incoming *orịṣa* may find its special niche (as the deity of the new yam, or smallpox, or hunting) already occupied, or it may seek to carve out a new niche for itself. Even the thunder god Sango, who seems the most essentially male of deities, can come to be represented as female where he is a latecomer to a community that already has a male thunder deity.[51] The unending push and pull between the homogenization and the differentiation of cults that takes place in the Yoruba religious marketplace means that no single cult can be considered in isolation.

As the god of the farm, whose main cult emblem was an iron stave made from hoe blades, Orisa Oko overlaps with Ogun in respect of the application of iron technology to agriculture. Though variously described as male or female, Orisa Oko is most commonly represented in myth as a hunter who turned to farming. His/her main cult center was at Irawo, a small town in the far northwest of Yorubaland, where there was an important shrine for the settlement of witchcraft accusations. According to the Rev. Thomas King, an Egba, Orisa Oko was the most esteemed and prominent deity worshipped by women at Abeokuta and was handed down in families, where its first acquisition "was always originate[d] from the accusation of witchcraft and sorcery."[52] Initiation was expensive, but membership carried social privileges: devotees (recognized by red and white marks on the forehead) could not be seized for debt, might cross war lines, and were exempt from tolls.[53] The interdict against their coming into contact with corpses suggests the relevance of the same complex of ideas about pollution and death that pertain to the cleansing role of the blacksmith's forge. A striking case of functional overlap at Abeokuta between Orisa Oko and Ogun was evident when, in order to promote cotton as a cash crop, the CMS introduced a roller gin to clean the raw cotton. Its erection and operation aroused great interest among the Egba, some reckoning it to be "a sort of mysteriously acting fieldpiece . . . for the use of the Egbas against their enemies," while others, contemplating it in silence, took it to be a manifestation of Orisa Oko.[54] In view of Ogun's celebrated adaptation to modern technology, it is noteworthy that in this instance from the mid-1850s it was Orisa Oko who took that part—as "a god represented by iron," explains our witness.

In the CMS reports from Ibadan, Orisa Oko figures rather differently. There is less emphasis on the elite status of Orisa Oko's devotees, and more on the communal importance of the cult. Because Abeokuta was founded as an amalgamation of many small towns, which kept each its cultic peculiarities, there was virtually no cult that embraced the whole town save that of Oro, the collective ancestors.[55] Ibadan's population was even more heterogeneous in its origins, but its early settlers were so scrambled that townwide festivals could coalesce more readily. The Egba pastor of Ibadan, Daniel Olubi, considered that, because "the whole town" was involved in them, the three principal deities of Ibadan were Orisa Oko, in whose honor "every gate and street are full of soup and pounded yams," along with Ogiyan (one of the "white deities," related to Obatala), and Oke'badan (Ibadan Hill, the *genius loci*).[56] Orisa Oko's importance, shown by his association with the New Yam festivities, rested on the Ibadan people's recognition of his key role in the annual reproduction of their community. When the second rains of 1883, much needed and expected, arrived in a nightlong downpour in mid-August, a pastor overheard many people in the street the next day attribute them to Orisa Oko, whose feast was due at the next new moon.[57]

All this seems to be just what we would expect for the chief agricultural deity; and insofar as Ogun could also have agricultural functions, we can consider Orisa Oko to have taken some of the semantic space in the West that Ogun occupied in the East. The exact converse has been noted by J. R. O. Ojo in a western Ekiti town where Orisa Oko had been introduced from an Oyo source: finding Ogun already clearly associated with farming, Orisa Oko had to assume a much more general role, as healer and protector against witchcraft and the like.[58] Another illuminating case is provided by Ila-Orangun, the main Igbomina town, which stands on the border between the East (where Ogun is the major civic deity) and the Center/West (where Sango and Orisa Oko have a strong presence). Here, according to John Pemberton's careful analysis, Ogun stands in a complementary relationship to Orisa Oko as hunter to farmer, the two aspects of subsistence provision.[59] But the ceremonial placing of the New Yam ritual was not simply a matter of anchoring it to the festival of the main agricultural deity. While it *was* very widely attached to Orisa Oko in the Center/West and to Ogun in the East, other *oriṣa* figured too: most commonly Obalufon, but also Oro at Iseyin, Ifa at Ilesha, Oramfe at Ondo, and even Sango at Ijaye.[60] Its linkage with a particular *orișa* seems to have been governed by local and practical considerations as much as by what was symbolically most appropriate, though in the towns of the East (as well as some old towns in the Center/West, such as Iseyin and Ede) Ogun was always bound into a ceremonial sequence that linked him with collective and royal ancestors, and with the forces of annual renewal, of which eating the New Yam was a powerful symbol.

OGUN AND SANGO

As a force to build empire, Ogun is challenged by Sango, the early *Alafin* of Oyo deified as the god of thunder. J. L. Matory has persuasively shown that Sango was much more than just the official cult of the Oyo regime: he was the very icon of the means and manner of the *Alafin*'s rule through his messengers (the *ilari*), the royal wives, and the Sango priests, who all stood symbolically as wives to the god-king as possessing husband.[61] Matory goes on to contrast Ogun with Sango as a deity who was more effective as a pathfinder or culture hero than as a ruler, and whom myth represents as failing to sustain his marriage with Yemoja. This is fair enough for Oyo but does not capture the manner in which Ogun's cult realized its communal importance, particularly among the eastern Yoruba. The central feature is that, despite his linkage with royal ancestors, Ogun's was typically a civic rather than a royal cult: a deity worshipped "from the king to the poorest man," as M. J. Luke put it for Ilesha in 1889.[62] A clear sign of this is the occurrence during Ogun festivals—as at Ilesha and Ila—of mock battles between palace and town chiefs, ritual dramas that present the expression and resolution of conflicts between the king and the people as lying at the heart of the public life of the community. At Ilesha, it was chiefs particularly connected with Ogun/iron who mediated the tensions between the king and the people.[63]

In the 1820s the imperial order of Old Oyo gave way to seventy years of turbulence among its successor states and their neighbors, which Matory sees as an Age of Ogun following an Age of Sango. The newly dominant social forms of the period—the warlords (*ologun*) and their retainers or "war boys" (*omo-ogun*), their vast military households, their prominence in the title systems of new towns such as Ibadan, Abeokuta, and Ijaye—have been well described by historians.[64] Matory's is quite a Yoruba way of putting it, in terms of successive ages (*aiye*) that have each its distinct character, and there is some evidence that contemporaries saw it this way too. A *babalawo,* in discussion with an African catechist in Ibadan in 1855, put down the wars to God's having sent Esu (disorder) and Ogun (war) "to execute His vengeance on men upon the earth for their disobedience."[65] Two decades later, a rather similar diagnosis was made by another *babalawo,* also in Ibadan.[66] God had sent Ogun and Sopona (the god of smallpox) into the world to "render unto everyone according to his deeds." As he went on, "Ogun is armed with four thousand short swords, and he goes out daily on the earth to slay, for his meat is to drink the blood of the slain." The *babalawo* ended by referring to Sango, "a very mighty god, and when he is about to go [into] the world, he is always cautioned by Ifa and Orisanla to deal gently with their own special worshippers." So both Ogun and Sango, like Esu and Sopona, are here seen as destructive deities, in contrast to the saving deities Ifa and Orisanla (Obatala). But the overall message is less that Yoruba considered this as *uniquely* Ogun's age than that they recognized Ogun as one of the major forces shaping it.

For as far as levels of individual devotion go, there is no evidence that Sango was displaced by Ogun. On the contrary, by the CMS evidence, Sango appears alongside Ifa as the most popular deity of late nineteenth-century Yorubaland, though less pan-Yoruba in the spread of his appeal than Ifa. Accounting for as many as 38 percent of all *oriṣa* referred to in Other Oyo towns (see table 3.1) and 27 percent in Ibadan—a difference explicable by Ibadan's significant population of non-Oyo origin—Sango attains 16 percent at Abeokuta, and still reaches 8 percent, equal to Osun, in the East, right outside his home territory. References to Ogun run at much lower levels, except for the East (where Ogun stands at 14 percent). Though these two sets of figures for Ogun and Sango are misleading as direct measures of their relative importance, they do shed valuable light on the social character of the two cults. For I suggest that the number of reports of Sango expresses not merely his popularity but also the sometimes spectacular appearance of his cult and the zeal with which he was promoted, both of which gave it a very high profile in nineteenth-century Yoruba towns. Sango's cult survived the collapse of the old imperial capital where it had been based, and it thrived vigorously in the new world of the warlords. It made its way through the belief of its devotees in its protecting power, through the way that it both frightened people and offered them relief from their fears, and through sheer predation, in the form of the purification fines or fees, backed by the threat of violence, that it levied after a house had been struck by lightning.[67] While priests of Ogun are never mentioned in the CMS reports[68] (except to the extent that a blacksmith might implicitly serve as one), priests of Sango are the next most frequently mentioned religious specialists after *babalawo* and Muslim *alfa*. The senior Sango priests at Ibadan were clearly formidable figures who had to be treated with circumspection by the ruling war chiefs of the town,[69] whereas the cult of Ogun does not appear as a distinct force in the politics of the town at all.

The adaptability of the Sango cult shows up equally at whichever end of its range we view it. As an instrument of rule, its potency was most evident at Ijaye, which until 1862 was Ibadan's only rival as the military successor state to Oyo. Ijaye's ruler Kurunmi—functionally a man of Ogun, if ever there was one—took the headship of the Sango cult himself and made it a mainstay of his regime. But Ijaye was an Oyo town, whose people already held Sango in awe. More impressive in its way was the extent to which Sango started to make inroads into Ogun's heartland of the East, regions that war and trade had opened to Oyo influence as never before. At Ilesha by the late 1880s, the Sango cultists were wielding a new influence over the king,[70] and their confident public praises of their god excited some popular resentment.[71] The reasons for these developments at Ilesha are obscure, but for Ondo we have a much better picture. In the late 1870s Ondo was afflicted by a run of smallpox epidemics. Though Sango was said in 1877 to be "worshipped here by only a few . . . [and] looked upon with some degree of contempt by the mass of the people," two years later he had "many worshippers," who conducted an impressive festival.[72] In 1879 and 1880 the chiefs gave large amounts to some newly arrived Sango cultists for sacrifices to expel the disease. The sheer chutzpah of the Sango people in promoting their god as the solution to the epidemic—something for which he was not previously known—can only be wondered at, especially when they called at the CMS compound afterward to mock the Ondos for their gullibility.[73]

Ogun's relevance to the public sphere was realized differently from Sango's. In all areas of Yorubaland, the nexus of killing, pollution, purification, and retributory justice was cardinal to it. Kurunmi, who avoided close contact with his mother's cult of Ogun as snake, is reported to have turned to Ogun on two occasions, which both involved the claim to righteous vengeance. An adulterous wife of his was killed, and her organs were torn out "in the front of his house before his Ogu, his god of iron"; and an old woman was killed for an unspecified offense at his Ifa festival, again before his Ogun, who this time received his usual sacrifice of a dog.[74] At Ota the place for executing criminals was a little grove of trees near one of the town gates, known as Ojugun (The Face of Ogun).[75] Ogun's role as the sanction of justice, which was most usually expressed in the practice of swearing on iron, is closely linked to his role in purifying the just shedder of blood. Here every blacksmith's shop was potentially a shrine: after the *egungun* at Ibadan had executed the adulterous wife of a chief, the actual killer had to sleep in a blacksmith's shop for several nights, to be released from blood guilt.[76] Both sides at the Kiriji battlefield had shrines of Ogun whither heads of the slain were taken,[77] which sound similar in their general form to the hunters' shrines of Ogun marked out by the cheekbones of elephants.[78] That of the Ekitiparapo was a grove in the middle of the camp where sacrifices were made, and there was also a smithy that could serve as a sanctuary, like other blacksmiths' shops.[79] Ogun, even in relation to the butchery of war, was far from being gratuitously bloodthirsty. He was not even always the deity who received human sacrifices: when the war staff (*opagun*) was propitiated at the beginning of Ibadan's campaigns, it was Oranyan, not Ogun, for whom a man was killed.[80] Unlike Sango's, the cult of Ogun was not predatory.

OGUNDIPE AS MAN OF OGUN

Yoruba religion is distinguished equally by the variety of its *orịṣa* and the reality of personal cultic choice. It has long been suggested that as a result there might be a close match between the personality of the devotee and the character of his god. This idea is strikingly confirmed in the case of that individual worshipper of Ogun about whom the CMS missionaries tell us the most, the Egba chief Ogundipe. A revealing incident is told by the English missionary J. B. Wood, who reckoned him a friend and had many dealings with him.[81] Ogundipe trained as a blacksmith, and even into his old age—he was now around seventy—continued to work at his forge. Wood once called to see him and knew he was at work from the smoke curling up in the evening air from the back of the house. Since no member of Ogundipe's household dared to interrupt him in his smithy, Wood had to wait and finally had to leave after more than an hour without seeing him. The story discloses not only Ogundipe's commitment to his "mystery" but the awe, even fear, in which his people held him. Like other great warlords, he maintained a large, polygynous household, which he ruled as its absolute master. If a wife or a slave absconded, he would pursue his rights with ferocious persistence, and on at least two occasions he killed adulterous wives.[82] His end was tragic. In failing health and fearing plots against him, he kept revolvers and a rifle always at his side, and he shot one of his wives, whom he suspected of poisoning his sleeping mat.[83] His death a few days later was suspected to be by his own hand—or perhaps someone in his household could stand his rage no longer.

If all this recalls the myths of Ogun's propensity for violence and his own fraught marriage, other sides of Ogundipe's life fit more positive aspects of the mythical template. The Methodist missionary J. F. T. Halligey called him "not only a brave warrior, but a very skillful mechanic—quite an artist in metal work": he made his own staff of brass, ornamented "with curious figures."[84] Ogundipe's artistic interests extended to music as well as to metalwork: he composed songs, which he set to his own music and had sung by a choir of his wives. Halligey actually met him "engaged in one of those interesting rehearsals," conducting some twenty-five women who accompanied their singing with a gentle rhythmical swaying and clapping. The words of the song, alluding to recent conflict in the town, were as follows:

> They who destroy other men's houses really destroy their own;
> The war chiefs sent their men to pull down the houses of the white men.
> The houses of the war chiefs must now come down.
> Cowards and thieves these war chiefs are.
> Strangers who visit us in peace they plunder.
> Ah! When the Dahomians come, these chiefs will flee.

We seem here to have a synthesis between the topical chants associated with the Oro cult (performed by men),[85] the Christian practice of conducted choral singing, and perhaps an element of praise poetry (*oriki*, performed by women). The expressed sentiment of retributive violence, of course, is most thoroughly Ogun's.[86] And even as they sang their husband's praises, the women could not have forgotten that like Ogun he was capable of doing terrible things in his anger.

Yet despite Ogundipe's capacity for violence, J.B. Wood insisted that in the public life of Abeokuta "he was admired, feared and *respected.* As a judge he was well-liked, since his judgments were regarded as fair, whilst his charges were moderate."[87] The Egba attributed the failure of the second rains of 1887, shortly after his death, to the passing of a great man.[88] He had first come to attention in the 1850s as the lieutenant of the enlightened chief Ogunbona, on whose death he became in turn the chief patron of the missionaries. He staunchly supported them during the crisis of 1867, when the Europeans were expelled from Abeokuta in response to the policies of the British governor of Lagos. Ogundipe's policy was always to keep trade routes to Lagos open and to encourage cultural innovation. When he argued, against those who wanted to maintain the blockade of the river linking Abeokuta and the lagoon, that "the river was made by God and is for him, and that whatever is made by God is made for the Common use of all his creatures,"[89] the Ogun theme of open roads converges with ideas of Christian enlightenment.[90] Ogundipe was widely known by the sobriquet *Alatiṣe,*[91] a name that alludes to a proverb promoting the ideal of active responsibility: its meaning comes close to "a man's got to do what a man's got to do."[92] Toward the end of his life he modified it to the title *Alatunṣe* (The One Who Restores Things).[93] Though this seems to allude directly to his role in the installation of an *Alake* (the Egba paramount) in 1884, it also clearly echoes a recurrent missionary theme: that their preaching was about *atunṣe aiye,* "the restoration of the world" from its present state of confusion.[94]

OGUN IN HISTORY

Of the two main ways in which anthropology can be historical—in dealing with the past as other and in addressing the problem of change—this chapter has concentrated on the former, attempting to give an account of the cult of Ogun as it was in the second half of the nineteenth century. The variations that have concerned us have chiefly been variations across space, not across time, and particularly as they link with variations in levels of missionary reportage of different *oriṣa.* The problem of Ogun's greater prominence in the Yoruba East proved less intractable than that of the apparently low level of his reportage in the Center/West when compared with that of some other *oriṣa,* notably Sango. To some extent, functions ascribed to Ogun in the East are taken up by other *oriṣa* in the Center/West, such as the agricultural deity Orisa Oko. The case of Sango, however, was quite otherwise: it was a matter less of competition for the same functional niche than of a general challenge posed by a cult that was distinctly organized, aggressively promoted, and endowed with formidable sanctions. Ogun, by contrast, was a cult much more implicitly grounded in a range of mundane activities that were vital to the welfare of the community, all arising from the perceived importance of iron. These respective characteristics ensured that Sango would get the maximum publicity in missionary reports whereas Ogun would tend to be underreported.

When the otherness of past practice is clearly shown—as here, most strikingly, with the largely female cult of Ogun as snake—the problem of change soon demands attention too. The conundrum here is that, although it is the differences between present and past that pose the problem, the past has to be seen as providing essential conditions for the present. The great fact about Ogun's recent history is his singular relative success, over a period in which *oriṣa* cults in general have been in marked decline, in adapting to the circumstances of modernity. Whereas Orisa Oko has declined with the marginalization of subsistence agriculture and the Sango cult has lost its most potent sanctions, Ogun never depended on such sanctions and still possesses a large field in which he is the implicit controlling force. Though some of his areas of functional relevance have shrunk in importance—subsistence farming, hunting, local warfare, and mining/smelting operations—there has been a vast expansion in others, such as the use and repair of iron implements. If we see Ogun qua iron in the center of the picture, then it is a shift away from the producer to the user end of iron technology. I suggest that the demise of Ogun's snake cult was an aspect of this shift. Most notable of all, perhaps, have been the uses of iron in relation to modern travel, where Ogun's traditional connection with the open road has been reaffirmed. The nexus of mechanics, drivers, motor-park touts (*agbero*), party thugs, and so on—the milieu memorably depicted in Wole Soyinka's play *The Road*—extends back to some of the values of the nineteenth-century war boys.

How far the modern manifestation of Ogun has been affected by his perception as a culture hero or as the archetype of the artist, as Soyinka has expressed it,[95] is hard to say. Suffice it to note that, whatever his personal religious beliefs, Soyinka stands directly in a tradition that runs back to the central figures of late nineteenth-century Egba Christianity. His great-grandfather, the Rev. J. J. Ransome-Kuti, was doubtless among the clergy and elders whom the Rev. Tom Harding assembled at Ake church in 1888, the year after Ogundipe's death, to provide collective answers to a questionnaire about Egba religion and who gave it as their view that Ogun was "the chief of all the many gods of the Yoruba people; . . . when other gods are consulted, their reply is 'worship Ogun.'"[96] The aggregate evidence of the CMS archive is hardly compatible with quite such a sweeping view. But perhaps we may interpret the opinion as a sign for the future as well as a statement about the past, as showing that a body of leading Yoruba Christians was already prepared to regard Ogun as an acceptable symbol of some widely shared values of their culture.

4

Divergent Modes of Religiosity in West Africa

The intellectual ambition of Harvey Whitehouse's project on divergent modes of religiosity (hereafter DMR) compels respect:[1] no less than to develop a general theory of religion.[2] Though there have recently been others,[3] what makes Whitehouse's somewhat different is that it has grown out of the ethnography of a particular region, Melanesia: one marked by a religious scene of remarkable diversity, where the confrontation between local tradition and missionary Christianity has not only produced a range of movements drawing on both, but has forced the contrast between different kinds of religion to the center of analytic attention. The tension between anthropology's ambition to develop a theory of a general, even universal, scope and its main research practice of regionally based ethnography is, of course, very much what drives it as a discipline. Yet if the history of anthropology shows anything, it is that its high ambition to be a science of man or a natural science of society has continually faltered in the face of the problems of regional and historical specificity that ethnography throws up. While it is true that ethnographic research has sometimes been inspired by theoretical concerns of high generality, what has happened repeatedly is that what were born as theories have survived as models: that is, as conceptual instruments for the more precise description and analysis of particular cases. The subject has tended to be centrifugal, in that theories are evaluated on the grounds of whether they are useful or have heuristic value in relation to the problems thrown up by particular local (or, at most, regional) studies. Whitehouse's aim is centripetal, in that it seeks to draw on local studies to test and refine the theory.

As Whitehouse points out, his distinction between imagistic and doctrinal modes of religiosity has a definite affinity with many of the other dichotomous contrasts that have been proposed in the sociology of religion, from Weber and Durkheim onward.[4] The central focus of these dichotomies has usually been on the content of the religions: with what they are about or with their orientation to life and the world. Thus Ruth Benedict's contrast of Apollonian and Dionysian religions is to do with the ethos that they express and promote; while Turner and other anthropologists of Africa have distinguished between cults that are primarily oriented to ancestors, or forces of society, or to deities/spirits of the land, or forces of nature. Of course, such variations in content will tend to be linked to other attributes, such as with their forms of organization or with their range or scale, but it is the linkage of such features with content that has tended to be the crucial issue both in sociological arguments about the functional importance of various features of religion and in historical arguments about the impact of particular religions on the direction of social change.

The distinctiveness of Whitehouse's approach shows up most instructively when we contrast it with Weber's, since there is much overlap in their content. Weber's sociology of religion pivoted on a distinction between traditional, primitive, or small-scale religions and world religions. Though this may seem to imply a primary concern with the effects of scale, Weber was essentially concerned with differences in their soteriological content: with whether salvation is a material, this-worldly matter or whether it has other-worldly objectives, as is the case with world religions; with the various directions that the search for salvation may take; with the affinities between different notions of salvation and the orientations of particular status groups; and with the consequences of these cultural choices for other areas of life. For several decades now the most impressive work in the Weberian tradition that covers much of the same subject matter as *Arguments and Icons* has been Bryan Wilson's *Magic and the Millennium*.[5] Its comparative analysis of movements in Africa, North America, Melanesia, and elsewhere is based on a sevenfold typology of their responses to the world. The sheer empirical variety and complexity of religious phenomena that led Wilson to this diversification of the original Troeltschean two-term typology of sect vs. church is for Whitehouse a means to the more strenuous testing and refinement of his dichotomous typology and its theoretical underpinning. Wilson points out that sociologists of religious movements have been largely preoccupied by the issues of doctrine, organization, and the relations between them (and that often in ways shaped by their Christian antecedents). But for Whitehouse it is neither the content of doctrine (or as he prefers, revelation) nor organization that is the pivot of his typology but the way in which the core revelation of a movement is encoded and transmitted. It looks to Darwin rather Weber, since it is about what religions have to do/be in order to survive and perpetuate themselves; and its premises are drawn from cognitive psychology.

Any revelation's accurate transmission over time depends upon the mechanisms of memory that it can call upon. Again, the emphasis of the theory of DMR is not on how the *content* of memory may be influenced by external forces but on the effects of different *forms* of memory.[6] These are of two kinds: episodic memory, which is of particular personal experiences; and semantic memory, which is of the generalized knowledge, whether practical or theoretical, that people acquire or have been taught as members of a community. Corresponding to these are two ideal-typical modes of religiosity: an imagistic mode, wherein adherents' grasp of their religion is encoded in personal recollections of relevant experiences, particularly of an emotionally arousing kind, such as of a terrifying initiation or a dramatic conversion; and a doctrinal mode, which derives from such means as sermons, catechizing, and rituals of a more routine kind. From an evolutionary viewpoint, each mode has its own limitations. The imagistic mode, since it depends on the recall of exceptional, irregular, and personally variable experiences, tends to generate cults that are limited to small, local communities and are susceptible to constant modification. The standardized and constantly repeated forms of the doctrinal mode do facilitate its spread to populations of varying local circumstances and ensure a relatively faithful transmission of its revelation. The main problem faced by the doctrinal mode is that repetition creates boredom and so reduces the motivation of participants. Any religion that managed to combine appropriate elements from both modes would find the prospects for its transmission and spread greatly enhanced.

As already noted, the first impetus to the theory of DMR came from trying to make sense of the religious diversity of Melanesia, where the initiation rites of peoples like the Orokaiva or the Baktaman suggested the imagistic mode; and the very different face of mission Christianity, the doctrinal mode. Whitehouse insists that, though the two modes are only tendencies and most actual traditions contain elements of either, the strength of their respective internal logics means that in practice Melanesian traditions "gravitate strongly" to one or the other, or if toward both, they do so "within readily distinguishable domains of operation." The evolutionary framework of his argument enjoins us to look less at what gives rise to either mode in general than to what enhances the survival prospects of particular cults or religions.

Yet the question of origins is pertinent to the general argument in one respect. It seems highly likely that the imagistic mode is more ancient, possibly going back to the Upper Palaeolithic era, and that the doctrinal mode, since it depends so much on codification by means of writing, came much later. So it is not surprising that Durkheim, when he came to characterize the forms of religion in general, drew his example from a Stone Age religion of a markedly imagistic kind. Here Whitehouse is led to comment that Durkheim overgeneralized, ignoring the different ways in which the doctrinal mode operated. But it is less the deutero-Durkheim of *The Elementary Forms* than the proto-Durkheim of *The Division of Labour* who comes closer to the matter.[7] For having first proposed that there are two forms of social solidarity, mechanical (deriving from *conscience collective*) and organic (deriving from the division of labor)—of which the former progressively gives way to the latter as society becomes modern—Durkheim turns round to argue that *conscience collective* nevertheless remains basic to the very existence of society. So too, it seems, with modes of religiosity: though the doctrinal is more characteristic of modern and world religions, these cannot altogether dispense with the imagistic. For the vitality of any religion must depend on its adherents feeling that their doctrines articulate the past occurrence, and the possible reoccurrence, of some more-than-ordinary contact between the human and the divine, which calls for the imagistic mode. Weber made much the same point with his argument that an access of charisma is the foundation of all religions, however much it is later institutionalized.

A theory such as DMR is one of those middle-range theories that social scientists have often asked for, mediating between highly abstract propositions drawn from cognitive psychology and ethnographic-*cum*-historical material of great empirical richness. So there are two broad approaches toward applying it. One would use a particular body of empirical data to test and refine the relations postulated between the variables of the theory at the abstract level; the other would apply a more pragmatic test and ask how far the theory enhances our understanding of a particular body of regional data. Here I shall take the latter approach, and especially with respect to what seems a crucial possibility suggested by the DMR theory: how the two modes may be combined or integrated in particular cults, religions, or local systems of religious provision.

. . .

As an ethnographic region West Africa has some similarities to Melanesia. It too is an area of diverse local religions, which over the past century and a half has witnessed extensive activity by Christian missions and large-scale conversion to them against a background of sweeping social change induced by colonialism. The cultural gap between the two kinds of religion, the pressures of colonialism, and the desire of Christian converts to seek power according to their own understanding gave rise, as in Melanesia, to movements of substantially Christian idiom, initiated by charismatic local leaders, that have variously been termed syncretist, prophetist, millenarian, and so forth. These similarities have often led to the inclusion of movements from West Africa and Melanesia within the same comparative and analytic frame. Yet in other respects the West African setting is very different. Most of its communities were far larger, including precolonial kingdoms with complex political hierarchies, large settlements with developed class and occupational structures, markets, and long-distance trade. Consequently, many indigenous religions and cults were much more extensive in scope and scale than in Melanesia; and there was the centuries-old existence of Islam—itself testimony to the region's extensive links with the outside world—which interacted in complex ways with indigenous cults, and in some areas both anticipated and complicated the encounter between them and Christianity.

The DMR dichotomy evokes several of those current in the West African literature, and so we are led to ask whether it offers a more precise and profound characterization of differences already and independently recognized as real and significant. But here a caution needs to be registered: a theoretically cogent dichotomy is a powerful cognitive magnet, tending to draw other, related distinctions into itself. Then dichotomies get stacked up on top of one another, so that significant differences of emphasis get elided or reduced to aspects or implications of the master dichotomy. Two dichotomies in particular have been much used in studies of religion in West Africa. First, between traditional (or primal) and world religions, or preliterate religions and religions of the Book, which is the same distinction empirically but viewed from a different angle. There is a more theorized version in Robin Horton's contrast between microcosmic and macrocosmic cults, which embodies a crucial shift of emphasis since it expressly allows for representations of the macrocosm to occur within the idiom of traditional religion.[8] Second, within the latter, anthropologists have made various closely related contrasts between two kinds of cult found widely in indigenous African religion: ancestors vs. deities, spirits of society vs. spirits of nature, political vs. fertility rituals. In all these cases distinctions that are manifest in empirical or synthetic form may be reworked analytically so as to highlight aspects considered to be of particular theoretical relevance.

So how far may either of these distinctions (traditional vs. world religions, ancestor vs. nature cults) be aligned with the DMR antithesis of the imagistic vs. the doctrinal? It is obvious how the former does, but its pertinence to the latter is not so clear. The argument to follow rests on the assumptions that the imagistic mode is primary (both in the sense that it emerged first and that it remains basic to the appeal of religion) and the doctrinal mode came later. The semantic memories sustained by the doctrinal mode are the generalized codification of what is taken to follow from the original episodic memories—that is, of those individuals who experienced divine revelation and communicated it to their fellows—on which all religious establishments and many social orders depend. It explores, first, how the ground for the doctrinal mode was prepared within the traditional religions of West Africa, later to be realized in a fairly pure form in the evangelical Christianity brought by the missionaries in the nineteenth century; and second, how the imagistic mode has been reconstituted within the born-again Christianity that is its dominant manifestation in West Africa today.

For our present purposes what most crucially distinguishes cults of the ancestors and of the earth or natural spirits is that the former are highly embedded socially, often to the point of being hardly more than the ritual aspect of the lineage structure that they regulate. Their membership is ascriptive and closed, whereas the latter tend to be freestanding religious institutions that have to take deliberate steps to reproduce themselves, for their memberships are open and fluctuating. Many ancestor cults, indeed, seem almost to stand outside the imagistic/doctrinal contrast, needing neither doctrine nor high-arousal experiences to motivate their practices but merely the habitus of quotidian relations with elders and the spontaneous remembrance of them after their decease, autobiographical memory gradually blending into semantic.[9] So it is understandable that ancestral cults in Africa tend to be poorly supplied with such mnemonic devices as myths or images. It is significant that in the Yoruba case, it is in the cult of a lineage's and town's *collective* ancestors, called *egungun* (as also with royal ancestors of importance to the community at large), that iconic representation bulks larger, with specialized priesthoods, annual festivals, and in general some degree of assimilation to the other kind of cult, of *oriṣa* or spirits of nature.[10]

The Yoruba *oriṣa* are a highly developed example of this category, since (though associated with natural features or substances) they were imagined as personalized deities, many of them with specialized functions or pronounced personal characteristics. Since, unlike ancestors, the *oriṣa* cults did not ride on other institutions, they needed to develop specific ways to ensure their survival: they had to motivate their adherents—which meant above all to provide cogent evidence of the presence and power of their god—and they had to offer an adequate rationale of the ritual and behavioral requirements of the cult. In respect of the former, their dominant mode was strongly imagistic: if an individual had not been dedicated at birth, it was often an acute personal crisis interpreted by the diviner as a call from the *oriṣa* that first drew members into the cult; *oriṣa* on occasion possessed their most active adepts and priests, who temporarily became their vessels and might offer further revelations; the cult members met regularly to renew their special relationship with the *oriṣa* through shared sacrifice; at annual festivals, accompanied by drumming and dancing, praise singing, and public parade of their images, links between the community and the *oriṣa* were reaffirmed. All this was highly performative—devotees were said to manifest their *oriṣa*'s active power by playing or enacting them[11]—and often generated states of high arousal.

There was a doctrinal aspect too. Partly it was implicit in the epithets of the praise poetry and in the symbols and images of the *oriṣa*—the red and white clay beads on the forehead of the Orisa Oko devotee, the thunderbolt-axe of Sango, Obatala's white cloth—because such served as mnemonic pegs for stories (*itan*) about their origins and attributes. Cult knowledge was esoteric, and authority within any social unit—whether cult, craft, lineage, or town—went with mastery of relevant *itan*. So access to knowledge was both highly stratified—priests and adepts having a deeper knowledge than ordinary adherents, and these than outsiders—and segmented into parcels not shared by everyone. But there was a body of generally knowledgeable people in the *babalawo* (fathers of secrets), the practitioners of the system of divination known as Ifa. The corpus of Ifa divination verses was the largest archive of myth and cosmology available to the Yoruba, and (since most people consulted *babalawo* occasionally and heard some of these verses) was probably the most widely available source of general religious knowledge. Of Ifa itself, more shortly.

Taken as a whole, Yoruba *orișa* cults were remarkably effective in staving off the two threats to survival that, according to the DMR theory, all cults face. The major cults, at least, were able to generate enough motivational interest—partly through their attachment to the major crises in human lives, which created a high level of personal identification with them, and partly through their own vivid presentation of *orișa* power at festivals, through possession, and so forth—as well as sufficient understanding of their theory and practice to achieve both wide geographical spread (extending in some cases well beyond the Yoruba-speaking area) and impressive stability over time. In this achievement of spatial and temporal extension, they may be contrasted with the nonlineage cults among peoples such as the Akan and the Kongo, whose spiritual forces—respectively, *abosom* or deities and *minkisi* or fetishes—not only lacked the personality and cult organization of the major *orișa* but, apparently like many traditional cults in Melanesia, showed a cyclical pattern in their rise and fall, as old ones lost their appeal and new crises led to the emergence of new ones.[12] Here cults established in conditions of social crisis, high emotional arousal, or both, seem to have lacked either the doctrinal elaboration or the social infrastructure to keep them perduringly in existence, though the cultural conditions for later revivals of similar movements remained in place.

The historical terrain created by missionaries in their project to convert adherents of indigenous religions to Christianity is likely to be especially fruitful for examining the interplay of the two modes of religiosity. For it contains movements that reach out in either direction: anticipations of the doctrinal within religious systems predominantly imagistic in character and movements to recover the power of the imagistic by those placed within strongly doctrinal settings like missionary Christianity. Of the former an excellent example is provided by the Yoruba divination cult of Ifa, which was held to be the special province of a particular deity, Orunmila. It was not the only system of divination, for the priests of other deities gave oracular guidance too, typically through some form of trance or possession. Ifa, however, relied not on its *babalawo*s being possessed by their *orișa* but on their mastery of a technique that entailed the capacity to remember a vast corpus of verses. The *babalawo* began by manipulating a handful of palm nuts to produce one of 256 (16 x 16) configurations (*odu*), to each of which corresponded a sequence of verses that described mythical precedents; these were then recited by the *babalawo,* and the client selected one that spoke to his situation. The source of the problem and the steps to be taken to resolve it, by a specified sacrifice to a particular *orișa,* would then be clarified by casting lots in response to the client's questions. Though Orunmila thus sustained the system of *orișa* cults as a whole (which indeed he belonged to), he also represented himself as somewhat above and outside it, as the sole channel of wisdom from the supreme being, Olodumare, who was the source of the Ifa verses. And as if to underscore this autonomy from the rest of the *oriṣa,* Ifa sometimes advised its clients that the answer to their problem was to become Muslim or Christian—that is, to worship God directly, rather than through the *oriṣa.*

It is thus not surprising that missionaries accorded considerable respect to *babalawo,* who were ready dialecticians and their most astute critics but also very ready to learn from them.[13] Moreover, the marks indicating the selected *odu* that the *babalawo* drew in the sacred powder on his ritual tray were widely interpreted by Yoruba pagans as a kind of literacy *avant la lettre,* and the reception of both Koran and Bible was conditioned by what was required of Ifa verses: to predict and to solve problems. In fact this degree of preadaptation to some of the features of the doctrinal mode may well have been written into Ifa from its origin, for it appears that the sixteen-options systems of divination, found widely throughout sub-Saharan Africa and Madagascar, all ultimately derive from Islamic sources.[14]

Yet though Ifa was the most doctrinal of the *oriṣa* cults and provided a doctrinal component to the system as a whole; though it became the most pan-Yoruban of all cults, and spread far beyond the Yoruba-speaking region, east to the lower Niger and west to the Volta region;[15] though its practitioners were able to enter into a serious engagement with Muslim and Christian clergy, it still fell short of being a full-blown realization of the doctrinal mode. First, it remained dependent on oral modes of transmission. Hence, though it was considered as sacrilegious to add to or subtract from the corpus, and steps were taken to prevent these (by such means as the stringent training of neophytes and Ifa-recitation competitions between experienced *babalawo*), there was almost certainly a slippage of content as well as some regional variation in what was put out. Second, since Ifa was a pragmatic and client-centered system of oracular consultation and not a congregational religion, it worked in practice to embrace a multitude of individual perspectives (albeit within a common framework of cosmology and ritual practice) rather than impose any kind of collective ideology—hence, indeed, its openness to Islam and Christianity. Third, it enshrined the principle of secrecy, for the expertise of the *babalawo* was that only they knew how to access secrets or hidden things (*awo*). Secrecy is bound to undermine the diffusion of standardized, common understanding of religious knowledge, which is at the heart of the doctrinal mode.

. . .

By contrast, missionary Christianity was in the strongest sense a religion of the Book, its converts being initially known in Yoruba as *onibuku* (book people). Instead of the pragmatic and personalized advice of Ifa were universal ethical injunctions; and instead of Ifa's emphasis on secrets (*awo*) it was vital that the Word of God should be made openly available in the language of the people. The other religion of the Book, already well ensconced by the mid-nineteenth century, had already been modified by the demands of Yoruba culture. The not-to-be-translated Koran lent itself to esoteric and magical uses, and quite a lot of the doctrinal/imagistic distinction seems to appear in the contrast between two faces of Yoruba Islam: the one communal and egalitarian, associated with public worship, Koranic exegesis, and sermons, and learning to recite the Koran; the other individualist and hierarchical, when people consulted *alfa* for Koranic charms or sought access to esoteric power through Sufi shaykhs. While there are difficulties in simply labeling the latter popular or heterodox—since it always drew in learned Muslims and had deep roots in the mainstream—there is no doubt that it could attract the criticism of preachers for encouraging wrong attitudes and is the target of contemporary reformism. Yet it provided a way to meet some basic Yoruba religious expectations that missionary Christianity found difficult to match. This was a primary stimulus to the independent religious movements and churches that burgeoned in the early decades of the twentieth century.

Here we come to the reassertion of imagistic practices within African Christianity, as against the anticipation of doctrinal ones within traditional religion. African independent churches (or AICs) have given great scope for typology.[16] While most classifications are derived from labels used by the churches themselves—such as Ethiopian/Zionist in South Africa or African/Aladura in Nigeria[17]—they have given rise to binary typologies of a more analytic character. So, for example, James Fernandez constructed four types based on two cross-cutting continuums: one (nativistic/acculturated) dealing with the movements' primary cultural orientations and the other (expressive/instrumental) having to do with the manner of their responses to the colonial situation.[18] Neither of these has much to do with the imagistic/doctrinal contrast. Yet the DMR theory does seem, in retrospect, to be pertinent both to certain empirical contrasts made in my study *Aladura* (1968) and to the searching critique of its approach expressed by Fernandez in an influential general review of the field.[19]

The Aladura are a cluster of churches founded by African religious innovators who triggered a series of revivals—involving healing through sanctified water, witchcraft confession, mass destruction of idols, and some millennial preaching—between 1918 and the mid-1930s. Their basic aim was to make the power of prayer (*adura:* hence their name) more available than it was in the older Protestant missions for such this-worldly objectives as health, fertility, protection against witchcraft and danger, guidance, prosperity, and success—in sum, that state of all-round well-being that the Yoruba call *alafia*. While Aladura's theological content is strongly Christian, its ritual forms as well as its ontology of the spirit world owe much to the indigenous religious background. Dreams, visions, and ecstatic tongues—gifts of the Holy Spirit—are seen as vehicles of divine power and guidance, recalling aspects both of *orișa*-cult groups and of Ifa divination, but with prayer substituting for sacrifice as the medium of human address to God.[20] There had been early influences from an American faith-healing group called Faith Tabernacle, but a more significant external input came when, from 1930 onwards, the Aladura became somewhat variably subject to the influence of Pentecostalism, initially through a British group, the Apostolic Church. The outcome was a spectrum of churches ranging from some of a more home-grown idiom (with African-style music and liturgy, the wearing of white prayer-gowns, elaborate hierarchies of spiritual offices, a rich repertory of ritual symbols, and the use of such items as candles, incense, and holy oil) to those more conformed to Euro-American Pentecostal norms, with their emphatic scripturalism and aversion to complex ritual symbolism. *Aladura* took for comparison two churches standing toward either end of this spectrum: the Cherubim and Seraphim (C&S) and the Christ Apostolic Church (CAC).

The approach of *Aladura* was intellectualist, in that, in contrast to studies of new religious movements in the Third World of Marxist and/or functionalist inspiration,[21] it sought to explain Aladura belief and practice as intellectually cogent responses, granted the cultural premises of young Yoruba Christians, to the problems and dilemmas they confronted at a time of midcolonial crisis. But from their shared roots C&S and CAC tended over the years to diverge. I was struck by how C&S, with its more African idiom, tended to revert to what may be called the Yoruba cultural default system, becoming flexible and pragmatic in its search for spiritual power, whereas the more consciously Pentecostal CAC held much more to doctrinally grounded lines of conduct, even against the promptings of Yoruba culture (e.g., its rejection of polygamy or its categorical ban on any use of medicine). I further related these differences to organizational ones:[22]

> The C&S see themselves . . . as a society of people which God had supremely invested with spiritual power, and the prophet or "spiritualist" . . . is their most distinctive religious type. The spiritual clientage is the form of grouping associated with such a man; and this is modified to being the general clientage of a big man, or an association of people after the same spiritual goal. . . . Wider organization than these they have found difficult.
>
> CAC members are equally concerned with the fruits of spiritual power, but they are being educated by their leaders to explain it differently. Personal authority of various kinds has always been, and still is important, but the possessors of it have used it to spread the idea that their church is the one which embodies correct doctrines, and so has spiritual power. This has been the work of intellectualist pastors. . . . Doctrines are open, public, arguable things, and favour the growth of pastors who expound them; the pastors derive their legitimacy from the church, the embodiment of the doctrines.

It is evident that this contrast may be rephrased in terms of the DMR theory: the C&S being more imagistic, the CAC more doctrinal—within a fairly narrow band of difference, it is true, but still with the organizational correlates that Whitehouse argued for.

There is a complex ebb and flow at work here. The C&S responded most directly to the dissatisfaction of African converts with an insufficiently inculturated British evangelicalism: its apparent inability to summon prayer power for mundane needs and, more diffusely, their hunger for symbolically (that is, imagistically) richer forms of engagement with the divine. The CAC, by contrast, thanks to the influence of Pentecostal mentors, seemed in some ways to have moved back some way toward the evangelical baseline—a less imagistic (or at least more doctrinal) form of faith—but yet seemed no less successful for that. I interpreted this in terms of a long-term process of religious rationalization, *à la* Max Weber, which I linked to the fact that its social bearers were modernizing, educated young men. It was this assumption that Fernandez called into question.[23] He argued, in terms that almost uncannily anticipate those of the DMR theory, that my intellectualist approach to Aladura and to African movements more generally projected a kind of imageless thought onto them. Instead, because African thought is socially embedded, analysts of religious movements needed to attend to the argument of images that they employ. This was applied in his analysis of the Bwiti cult among the Fang of Gabon and the former French Congo, one of the finest studies of an African religious movement ever done.[24] The colonial experience was extremely traumatic for the Fang, but what Bwiti offered was less a monovalent solution to its problems than a microcosmic pleasure dome created through a complex play of symbols and ritual, syncretizing themes from Christianity, the ancestral cult, and images from the rain-forest environment, from which any adept may take what s/he needs. Bwiti is one of the very few African cults to make use of a psychotropic drug, *eboga*, in its rituals. Its use of symbols is highly polysemic, and its sermons employ what Fernandez called "an elliptical riddling style" to produce "edification by puzzlement."[25] If it is a mark of the imagistic mode, as Whitehouse observes, to generate a "dynamic . . . towards creative elaboration rather than faithful repetition, and the production of local differences rather than regional homogeneity,"[26] then Bwiti fits the bill perfectly. But at the same time, this implies that the approach advocated by Fernandez, with movements of this type in mind, will be less helpful for those that stand closer to the doctrinal pole, such as the Nigerian CAC.

. . .

It is not easy to generalize about the direction of change within African Christianity as whole over the last three decades, but if there is a single dominant trend, it is the rise of neo-Pentecostal or (as it is colloquially known in Nigeria) born-again Christianity. The Africanizing ethos of the older AICs like the C&S, with their local idioms and resonances, yields to something a great deal more nearly universalist in its sense of itself. Neo-Pentecostalism is a global movement in Christianity, with much circulation of people and media between West Africa, its epicenters in the American South and West, and even such places as Brazil or Korea. While this is certainly a response to wider processes of globalization, it does not mean that churches of a strongly local idiom do not continue to attract many Nigerians.[27]

Surveys of churches in the Yoruba metropolis of Ibadan in the 1990s showed a great burgeoning, not merely of the newest born-again churches or "ministries" (as they often style themselves), as well as of older Pentecostals such as Apostolic, Foursquare Gospel, Assemblies of God, and others, but also of the Celestial Church of Christ, a C&S-related body that has the most ritualized practices of prayer, healing, and prophecy of the "White-garment" churches, as the Aladura nowadays are often described. Of the churches once regarded as Aladura, it seems that it is those at either end of the imagistic/doctrinal spectrum (e.g., Celestial and CAC) that have grown the most, whereas churches in the middle—most C&S branches or Church of the Lord (Aladura)—that have languished. One great irony is that though Pentecostalism first entered Yoruba Christianity *through* the Aladura movement in 1931, the terms "Aladura" and "Pentecostal" are now regarded as mutually exclusive, falling into different sections of the national umbrella body, the Christian Association of Nigeria. CAC is now emphatic that it is Pentecostal, not Aladura, and has had close relations with some of the newer born-again groups, especially Deeper Life. A further irony is that the current market leader among born-agains, the Redeemed Christian Church of God, actually began as a breakaway from the Eternal Sacred Order of Cherubim and Seraphim but was radically reconstructed by its well-educated second leader, Pastor E. A. Adeboye. Like other born-again churches, it is anxious to make out that a chasm separates it from the Aladura, who are stigmatized as mixing pagan or demonic elements into their practices. Former members of the Celestial Church sometimes denounce it in testimonies given at Redeemed revival services as engaged in works of Satan, to be renounced by the born-again.

The fact that people can still be drawn in large numbers to Africanizing churches like the Celestial Church of Christ, even though the main flow of preference is to the more globally oriented born-agains, should counsel us against seeking to explain the success of the latter simply as an adjustment to the spirit of the times. Pentecostalism *is* a global form of Christianity, but then so is Catholicism, even though since Vatican II inculturation, or the adaptation of its theology and liturgy to local cultures, has been strongly promoted. But granted that the ethos of global modernity projected by neo-Pentecostalism is part of its appeal, and that this pushes it toward the doctrinal mode since it has to rely on semantic memory to create understandings that can be shared across an international community of believers, how is born-again Christianity so successful in combating the tedium effect (with consequent loss of motivation) that threatens all forms of Evangelicalism, with its austere symbolic repertory, sustained Bible study, long sermons, and so forth?

Here we may return to Whitehouse's view that the source of the doctrinal mode presented in missionary Christianity (of all denominations) lay in the Reformation's onslaught on the imagistic practices of late medieval Catholicism.[28] A weakness in his argument at this point is that, in jumping directly from the sixteenth century to the nineteenth, it elides some critical shifts in how the two modes have figured within evangelical Christianity. We may distinguish three main paradigms in chronological order: Puritanism, Evangelicalism, and Pentecostalism. In the first of these, Puritanism up to the end of the seventeenth century (or in America the early eighteenth), the doctrinal mode in a fairly pure form could often be applied in religiously uniform communities—Geneva, Scotland, New England—where the tedium effect could, at some cost, be suppressed by social controls. It is hardly a historical accident that it was when these started to break down, in the early eighteenth century, making it necessary to find some other means to revive motivation, that a new form of the imagistic mode came into being. Hence Evangelicalism, distinguished sociologically from Puritanism by its focus not on the closed community of the Elect but on the perception (in John Wesley's words) of the world as its parish, and theologically by its voluntaristic conception of God's saving grace freely offered to all who would receive it. Evangelicalism saw itself not as disclosing new doctrinal truth but rather as reviving the faith of the believer. So in the terms of the DMR theory there was the paradox that, though in one sense it was as doctrinal as any other version of Protestantism—as dependent on preaching and reading the Word—Evangelicalism also made vital use of a new form of the imagistic mode. For it created powerful experiences of divine grace, whose deposit in autobiographical memories—of ecstatic revival meetings, of the moment when one first *knew* the Lord Jesus—would supplement the semantic memories of routine religious instruction. Hence the Methodist societies as they initially related to the Established Church markedly resembled such splinter groups of the mainline Paliau movement as the Noise or the Second Cult.[29] Compare the name assumed by the movement in colonial America, "the Great Awakening," with the Melanesian cultists' use of the metaphor of waking up. "Imagistic" is a term that may mislead if it is felt to point exclusively to visual icons; for the autobiographical memories activated in the evangelical religion of the heart depended not on visual images but on words and music.

With its institutionalization in churches, evangelical religion tended to slip back to a greater reliance on the doctrinal mode, with little iconic or ceremonial richness to offset the danger of tedium. As John Wesley himself said, in a passage famously quoted by Weber: "I do not see how it is possible, in the nature of things, for any revival of true religion to continue long."[30] So too the evangelical missionaries of the Anglican CMS in Yorubaland came to lament the cold, formal religion (which, reversing Wesley's line of causation, they thought gave rise to worldliness) of their flock in the second generation.[31] Yet revival—a form of religion in the imagistic mode—was still contained within evangelical culture as a memory and a hope, at both individual and collective levels, to be periodically reactivated.

The 1859–60 revival in Britain and Ireland (monitored from afar by missionaries in West Africa) led on to the Keswick Convention from the 1870s, which over the next three decades sent out a series of evangelists to conduct revivals at the behest of the Lagos churches.[32] African CMS candidates for ordination in the 1880s and 1890s, many of whom were converted at these Keswick revivals, were asked to write autobiographical statements, of which a key element was their account of this experience.

An issue that needs to be explored in relation to mission is how this evangelical culture of periodic revival interacted with indigenous historicities in which there were cycles of social renewal, involving such imagistic episodes as antiwitchcraft movements or the accession of new sources of power. Take the case of the Ulster evangelicals who set up the Qua Iboe Mission among the Anang of southeastern Nigeria. Its pioneer, Samuel Bill, was moved first in the late 1870s by the visit to Belfast of the American evangelists Dwight Moody and Ira Sankey in one of the "last waves of the Ulster revival"[33] and started out in Nigeria in 1887. By the 1910s the mission was making fair progress under the aegis of colonial rule, opening churches and schools, winning converts, but yet dissatisfied: "The Christians in Ikotobo . . . have not grown in grace as they have grown in numbers. . . . The missionary, joined by a few earnest souls, has been much in prayer for a true revival."[34] Over a decade later it was still reported that "our churches and services and all our carefully built organisation are futile for doing God's work without the life-giving Spirit."[35] It finally came in 1927, triggered by a young teacher but taking the mission completely by surprise, to produce what was known as the Spirit Movement, marked by witch confessions, mass destruction of idols and charms, contagious enthusiasm, glossolalia . . . The missionaries, of course, saw it in terms of the archetypal Day of Pentecost, and of precedents such as the Ulster revival or the Welsh revival of 1904. The Anang precedents are less easy to discern, and certainly some of the immediate conditions, arising from tensions produced by colonial rule, were strictly *un*precedented; but later cycles of upheaval suggest that this fluid society, with rather unstable chiefly authority—in that, more like Melanesia than the Yoruba were—was prone to cycles of routine and revitalization.[36]

Faith missions like the Qua Iboe were already on the cusp between classic Evangelicalism and Pentecostalism, the third main manifestation of the Protestant tradition. The ideal of being born again in the Holy Spirit had been present within West African Evangelicalism from its very origins: it was a prominent theme in the preaching of Rev. W. A. B. Johnson, the famous German CMS missionary who converted hundreds of liberated Africans during his ministry at Regent in Sierra Leone, as far back as 1817–23. So what exactly did Pentecostalism bring that was new? Pentecostalism incorporates several of the recurring features of nineteenth-century American Protestantism—perfectionism, premillennialism, fundamentalism, dispensationalism—and also draws down, through its African-American origins, a strong current of African religious sensibility (which would of course reconnect potently with local cultural demand when it got to Africa). Perhaps what most set it apart it from earlier (and largely European) expressions of evangelical religiosity was the emphasis placed on the physical tokens of divine favor, notably speaking with tongues as the mark par excellence of baptism of the Holy Ghost, and miracles of healing. As studies of its worldwide diffusion show clearly, Pentecostalism is an extremely protean phenomenon, even within particular countries or churches.[37] Whether its impact is politically conservative or culturally radical, what its natural class affiliation is, what its main practical thrust is—whether holiness teaching, divine healing, gospel of prosperity, deliverance from demons and ancestral spirits, predictive prophecy—are questions all hotly debated (probably because each and all of these alternatives comes up in the appropriate context). Neo-Pentecostalism taps as deeply into the springs of indigenous African spirituality as the older AICs but manages to do it in an attractively modern and transnational idiom. Its success may be seen, in terms of the present argument, as arising from its unique ability to bring together, sometimes close to the point of fusion, the two modes of religiosity.

The DMR theory is about how the ability of a religion to pass on its revelation is affected by the way it is encoded in memory, not about how the content of that revelation may relate to its context. Still, the connection between religious content and mode of religiosity will always call for attention. Here I come to a final dichotomy apparent in the fluctuating religious orientations of both Aladura and born-agains, which may be called holiness vs. empowerment. Holiness is essentially a concern to conform oneself to the will of God, following the dictates of scripture and prayer, typically by living a life of spiritual self-discipline. Empowerment is whereby one seeks to enlist the power of God, above all through prayer and revealed means, to achieve a full, rich life and to defeat any forces that oppose it. While holiness looks *inside* the self for the solution to existential problems, empowerment looks *outside*. Yet despite this contrast the two orientations have common elements, and holiness can easily flip over, as when self-discipline comes to be regarded instrumentally, as a means analogous to sacrifice in gaining the favor of a god. In their first encounter with religious modernity, the Yoruba had an early version of the holiness solution presented to them by evangelical CMS missionaries—change yourselves inwardly, and then your institutions will be transformed, and your country will become good—while they looked to the mission for direct techniques of empowerment.[38] It goes without saying that the missionary version of holiness teaching was firmly in the doctrinal mode.

The trajectories of Aladura (from the 1920s) and the born-agains (from the 1970s) show striking similarities. Both began as prayer and Bible-study groups largely composed of earnest young people with a marked orientation toward holiness. Faith Tabernacle (CAC's precursor) and the Praying Band of C&S were composed of young literates,[39] and fellowships of campus Christians were the germ of the massive born-again ministries of recent years.[40] Chastity and monogamy, abstention from alcohol, regimes of fasting, reliance on prayer alone for healing, not wearing jewelry (in the case of women), and a generally disapproving attitude to the flamboyant display of Yoruba social life were some of its hallmarks. So what are the conditions under which it becomes plausible, even compelling, so to go against the grain of Yoruba culture? Holiness, presenting oneself to God as a living sacrifice, is an appropriate response to the expectation that the millennium, the end of the present dispensation, is imminent. Premillennialist anticipation was widespread in Nigeria in the years after 1918 into the early 1930s and still animates the more holiness-oriented of the larger born-again churches, such as Deeper Life. But a complex blend of zeitgeist and Bible-based teaching is needed to hold the holiness orientation in place, and if either condition fades, it may be expected to yield to the perennial Yoruba search for empowerment, where its moral restraints will be resignified as conditions for effective prayer. The concern for empowerment tends to reassert itself when what start as small holiness fellowships grow into large ministries, though differences of emphasis may still remain: of the larger bodies, Deeper Life still stands toward the holiness end of the spectrum, whereas the Redeemed Christian Church of God or Winners' Chapel stands toward the empowerment end.[41]

In asking how the holiness/empowerment distinction correlates with the DMR contrast, it helps to consider what challenges the two tendencies respectively have to face. Holiness groups need above all to keep their members from slipping over to born-again churches closer to the general cultural mainstream—that is, those of the empowerment tendency. Their integrity is grounded in the doctrinal mode, in Bible study, sermons, and pamphlet literature, but this is motivationally boosted by the imagistic impact of intense emotions aroused by prayer and the work of the Holy Spirit, particularly in small fellowship groups. The challenge facing the empowerment tendency (which includes most of the largest and highest-profile born-again organizations) is more from rival operators offering similar products in the same crowded religious marketplace, including Aladura churches like the Celestial Church of Christ. What they most have to do, rather like *oriṣa* cults in the nineteenth century, is project a clinching public image of their effectiveness as mediators of divine power. So here the relative importance of the imagistic and the doctrinal tends to be reversed.

Revival is here more of a continuous preoccupation than in the older evangelical churches: Redeemed has a Holy Ghost Night every month, drawing tens of thousands of people to its Redemption Camp off the Lagos-Ibadan expressway. In cities like Lagos or Ibadan big revivals and crusades take place almost continuously, often with visiting pastors on the born-again circuit (including prestigious figures from abroad). They are attended by much advance publicity and make full use of all the techniques of religious showbiz as developed in the United States. I earlier noted that the term "imagistic" may seem oddly applied to Evangelicalism, granted its poverty of visual icons, as witness the declination from the Catholic crucifix to the plain cross of the Protestants to no cross at all in many neo-Pentecostal auditoriums. But visual imagery has been able to stage a triumphant reentry through the born-agains' confident exploitation of electronic media: TV coverage, videos of preachers and revivals, and video movies such as those made by Mike Bamiloye's Mount Zion Faith Ministries. Yet even here all is not imagistic. Complementing these revivals is a network of prayer fellowships and Bible-study sessions, where the doctrinal mode is paramount. Within a fortnight I have seen the leader of the Redeemed Christian Church of God, E. A. Adeboye, conduct a studious afternoon Bible-study meeting at the University of Ibadan's Protestant chapel and preside at the tumultuous praise worship and ecstatic spiritual effusions of a Holy Ghost Night. It is in how it has found ways to combine imagistic and doctrinal modes of religiosity that much of the effectiveness of the born-again movement is to be found.

5

Postsocialism, Postcolonialism, Pentecostalism

We live in a world of expanded limits and in an age that we are no longer certain how to categorize.[1] Our use of terms like "postsocialism" and "postcolonialism" (like several other "posts") indicates our reluctance to give a positive definition to the character of our age at all and suggests that we may have finally thrown off a notion that has been basic to Western social theory since the Enlightenment, that the salient features of every age can be best made intelligible in terms of its place in an evolutionary sequence of stages leading to a determinate climax. Now at last it seems to be goodbye to all that—or at least seems so to those who prefer to pluralize the age as one of modernities. It is outside the West that the most definite conceptions are now entertained of what modernity is, along with the aspiration to progress in that direction. The concept of late capitalism—a last echo of the Marxist variant of social-evolutionary thought, absurd because it implies a time schedule that makes sense only within the terms of a historicism that is ostensibly disclaimed—has given way to neoliberalism, a less tendentious way of characterizing our age. While neoliberalism's primary reference is economic, to the hegemony of the free market, it is also usefully suggestive of other freedoms, particularly (in this context) of religion in formerly socialist states, where a plurality of competing faiths has largely replaced states' attempts to control, monopolize, or eliminate the expression of religious belief. With the removal of many of the previous barriers to the circulation of religious messages, the activities of transnational religious organizations have burgeoned. State socialism fancied itself as postreligious; postsocialism has seen the revival of religion. In that respect the Soviet bloc, whose historic aim had been to blaze an entirely different trail for the social evolution of humanity, has rejoined most of the rest of the contemporary world, though in a very different situation from the one in which it left it.

The opening up of the former Soviet bloc to new religious influences has occurred at a time when, owing to religious developments elsewhere in the world, transnational flow-patterns of religious influence have become much more polycentric and multidirectional than we have hitherto thought of them as being. Catherine Wanner presents a particularly striking instance of this:[2]

> When a Nigerian opens a church in Ukraine that sends Ukrainian believers to the US, Germany and elsewhere to save the unsaved and church the unchurched, it is no longer a case of core exerting influence on the periphery. Rather the interconnections and the cultural flow of ideas, objects and people are also significant among non-Western regions and from the so-called Third World to the West.

What she describes as occurring in Kiev is an entirely novel conjuncture of religious currents, of the postsocialist and the postcolonial. A full account of the Nigerian background will open the way to a full appreciation of the paradoxical way in which the postcolonial has here come to the postsocialist world.

The founder of the Ukrainian Pentecostal church known as the Embassy of God is a Nigerian, Pastor Sunday Adelaja, who came to the Soviet Union as a student (like many Nigerians before him) in 1989. His name tells us he is not just a Yoruba but an Ijebu. The Ijebu are one of the most distinctive of the Yoruba subgroups, inhabiting a cluster of towns once organized in an ancient kingdom in the close hinterland of Lagos, Nigeria's largest city and former capital. They were conquered by the British in 1892 in order to break their stranglehold on the trade route that ran from Lagos to the interior; but after the conquest (having previously excluded missionaries) many Ijebu embraced the world religions—both Islam and Christianity—with alacrity.[3] Now, it happens that there was an earlier Pastor Adelaja, a trader who migrated in the 1920s to Kano, in Northern Nigeria. He was active in a prayer circle called Faith Tabernacle and later played a key role in the establishment of Nigeria's first independent Pentecostal church, the Christ Apostolic Church.[4] It is almost certain that *his* father was one of those who became a Christian—very likely an Anglican—in the great wave of Ijebu conversion after the conquest of 1892. Perhaps this first Adelaja to be a Christian was even the John Adelaja, an Ijebu migrant rubber trader, who headed the tiny congregation at Ife in 1899.[5] Pastor Adelaja of Kiev may or may not be the great-grandson of this John Adelaja or the grandson of Pastor Adelaja of Kano, for Adelaja is not an uncommon name among the Ijebu. But if we imagine he was, then we have a hypothetical patriline of four generations that encapsulates the whole history of Ijebu Christianity as it developed over the colonial and postcolonial periods: the early convert to evangelical Anglicanism in the wake of the British conquest; his son who left Ijebu as a trader to Northern Nigeria and was active in one of the new independent Aladura churches, a man whose life span fell entirely within the colonial period; a putative grandson whose life must have spanned the rise of nationalism and the early decades of independence; and fourth in line, Sunday Adelaja himself.

This fourth Adelaja came to adulthood in a grim period of Nigeria's history, one of corrupt military rule and chronic economic mismanagement. It was also marked by new levels of religious enthusiasm—for born-again or neo-Pentecostal Christianity and for newly reformist and politically engaged forms of Islam—and by the growing public saliency of religion, extending to episodes of violent conflict.[6] The sequence that runs from the missionary evangelicalism to which Adelaja I converted, through Adelaja II's adoption of an independent Christianity that turned Pentecostal in the 1930s, to culminate in the globally oriented born-again Christianity of Adelaja IV represents not just a consistent religious trajectory but a series of mediated responses to the colonial and postcolonial experiences of Nigerians. The liftoff of neo-Pentecostal Christianity in Nigeria, as in many other countries, is linked to the deepening crisis of the postcolonial state from the mid-1970s onward, though it is surely not to be reduced to it.

Historically, most missions have gone from the advanced, richer, and more central society to the backward, poorer, and more peripheral one; so what is the import of missions going the other way? The Adelaja sequence shows that Yoruba Pentecostalism, despite its American ancestry, still stands in an orthogenetic local tradition in Nigeria now going back more than a century. How then can Pentecostalism, seemingly more than any other new religion, manage to graft itself so successfully into a society such as the Ukraine, with an ancient Christian tradition to which it seems radically exotic, or into diverse other local cultures in the former USSR? Far-reaching questions are raised here about both society and religion. What is it about the postsocialist situation—really a range of situations, as the diverse studies in Mathijs Pelkmans, ed., *Conversion after Socialism* (2009), show—that creates needs and opportunities to which Pentecostalism has so widely been such a cogent response? What is it about Pentecostalism that has enabled it to offer this solution, and thus to become such a remarkable bridge between peoples in such diverse social contexts?

. . .

Katherine Verdery has already made a strong case for bringing the study of post-socialist and postcolonial societies together, essentially on the empirical basis that there has now come about "the full incorporation of both the former colonies and the former socialist bloc into a global capitalist economy."[7] While that perception is cogent enough, it is still worth reminding ourselves that the globalization that is everywhere spoken of today is neither so novel nor so essentially economic as Verdery's view may be taken to imply. Socialism, an *ideology* of economic organization before it became anything else, was initially a response to the emergence of capitalism as a systematic material reality in the late eighteenth century. Whereas the socialist internationals were a response to the global outreach of capitalism from the late nineteenth century, the most prominent religious internationals of our own day—Catholic, Muslim, and Pentecostal—are based on universalist faiths that do not just rest on specific theological assumptions but are inspired by historical traditions reaching back to the empires of antiquity. (Let us not forget that the Soviet Third International was in a sense the legatee of Holy Russia's claim to be the Third Rome.) The European colonial empires of the twentieth century were not able to stop socialist ideas entering the late colonial world as part of anticolonial ideology and becoming a major theme of African and Asian nationalism. Yet despite this influence from the Second to the Third World, it is still essential—especially in the light of later religious convergences—to begin by drawing out the differences between the African colonial world and the Soviet Eurasian world as regards the relations between socialism, nationalism, and religion.

In the USSR there was a full-blooded state socialism and, among its many constituent communities, a number of ancient and coherent nations. Marxism had always seen the proletariat as the universal class that transcended all national boundaries (though it could regard certain nationalisms as situationally progressive and give them conditional and pragmatic support).[8] The policy of socialism in one country, adopted in the 1920s, entailed a certain reinterpretation of the internationalist ideal, in that the destinies of the universal class were now seen as contingently aligned with those of the Russian state; but other nationalisms were still regarded as potentially dangerous and reactionary. Stalin's nationalities policy—the limited recognition of nations as entities within the Soviet overarching state, the folklorification of national cultural forms, and so forth—was intended to neutralize nationalism, and for a long time seemed to have succeeded in doing so; but the USSR's collapse rapidly led to a renewed assertion of national identities, often with religion as an integral part of their expression.

African states, by contrast, were in nearly all cases externally imposed by the colonial powers and rarely had any significant link with any preexisting indigenous nations (of which few can be said to have existed). African nationalism was a movement led by educated colonial subjects to take control of these states from the metropolitan ruling cadres, but it was undertaken in the name of the mass of colonial subjects whom the nationalist elite claimed to represent; but their claim rested more critically on their sharing a racial rather than a cultural identity with the mass. It was by a kind of courtesy that these states, upon their independence in the 1960s, were referred to as nation-states or new nations, as if political independence was itself enough to create nationhood. In fact, the nationalist leaders who came to power at independence were intensely aware of just how weak their nations were, how prone to faction and fission based on ethnic and regional loyalties. And thus in Africa socialism, so far from being threatened by nationalism—in some form it was professed by most nationalist leaders—was seen as part of the answer to the weakness of the nation. This was so in two respects. First, it gave legitimacy to the single-party states that became widespread in Africa in the decade or so after independence as the best means for forging the nation, in a collective march toward political and economic development. In this, Eastern Europe seemed to offer an attractive model, and the USSR exploited this situation in its bid for African allies for its own *Weltpolitik*. Second, socialism—more particularly African socialism—enabled the African past, with its communal values, lack of private property in land, and supposed classlessness, to be seen as a springboard to the future. Few things are more consoling than to believe that an aspired-to future—a developed nation—is somehow prefigured in the past. But in reality the weak nations of Africa exhibited a weak, largely rhetorical form of socialism. Paradoxically it was more about building up a new, postindependence class based on political access than about demolishing old classes based on control of the means of production.[9]

The key comparative question to be asked is: How did religion stand in relation to the two other great ideologies, socialism and nationalism, as between the two regions? Marxist-Leninist dogma objected to religion on two distinct grounds: first, that it was offensive to scientific reason and so a source of backwardness; and second, because it served to legitimize the position of the ruling class. So in the Soviet Union religion was at the worst suppressed, though on occasion or in certain circumstances it had to be tolerated or could be used by the regime to its own ends—mainly because of its linkage with particular ethnic or national interests. Things were very different in colonial Africa. There was little general antipathy to religion on the first of these grounds: first, because spiritual forces were generally regarded (by elites as well as by the masses) as governing the real conditions of existence and so compelling respect;[10] and second, because Christianity—I shall here leave Islam out of consideration—was so strongly linked with modern education that it was more plausibly regarded as a force for progress rather than for reaction. It was only during nationalist mobilization, continuing into the period of postcolonial socialism, that many elites came to feel distinctly ambivalent about Christianity (despite the fact that most of them had had a mission education), because it was seen as having legitimated colonialism. Yet it was rare for this feeling to be extended to independent African churches, still less to a generalized antagonism to religion as such.

. . .

These generalizations are best made concrete through a consideration of three countries that constitute varying degrees of exception to them on account of their having tried most seriously to emulate the Soviet socialist model: Benin, Mozambique, and Ethiopia. I shall consider them in sequence from the least to the most like the situation of Soviet Russia.

Benin (the former French colony of Dahomey) stands closest to the African norm, in that it had no European settlers and gained independence in 1960 without a violent anticolonial struggle. It was a society that had both a traditional religion of great tenacity—the source of Haitian Voodoo—and the most educated elite of French West Africa through the efforts of the Catholic Mission. A decade of extreme political instability, arising from acute ethnoregional factionalism played out against a deepening economic crisis, resulted in a coup in 1972 that brought to power Colonel Mathieu Kérékou. In 1974—significantly, at the place where the last king of Dahomey had surrendered to the French; for this was about nationalism as much as it was about socialism—Kérékou declared Marxism-Leninism to be the ideology of the state. Yet the superficiality of Benin's socialism—in popular humor it was mordantly known as *Laxisme-Beninisme*—expressed the absence of the social structures and historical experiences that are needed to give weight to a revolutionary agenda. Its coercive, incorporative statism was always more apparent than real, with the Roman Catholic Church, as easily the largest and most powerful institution of civil society, the obvious prime target. While the takeover of church schools was understandable for a regime that saw itself as committed to scientific socialism, it is some measure of how shallow and desperate this project soon became that it adopted Vodun as the state religion: a gesture of nationalism because a cultural rebuff to the church. Yet the church kept its grass-roots support, and as the regime staggered to its end in the late 1980s, its social strength made it the only force that could chair the national conference that paved the way for a return to multiparty politics in 1991. Kérékou lost the election despite announcing that he had become a born-again Christian, but he was elected again in 1996, one of the great survivors of African politics.[11] Since the 1990s, under a democracy renewed "at a chameleon's pace,"[12] there has been a diverse resurgence of religions, from the neo-traditionalism of the irrepressible *vodun* cults to a Pentecostal boom, flooding in from Ghana and Nigeria along the coastal corridor with a message of modernity, rupture from the past, empowerment, and openness to the world, especially to the Anglosphere.[13] One Pentecostalist quoted by Claffey drew a contrast between "a suffering Christianity as Francophone and Catholic . . . [and] his own, which he [saw] as American and Protestant with a strong emphasis on health, wealth and success."[14]

In Mozambique colonialism began much earlier and lasted nearly twenty years longer than in most of Africa. Though the Portuguese first established coastal footholds in the sixteenth century and created settler estates up the Zambezi Valley in the seventeenth, the colony did not assume its modern form till the end of the nineteenth century. Since Portugal was one of the poorest countries of Western Europe, its colonialism was correspondingly archaic and undercapitalized, relying heavily on forced labor and the supply of contract labor to South Africa. In accordance with the right-wing dictatorship of Antonio Salazar in Portugal (1926–74), the Catholic Church was a key ideological mainstay in all its colonies and held a privileged position in the field of African education. As a result the nationalist leadership (much of it drawn from Protestant mission schools) was markedly anticlerical. Further radicalized by Portuguese political intransigence, the main nationalist party, FRELIMO, turned to armed struggle. Independence came only in 1975, after disaffection among the Portuguese military had spread to Lisbon and led to the overthrow of the Salazar regime. In 1977, amid the economic wreckage from years of war, FRELIMO adopted Marxism-Leninism and soon took measures against religion as superstitious and counterrevolutionary: churches closed, activities banned, missionaries excluded, property confiscated.[15] There ensued more than a decade of civil war against regional and other opponents, backed by white South Africa; but before it ended in 1992, FRELIMO had abandoned socialism for the World Bank's prescriptions. The establishment of a free market in religions had occurred some years earlier, resulting in a phenomenal growth in Pentecostalism in particular. In this, southern Mozambique was much subject to influences from South Africa; the refugee camps were a fertile terrain for the propagation of charismatic religion; and the Lusophone connection prepared the way for the entry of dynamic groups of Brazilian origin, notably the Universal Church of the Kingdom of God, reputedly the largest Pentecostal church in the world.[16]

Our third case, Ethiopia, comes closest to the Soviet paradigm. Here was an ancient sacred monarchy closely bonded with an Orthodox Church that was the cornerstone of national identity. These institutions rested upon a material base more characteristic of Eurasia than of the rest of sub-Saharan Africa: namely a plow-based agriculture and a feudal class structure wherein landlords held estates under service tenure from the emperor and extracted rents from a peasantry.[17] In the late nineteenth century the core Christian kingdom not only beat back European colonialism but engaged in imperial expansion itself, bringing under its sway a vast area to the east and south, ethnically very diverse and overwhelmingly non-Christian in religion. The revolution of 1974 was the work of a radicalized intelligentsia (extending into the army) that, disgusted with the failure of Emperor Haile Selassie's attempt at a form of conservative modernization, saw a Marxist-Leninist command state as the only solution to the country's backwardness. Its own mistakes (particularly in the agrarian sector), natural catastrophe, and the draining effect of war against Eritrean secessionism kept the regime—known as the *Derg* or revolutionary council—in fairly permanent crisis, despite Soviet aid and backing. When this dried up in 1989, the socialist experiment was abandoned; and the *Derg* collapsed in 1991, a pendant to the final debacle of state socialism in the USSR.

The vicissitudes of religion in the trajectory of Ethiopian socialism have been brilliantly analyzed by Donald Donham from the perspective of one of the southern peripheral regions of Ethiopia, Maale.[18] (The story evokes several parallels with the experiences of the peripheral non-Russian peoples within the Soviet Union, such as the Nenets and Chukchi.)[19] Though the Orthodox Church reached Maale as part of the structure of imperial overrule in the 1890s, its local impact was minimal, and Christianity made slow progress until the Sudan Interior Mission (SIM) started to make significant numbers of converts in the 1950s. The great irony was that, while the

SIM had originated in Canada as a fundamentalist-faith mission strongly opposed to the liberal Protestantism of the day—and to that extent was antimodern—in Maale it became the very epitome of local modernization (and as such opposed to the Orthodox Church, which seemed both reactionary and a tool of alien control). As a result, when the revolution spread from the Ethiopian heartland, the young converts of the SIM were naturally its first allies in Maale. But a few years later, when the *Derg* was forced into defensive turmoil by Somalia's invasion of the Ogaden, it sought to consolidate national morale and its own legitimacy by reversing its policy of hostility to the church (in a manner strikingly reminiscent of Stalin's rehabilitation of the Russian Orthodox Church during the straits of World War II). Then, in line with the replacement of the USA by the USSR as Ethiopia's major foreign ally and arms supplier, a further shift in the regime's religious alignment took place: Protestant churches of North American origin (so recently local supporters of the revolution) found themselves stigmatized as antirevolutionary fellow travelers of imperialism and capitalism, foreigners who "rejected the nation and the revolution."[20] It is interesting that they were also labeled as Pentecostals or "pentes," even though none of the major missions such as the SIM or the Lutherans was Pentecostal and there were as yet very few Pentecostal missionaries. Only in 1967 was Ethiopia's first Pentecostal church founded, among students in Addis Ababa, though the imperial government refused to recognize it. But the *Derg* rightly divined its ominous potential, a straw in the wind that would blow strongly after Ethiopia was liberalized in the 1990s. There are now estimated to be several million Pentecostalists in Ethiopia.[21]

So the soft socialism that usually accompanied African nationalism turned in a handful of cases into a much harder kind when hopes for national development faltered in the 1970s. The weaknesses of the Soviet model were not yet apparent, and the geopolitics of the Cold War created opportunities. But there was another predisposing condition, which points the way to appreciating how religion fitted into both the rise, and the demise, of these socialist regimes. The more a regime is founded on an integral bond between the nation/state and a single church or religion, the more likely it is that, if that regime is challenged or overthrown, it will be replaced by an alternative of the left that mirrors its integralist character but with an inverted, antireligious content. Thus, strongly Catholic or Orthodox national regimes, as in Spain or Russia, were much more likely to generate anticlerical attitudes and vigorous communist movements than Protestant regimes were, whether the latter had state churches of nearly universal membership along Scandinavian lines or a high degree of religious pluralism as in Great Britain and (to an even greater extent) the United States. Something of the same correlation is also seen to occur in Africa when we contrast former British colonies, none of which—not even the most left-wing ones, like Nyerere's Tanzania or Ghana under Nkrumah—took its socialism to the extreme of Marxism-Leninism with the three countries we have considered. For British colonies tended to have more missions operating in them, missionaries of more diverse national origins and a higher proportion (if not a majority) of Protestants—all making for a more plural religious scene—than French or Portuguese colonies did, and a fortiori than a country like Ethiopia.

Moreover, this pluralism, besides being unpropitious for the emergence of an antireligious socialism, was also the best climate in which Pentecostalism might take root and flourish. Late fruit of the evangelical revival, Pentecostalism first arose in the most plural of all religious contexts, the United States, and soon after in the more peripheral regions of Protestant Northern Europe. Unsurprisingly, it found its first African footholds in English-speaking milieus like South Africa and British West Africa (Nigeria and Ghana) in the first decades of the twentieth century.[22] But in countries outside the Anglosphere like Benin, Mozambique, and Ethiopia—to say nothing of the countries of the former Soviet bloc—a turn to Pentecostalism after Marxism-Leninism represented a radical change of cultural direction.

. . .

The sociological explanation of religious change consists largely of showing the fit between the demands of a novel social situation and the potential of a religious tradition. Or, if this sounds too functionalist, it is about why and how answers to the predicaments that people newly find themselves in are drawn from particular traditions. Before we ask why Pentecostalism has so widely been taken as the answer to the predicaments of the present age, it is worth emphasizing the link between the extraordinary diversity of the situations that Pentecostalism has answered and (what has made this possible) the extremely protean quality of Pentecostalism itself. Simply on the basis of examples from the papers presented at the Halle conference entitled "Conversion after Socialism," Pentecostalism and closely related forms of evangelical Christianity have made significant headway in at least four quite different kinds of setting in the former Soviet bloc: first, among Roma or Gypsies in Eastern Europe; second, among some peoples of the northern peripheral regions, such as the Nenets and Chukchi; third, on a small scale, among some Muslim peoples of Central Asia, such as Uighurs and Kyrgyz; and fourth, the Embassy of God in the heart of Ukraine. There could hardly be more variety here—in prior religion, cultural context, rural or urban location, mode of life, political placement—so what accounts for the extraordinary range of Pentecostalism's appeal?

We may see grounds for the adoption (or rejection) of a new religion or church in terms of two very general criteria of religious value.[23] The first is that potential converts must feel that its message expresses the reality of things: what we may call its truth value. The second is that they must regard the identity conferred by joining the new religion to be compatible with what they feel or want themselves to be, in relation to other identities, especially communal, ethnic, or national ones: what we may call its identity value. In stable religious situations, truth and identity values are likely to be in accord, and in periods of steady adaptive change, truth values may be adjusted without identity values being undermined. In times of crisis, the truth value of a religion is perhaps more likely to be first called into question, and if conversions to an ostensibly truer religion result, it may create tensions with existing identities. This was often the case with early Christian converts in Africa who thereby became estranged from their communities, resulting in an agenda for the Africanization of Christianity. On the other hand, it was often those whose identity attachments had been undermined (e.g., by being sold into slavery) who were most responsive to the preaching of Christian truth; whereas provided that communities (and the identities they sustained) remained viable, prosperous, unchallenged by defeat or natural disaster, they were likely to remain content with the truth that they had.

Pentecostalism now goes back a century, and the wide variety of forms it now exhibits is ample proof of the adaptability of its basic themes.[24] Its core truth has always been its vision of the self as reborn and empowered through the Holy Spirit, as described in the charter biblical narrative of Acts II. Bible and Spirit are indeed the two cornerstones of the movement, and many of its current tensions and options can be seen in terms of the emphasis distributed between impulses that flow from either of them. Pentecostalism's first constituency in America was drawn from poor, recently rural people, both white and black, experiencing the dislocations of urban life in a quickly developing capitalist economy. The fundamentalism of its use of the Bible as a source of validation came out of a long tradition of popular Evangelicalism. But its great innovation was to complement the ascetic disciplines of Protestant morality with a lively sense of the corporeal gifts of the Spirit. These ranged from the ecstasy of speaking in tongues (which was the main thing immediately distinctive of the new movement), to divine healing, prophecy, the casting out of evil spirits, efficacious prayer, and the possibility of miracles. In effect this new orientation represented a fusion of two distinct strands within American religion: the perennial this-worldliness of African belief mediated through African-American practice, and the new acceptance within Protestantism at large of wealth, health, and happiness as legitimate rewards of faith.[25] Finally (and somewhat paradoxically in the light of the last point), a kick of urgency was given to the new teachings by a fresh wave of millennial expectancy.

This repertory of themes proved highly flexible in application, enabling Pentecostalism both to connect with the aspirations of diverse audiences and to move with the times. Its two sides, the scriptural and the pneumatic, enabled members to strike a variable balance between discipline and ecstasy, adjustment and mobility, as their particular circumstances required. Because the gifts of the Spirit might be variably construed in terms of intrinsic or expressive rewards and of external or instrumental ones, Pentecostalism could connect both with the self-improvement techniques of popular psychology and with rituals to exorcise evil spirits that block one's progress. Though "an option for and of the poor"[26] (which still remains a fair characterization of the bulk of its adherents across the world),

Pentecostalism has never encouraged class *ressentiment;* but neither has it worked to reconcile the poor to their poverty—rather to empower them within it so that they may move up out of it. So, sidestepping Marxism's strategy of class action, it has facilitated social mobility, initially of individuals but also (especially where adopted by ethnic minorities or in peripheral regions) collective self-enhancement.

Pentecostalism soon started to move up in the world. By 1950, it was no longer solely a religion of the poor and marginal: it had risen with the growth in population and wealth of its American heartland in the South and West, and some churches were acquiring fine buildings and facilities. Of the various doctrinal developments of the following decades, none was more telling than the so-called faith gospel, also known as the gospel of prosperity, which was reciprocally related to this growth: it both appealed to members' material aspirations and generated large revenues for church expansion. To the small, egalitarian congregations of earlier days were added a number of megachurches run by high-profile and wealthy charismatic preachers, prominent among whom was a handful of celebrity televangelists, for Pentecostalism had responded with alacrity to the new opportunities offered by the electronic media. The movement became more consciously identified with American values, and it entered into a phase of energetic transnational outreach and exchange: in Africa and Latin America Pentecostal missionaries now far outnumbered those of mainstream denominations. Yet this was never a univocal or one-way process, never *just* a matter of "exporting the American Gospel,"[27] since Pentecostalism lends itself so readily to selective appropriation. In Africa the 1970s saw a massive takeoff of neo-Pentecostalism, initially in Anglophone countries like Nigeria and Zimbabwe, where it could build on an existing Pentecostal tradition going back many decades.[28] Yet even though this depended on African initiatives, it adopted a markedly more internationalist (which means in effect American) style. The economic and political backdrop of this—the crisis of the postcolonial state—was, of course, what had also led to the Marxist-Leninist turn in Benin, Mozambique, and Ethiopia.

Now that state socialism, as a form of political and economic organization, is exhausted, some variant of neoliberalism is pretty well the only main course on the menu. Whereas Marxism-Leninism, like its integralist predecessors, aspired to be a total social system and tried to generate its own cultural underpinnings—and when it came to religion, fell down badly—neoliberalism can afford to be more eclectic. As a main course, it can be combined with cultural side dishes *à l'africaine, islamique, russe,* or whatever, but it has to be said that few religions match its flavor better than Pentecostalism. As a product of the most demanding religious marketplace in the world, Pentecostalism is better able than most other religions to express the experiential truth of the conditions in which people and communities in today's world have to seek development. And this is also a practical truth, since Pentecostal churches, by their lifestyle teachings and social support systems, also do much to equip their members to survive—and in some cases to prosper—in the neoliberal environment.

Pentecostalism is also persuasive in another way that expresses the spirit of modernity. Compared with the two other great transnational movements of our day, Pentecostalism has nothing of Catholicism's hierarchical structure, or of the central places of Islam and Catholicism, or a unifying ritual like the Muslim *hajj*. Its unmistakable unity in diversity is realized through a dense, many-stranded, noncentered global network of exchanges, employing a distinct but ever-shifting stock of themes and motifs. This permits its participants both to feel their fellowship as part of a movement across which there is much sharing and borrowing, and to draw on this stock and to innovate as they respond to the demands being made in their part of the network. The unbounded and noncentered unity of global Pentecostalism strongly evokes the character of the Internet. Like the Internet, Pentecostalism bears many signs of its American origins, and America is where the mesh of exchanges within the whole system is at its densest. But despite its influence, America is not *formally* privileged as its center: Pentecostalists may look to it as the epitome of modernity but not in the way that others look to Rome or Mecca.

Accepting the truth of Pentecostalism brings a new identity with it: indeed one may say that its truth and identity values fuse in the figure of the person who is born again through the Holy Spirit. This self-defining experience serves to mark off the born-again in two dimensions: from their own past and from other individuals who are not reborn. Clearly, any act of individual conversion implies some degree of dissatisfaction with the personal past as well as a readiness both to break from it and to associate with a new group of people: an act of both severance and attachment. In Pentecostalism's early days, the wider identity implications of this were limited in two respects. First, the born-again came from the same Protestant American milieu as the unregenerate, and—insofar as they had a wider message—it was largely to *re*call them to traditional values that they had neglected. Second, Pentecostalism was the product of a highly individualistic society, and its regeneration was imagined as extending not to society as a whole, merely to the aggregate of other born-again individuals. (In one widely held Pentecostal belief the born-again are to be raptured into heaven at the end time, leaving the mass of the unregenerate to their fate.) But when Pentecostalism went abroad, these two conditions were often not met, so the issue of how it would sit with other identities became more pressing. In postcolonial and in postsocialist societies, it typically came as a religion bearing American attributes with the promise of modernity and global mobility. At the same time, despite its appeal as a powerful vector of individualism (especially among the young), it was also often looked to as a vehicle of collective regeneration. So in Nigeria in recent years, it has become commonplace for Pentecostal leaders to offer renewal, deliverance, and prosperity to the *nation*, as if in reproach at the failure of the nationalist state to deliver the fruits of development. (See chapter 10)

Now, where a community is the focus of renewal, such that the Spirit is anticipated to work its signs not just on the human body but also on the body politic, the issue of the balance between rupture and continuity presents itself in a particularly acute form. For this implies that the community, by the very fact of its being worth renewal, is seen as a site of positive value. But since Pentecostal conversion rests on the conviction that the prevailing state of affairs is profoundly corrupt, there is inevitably a problem about how to reconcile the rupture that this implies with the continuing value that attaches to the communal identity of its potential converts. A resolution is not always easy to achieve, and the shifting and variable outcomes have led to some interpretive schizophrenia, at least in the literature on West African Pentecostalism. Some observers, following the common self-representations of Pentecostalists, have perceived a radical rupture, "a complete break with the past,"[29] of which the demonization of ancestors and local spirits, and the provision of rituals of deliverance from them, are a conspicuous sign; whereas others have seen in the emphasis on healing and prosperity the strength of values drawn from primal or traditional religion.[30] The concrete reality is always a mix, and it is a mix whose formula can only be worked out in situ. It is in the protean genius of Pentecostalism that it has so often enabled this to be done, turning rupture into redemption.

Several of the postsocialist cases illustrate how the tensions between rupture and continuity may work themselves out.[31] At one pole is the Embassy of God in Kiev, an American-style megachurch like several other Nigerian ministries, which has succeeded in implanting itself as a genuinely Ukrainian movement: a singular achievement when one considers that such a church in London (of which there are several) would have been strongly tied to a mainly Afro-Caribbean constituency.[32] Ukraine's own tradition of religious pluralism was helpfully permissive, but the critical factor for the Embassy of God's success was how it linked its truth for individuals—its message of redemption from alcohol, drugs, and other personal problems—with a cogent claim to share the identity of the new, democratic Ukraine and to be a positive force in the rebuilding of its civil society.

At the other pole stand the cases where Pentecostalism (or evangelical Baptism, which is close to it) has been taken up not at the heart of a large historic nation but among marginalized ethnic minorities. Take the case of the Nenets:[33] here the tension between truth and identity presents itself more starkly yet is resolved with a striking paradox. With the survival of much of the old shamanic worldview and the influence of Russian Orthodoxy largely erased by decades of official atheism, both face the challenge of reframing their identities after the collapse of the Soviet order. Laur Vallikivi describes the faith of Nenets Baptists (many of whom are born-again) in terms that recall the discourse of African Pentecostalism: "total transformation," the old spirits pushed into a "demonic periphery," the "negation of the past," and so on. Yet he also characterizes their use of language in prayer as "represent[ing] at the same time continuity and rupture" and "creating a clear continuance with the past" in their conviction of the power of the Word in relations with the spirit world.[34] At the same time, the new faith serves both to integrate the Nenets into the wider society by its adoption of the Bible in Russian and to preserve their identity within it by a faith that stands in contrast to Russian Orthodoxy.

One way in which rupture may be reconciled with continuity is through their placement at complementary levels, individual and collective, respectively, as Ludek Broz shows in his account of evangelical Christians in the Altai Republic of southwest Siberia.[35] Here, because the core truth value of Evangelicalism lies in its promise of individual self-renewal, of liberation from an old life of sin and addictions like alcoholism, the theme of rupture from the past is most strongly evident in what Broz calls "personal narratives of discontinuity." But while a new and foreign religion is well suited to be a vehicle of such personal liberation, the charge of alienness—which its rivals throw at it—is embarrassing; so it makes sense that evangelicals have responded by being warmly enthusiastic in their support for Altai language, music, and customs. This is a claim to belong through the assertion of continuity with the local cultural past. Here the Altai evangelicals faced a problem similar to one that challenged the inculturation of Christianity in Africa. Though there was no indigenous Altai concept of religion, local identity was deeply bound in with practices that evangelical Christians could not but regard as heathen, such as some of the rituals involved in *Chaga*, the celebration of the New Year. As often in Africa, the solution was to draw a novel distinction between what was religion and what was culture, so that the latter could be embraced as part of Christian practice. Thus the demands of truth and identity might be reconciled in a specific blend of rupture and continuity.

Of course, Pentecostalism does not always manage to achieve this elusive reconciliation, as Johannes Ries's study of Pentecostalism among the Transylvanian Gypsies shows.[36] Of the two main components of the Gypsy population, the relatively privileged Corturari, who retain much more of Roma culture, have been impervious to the appeal of Pentecostalism, whereas it is the impoverished but culturally more assimilated Tsigani who have started to turn to it. Rupture would cost the Corturari too much by way of ethnic identity loss; by contrast, the cultural value attached to Tsigani identity has been so far eroded that Pentecostalism can offer the converts an altogether new kind of solidarity, as members of a trans-ethnic family of God. Elsewhere, movements other than Pentecostalism have met the yearnings of the postsocialist world, though it is notable how often they echo Pentecostal messages and have Pentecostal groups as their main competitors.

. . .

The range and flexibility of Pentecostalism have enabled it to put down roots in very diverse social contexts. The two very broad categories of context that I have considered here, the postsocialist and the postcolonial, though each of them is now the designation of a distinct academic subfield, are themselves internally very heterogeneous as well as overlapping. In relation to the new religions that now flood across them, their main overarching feature is that they both have had to come to terms with the exigencies of the neoliberal order. Behind that lies the failure of the state, whether (in the case of the former Soviet bloc) of long-established socialist states, or (in the case of the African Marxist-Leninist countries) of postcolonial socialist regimes that lasted barely two decades, or of the majority of African former colonies, including the Anglophone ones, that had adopted a softer African socialism. When the crisis of the postcolonial state first hit Africa, in the 1970s, there were two very different responses: a turn to Marxism in a handful of cases and a dramatic surge of Pentecostalism in others. Of course these cannot be seen as strictly analogous or alternative options, though it is significant that as responses they could not be combined. But when Marxism-Leninism's failure became evident, at the end of the 1980s, Pentecostalism was widely seen to be some kind of answer. But an answer to what, and what kind of answer? Religions just don't have viable answers to the problems of political and economic organization posed in today's world, though some Muslims think they do, in such forms as Sharia law or Islamic economics.[37] But Pentecostalism is happy to leave this task to the engineers of neoliberalism and to complement it by fashioning subjectivities that enable individuals to make practical sense of the experiences of living in a world so organized.

If the operational requirements of neoliberalism, then, are lessons that tend to flow from North to South or West to East (via agencies like the World Bank), the modes of experiential adaptation to it—of which, I have argued, Pentecostalism is one—now often move in other directions: South to North (or from the old Third to the old Second World), as from Nigeria to Ukraine, or South to South, as from Brazil to southern Africa. This is not surprising, since experiential solutions have to take account not just of the objective external conditions but of the cultural personalities of those on whom the adaptation is imposed. In creating these transcontinental bridges, Pentecostalism has the great asset that, behind the North-Americanness of its expression, its ease with the electronic media, its modernity, and its individualism, it is also the bearer of a much older religious ethos, concerned with healing, visionary guidance, the various ways in which the spirit may imprint on the flesh. This is what has enabled it so often to click with newly urbanized ex-peasants, or tribal populations caught in the peripheries of modern states, or transnational migrants in search of a better life, to achieve, in some cases, paradoxical combinations of the old and new or unexpected fusions of rupture and continuity.

PART TWO

6

Context, Tradition, and the Anthropology of World Religions

The world religions present social anthropology with a serious challenge. It came to them relatively late but with a body of theory and method honed on the analysis of primitive or tribal religions. The larger project by which the classic monographs were framed was in one sense paradoxical: it was to use materials from societies few of which had so much as a concept of religion to develop theories about what religion (or else ritual) was in general. But now we have to move from a large number of small religions to a small number of very large ones; from religions that have no awareness of themselves as such to religions that are highly self-conscious of themselves and of their boundaries; from religions that had to be treated as having no time depth to ones that not only are "the longest lasting of civilization's primary institutions"[1] but have complex ways of remembering their own pasts. It is these world faiths that have been spreading through mission and migration, generating new forms of religious expression and new situations of pluralism and conflict.

So it is hardly surprising that over recent decades a fast-growing number of impressive studies of particular world religions has appeared and that attempts have begun to be made to organize them intellectually as subfields, in the form of programmatic statements for anthropologies of Islam (most elaborately), Christianity, and Buddhism. These various attempts have typically been based on the corpus of studies of the particular religion, referring to the salient empirical questions to which it has given rise and to more general criteria of anthropological reason; but they have made little use of the notion of world religions or employed comparisons between them as a means of deepening their analysis. That may not matter so much if the religions exist as cultural isolates, but there has been much historical interaction between them—notably between Christianity and

Islam—and they coexist in a growing number of situations in the contemporary world, where people compare them in practice and so encourage various kinds of exchange to occur between them.

Our primary framing category of world religions stands against one of tribal or primitive religions, in terms of a complex of interrelated features: that they have written scriptures, seek (or at least acquire) converts, tend be transvaluatory, and so on.[2] But the distinguishing feature that I want to start from is the differentiation of religion and society. The classic ethnographers—Raymond Firth, John Middleton, E. E. Evans-Pritchard, say—soon found themselves having to refer to religion when they set out to elucidate such things as Tikopia chiefship, Lugbara lineages, or the Nuer's relationship to their natural environment. By contrast, the links between world religions and the societies or communities where they are practiced lacks this quality of immediate and necessary mutual implication. Even where a world religion is strongly held by everyone to the exclusion of any other, provides the charter for the basic forms of social life, and is regarded as a key component of group identity, people are aware that it has come from another time, or place, or both. They know that their forebears converted to it; and their clergy—whatever exact form these take—have to remind them regularly that their practice of it falls short of its highest normative standards. Implicit here is comparison: with the practice of another place or time (or both), or with the practice of other religions. This gap between religion and society means that the analysis of world religions can never be purely contextual and functional, as the classic monographs of primitive religion have been. It must be both comparative, because of world religions' inherent awareness of alternatives, and historical, because their normative ideals have a once-and-future character.

Paradoxically, all this may be better appreciated when we take a view not from the heartlands of a world religion, where it has been long practiced and become deeply woven into local culture, but from its frontiers or periphery. The point has been made before. Fernand Braudel remarked that "it is most often on the border that the most characteristic aspects, phenomena and tensions [of a civilization] are found."[3] More recently, the historian of medieval Islam Richard Bulliet has argued that the growth of the Muslim *umma* as a transcultural entity is better understood by taking a "view from the edge" (in this case from Khurasan)—that is, to look at how Islam's non-Arab converts were brought into it—rather than by following the conventional approach of tracing its expansion outward from its Arabian point of origin.[4] So too with the Yoruba. What makes their case even more exemplary is that the age of conversion, being for most people only two to three generations back, has not entirely faded from the communal memory; and everyone is aware that there are alternatives to the religion that they practice, for they are also divided roughly half-and-half between Islam and Christianity. As a result, history and comparison are inherent in the religious situation—part of the lived experience of every Yoruba—and not brought to it, or imposed on it, by the external analyst.

II

It is quite possible for excellent, even classic, studies to be written about particular Christian or Muslim groups or movements by authors who are not interested in asking questions about the inherent or distinctive attributes of the religion as such. Such was the case for a long time with anthropological studies of Christianity—a religion that presented the additional problem that it seemed so close to the culture that had produced the anthropologists as not to merit their attention in the same way as religions deemed exotic to Europe. Their focus was divided between two distinct spheres, which gave rise to two bodies of literature about different kinds of Christianity, seemingly almost unconnected with each other. First, there were studies of peasant or folk religion in areas long Christian, such as the Catholic or Orthodox Mediterranean or Latin America. These generated the well-used distinction between great and little traditions, which spread into the study of other world religions and so worked against, rather than for, any deeper inquiry into the character of Christianity as such.

Second, there were forms of Christianity arising in the wake of European mission and colonial expansion: cargo cults in Melanesia, nativist movements employing Christian symbols in North America, prophetist movements and independent churches in Africa. Here, the question of how far, or in what ways, they were to be seen as Christian usually did not interest anthropologists, though it was a preoccupation of many missionary writers under the rubric of syncretism.[5] Insofar as it concerned them at all, the Christian expression of these movements was treated as incidental rather than integral to them: anthropologists were much more concerned to show how it was underlain by indigenous, pre-Christian concerns and beliefs. (A partial exception to this may be seen in the comparisons sometimes drawn with earlier outbreaks of Christian millennialism, for example through Norman Cohn's classic studies of the Middle Ages, though here too what gave more satisfaction was the discovery of indigenous notions of periodic societal renewal.)[6] Often the framing questions were more to do with politics than religion, as in the debate about how far they were to be seen as movements of anticolonial protest and precursors of nationalism.[7] Were they better explained with reference to a Marxist analysis, in terms of interests, or a Weberian one, in terms of ideas?[8]

Still, Christianity slowly rose up the anthropological agenda, of which a significant marker was Wendy James and Douglas Johnson's *Vernacular Christianity* (1988). Important as this was in arguing for the gap between the two literatures to be closed, it was still some way from adumbrating an anthropology of Christianity as that has developed in the last decade through such scholars as Joel Robbins, Fenella Cannell, Matthew Engelke, and others.[9] These scholars typically had their roots firmly in one or the other of the two spheres of Christianity distinguished above—like Cannell on popular Filipino Catholicism or Robbins on Pentecostalism in the New Guinea Highlands. As we shall see, their specific proposals for an anthropology of Christianity tend to bear the imprint of these backgrounds.

The aim of the anthropology of Christianity (as of other world religions) is to give a sharper intellectual organization to a spread of empirical inquiries that are cognate (in that closely related thematic issues keep cropping up within it) and also disparate (in that diverse local concerns clutter the foreground). It embraces questions both of method (i.e., how the study of religion *X* should be set about) and of substance (i.e., what concrete issues are central to its study). Though there is no sharp distinction between these two kinds of question, the main emphasis of different authors may be directed one way or the other. A common strategy for anthropologies of religion *X*, *Y*, or *Z* is to select some substantive feature deemed particularly characteristic of the religion, which is then treated as a fixed point to which studies of its diverse manifestations may relate. So Robbins proposes that discontinuity be seen as a central feature of Christian culture. The problem about any such particular proposed focus is that, however plausible it may be, it is likely to be at once logically arbitrary and factually overdetermined by the researcher's own research area. So while Robbins's idea of discontinuity fits very well with his research on Urapmin Pentecostalism, does that make it paradigmatic for Christianity in general? If he had worked on, say, Coptic Christianity in Egypt, is it conceivable that he would have proposed discontinuity as *the* leitmotif of Christianity? The key principle of method here is that no particular form of a religion can be privileged over any other as the starting point of an anthropology of it.

Cannell's proposed focus is quite different: Christianity's propensity for various kinds of dualism, especially as between the transcendent and embodied dimensions of faith—the unresolved character of which leads her to dub it "the impossible religion."[10] This perspective can surely yield real insights for the study of Christianity; but like the problematic of great vs. little traditions with which it has an obvious affinity,[11] the idea of a tension between the transcendent and the embodied does not seem to be peculiar to Christianity. Is it not equally a tension in other world religions (as her own passing references to work on Hinduism imply)? Taken together, the proposals of Robbins and Cannell highlight a general problem of method: how to steer a middle course between the Scylla of too much specificity and the Charybdis of too little.

As these questions imply, any proposal for a substantive agenda for an anthropology of religion *X* or *Y* carries comparative implications, whether or not these are explicitly addressed. The obvious kind of comparison is substantive: What concrete features of religion *X* most usefully serve to distinguish it from religions *Y* and *Z*? But sometimes the comparison has to do more with method: Robbins's argument for the anthropology of Christianity to be grounded in the notion of *dis*continuity is counterposed to what he sees as the continuity thinking ingrained in anthropology's approach to cultural phenomena. He has a good point here; for certainly the study of movements like cargo cults and African prophet movements has been strongly disposed to emphasize their roots in precontact local culture and to downplay their Christian originality. What is curious about Robbins's argument is that implicitly it runs against one common criticism made of the anthropology of religion: that it imports assumptions derived from Christianity (especially liberal Protestantism) into its analysis of other religions. That precisely was the thrust of Talal Asad's well-known and widely accepted critique of Clifford Geertz's seminal essay "Religion as a Cultural System."[12] It is Cannell who stands closer to Asad here, with her idea that Christianity has functioned as the repressed—an active but unacknowledged force—within the culture of anthropology itself. Perhaps it is not so unacknowledged as she claims. For as David Gellner shows in his masterly review of the anthropology of Buddhism, European scholars—both anthropologists and orientalists—have made much use of the categories of Protestantism and Catholicism to get a theoretical fix on the many variants of Buddhism: Mahayana and Theravada, traditional and modernist.[13] Nor is this necessarily distorting, provided the comparisons are sufficiently tentative and provisional, used as methodological scaffolding rather than as substantive rafters for the anthropology of Buddhism.

Now, if there is one general problem of method that is relevant to the anthropology of *any* world religion, it is how to conceptualize it as a theoretical object without essentializing it. Essentialism, one may say, is pretty much anthropology's Sin Against the Holy Ghost. By contrast, most believers consider that there is a timeless, essential, transcontextual core to their faith. Typically this also has a normative force, providing criteria for defining certain beliefs and practices as illegitimate and excluding deviants from the faith community. Anthropology, of course, cannot get into the business of religious norm-setting by privileging one form of a religion against others. What a large majority of believers may consider as heterodoxy or deviation, even to the extent of placing it outside the faith community altogether, anthropologists will rightly wish to see as standing in the tradition of that religion as much as its dominant or mainstream forms. Indeed, a religion's tradition may be very fruitfully viewed precisely as a set of running arguments about just what *is* essential to it.[14]

One seeming solution to the problem presented by the contrast between the essentializing faith of the believer and the variety of forms encountered by the anthropologist is to try to dissolve it by pluralizing the religion, making as many Christianit*ies* and Islam*s* as there are contexts in which they are practiced. That would be to abandon any serious program for the anthropologies of religions *X* or *Y*, and a fortiori any comparative anthropology of the world religions at all. But it is hardly a solution, since particular variants or versions of a faith, or groups or communities that consider themselves to practice it, all presuppose the prior existence of a body of diverse but cognate traditions such as is implied by the notion of a world religion. Those complex, variegated, historically given ensembles are bound to be fuzzy at the edges—Does Mormonism belong to Christianity? Do the Druse or Ahmadiyya belong to Islam? Does Chrislam[15] belong to either, or to both?—but it surely suits the purposes of anthropology to take an inclusive view and count marginal cases as being in rather than out. The strategy of pluralizing world religions, rather than accepting them for the complex unities that they are, ignores both the prime source of their resemblances and the issue of why their disparate members are typically so keen to claim for themselves the name of what *they* assuredly see as *one* religion.

An extreme form of this pluralizing strategy to deal with the problem of reconciling the linked tensions between unity/diversity and believer/outsider perspectives has been proposed by some anthropologists of Islam.[16] This is to regard Muslims, rather than Islam, as the object of anthropological inquiry. Daniel Varisco goes further, to argue that, "the anthropologist observes Muslims in order to represent their representations of Muslims; only Muslims can observe Islam."[17] An initial appeal of this solution is that it neatly gives unity to the believers and keeps diversity for the anthropologists, thus keeping the latter well away from the lure of essentialism. But can it possibly make sense for anthropology to be restricted to a study of believers' representations? Of course it is widely accepted across the whole field of religious studies that believers *must* be treated as the privileged witnesses of their own faith; and that includes their representations, as they are evident to the anthropologist in the context of his field encounters.[18] Data of this kind are surely the starting point for anthropology's distinctive contribution to the study of world religions. But if we want to go beyond this in the description of a religion, or to advance from description to comparison and explanation, then a very large part of the evidence, such as the social and material conditions of those representations, the whole of the religion's past (including its scriptures), its institutional forms, and so forth, is not subject to believers' privilege. In so doing, we will be talking about the world religions as given bodies of tradition that provide preconditions for the beliefs and practices of their contemporary adherents. The complex historical reality of Islam is presupposed by the existence of the contemporary Muslims, with all their diverse views of what true Islam is, who are encountered by anthropologists. The same must be true, mutatis mutandis, for any other world religion.

III

It is more than odd that the programmatic wave of writing on Christianity should refer so little to work on Islam, and not just because the anthropology of any world religion is at least implicitly comparative with respect to the others. For the anthropology of Islam is unquestionably much more developed, with a lively critical literature (now going back more than 30 years) in response to the impressive build-up of monographs.[19] No single contribution to it has occasioned as much comment as Talal Asad's essay *The Idea of an Anthropology of Islam* (1986). Since it offers the most cogent attempt so far to steer a viable course between pluralism and essentialism in the analysis of a world religion, it has lessons for those interested in other religions, though these are not Asad's main concern.

Asad's question is how Islam may be conceptualized as an object of anthropological inquiry. He quickly disposes of two answers: that Islam is merely a convenient label that covers all its concrete instances, as emically defined (the position of Michael Gilsenan); and that Islam has no value as an *analytical* category at all (as Abdul Hamid El-Zein argued). What he is especially concerned to critique are the views of those like Ernest Gellner and Bernard Lewis, who see Islam in *substantive* terms, as a historic formation that has shaped the life of Muslims and the forms of their societies in particular and distinctive ways. Inevitably, comparison comes quickly to the fore here, but Asad is oddly resistant to it. He brushes aside, rather than engages with, still less refutes, Gellner's contention—hardly original with him—that a highly distinctive and historically momentous feature of Islam, compared with Christianity, has lain in its relationship with political power. Islam offers, Gellner argued, the "blueprint of a social order," a political aspiration consolidated by its rapid ascent to being a world empire. By contrast, Christianity's normative separation of the things of God and Caesar is to be referred back to its early formation among the politically marginalized. Asad, however, finds it "impossible to accept" that Christianity throughout its history has been less intimately concerned with political power, citing cases from the emperor Constantine to "colonial missionaries."[20] His refusal to recognize difference at this point begs quite a few questions about the precise *modalities* of how the two religions have related to political power. As if sensing this, Asad at once avers that he has "nothing in principle against comparison between Christian and Muslim histories," and instances a couple of cases;[21] but these are perfunctory and play no role whatever in his argument. It is clear that for Asad the path to an anthropology of Islam does not lie through comparison with other world religions as regards substantive features of any kind, that derive from its origins or early history and exert some characteristic effect on its subsequent instances.

So where does Asad look for it instead? He wants to find a framework that can encompass the many diverse realizations of Islam that anthropologists encounter without privileging any one of them in terms of its substantive content. He finds this in a notion of Islam as a discursive practice, a tradition of argument among Muslims about the correct forms of belief and practice. Such a discursive tradition is necessarily both rooted in, and oriented to, the past, but it is always conducted in some particular present, which is where it becomes the object of anthropological analysis. Now, while this is pitched at a very general level and appears as more methodological than substantive in its import, it is not hard to see something more concrete glimmering behind it (rather as Pentecostal revivalism glimmers behind Robbins's notion of Christian discontinuity). I mean the absolutely central role within mainstream Islam of argumentative recourse to the Koran and the *hadith* in the ongoing normative self-constitution of the community of Muslims, the *umma*. Of this, Sharia is the consolidated summation.

That is, if you like, the strong version of Asad's argument, perhaps stronger than he wants to make it, since he does not explicitly mention Sharia. But we may also see a weaker version, which has the potential to serve as starting point for other world religions too. The relation between the present and the past, or rather the way that the present serves as the fulcrum between the past and the future, is absolutely central to *all* religious traditions and to all religions *as* traditions. A body of knowledge and practice is received from the past, but never inertly: it has to be engaged with, worked upon, and so its reproduction is also, to varying extents, always a process of development or transformation. *Pace* Robbins, while we cannot ignore the ruptural potential of Christianity, the latent continuities must not be neglected either—even in its most ruptural forms, like Pentecostalism[22]—for in a larger view it is the tension or balance between rupture and continuity that marks the reproduction of all religious traditions.

Yet despite its promise, Asad's program for the anthropology of Islam leaves one with a pronounced sense of anticlimax. Substantive lines of inquiry pursued by other anthropologists are dismissed, yet his own core concept of discursive tradition remains very sketchy, almost empty of content. He has little to say about what distinctive cast may have been given to Muslim life by the vehicles of this tradition: the Koran, ancillary media such as *hadith, tafsir,* legal commentaries, and so forth; then historical works—both copious and distinctive[23]—from the *sira* (biography) of the Prophet onward, and other traditions that give Muslims a sense of their past, including mnemonics set in ritual practices (such as the *hajj*); and, moving further from Islam's normative mainstream, forms of custom and culture linked to Islamic identities in particular ways. And beyond all this, is the tradition of Islam to be seen purely as a matter of discourse? Does it not carry definite institutional implications? Asad implicitly points us toward this when he writes of "the *alim* [scholar], *khatib* [Friday preacher] or Sufi *shaykh*" as among those who activate the discursive tradition of Islam.[24] For these all denote statuses that are socially instituted in enduring structures that are distinctive of Islam—statuses that may be contrasted with those of other world religions, such as the monks of the Buddhist *sangha* or the clergy of a Christian church. Why is it so difficult for us to imagine Islam as having monasteries, or Christianity Sufi brotherhoods?[25] It is as if Asad's argument describes a circle: he has begun by leading us away from the substantive approach of an Ernest Gellner, but ends—albeit inadvertently—by leading us back to the kind of substantive question about the impact of Islam over time that engaged Gellner.

IV

The two basic components of the anthropological analysis of world religions are context and tradition. Ever since the revolution that displaced the older evolutionary paradigm and created modern anthropology in the 1920s, it has been widely agreed that its central interpretive strategy is to proceed by "placing social and cultural phenomena in context."[26] The notion of a context may be understood in various ways: subjectively, as the epistemological frame for the questions the anthropologist asks of the phenomena, or objectively, as the given conditions that frame the existence of the phenomena themselves. In the latter case—which is what concerns me here—it is vital to distinguish between, rather than to yoke or conflate, social and cultural notions of the context. It helps to bring out the theoretical difference by noting what they are respectively set *against*. To emphasize the *cultural* context is to insist that social and material conditions, routinely treated as predictably leading to similar effects in all contexts where they are present, are insufficient to explain the phenomena. In other words, in the name of cultural variation between contexts, it is a protest against an oversimplifying universalism. On the other hand, an emphasis on explanation in terms of the *social* context tends to go with a distinct presentism: things are to be made intelligible in their concrete immediacy solely through their mutual relations with other features of the context. This is above all a protest against any recourse to the past, any attempt at explanation of the phenomena in terms of how they have come about, or to what has preceded them. Of these, the former is typical of American anthropology in the Boasian tradition; the latter, of British social anthropology, particularly after Radcliffe-Brown gave a more strictly sociological cast to the presentist functionalism pioneered by Malinowski.

It is only superficially a paradox that, when our objective is to analyze a cultural phenomenon, such as a world religion viewed as tradition, the *social* context is the best place to begin. What makes the notion of cultural context unhelpful as a starting point is that it tends to take for granted precisely what we are seeking to explore: how religions realize themselves over time, as they pass through successive contexts. Culture being "precisely the organization of the current situation in the terms of a past," as Marshall Sahlins has put it,[27] if continuity between past and present is presumed, then invoking the cultural context is all too likely to lead to a vacuous redescription of what we are seeking to explain in the first place. Of course, in nearly all settings there will be important long-run continuities from past to present; but the relationship between them needs to be examined open-mindedly. So although no one would be proud to call himself a functionalist now, it makes good sense that anthropologists still usually start their analyses by looking at how the thing that they are interested in is conditioned by its immediate material and social circumstances.

The notion of social context is a static conceptualization, a synchronic model of the interplay of social forces that corresponds to the present of the anthropologist's encounter with his subject. But viewed concretely, it is also a site through which multiple temporalities flow, from the relatively short span of individual lives to the longer-spanned lives of institutions, with world religions virtually the longest-spanned of all. How should we characterize the relations of present and past represented by the tradition of a world religion? The obvious and to some extent inescapable way is to see it in terms of a descent, the transmission of an inheritance or deposit from the past, subject to a degree (often large) of variation from its original form through the impress of later circumstances: that is, of the cumulative effect of the successive contexts through which it has passed. Tradition and context thus stand in a two-way relationship. Contexts are given to religious traditions at every moment of their empirical instantiations, but they are also subject to modification by them, as they strive to realize in novel situations the specific and distinctive forms that they bring from their pasts. Thus it is that as traditions pass through successive contexts of practice, they are partly reproduced and partly transformed.[28]

The utility of a notion of tradition here may be reached by another route. In order to recognize the multiple commonalities among the members of a class without making the assumption of a single underlying essence—as sociocultural phenomena of all kinds typically require—anthropologists have often invoked the idea of polythetic classification.[29] This derives from Wittgenstein's metaphor of family resemblances, but a fruitful implication of this metaphor is rarely drawn out: that such resemblances are intelligible only on the basis of shared descent from a common ancestor.

If we apply a neo-Darwinian model of descent with modifications, as suggested by W. G. Runciman for cultural and social phenomena of all kinds, this may be expected to lead to a gradual but continuous drift away from their original forms.[30] But in the case of world religions, a countervailing force comes powerfully into play, one that we may call recursion. This arises from the fact that the past is not just an objectively given anterior state to the present, the baseline on which change works, but is often regarded as something of such intrinsic positive value that serious attempts are made to download it for contemporary application. However, this does not lead to a unified or determinate relation between past and present. Valuing the past may lead to an active concern to preserve its institutional, monumental, and documentary traces, so that it can be genuinely known for what it was and so be a means for genuinely assimilating present to past. But where the demand for normative support from the past is strong but the means to recover it are weak, the past easily becomes more like a site on which present interests are projected, as Malinowski famously argued.[31] So we have the paradox that, for all their supposed traditionalism, the religions of preliterate peoples are particularly likely to be labile, though for lack of evidence their histories are notoriously hard to recover.[32] Even when literacy enables religious truth to be fixed in a scriptural canon, the very prestige of a source that is viewed as giving access to an authoritative past, like *hadith* in Islam, may encourage traditions to be invented on a massive scale.[33] A world-religious tradition may alternate between periods when the past is largely replicated, but within a slow drift of little-noticed change, and other periods, perhaps triggered by some sense of crisis, wherein the past is deliberately turned to as a source of guidance[34]—sometimes with far-reaching transformative effects, as notably with the Protestant Reformation.

But while recursion plays a key role in the actualization of world-religious traditions, it is powerfully constrained by what they make immediately available, even when allowance is made for the possibility of drawing on the resources of the remoter past to leapfrog the bequest of the more recent past. Now, whereas the anthropologist is chiefly concerned with the most recent past, since that is what a religion's adherents practically engage with as they reproduce and modify its tradition, these latter will usually set much more store by what they believe of its remote foundational past, which they access through scriptures, mnemonic rituals, and the institutions that carry and interpret them. Since this past serves as the common point of reference for all the diverse contemporary manifestations of their faith, it also serves as a key reference point in the marking of religious identity at the global level. Yet despite the mythologization to which it is invariably subject, all students of the religion have to take this past as standing in *some* sort of relationship—however highly refracted—with a definite historical reality, namely the religious entity as it was when it started its movement through time and space down to the diverse contexts of the present.

Between these two points stretches a vast historical terrain crossed by tracks that diverge, sometimes intersect, and occasionally converge, since they are subject not just to the continuous impress of influences specific to each new context that they pass through but to less frequent movements within the imagined *oikoumenē* of each religion that cut radically across contexts—such as (say) the Evangelical Revival in Protestant Christianity or the Wahhabist movement in Islam, both coincidentally originating in the eighteenth century. Religions go through golden ages and periods of decline, episodes of restoration and revival, all of which further inflect their traditions in particular ways. Over time, world religions acquire many additional attributes, whose historical contingency does not make them any less consequential, at least for a time. They establish alliances with various cultural and political formations, and though these have their own distinct historical trajectories, the concurrence between them and the world religions, with the two-way influences that result from it, may result in what amount practically to near-fusions of religion and culture or polity. So Islam's linkages with some particular peoples—such as the Turks (so that, in a seventeenth-century Christian European perspective, to become Muslim was to "turn Turk")[35] or the Fulani in parts of West Africa[36]—were of great contextual importance, though of course neither had the foundational character that created the integral bond between Islam and Arabic. Christian history evinces two long-lasting phases of the near-fusion of religion and culture, far-reaching in their effects but still in the end time-limited. The first was the medieval emergence of Christendom, a joint effect of the papacy's ambition to turn itself into a universal monarchy, the absorption into the Western Church of so much of the value system of a Germanic military aristocracy,[37] and the confrontation with Islam. Undermined by the Reformation and the rise of the nation-state, Christendom eventually mutated into "the West"—but only after a long period in which Christianity was seen throughout much of the world as the white man's religion, the ambiguous traveling companion of Europe's imperial outreach.[38] Then as Christianity has moved south over the past two centuries while Europe became more secular, the contingency of its long and intimate concurrence with Europe's history has become increasingly apparent.

If we emphasize those features that a world religion derives from the political and cultural context of its first emergence and treat them as a deeply engrained, primary deposit within its tradition, we clearly open ourselves to the charge of essentializing it—that is, to treat it as if it stood outside history. To this, two responses may be made. First, a world religion's early years are *in fact* likely to have the most far-reaching and wide-ranging relevance for its later manifestations. We are speaking here not just about its scriptures, especially if they are seen as a foundational revelation absolutely prior to any institutional development of the religion (as believers often suppose), but also about the ritual and institutional forms with which they are closely implicated. But, second, what is at stake here is not features assumed to be necessarily present in *all* instances of a particular religion, as an unvarying and essential ground of their being such, but something less than that: features so characteristic of a religion and attributable to its early history that they repeatedly recur in diverse later contexts and, when taken in the aggregate, serve to distinguish instances of that religion from those of others. But as the metaphor of family resemblances suggests, we can regard mandibular prognathism as being a characteristic feature of the Habsburgs without seeing it as an invariable trait, still less a defining attribute, of all the descendants of the emperor Frederick III.

We may illustrate this by comparing how the formative years of the three great world religions endowed them not just with characteristic answers to the problems posed by human existence, but in particular with very different core social institutions: the Christian church (*ekklēsia,* "assembly"), the Muslim *umma,* and the Buddhist *sangha.* The church is a collectivity of believers that presupposes the parallel existence of a secular collectivity, even where their memberships closely coincide, whereas the *umma* unites the faithful in a single collectivity that originally and ideally is both religious and political. The basic conditions of this difference are much as Ernest Gellner suggested: that Christianity grew up within a state that it did not create (though it eventually "annexed" it), whereas Islam created its own state. But whatever their links to the state, religious collectivities soon require organization, which inevitably has a political dimension; and the structures that the two faiths developed again corresponded to their respective political placements. In the case of Islam this was tantamount to the organization of its own polity, which is why its fundamental (and enduring) internal cleavage of Sunni vs. Shia concerned the nature of legitimate authority within the early Islamic state.[39]

The Christian Church, by contrast, had little alternative but to develop a specifically *clerical* hierarchy. While facilitated by belief in the mediated sacred power of the priestly heirs of the apostles—something abhorrent to early Islam—this was really necessitated by Christianity's development over its first three centuries as an entity outside the state. Paradoxically, lacking organizational models of its own, in this process it borrowed extensively from Caesar's domain: territorial dioceses, priestly vestments copying those of secular magistrates, great church buildings modeled on the law courts (basilicas) of imperial Rome, and so forth. But being no more than a quasi polity, the Church still needed to look for a mutually supportive relationship with rulers whose original legitimacy came from elsewhere but who could be remodeled as Christian kings. Here there are notable parallels with the independent case of Buddhism, which also developed outside the state.[40] Where early medieval Europe had its Woden-descended kings, southeast Asia had its Hinduized sacred monarchies; and in both cases, convert kings derived new legitimacy from such pious acts as endowing monasteries.[41] But there is a major difference. While both Buddhism and Christianity have a laity in a sense that Islam lacks, the *sangha,* as a corporation of monks, is not a kind of church. For Buddhism, unlike Christianity and Islam, is not a congregational religion—a feature that the latter two derive from their shared Judaic roots. This three-way comparison, which puts Christianity in the middle, rests on two axes of variation. The first, dealing with the structural context of its emergence, gives rise to the parallel with Buddhism, whereas the second, deriving from the religious tradition from which it came, produces the affinity with Islam.

Clearly, these classical forms of the three religions, with the values and roles that ride on them, are not guaranteed to reproduce themselves fully (or even, on occasion, at all) in all subsequent instances, owing to the contingent circumstances of history. For considerable periods in the history of Buddhism in South Asia, according to Michael Carrithers, the *sangha* virtually disappeared.[42] For us, the contrasting trajectories of Islam and Christianity are especially illuminating, not just for their vicissitudes but for the ways they impacted on one another. The primary ideal of the *umma*—a community of believers undifferentiated horizontally as between religious/political or vertically as between laity/clerics—started to come under pressure almost at once, with the death of the Prophet and the rapid conquest of a vast empire. Eventually there emerged a social group that ever since has been regarded as distinctive of Islam: the scholars or *ulama,* those credited with the authority to determine the content of prophetic tradition that was critical to the systematization of Sharia law, which was starting to occur around this time (eighth and ninth centuries C.E., 150+ years A.H.).[43] Their rise was a response to the fading of direct oral memories of the founding years, coupled with the rising flood of non-Arab converts seeking normative incorporation into the *umma*. The political alignment of the *ulama* was uncertain: the legal advisors and so usually the allies of the rulers, they were also sometimes the focus of popular opposition to them (especially where the latter was of alien origin). Yet despite these developments, the *ulama* were always very different from a Christian clergy, just as Sufi shaykhs and *muqaddams*, new religious roles within Islam that emerged a century or so later, differed from the ascetic spiritual guides that were primary within Buddhism. For it remained the case that these new roles were set within a wider institutional and ideological matrix that was a particular and unique product of Islam's earlier history.[44]

Islamic institutions would face a more complex challenge where Muslim populations came to exist as minorities under non-Muslim rule—as in large parts of South and Southeast Asia, sub-Saharan Africa, and (latterly) Western Europe—and so lacked the political means to guarantee the routines of Muslim life as originally imagined. As Olivier Roy argues for Muslims in the West today, a whole range of responses to this predicament is available in principle, from the radical ones of following the Prophet's precedent of *hijra* or withdrawal to a Muslim-ruled territory or trying to annex the country to Islam by jihad, to various forms of accommodation, such as creating religiocultural enclaves or settling for a much more church-like social existence, based on local congregations.[45]Across the long span of Islam's existence in Nigeria, several of these options have been realized as the varying circumstances of time and place have allowed. Roy suggests that among Muslims in the West, several reduced forms of the *umma* exist concurrently: most concretely as a local congregation; as an imagined but deterritorialized world community; or and as a virtual community accessed through the Internet. Even where the adherents of a religion are able to realize, or are happy to settle for, much less than its normative ideal—that is, for Muslims, the *umma* as a religious community politically organized within its own space—it tends to retain a potent and recurrent appeal, especially for its clerics and literates, who know it from its scriptures and traditions, or from its practice in the past or in other places. Even though the characteristic traits of a religion are not invariably reproduced, their presence in past tradition makes it more likely that they rather than randomly possible others will recur; and—to anticipate the Nigerian case study to come—a comparison of the divergent features of two religions in a single situation may bring out sharply the potentiality of what lies latent in their distinctive traditions.

V

"Compare and contrast" goes the old cliché of examination papers. The implication of this phrasing—that comparison looks for similarities; and contrast, for differences—is misleading, since productive comparison always depends on finding the right interplay between similarities *and* differences. Even so, comparison shifts between moments where one or the other mode predominates. Anything can be compared with any other thing, however unlike; but to be fruitful the process has to begin from establishing a similarity, some shared features to provide a frame within which questions about difference can be posed. When faced with puzzling novelty, the first human impulse is to get some kind of preliminary fix on it by looking for similarities with what is already familiar. Thus the Spanish conquistadors initially called Aztec temples "mosques"—the impressive buildings of an alien religion[46]—or (as implausibly) the London *Evening Standard* suggests to its readers that Professor Tariq Ramadan may be seen as Islam's Martin Luther.[47] Such ad-hoc comparisons are very likely to be tendentious, because cognitive considerations are subordinated to practical ones, such as the pressure to reassert moral boundaries challenged by otherness, or to quell anxiety by domesticating the alien.

It is when the grounds for comparison are elaborated and the two comparanda are subsumed under some more general notion that the real cognitive possibilities of comparison open up. Such a notion is fundamentalism. Curiously, this term initially implied only an intra-Christian comparison, since it was used around 1920 as a self-identification by conservative evangelicals to distinguish themselves from liberal Protestants given to a nonliteralist reading of Scripture. Only later was it turned the other way, often by secular-minded commentators, to stress—usually with negative overtones[48]—the similarities between diverse contemporary movements within Christianity, Islam, and other faiths. Subsequent attempts to theorize the term have not proved very productive, because the phenomena themselves are so diverse; so that what we are left with is the valid but much watered-down claim that there are many partial and overlapping resemblances among the movements so designated. I shall argue later that the careless use of the term has led, in the Nigerian context, to the ignoring of important differences between Muslim and Christian forms of so-called fundamentalism.[49]

Drawing out the similarities between world religions can shed much light on some key features of their operation, especially those that arise from common structural conditions. To take one example, we may abstract and generalize from a trajectory that Carrithers identifies in the history of Buddhism, by which the renouncer, the monk devoted to the individual exemplary pursuit of spiritual merit, becomes the specialist, someone whom that very merit enables to provide ritual and magical services for a lay community. Something analogous can be seen in other religions: for example, in the way in which Sufi shaykhs in West Africa came to be valued more as miracle workers than as mystical guides, or (a less exact parallel) in the transit of West African Pentecostal churches from a primary focus on the pursuit of holiness through ascetic self-discipline to the provision of effective prayer for mundane needs. The sheer diversity of the settings in which something like this trajectory shows up indicates a recurrent dilemma that world religions face. They all originated in a radical, world-rejecting vision that downgraded the significance of the here-and-now in favor of a transcendental vision of reality.[50] It is surely significant, as Max Weber emphasized,[51] that this perspective was typically grounded in the experience of social groups—traders, craftsmen, officials, minor aristocrats, and so on—who were marginal to the imperatives of subsistence production in overwhelmingly agricultural or pastoral societies. But as the religions spread, the old this-worldly pressures—especially for healing and magical services—inevitably reasserted themselves. The tension between the two orientations became a perennial stimulus to reform movements as it came to be felt that the founder's elevated vision had got too overlaid with baser concerns. At this point, however, our comparative focus needs to shift back from similarity to difference, for the responses to this situation are also strongly inflected by the traditions of each particular religion. So notwithstanding the existence of what has been called Protestant Buddhism in Sri Lanka in the nineteenth century,[52] it would seem that Buddhism is less prone to reformism of the sort just outlined than are the two Abrahamic faiths, since lacking their monotheist and exclusivist character it can more readily offload the provision of health, fertility, prosperity, and suchlike onto cults of local deities that can easily coexist with it without compromising its transcendental message.[53]

When anthropology moves from its primary task of contextual analysis to comparison, it usually has to *de*contextualize its objects of analysis. Taking religions out of their social context and treating them for comparative purposes as things in themselves is routine in the field known as comparative religion, whose aim may be no more ambitious than to show the comparability of religions through applying phenomenological categories taken to be universal.[54] It is presumed in any project whose aim is to compare them solely in terms of their theologies or internal logics or how they address what are taken to be universal problems of human existence, such as John Bowker's study of the ways they respond to human suffering.[55] But decontextualization *does* pose a problem for the social-scientific study of religion insofar as that aims to explain the variable social impact of the world religions, because the myriad contextual circumstances in which this occurs cannot be controlled. The ceteris-paribus proviso that is presumed in any rigorous analysis of the social impact of differences between religions can hardly obtain if the contexts are full of random variation. There is no doubt that this is a major methodological problem that dogs Weber's *Sociology of Religion,* master work of historical sociology though it is.[56]

The logically optimal conditions for comparing world religions are not easily met, as we see in the case of Geertz's *Islam Observed,* widely regarded as a foundational text for the anthropology of Islam.[57] Because this treats Islam as the constant, and the two cultures in which it has found a context—Morocco and Indonesia—as variables, it ends up telling us less about Islam than about the two cultures that have each imprinted a very different ethos on it. The book's most general message—that Islam is susceptible to enormous variety in its concrete realizations—is mere conventional wisdom for anthropologists, whereas it may be found challenging by Islamicists and even more so by orthodox Muslims. What is essentialized by Geertz here is not Islam but the two cultures in which it is set. They are portrayed in the manner of Ruth Benedict's *Patterns of Culture,* consistently opposed to each other in a series of maximally heightened contrasts, whereas Islam itself, though described in its local specificities, never receives any kind of overall characterization.[58] In Geertz's shorthand, Islam in Morocco is maraboutism, whereas in Indonesia it is illuminationism.[59]

But when Geertz comes to his longest, pivotal chapter, entitled "The Scripturalist Interlude," which deals with the contemporary religious situation as observed in the present time of his own fieldwork, there is a notable shift in the balance of similarity and difference in his argument. He sees the Islamizing movements in both countries as astonishingly similar, though differing in the details of their local course and impact.[60] To explain this he invokes three conditions: Western colonial domination, the growing influence of a new kind of legalistic, scriptural Islam, and the emergence of an activist nation-state, all of which working together have shaken the old order of things in a manner analogous to the complex joint impact of Capitalism, Protestantism, and Nationalism in Europe.[61] One cannot but be struck by the contrast between his thoroughly anthropological emphasis on difference in his characterization of the two classical cultures and his readiness, when he switches into macrosociological mode, to stress sweeping similarities between expressions of religion across great gulfs of historical time and cultural space. Resemblances on this scale obviously require explanation in terms of broadly similar and highly general social-contextual conditions, such as are here denoted by the overarching labels of Capitalism and Nationalism.

But the third condition, "the increasing influence of . . . scriptural Islam" (or, Geertz implies, of a kind of Protestant Islam), is different from the other two. For it is a cultural rather than a social condition, and it brings with it the ambiguity so common with cultural explanations: it seems to be as much part of the *explanandum* as one of the *explanantia.* For what we are dealing with here is the operation of a tradition, reaching back into the past and interacting reciprocally with other features of the situation or situations through which it passes. Geertz makes mention only of "the Koran, the Hadith and the Sharia, together with various standard commentaries on them," when he gets to the "Scripturalist Interlude," as if they had not been significant factors in the prior history of Islam in the two countries.[62] To use a musical metaphor, *Islam Observed* is like a pair of variations without any prior statement of the theme: we have maraboutism and illuminationism first, placed in contrasting *cultural* contexts, then their shared nemesis Scripturalism, which is placed in a mainly *social* context. But the operation of the

Islamic tradition as an object of anthropological inquiry—which would require the analysis of its reciprocal interaction with the contexts wherein it is taken up or of the interplay of the cultural and the social—is barely attempted.

VI

This interplay of the social and the cultural, or (what is the same thing) of context and tradition, is at the very heart of understanding how religions are realized in human practice. As in all other areas of social life, religious action is always doubly constrained: by the features of the context to which agents have to respond and by what tradition—beliefs, values, and institutions received from the past—makes available to them. But never is it completely determined. Virtually all contexts yield options for action, and traditions are open to be revised or reinterpreted. Tradition shapes the selection of options, and context inflects how tradition is received.

Granted this necessary dialectic, it is remarkable how often attempts are made—whether by social scientists or by lay social actors—to deny its operation by insisting that one or the other side of it counts for everything. Such perverse one-sidedness typically has its taproot in moral or ideological considerations regarded as being of overriding practical importance. Take a real-life case from Nigeria, which touches on matters to be considered later. The Right Rev. Josiah Idowu Fearon, Anglican bishop of Kaduna, is reported as having said of Boko Haram, the violent Islamist organization active in the northeast of Nigeria since 2007, that it "is a resistance movement against misrule, rather than a purely Islamic group."[63] Since it is quite possible (and it is in fact the case) that Boko Haram is both these things, why should he want to present it as a matter of either/or rather than both/and? The bishop is active in interfaith dialogue—very much needed in a city where severe religious rioting occurred in 2000 and 2002—and knows that many Muslims are strongly opposed to Boko Haram's activities too, and so he is reluctant to stress its Islamic character.[64] It may well be, too, that he wants to counter the common tendency among his fellow Christians to explain everything they see as negative in Muslims as being due to their Islam. (Muslims tend to view Christians through the lens of a similar religious essentialism, such homologies being routine features of religious confrontation.) If these are his motives, they are certainly not malign or ignoble ones. But an ecumenical spirit is not necessarily the best guide to a full and cogent analysis of why Boko Haram does what it does.

With less excuse, Olivier Roy takes a position similar to Bishop Fearon's but elaborates it methodologically, in an attack on what he terms "culturalism."[65] He sees this as widespread across a very wide range of opinion: Samuel P. Huntington of course, "orientalists" such as Bernard Lewis, "the man in the street," fundamentalist and conservative Muslims, even some "opponents of Islamophobia and . . . moderate Muslims."[66] Altogether quite a coalition of error! Roy's own stated approach is strongly of the either/or variety. "Neofundamentalism and radical violence are more linked with westernization than with a return to the Koran," he argues, so that we need "a transversal approach to Islam, rather than a diachronic approach [which would look] to history to understand the roots of 'Muslim anger.'"[67] So in trying to understand new trends among Muslim youth, it is more useful to look for parallels with other forms of modern religiosity than "trying to reread the Koran."[68] But again we have to ask: Why should it be a matter of either/or rather than of both/and? In fact, Roy has already undermined his own prescription—and his book is much the better for it—by its very subtitle, *The Search for a New Ummah.* For a "new Ummah" implies an old Ummah, which is at the same time (transversally) a distinctive element in how Muslims respond to the predicament of modernity that is absent from how Christians or Buddhists may respond to it, and (diachronically) one that entails the duality of reception and interpretation, the two-way exchange between present and past that is how religious traditions work. It is fine to begin from a transversal approach to religions in the modern world, but it is arbitrary to limit it to a search for similarities and to ignore the differences between them; and once difference is admitted, it becomes impossible to exclude the past from the analysis of the present. So when Roy says that "the key question is not what the Koran actually says, but what Muslims say the Koran says," he offers us another false choice.[69] For if arguments about the true import of the Koran and other sources of faith are a crucial part of how Muslims conduct their lives—as Asad was right to insist—it is hard to see how this work of interpretation can be understood by ignoring what it is that is being interpreted.

In examining the interplay between context and tradition, our method must not be to start with the origins of the tradition or its foundational texts and speculate about what their implications must be for its later practice, as some recent antireligious polemicists like to do,[70] but the reverse. We must place ourselves in the midst of a concrete realization of the religion and look to see what elements of its tradition are presupposed by it. A religion's tradition is thus seen as embodying a set of potentials that make particular outcomes more or less likely but that can be fully assessed only in their realization. This task is made much easier if it is possible to compare two religions in the same context, thus enabling factors specific to each religion to be identified—a strategy opposite to Geertz's: not one religion and two contexts, but one context and two religions. While there are many plural religious settings, the optimal conditions for such a comparison are not easily found, for the two religions need to be equally copresent. It is not easier to think of a case that fits the bill better than the Yoruba of southwestern Nigeria, who are divided roughly fifty-fifty between Islam and Christianity. So to this I now turn.

Though Christianity and Islam have coexisted since the very birth of Islam, their relationship has usually been very asymmetrical, as with two of its main contemporary modes: in the Middle East, where historic but rapidly eroding Christian communities exist, as they have for many centuries, within Muslim-dominated societies; and in modern Europe, where Muslim communities have come to exist through migration, mostly over the last few decades, amid a Christian or post-Christian majority. There is also a third mode: where Muslims and Christians, whether through migration or conversion, have come to coexist in settings dominated by a third religion, as in Susan Bayly's account of how Islam and Catholicism have adjusted to a Hindu context in southern India.[71] The Yoruba situation began like this, but over the past century it has changed to the point that the traditional religion has been drastically curtailed in its range and reduced to the preserve of a small minority (though its memory and ethos still exert a large, diffuse influence). Nowadays, the two world faiths are to be found in virtually every community, though their regional distribution is markedly skewed. The presence of Islam goes back much further in time, but both religions can now be regarded as fully and equally at home in Yoruba society and culture. There are high levels of social interaction between Muslims and Christians, and virtually no residential segregation between them. Interfaith marriages are not uncommon; many extended families contain both Christian and Muslim members; and mutual participation in each other's ritual festivities is a standard feature of Yoruba social life as well as a source of cultural pride.

Since this remarkable pattern of coexistence has come about over the past 150 years, comparison of the two religions cannot be a static exercise. It has to be analyzed as the evolving outcome of the interaction between the two world religions with the antecedent culture of the Yoruba, into which paganism had been seamlessly woven, and with each other. More than that, as Yorubaland has become ever more involved in the social and cultural networks that constitute Nigeria, inter-religious relations have been affected by developments at the pan-Nigerian level, particularly since the 1970s. Here another comparison becomes relevant, between the religious harmony of Yorubaland and the pattern of recurrent religious violence that has become endemic in Northern Nigeria. So the two religions are to be seen as dynamic entities, not just subject to change but initiatory of it, ever reworking both themselves and the social contexts in which they are active. This dynamic capacity, or determination to make history, which we see actualized in the agency of individuals and collectivities, is fueled by what each religion brings to the Yoruba and the Nigerian situation from its own past. The various ways for these distinctive heritages of Islam and Christianity both to enable and to constrain their ongoing self-realization must lie at the center of our comparison.

7

Conversion and Community in Yorubaland

The Yoruba have a sense of themselves as being exceptionally tolerant of religious difference—and now particularly as having harmonious relations between Islam and Christianity. Let me illustrate the point through two vignettes from field research in Ibadan in 2009.

The local-ward development committee in Yemetu Aladorin meets to launch a primary health-care program for women and children. It is chaired by a local imam, and the six committee members present comprise four Muslims and two Christians. At the end of the proceedings, the imam recites the *surat al-fatiha* (the short first *sura* of the Koran) in Arabic, and I notice even the Christians trying to follow it with their lips. One of the Christians then says a short informal prayer in Yoruba, ending with *l'orukọ Jesu Kristi Oluwa wa!* (In the name of Jesus Christ, our Lord!), to which everyone responds *Ẹ yin Ologo!* (Praise the King of Glory!).The imam rounds off by saying *Hallelu!* three times.[1]

> Two ladies from St. Paul's Anglican Church take me on a tour of the back alleys of Yemetu to explore the great variety of little churches and mosques to be found there. We come to the small Akabiako mosque, whose elderly imam belongs to the Bamidele sect. The two women teachers in the primary school attached to it are both *ẹlẹha* (wearing full black purdah). Before we get to our discussion, which might touch on sensitive religious differences, one of my companions recalls to the imam an incident a little while back. A female pupil of the mosque school had been knocked down by an *ọkada* (motorbike taxi) in the main road. The church lady picked her up, sorted her out, and brought her back to the mosque. The imam thanks her again warmly for what she had done, and our discussion proceeds. A common ground of Yoruba humanity has been reaffirmed. No surprise that the imam later says that

> Muslims and Christians, while they go their different ways for religious purposes, should still regard one another as *ọmọ-iya* (children of the same mother).[2]
>
> By and large this self-image is well justified, especially compared with the pattern of intermittent violent conflict that has developed in many areas of Northern Nigeria over the past thirty years. The Yoruba like to see their tolerance as an enduring cultural trait, and it does surely derive support from the live-and-let-live ethos of the *oriṣa* cults; but if we want to *explain* it, it is more fruitful to regard the relationship between Islam and Christianity as potentially conflictual, and also as one that is not static but evolves under changing historical conditions. In fact, we view it better as an ongoing historical accomplishment than as a cultural given, the product of the kind of ground-level interaction in local communities of the kind just described. Nowadays this takes place in full awareness not only of the situation in Northern Nigeria, where things are so different, but also of the strong rivalry between the two faiths in Yorubaland. I will suggest that the classic form of this interfaith harmony belonged to the late colonial period and lasted through independence, in 1960, but came under severe pressure from the late 1970s. Though substantially restored in the 1990s, it can no longer be taken so easily for granted as before.

So I begin by looking at the evolution of this pattern of interfaith relations since the beginning of the colonial period. My analysis will hinge on the concept of community: the overarching framework of the Yoruba community, the communities created by the two religions, and the relations between them. Here Yoruba community must be understood as an expanding hierarchy of levels: at its center the town or historic community known as the *ìlú;* below this the town's quarters, and (at the bottom) the family compound; above it a level of subtribes (Ijesha, Ekiti, Egba, etc.), often related to colonial administrative divisions, and at the top the pan-Yoruba level, which was progressively emergent over the colonial period.[3] In what follows, my narrative will move through three stages: the process of conversion, the formation of the new religions as communities within the wider community, and the impact of nationalist and postnationalist politics on the pattern of religious coexistence between them.

EXPLAINING YORUBA CONVERSION

From their modest numbers at the end of the nineteenth century, both world religions experienced a dramatic growth within a few decades after the imposition of colonial rule in the 1890s. By the later 1930s, probably a majority of Yoruba had become Muslims or Christians; by the early 1950s nearly 90 percent were; today virtually everyone is. This correlation suggests an obvious explanation, at least for Christianity: its association with colonial power—whether in a general, symbolic way, or as a mystical way of accessing the white man's power, or through such specific modalities as passing through the school system, which was largely set up and controlled by missions. But this explanation won't work for Islamic conversion unless that is seen as a path to empowerment that avoided symbolic identification with colonialism, or even as some kind of symbolic resistance to it. But neither of these views—which would treat conversion to the two faiths as presenting two quite different patterns and problems—fits with what we know of the local phenomenology of Yoruba conversion; and this suggests that the two processes ran concurrently along similar lines.

The problem of Yoruba conversion to the world religions has to be addressed in the light of two general principles:

1. What needs to be explained is a *single* overall pattern of change, where the two world religions advanced at roughly the same pace over time, but very unevenly over space.
2. Paradoxically, it proves easier to work down from the broad social trends to a rationale that makes subjective sense at the individual level, then to work upwards from personal reasons for conversion to explanation of the overall movement. The latter approach—such as I once employed in a household survey of Ilesha to collect, inter alia, family histories[4]—tends to produce a great array of personal motives and circumstances that tell much about the *How?* of individual conversion but will not yield a coherent answer to the overall *Why?* of the whole process.

Here Robin Horton's general theory of African conversion is promising on both counts, since it is so set up as to apply equally to both world religions, and it follows the classic Durkheimian strategy of treating social facts as things and relating them to other facts of the same order.[5] It explains the social fact of conversion not as a response to colonial power per se—as in explanations of the "adopting the religion of the conqueror" type[6]—but as an adjustment to a general social experience that colonialism contingently brought about: to wit, an increase in the scale of social relations, a move from the microcosm of life lived mostly in local communities to the macrocosm of lives opened to wider influences (such as labor migration, expanded trade networks, growing cash crops for world markets, the expansion of horizons by education and the press).

As to why such a change of experience should produce such an ideational change as a principal effect, Horton argues that it depends on the character of indigenous belief. From that perspective, Islam and Christianity are essentially cults of a High God, who functions as a general ground of being within the indigenous cosmology but receives little direct ritual attention. That mostly goes to subordinate deities, *orișa* in the Yoruba case, since they are seen as addressing the conditions of existence of people whose lives are mainly preoccupied with local concerns. A shift of focus from *oris̩a* to God can therefore be expected wherever the vital concerns of a population shift away from the microcosm to the macrocosm. Colonialism in Nigeria certainly provided a sufficient condition of such an outcome but evidently not a necessary one. From our viewpoint, the vital implication is that if Christianity gained converts under colonialism, it was less because it was the Europeans' religion than because it was locally the most available monotheism; and that where Islam was more available, then colonialism would deliver converts to *it*.

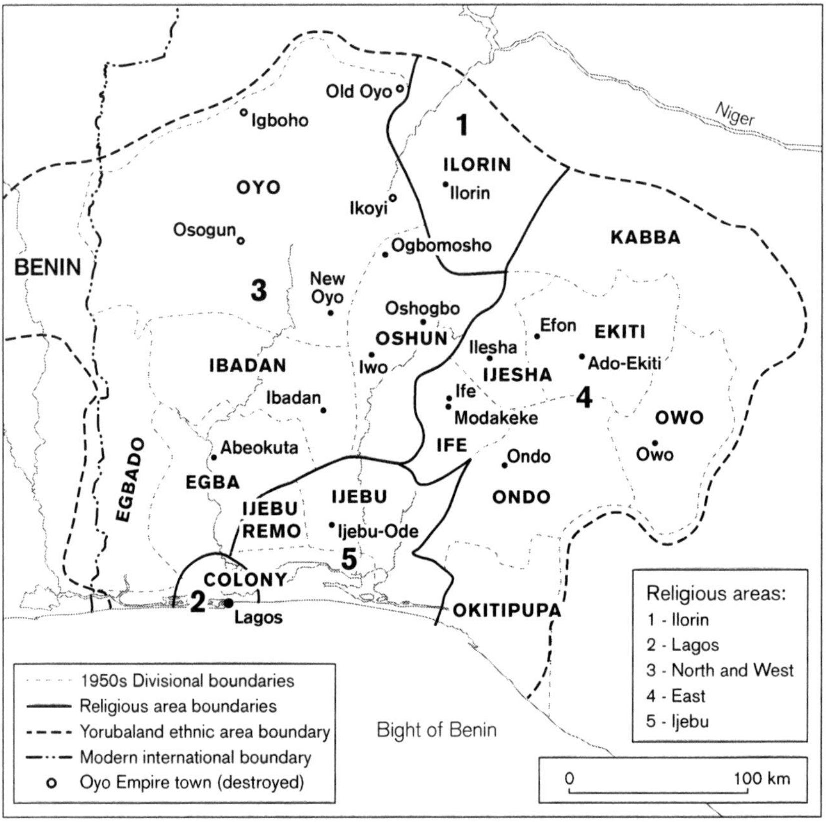

MAP 2. Yorubaland: Religious areas (based on the census of 1952).

So we have a coherent and elegant explanation of the temporal and geographical pattern of conversion to the monotheistic faiths in Yorubaland. It depends essentially on the relationship between two factors: first, the timing and intensity of the colonial impact (in terms of adoption of cash crops, communications, administrative presence, etc.), which tended to spread out in waves from Lagos toward the remoter parts of the North and East, and second, the relative strength of existing Christian or Muslim contacts and influence, when and where the general disposition to convert appeared. The first of these explains the *general* disposition to adopt a monotheistic religion, and the second explains which *particular* monotheism would be its principal beneficiary in any area.

In the light of the map, we can discern five distinct regional patterns.[7]

1. Ilorin. This was the only area of Yorubaland to be conquered in the jihad that established the Sokoto Caliphate, of which in the early 1820s it became the most southerly emirate.[8] Initially its Muslim ruling class presided over

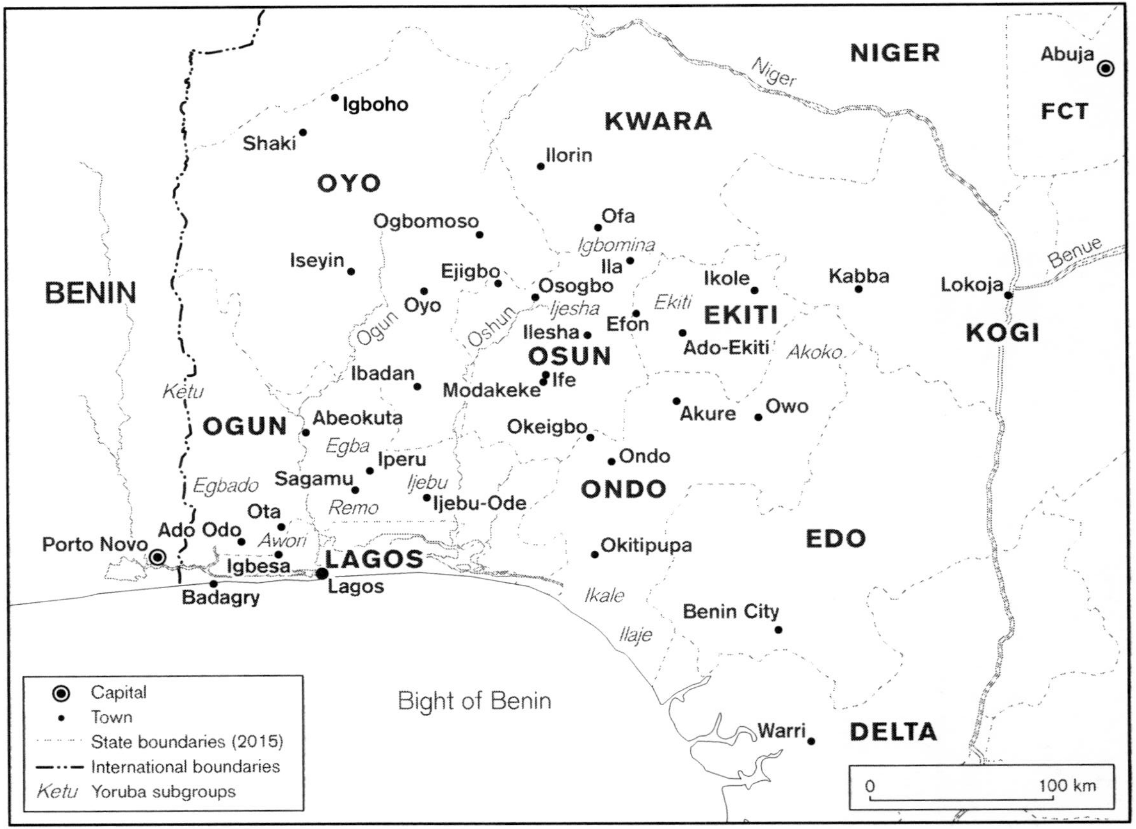

MAP 3. Yorubaland: General, showing state boundaries of 2015, most significant towns, some sub-Yoruba ethnic groups, and three main rivers.

a mainly pagan population, whether of slaves or of free peasants. Under colonialism it was assigned to Northern Nigeria, which impeded missionary activity and so facilitated Islamization, resulting in a large Muslim majority, though some peripheral areas to the east became more Christian.

2. Lagos. After a decade of informal control through what was called a consulate, British rule was imposed in 1861, more than thirty years before the occupation of the Yoruba interior. Islam had a significant presence well before the missions arrived, in 1851, and spread rapidly in the 1860s and 1870s, especially among the followers of the exiled king, Kosoko.[9] By the 1890s, to missionary chagrin, Islam had succeeded in claiming the allegiance of a majority of indigenous Lagosians.
3. The North and West. This embraces most of the savannah region and extends into the forest areas settled by Oyo in the nineteenth century. Here the missionaries established their early bases at Abeokuta and Ibadan in the1840s and 1850s, finding Muslims already there: not many, but the *alfa* were well placed, with networks ramifying toward the North.[10] When the conditions for mass change came, in a series of rising surges (the 1890s, World War I, the cocoa boom of the 1920s), Islam picked up more converts than Christianity did, particularly among Oyo-Yoruba.
4. The East. This vast area, extending into what had been Kabba Province of Northern Nigeria (now part of Kogi State), is mainly forest, fading northward into savannah woodland. It had been substantially beyond Oyo control or settlement, and Islam had little or no presence prior to Christianity. Missionaries reached Ilesha around 1860 and Ondo in the late 1870s, but the work of conversion came in strength only after the 1890s.[11] Here Christianity came to claim a large majority of the population, with the boom coming in the 1920s and especially the 1930s, when the Aladura revival created a mass conversion movement.[12] The proportion of Muslims rises somewhat in the far northeast (Akoko), an area subject to the influence of the Muslim Nupe in the late nineteenth century.[13] An instructive case is Ife itself, where back in the 1840s a party of Oyo refugees (when they must have been almost entirely pagan) were allowed to form an adjacent settlement called Modakeke. The importance of Oyo links as a vector of Islamic influence is shown in the fact that, many decades later, while indigenous Ife went mainly Christian, Modakeke went mainly Muslim.[14]
5. Ijebu is the most complex case of all.[15] Close to Lagos and athwart its main trade route to the interior, Ijebu had refused the missions all entry in the nineteenth century. By the 1880s there were close links with Muslims in Lagos and Ibadan, which had a fair number of Ijebu residents. Ijebu was the only Yoruba kingdom the British needed to crush with a full-blown military expedition (1892), and this defeat triggered within a few years the first mass movement toward the world religions. The theological response

> to the defeat, as noted by an African pastor in Ibadan, was *Ọlọrun ni a o sin!* (It is God we shall serve!).[16] But not exclusively the white man's God. The missions did indeed gain massively—by the 1920s over a third of Yoruba Christians were Ijebu, with many becoming teachers and clergy—but so did Islam. In fact Muslims came to comprise over two-thirds of the capital, Ijebu Ode. There is no way that the Islamic option can be regarded as anticolonial, since the chief who led it, *Balogun* Kuku, was the principal local ally of the British in the wake of the conquest. He built himself a grand mansion, Olorunsogo (God Has Wrought the Glory) House in the high-bourgeois style of Victorian Lagos.

But whereas Ijebu Ode went mainly Muslim, the smaller subordinate towns of the Ijebu kingdom went mainly Christian. Although this may partly be due to reaction against the capital's choice—Yoruba subordinate towns are always looking for the opportunity to assert their autonomy—the critical condition was that, being towns with populations of farmers rather than traders, they lacked the prior links with Muslims in Lagos and Ibadan that Ijebu Ode had.[17] A further feature of the Ijebu case sits especially well with Horton's theory. A major aim of the British conquest had been to break Ijebu's stranglehold on the trade route between Lagos and the Yoruba interior. A further effect of this, as well as the weakening of the capital's control over the district towns, had been to throw the Ijebu into a trading diaspora: they crop up everywhere along the new arteries of colonial trade over the next twenty to thirty years, often as pioneers of Christian congregations in other parts of Yorubaland or following the line of rail into Northern Nigeria.[18] Thus the scale of their social experience was more abruptly and radically expanded than occurred with any other Yoruba group, with just the religious effect predicted by Horton's theory.

A final general observation may be made about the conditions of conversion after 1892. Although Islam's expansion was greatly accelerated by colonial conditions, Christianity's overall *rate* of expansion, starting from a much smaller base, was undoubtedly greater. Two additional factors, which both stand outside the terms of Horton's theory, would seem to explain this: the enhanced attractiveness of the specific empowerment package offered by Christianity under colonial conditions;[19] and the greater effectiveness of Christian missionary institutions, compared with Muslim ones, in proactive outreach into new areas where neither religion had better prior contacts than the other. I shall return to the question of their respective institutional endowments shortly.

AFTER CONVERSION: PRAGMATISM, LOYALTY, AND TOLERANCE

So what did conversion to these monotheistic faiths, with their aspiration to create exclusive religious loyalties and to reshape individual and community life, mean for the new Christians and Muslims? What sort of faith communities emerged from the protracted conversion process? At their heart, I suggest, we may see a balance between three attitudes, all to some extent carried forward from the old religion and closely implicated with one another: pragmatism, loyalty, and tolerance.

Even after conversion, the Yoruba still largely rationalized their religious adherence in pragmatic terms—it often comes up when individuals talk about their personal religious choices: What does it bring by way of spiritual empowerment or secular advantage? These were not evenly spread between the two religions. Christianity's greatest relative advantage was its virtual monopoly of access to modern education in the early colonial period. Still, those who see this as the primary explanation for Christian conversion have to explain why those Yoruba who became Muslim were apparently indifferent to it. Islam also had its secular advantages—such as giving access to certain trading networks or craft skills or to chiefly patronage—but these may have been less important than the magicospiritual techniques deployed by its clerics (*alfa*). In time Christianity would develop its own responses to these, in the missions' various medical facilities and in the prayer power offered in the Aladura churches. In the early colonial period, Islam still had the negative advantage over Christianity that it demanded less from potential converts by way of cultural renunciation (e.g., in the matter of polygamy), though as the number of Christian converts grew, the churches perforce soon became more tolerant of Yoruba custom. Each religion was aware that it had certain weaknesses in relation to its rival, and so their competition, conducted within the shared moral framework of community membership, led to considerable interchange between them—a topic to be explored at greater length below in chapter 9.

At the same time, despite these pragmatic reasons and rationalizations, converts were rapidly drawn into new bonds of fellowship, expressed in each religion's distinctive rituals and activities, which fostered loyalty to their new faith. Intrinsic satisfactions and identities must have worked to reduce the likelihood that converts would be led by pragmatic considerations to subsequently swap their religion, though this seems to have been common right at the beginning, with many first-generation Muslims being prepared to send their children to school, even though it might well result in their conversion to Christianity. With the entrenchment of the colonial order by 1920, the appeal of education got even stronger, leaving committed Muslims—with some exceptions[20]—with a clear choice: to keep their children out of mission schools or to organize schools of their own.

A crucial challenge presented by the world religions to Yoruba society was how these new loyalties might be reconciled with their existing communal loyalties. One positive condition for this was the pragmatism that had powerfully underpinned conversion in the first place, since it worked to undercut the kind of exclusive identification with the transcendent values that world religions seek to instill in their converts. It encouraged Yoruba to view all religious attachments as provisional on their capacity to deliver benefits, as had been the case with the membership of the *orișa* cults. This view underlay and was reinforced by the large-scale shift of religious identities that occurred between 1910 and 1940. Membership of one's *ìlú* (town) or of its smallest subunit (the *ilé*, family, compound) was nothing like so provisional as that. Religious tolerance was a corollary of this combination of personal religious choice and the nearly absolute givenness of community membership.

The culture and practice of tolerance had deep roots in the past. An elder once expressed it in response to some unwelcome hellfire preaching from a Yoruba evangelist in Ijebu back in 1878: "Let the Ifa man worship his Ifa; let the orisha man worship his orisha; and let the slave follow his Shango priestcraft for his food."[21] Sentiments like this occur widely into the twentieth century, the *orișa* varying according to the locality: *Ẹ j'onifa o bọ Ifa, ẹ j'ọlọṣun o bọ Ọṣun, Ẹ j'elegun o bọ Egun rẹ, k'aye le gun* (Let the Ifa devotee worship his Ifa, let the Osun devotee worship her Osun, let the Elegun worship his Egun, that the world may be straight) was a song current near Osogbo.[22] Pragmatic considerations—the thought that because there were many powerful *orișa,* it was imprudent to neglect any of them—as well as a spirit of live and let live between cult groups, underlay the practice of tolerance. Even so, this tolerance was not unconditional: in many places both world religions were persecuted at the outset, whether because of their alarmingly absolutist claims or the fear that they would cause the neglect of local cults that local people regarded as essential for community welfare.[23] But tolerance returned as soon as it became clear that the new cults could be domesticated and were themselves keen to contribute to the well-being and solidarity of the community. The reassertion of tolerance during the period of mass conversion is uniquely described in many of the biographies of notable Yoruba men and women that have appeared in the past two decades. Here are two haphazard examples chosen from different parts of the country.

The first concerns Mrs. Folayegbe Ighodalo (b. 1923), the first woman to become a permanent secretary in the civil service of Western State, who grew up in a large compound in Okeigbo, a middling-sized and eventually mainly Christian town northwest of Ondo:[24]

Her father, Benjamin Akintunde, was baptized in 1915, but the compound head (*baale*), his great-uncle Bello Aromoye, was a Muslim. The compound had its own *egungun* (ancestral masked spirit), as well as shrines of other *orișa.* As a devout Christian, Akintunde forbade his children to enter any of the shrine rooms, to go out during the Egungun festival or to eat any of the sacrificial food of the *orișa* worshipped by some family members. "Still, he realized the futility of forbidding them to watch the entertainment part of the festivals and never defied the instructions of the [*baale*] that the eldest child of each family in his compound must attend the ritual slaughter of a ram during the Muslim festival, Id el-Kabir [Ileya]." Fola's brother attended, but under strict instructions not to eat any of the meat. Members of Akintunde's family "always contributed to and attended the naming ceremonies, marriages and funerals of their Muslim and traditionalist relatives, [and] Muslims in the family always attended the festivities . . . of their Christian relatives."

What is impressive here is how tactfully individuals manage to combine a fairly strict view of the lines they need to draw to meet the demands of their own faith within a shared social framework that requires their recognizing the equal claims of others—and more than that, how the Christians show respect to the Muslim *baale* by acknowledging the special status of his celebration of Ileya.

The second instance comes from a much smaller place, Joga-Owode, a village in Egbado (now known as Yewaland), the birthplace of Professor Biyi Afonja (b. 1936), an eminent statistician:[25]

> He grew up in a religiously mixed family: of his father's eight paternal siblings, only two were Christian, the others Muslim, but two others on his mother's side were Christian. But they all attended the major ceremonies of both faiths. "Every [New Year's Eve], our village church St John's was filled with as many Christian and Moslem worshippers outside as there were inside. At exactly midnight, the church leader would ring in the New Year by joyously shouting, *Da muso, muso!* [that is, "Hip, hip, hip!"] and the congregation would give a thunderous *Muso!* [Hurrah!]. As we all trooped out of church singing the hymn *Ọlọrun t'ọdun t'o kọja,* "O God Our Help in Ages Past," bonfires would be lit and the loud noise of bangers would rend the air. . . . Conversely, during Ramadan young Biyi would join his Muslim uncles at the 4.30 meal called *sari* before the day's fast and (though he didn't usually fast past midday), he'd be present at the evening prayer (*asamu*) before joining in the meal afterwards. At Ileya, his father would actually don a turban and accompany his Muslim brothers in the grand procession to the prayer ground.

In this small Egbado village, people clearly took a more relaxed view of what their religion required of them than in Okeigbo. One reason for strong Muslim attendance at the New Year service may be that, because the ritual calendar of Islam operates on a lunar cycle, the solar calendar of Christianity is better able to provide an idiom for annual transitions and is to that extent more compatible with traditional ideas about the need for a yearly fresh start. It is worth noting that the Christian villagers of Joga-Owode called Christmas *ọdun kekere* (the little festival), while the *ọdun nla* (the great festival) was the New Year. Life-cycle rituals, now expressed in Christian or Muslim idiom, rather than the public rituals of the new religions themselves, came to be the prime occasions for individuals to express solidarity across the Muslim-Christian divide.

But the public expression of communal religious amity still depended vitally on two institutions carried forward from the past, though both would be modified in the process. The first was the festivals of a small number of important *oriṣa* that were felt to embody the identity of the whole town, such as Sango in Oyo, Agemo in Ijebu, or Ogun in Ilesha, Ondo, and other eastern towns. For decades to come, Christians and Muslims continued to join in these annual festivals, though they gradually came to see them in more secular terms, as cultural events; or they reconfigured them in newly devised festivals aimed at community development.[26] The second key institution was the *ọba*ship. As a quasi-divine being himself—*ekeji oriṣa* (second to the gods)—the *ọba*'s most essential role was to serve as the point of articulation between the town and the *oriṣa* whose goodwill ensured public welfare. It is thus is not surprising that *ọba*s tended to be religiously more conservative than their subjects. But as the balance between the old cults and the new ones tipped in the 1930s, the *ọba*'s patronage shifted toward the world religions, though in a similar spirit as with the old cults. Whatever his own convictions, he had to be the father equally of all accepted faith groups in the town: attending their major festivals (usually with a small retinue of chiefs, attendants, etc.), receiving their leaders at the *afin* (palace), contributing to their building funds, and so forth. In any case, by this time increasing numbers of *ọba* were Muslims or Christians themselves, very often men who had lived and worked for some time outside the town, so acquiring a degree of *ọlaju* (enlightenment).[27] By the 1940s, so widely was it coming to be felt that a town's progress depended on having an enlightened *ọba* that several strongly Muslim towns were moved to choose a Christian to be their *ọba*,[28] on the grounds that he would be best able to represent their overall interests, a striking testimony to both their pragmatism and their tolerance.

INSTITUTIONS AND COMMUNITY: CHRISTIANITY

The two religions organized themselves as segments within the larger community in very different ways expressing their own prior institutional histories. Christianity's main institutional form was the churches or denominations set up by the missionary societies. By the 1920s, these were beginning to recede into the background as Yoruba pastors headed congregations, chaired local church councils, and managed church schools. European missionaries remained in power at the highest levels but were increasingly concentrated in educational, training, and medical work. Yoruba Christianity is predominantly evangelical Protestant, with Anglicans (CMS) historically the largest and most prestigious church, followed by Methodists and Baptists. The Roman Catholics, though important for their hospitals and schools,[29] were less numerous and remained dependent on foreign missionary priests for much longer.

The mainline churches became considerable bureaucracies, employing thousands of people (especially teachers); owning extensive property in church premises, schools, and other facilities like hospitals and clinics, training centers, presses, and bookshops; and developing systematic evangelization strategies. Apart from their training colleges like St Andrew's College Oyo or the Baptist Seminary at Ogbomoso, their apex institutions were grammar schools, the focus of intense local as well as church pride in places like Lagos, Abeokuta, Ibadan, Ijebu Ode—the top flight of these were known as the Aionian schools, a sort of Ivy League. And even when such schools were owned by the community rather than the church (as Ondo Boys' High School, Oduduwa College at Ife, or Ilesha Grammar School were), they were often headed by Anglican clergymen.

The clergy of the interwar years, the age of high colonialism—the sons of the nineteenth-century pioneers, the fathers of the postwar generation of nationalist politicians and professionals, so to speak—were major figures in their communities. The archetype of them all was the Rev. A. B. Akinyele (1875–1968), a member of one of Ibadan's oldest and most distinguished Christian families.[30]

> His early career was typical. From the CMS Grammar School in Lagos he went on to its training institution for native teachers and then, after a few years teaching (mostly in Abeokuta), he caught the attention of the bishop and was sponsored to attend Fourah Bay College, in Freetown, then the only institution of higher education in West Africa. Graduating in 1906, he returned to pastoral work in Ibadan and was ordained priest in 1910. When Ibadan Grammar School was founded, in 1913, under CMS auspices but with strong support from local people—land for it at Oke Are was given by a prominent Muslim chief, *Balogun* Shittu—Akinyele was the obvious man to be its first principal. He remained so for twenty years, and as such presided over the production of the next generation's elite. Church affairs apart, he was much consulted informally both by the chiefs and by colonial officers (some of whom he instructed in the Yoruba language) and was active in all the doings of his fellow *ọlaju* (enlightened people). A powerful axis of influence linked him with his junior brother, I. B. Akinyele, who was active in local politics, becoming a chief in 1933 and slowly climbing the hierarchy till he got to be *Olubadan* (king of Ibadan, 1955–64). In 1933, A. B. was appointed assistant bishop of Lagos, based in Ondo, but he returned to Ibadan as first bishop of its new diocese in 1952.

A proper social and cultural history of this important group of men remains to be written, though much of it can be excavated from the many commemorative local church histories that have been produced.[31] For the present, the most vivid evocation of this world is to be found in two memoirs by Wole Soyinka: the autobiographical *Aké,* mostly about his mother's family (the Ransome-Kutis) in Abeokuta, and *Ìsarà,* a quasi-fictional treatment of his father's circle of young *ọlaju* in a small Remo town.[32] These men stood outside the formal structure of the native authority, local government by *ọba* and chiefs, as sanctioned by indirect rule, but they were often their advisors. They tended to be active in the town improvement societies and progressive unions, which combined local patriotism with the promotion of *ọlaju.* Here they joined with educated traders (often former mission teachers), commercial or government clerks, and even a few educated Muslims—though the societies' ethos was distinctly but undogmatically Christian.[33] At the same time, there was an important pan-Yoruban dimension to their work lives: against local dialects they promoted the CMS-derived Standard Yoruba language in church and school; in their early careers (often starting as teachers) they were liable to be transferred all over Yoruba country, forming regional networks; a handful of them went annually to Lagos for the diocesan synod, the nearest thing to a parliament for the *ọlaju* of Yorubaland in the interwar years, where they discussed issues going far beyond the narrowly ecclesiastical.

These years of rapid church growth brought their conflicts and tensions, of which two waves of breakaway or independent churches were the outcome. What are known as the African churches emerged between 1891 and 1918: opposed to paternalist policies and the restriction of African advancement in the mainline Protestant missions, particularly the CMS, they advocated a greater acceptance of African culture and custom, but in doctrine and church order they remained close to the missions from which they had seceded.[34] At one level the Aladura or praying churches, emerging between 1918 and 1940, were a response to a widespread sense of social dislocation arising from the rapid growth of the cash economy in the 1920s followed by the depression of the early 1930s.[35] They offered a much farther-reaching Africanization that did much to close the gap with Islam though the provision of Christian techniques of healing, divination, and protection. The Aladura movement created new organizational forms, such as the followings of charismatic *woli* (prophets), but over time they tended to move back toward the template provided by the older churches as they too began to acquire property and needed to develop stable systems of leadership succession.

INSTITUTIONS AND COMMUNITY: ISLAM

The primary organization of the Muslim community differed markedly from that of Christianity (and still does), even though there has been some adoption of Christian forms. Islam famously has no church, which is because as a religion it set out to be none other than the organization of a spiritual polity. In Yorubaland, except for Ilorin, it spread without corporate institutions of any kind, bottom-upward rather than top-downward, without jihad or the constraining force of Islamic rule. The main agents of its expansion were Muslim clerics or *alfa*, a social category whose two defining features—some measure of Arabic learning and the provision of religious services—were extremely variable, though the most essential function of any *alfa* was to be a professional man of prayer.[36] They ranged from those with just enough Arabic to be able to offer magicospiritual services to clients both Muslim and non-Muslim,[37] to those whose better command of Arabic enabled them to run Koranic schools, as well as to perform the public prayers and life-cycle rites of the Muslim community.

Though the *alfa* began more as entrepreneurs than as missionaries, they readily organized those who gathered around them into congregations. As the numbers of Muslims grew, augmented by visiting traders and their local contacts, in every significant community there emerged a *jumat* or central mosque for Friday prayer, often located close to the *ọba*'s palace (even in mainly Christian towns like Ilesha and Ife). Here there clustered those *alfa* with the greatest reputation among their peers for Arabic learning, often the descendants of pioneers who had come from Ilorin, Hausaland, or farther afield. They occupied the chief imamship and other offices of the central mosque, which tended to become hereditary among their descendants. Spread throughout the town were many small, so-called *ratibi* mosques, usually set up by an *alfa* under the patronage of the *baale* or compound head, where local residents gathered for the five daily prayers. These might be no more than a large room in a house or a small building within the compound and were typically known by the name of the founding *alfa* or the compound itself, being regarded simply as a Muslim spiritual facility for the neighborhood. This has led some to regard conversion to Islam as being collective—the coresident members of a lineage deciding to convert together—in contrast to Christian conversion as individual. I see no good evidence for such a contrast, though the conversion of a big man might lead many of his followers to convert, as with the *Arẹ* Latosa in nineteenth-century Ibadan or *Balogun* Kuku in early twentieth-century Ijebu. The central mosque apart, mosques thus tended to be more numerous but smaller than churches.

This basic pattern became more complex as Muslim numbers grew and the varieties of Islam diversified. As the population of Ibadan rose to more than a million in the course of the colonial period, with over 65 percent of its indigenes Muslim, the simple structure of central and *ratibi* mosques became insufficient. From the mid-1950s onward, a middle tier of more localized central mosques for Friday prayer emerged throughout the main localities of the vast town, thus replicating the urban hierarchy of town, quarter, and compound. In addition, over roughly the same period, various sects and societies established their own mosques, which formed their own groupings more analogous to Christian denominations, with some having their own central mosques for their fraternities in the town as a whole. Here the way was led by modernist Muslim organizations, such as Ahmadiyya, which came to Lagos in 1916 and operated much like a Christian missionary society, with a directing overseas headquarters (in the Punjab), moving into the interior and opening schools, among which Ahmadiyya Grammar School in Ibadan proved especially important.[38] It showed the way for other societies of modern-oriented Muslims, which also opened schools and had their own mosques: Ansar-ud-Deen (1923) and Nawair-ud-Deen (1936).[39] At the other end of the spectrum were societies like the Zumratul Mumin, popularly known after its founder as the Bamidele, a religiously conservative group founded in Ibadan in the 1940s whose branches operate more like Aladura churches (including a certain proneness to factional splits).[40]

So Islam, weak in principles of corporate organization above the level of the single congregation, made some use of the denominational form characteristic of Christianity but relied mainly on whatever structures of community prevailed locally. Whereas churches are a distinctly religious form of organization, differentiated from the communities they work in and also working across many communities, Yoruba Islam aspires to be, as it were, the community in its Islamic aspect. Some very characteristic effects of this have appeared in patterns of leadership and conflict, particularly in strongly Muslim towns, such as indigenous Lagos, Ibadan, and Ijebu Ode.

There has often been a strong mutual influence between the chiefly hierarchies of the town and the Islamic community, especially around its central mosque. At Ijebu Ode, it was the custom that appointments to the two senior Muslim posts, the chief imam or *Lẹmọmu* and his deputy, the *Noibi,* were ratified by the *ọba*—something that no church would have judged appropriate—which meant that it might fall to a Christian *ọba* to install the chief imam by capping him.[41] This went with the obligation of the *Lẹmọmu* and his fellow *alfa* to go and pray for the *ọba* every year at the Ileya festival. In Iseyin, a town where Islam was established very early, the imamship came to rotate between the four quarters of the town much as an *ọba*ship might rotate between the main segments of the royal lineage.[42] Ibadan developed its own unique system of succession to the imamship, which again mirrored that of the town.[43] Because it had been founded in the nineteenth century as a war camp and lacked a crowned *ọba,* it came to be governed by two parallel ranked lines of chiefs, respectively civil and military. Men from the leading families were appointed to a low rung on either of these ladders and progressed upward as deaths opened vacancies above them, while succession to the headship of the whole town alternated between the two lines. Over the twentieth century, a norm emerged for Ibadan's central mosque to be governed by two lines of chiefs, known as the *Mọgaji* and *Alfa* lines, filled respectively by sons of previous imams and by self-made men of Islamic learning. (A *mọgaji* in Ibadan is the heir to the headship of one of the major families.) This can be seen as a way of recognizing both descent and learning as criteria for the imamship, but the system of choosing the imam from the two lines alternately has often not worked smoothly in practice. There are various criteria for choosing an imam—learning, popularity, descent, character—and they rarely converge in one man. So to the regret of many educated Muslims, especially those aware of normative patterns elsewhere in the Islamic world, imamship succession disputes have tended to resemble Yoruba chieftaincy disputes in general.

A further result of the interpenetration of Muslim and town organization has been that conflicts arising in one sphere have readily spilled over into the other, in a way that has rarely happened with Christianity. These cleavages—whether originating over doctrinal or ritual issues (or both), or over rivalry for office, or matters of mosque management or control—might run on for years, morphing over time from one leading issue to another. Muslim unity in Lagos was first fractured by an *alfa* from Ilorin who during Ramadan 1875 preached the all-sufficiency of the Koran, without recourse to *hadith*, for determining Islamic practice. His followers thus came to be known as the Alalukurani or Koranic Muslims. So heated did feelings become that the governor felt it prudent to post troops during Id al-Fitr to prevent violence and later presided at reconciliation meetings; but he refused requests to use his authority to ban the Alalukurani.[44] In 1901 another cleavage opened up, initially over the management of the central mosque, one faction following the chief imam, hence known as the Lemomu group, the other as the Jama'at (congregation) group. The great flashpoint in secular Lagos politics in the early twentieth century was the government's plan to introduce a water rate, which polarized opinion into anti- and pro-government parties. By 1916, the existing split among Lagos Muslims had become aligned with this, the Lemomu group supporting the government, while the Jama'at people opposed it, thus becoming the popular base for what evolved into a protonationalist party, the NNDP.[45] The leadership of the NNDP was provided by educated Christians—notably Herbert Macaulay, the grandson of Bishop Crowther—but they were involved as individuals, not as a faction of any church or of the Christian community at large.[46]

At Ijebu Ode too, cleavages in town politics impacted reciprocally on those in the Muslim *umma*. In the late 1890s, a dispute over the quality of the Arabic learning of the chief imam (*Lẹmọmu*) became entangled with the main conflict in the town at large, between the king (*Awujalẹ*) and his overly mighty subject, *Balogun* Kuku. Whereas Kuku gave his backing to the *Lẹmọmu*'s critics, the *Awujalẹ* supported him; and by 1907 the Muslim cleavage had hardened to the point that there were two *Lẹmọmu*s and two *Noibi*s, with occasional fights between the two factions. It took eleven years for the conflict to be resolved, and finally only through the intervention of the district commissioner and town council, which included several lay Christians.[47] A running sore of Ijebu Ode politics in the late colonial period was the unpopularity of *Awujalẹ* Gbelegbuwa II (1933–59), whom the British virtually forced on Ijebu as they wanted an enlightened ruler, despite the general view that he was ineligible by descent and excessively high-handed in his dealings with people. Gbelegbuwa was a Christian, and as such drew some support from his coreligionists, though his most doughty opponent, Chief Timothy Odutola, was also a Christian; and not just that, but a member of the same church (St Saviour's Anglican), with the title *Asiwaju* (leader) of Ijebu Christians.[48] This was in recognition of his being, as a highly successful entrepreneur, the wealthiest Ijebu of his day. As a subject fit to rival his king, Chief Odutola was rather like a latter-day Kuku. Yet the dispute came to affect the Muslims of the town more than the Christians, since different quarters of the town split over the imamship, and rival candidates were anti- or pro-*Awujalẹ*, even with an *Awujalẹ* so generally unpopular among the mass of Muslims as Gbelegbuwa was.[49]

LEADERSHIP AND THE YORUBA MUSLIM DILEMMA

At least since the early twentieth century, Yoruba Muslims within Nigeria have faced a continuing dilemma, whether in religion, culture, or politics: How far do they orient themselves toward their Christian fellow Yoruba or their non-Yoruba fellow Muslims? The dilemma arises from a double sense of inferiority that has challenged them: the sense of being regarded as less enlightened than their Christian compatriots, and as less complete Muslims than their coreligionists in Northern Nigeria. Education was critical to addressing the problem on both fronts.

On one side, the virtual Christian monopoly of Western education in the early colonial period was an enormous disadvantage to Muslims, felt especially in Lagos. The government took some steps to rectify this, appointing Edward Blyden as director of Muslim education (1896). But Muslim parents still tended to be suspicious, not least since the government's aims were sometimes undermined by the appointment of Christian teachers. On the other side, there was the low level of Arabic scholarship of most Yoruba *ulama*. For many of them, this did not extend to much more than a few years' attendance at a local Koranic school, which gave them just enough Arabic to make a living by selling charms and divining. The necessary dual upgrading took place over many decades, and involved not just some synthesis of Arabic and Western syllabuses and educational methods but drawing on links with Ilorin, the North, and the Middle East.[50] By the 1940s, some Yoruba had attended Al-Azhar in Cairo, and in the 1950s two major centers of higher-level Arabic/Koranic training were established at Elekuro in Ibadan and Agege, near Lagos. The latter, the Centre for Arabic and Islamic Studies, was founded in 1955 by an Al-Azhar graduate from Ilorin, Shaykh Adam Abdullah al-Ilori (1917–92), the greatest Yoruba Arabic scholar of his generation, trained entirely outside Western institutions.[51] In his own writings in Arabic, al-Ilori showed himself to be well aware of the two sides of the Yoruba Muslim dilemma. He responded critically to the Rev. Samuel Johnson's pro-Christian account of Yoruba origins and history; but he also asserted the integrity of Yoruba Islam, defending it from "reckless accusations of infidelity" by the overzealous orthodox, including the leading Salafist intellectual of the North, Abubakar Gumi.[52] In the last thirty years, another source of Arabic expertise has come into play: Yoruba graduates of Saudi universities, especially the Islamic University at Medina. They pride themselves on the fluency of their Arabic, and there is some status rivalry between them and the Nigeria-trained *ulama*, who regard them as narrow in their attitudes. They were the core of an organization founded in 1982, Tadamun al-Muslimin (Islamic Solidarity), which with some others under the umbrella of a larger grouping calling itself Ahl us-Sunna (People of the [Prophet's] Way) has promoted a Salafist perspective within Yoruba Islam, though so far with limited success.

In theory, Islam has no priesthood, but here there is the paradox that in a non-Arabic-speaking society like Yoruba the sacred and esoteric prestige of Arabic for Muslims inevitably produces a distinction between *ulama* and laity that is in some ways more marked than that between pastors and lay people in Yoruba Protestantism. Though churches are institutionally distinct from society, the culture of Christian *ọlaju* is shared by clergy and educated laymen, as witness the ease with which university lecturers (often in scientific subjects) have become the leaders of Pentecostal churches. They are distinguished from their members less by their possession of specialist knowledge than by the charisma that is attributed to them. But among Muslims, Arabic learning and Western education remain distinct sources of authority, and their respective possessors—the serious *ulama* and the educated Muslim laity—vie with one another to speak for Islam, since few people stand really high in both categories apart from university graduates in Arabic and Islamic studies. Thus there is some tension between the League of Imams and Alfas (LIA), an organization of and for the Yoruba *ulama* across a broad spectrum, and a body like the Muslim Ummah of South-Western Nigeria (MUSWEN), inaugurated in 2008 after several years' discussion among modern Muslim professionals (lawyers, academics, doctors, etc.). They felt that the LIA leadership was not educated enough to articulate the collective Muslim interest under the peculiar conditions of Yorubaland, where Christians were so much seen as the bearers of modern civilization.[53]

The third source of leadership in the Muslim community is wealthy laymen, typically traders or businessmen. Some of them have a smattering of Arabic, and most have a measure of Western education, but it is their power of material patronage that gives them standing and influence (e.g., to appoint imams to mosques they have founded or to settle disputes within the *umma*). Until his death in 2014, the preeminent figure here was Alhaji Abdul-Azeez Arisekola Alao, who had a few years of Koranic school and completed his primary education at a CMS school in one of Ibadan's villages before getting a job as a distributor of agricultural chemicals.[54] His commercial activities diversified, but it was not till the 1990s that he really made it big through a contract, gained through his friendship with General Abacha, to supply food to the Nigerian troops in ECOMOG, the peacekeeping force in the Liberian civil war. After something of a playboy youth, he started taking his religion more seriously at the end of the 1970s, and in 1981 agreed to be turbaned as *Arẹ Musulumi* (Commander of Muslims). His most conspicuous work of patronage was his building a large mosque with a conspicuous golden dome on the Iwo Road in Ibadan, which he got the chief imam of al-Azhar in Cairo to come and open. Arisekola paid the salaries of at least three imams. Yet the style of his leadership owed more to the Ibadan warlords of the nineteenth century than to any Islamic paradigm,[55] as struck me forcefully when I visited him in his vast walled compound at Ikolaba, a respectable suburb in the northeast of Ibadan:

> We enter through great double iron gates set in a concrete wall about 15 feet high, in front of which runs a mucky stream which looks somewhat like a moat. Security

is intense: several tough-looking henchmen hang around a small guardhouse, and we wait in the car for over twenty minutes after having phoned to announce our arrival before being admitted, while other vehicles are checked as they come or go. Inside there is a large main house, other buildings including a mosque, plenty of parking and well-maintained grounds which are said to include a menagerie with ostriches. We are received in a large audience chamber upstairs, decked with drapes in the Nigerian colours of green and white, and in the corners are set enormous coloured photographic portraits of Arisekola's late parents on their return from the *hajj*, as well as of General Abacha. Arisekola's manner is relaxed, self-confident and genial. We sit on a sofa by a glass table on which he lays a small array of cell-phones, which ring periodically throughout the 90-minute interview. He answers briskly, *Tani yẹn?* ["Who is that?" or "Do I know you?"] to what appear to be requests for money or favours. Two or three times an attendant comes in and speaks in a low voice to Arisekola, who rummages in the front pocket of his big gown and brings out wads of banknotes to be distributed. On the way out, we pass by a large antechamber with thirty or more people still waiting to see the *Arẹ*: men and women, all sorts and conditions, but including several quite prominent people known to my companion (who is an experienced journalist).

Arisekola was not the only wealthy Muslim to receive a title from the League of Imams and Alfas: his friend and political associate, the late Chief M. K. O. Abiola from Abeokuta—of whom more shortly—was styled *Baba Adinni* (Father of the Religion). This conferment of pan-Yoruba Muslim chieftaincy titles was an organizational innovation at the time.[56] Titles have long been given to senior lay leaders in both Islam and Christianity, but usually at the level of the single congregation, as with the *Baba Ijọ* (Father of the Church) or *Iya Suna* (Mother of the [Islamic] Faith). In the extension of this to the highest levels of the communal hierarchy—like Oyo, Ogun, or Lagos States, or Yorubaland as a whole—we see again Yoruba Islam's propensity to draw organizational form from the wider community or polity in which it is set. These wealthy laymen offer a kind of leadership that has no close equivalent within Yoruba Christianity today. While their largesse is eagerly received, their power is also resented, especially by some of the *ulama*, who feel that those qualified by learning and piety for Islamic leadership should not have to defer to big men whose conduct sometimes falls short of the religious ideal. It is a tension that harks a long way back in Muslim history, recalling the attitudes of the *ulama*, then still emergent as a force within Islam, toward the Umayyad caliphs.

RELIGION AND NATIONALISM, 1940S THROUGH LATE 1970S

Nationalism—the movement after 1945 to take over control of the colonial state in the name of the mass of the African people—had its roots in the agitation by educated young men a decade or so earlier to challenge the system of Indirect Rule, which had restricted power in local communities to *ọba*s and chiefs. In both cases leadership was overwhelmingly provided by Christians, even in mainly Muslim towns, since they were so far ahead in the Western education needed to challenge the institutions of the colonial state. Because effective representation of communal interests was always the paramount issue, Muslims were on the whole happy to accept Christians as their community representatives. The main vehicle of Yoruba political aspirations, the Action Group (AG), was not strictly a Christian party, even though its leader, Obafemi Awolowo, and most of all his closest political associates were Christians, and its program was strongly infused with the Yoruba Christian value of *ọlaju*.[57] Still, *some* Muslims were uneasy about these affinities, and in 1957 a Muslim party, the National Muslim League, was founded—though it was quickly and effectively stamped on as religiously divisive. Measures were taken to gain Muslim favor, such as setting up a pilgrims' welfare board and more provision for Islamic instruction in schools.

Where party-political divisions in Yorubaland did come to have a religious aspect, this arose contingently, as a by-product of the religious profiles of particular communities, as we can see from a comparison of Ibadan and Lagos. Many of the same factors were present in both places, such as a strong Muslim majority among the indigenes, but under different local conditions they led to diametrically opposed outcomes. At Ibadan those chosen at the first elections in 1951 were mostly from the local Christian elite, members of the Ibadan Progressive Union drawn to a politics of *ọlaju*, and they naturally affiliated themselves with the Action Group at the level of regional politics. Popular disaffection with this elite arose less directly from the fact that the mass of Ibadan people were Muslim than that they were linked by ties of personal attachment to the compound heads or *mọgaji*, descendants of the warlords of nineteenth-century Ibadan, whose position was under threat from the rationalizing reforms to the court and taxation systems intended by the Action Group. What further alienated them from the Action Group was that, as a party with a strong pan-Yoruba identity, it had no option but to support the demand of the so-called native settlers to be allowed to acquire land rights in the town. These were immigrants to Ibadan from other Yoruba towns, especially the much-resented Ijebu—of whom Awolowo was one, with a house at Oke Ado, where his legal practice was based. There emerged a communal party, the Mabolaje Grand Alliance,[58] under the leadership of a flamboyant Muslim populist, Adegoke Adelabu, which allied itself at the regional level with the Action Group's rival, the NCNC.[59] Since Islam (though fairly recently adopted in most cases) had fused rather effectively with status values deriving from nineteenth-century Ibadan, Adelabu combined radical socialism at the national level with cultural conservatism at the local level.[60] Though as well educated as most of his Christian compeers and possessed of an excellent command of English, Adelabu was a polygamist who kept open house in traditional chiefly style, and he made good use of Muslim networks—such as the *ratibi* mosques—to build a strong popular base. He was well supported by the generality of the *ulama*, and in fact there was nearly a rebellion against the leadership of the chief imam of the day, Muili Abdullahi, because one Friday in 1957 he introduced Awolowo (who was Muili's personal friend) into the central Mosque.[61]

One might have expected the NCNC to have become the political voice of the Muslim indigenes in Lagos too. It had been founded in 1945 as the successor to Herbert Macaulay's NNDP, which (as noted earlier) had its popular base in the Ilu Committee, closely linked to the Jamaʿat faction at the central mosque; and the NNDP had indeed attracted "the traditionalistic, predominantly Muslim indigenous masses" of Lagos.[62] Now, this was a period when the population of Lagos was growing rapidly, through immigration not only from the Yoruba interior but from farther afield (including many Igbo), and the census in 1950 showed that as a result Christians had come to outnumber Muslims. The Lagos indigenes felt that they were becoming marginalized in their own city. Of the two main parties, up to the early 1950s the NCNC was master of the field in Lagos, so the Action Group faced the problem of how to break into it. Now, whereas the NCNC was more a pan-Nigerian party, the Action Group was more a pan-Yoruba one; and while this worked against it in Ibadan, where the indigenes saw the main threat to their position as coming from other Yoruba as native settlers, in Lagos the threatening outsiders were culturally much more diverse, and the Action Group—unencumbered by the wider ethnoregional commitments of the NCNC—was better able to target its appeal at the Lagos indigenes.[63] In particular, it built a network of effective support through the market women, led by such as the formidable (and piously Muslim) Madam Abibatu Mogaji. The effects proved long-lasting: there emerged a lineage of progressive Muslim politicians—L. K. Jakande, Bola Tinubu, Raji Fasola[64]—attached to the Action Group and its successor parties (UPN, AD, ACN, APC), which have controlled Lagos State down to the present.

Awolowo remained the political hero of most Yoruba, whether Christians or Muslims, for the rest of his life.[65] His reputation was only enhanced by his imprisonment for alleged treason between 1962 and 1966, at the hands of a coalition of his enemies, headed by the Muslim premier of the Northern Region, the Sardauna of Sokoto. At least on the Yoruba side, this opposition was always coded in terms of North vs. South, or Hausa vs. Yoruba, rather than Muslim vs. Christian. In fact Awolowo's onetime lieutenant, who was seen as having betrayed him to the Sardauna, Chief S. L. Akintola, was a Christian from Ogbomosho, and the acting leader of the Action Group while Awolowo was in prison was a Muslim from Abeokuta, Alhaji D. S. Adegbenro. Up to the late 1970s, the conventional wisdom was that religion—in the sense of the Muslim-Christian divide—was essentially irrelevant to Yoruba political conflict except as an occasional accompaniment to communal divisions.[66] But this would change.

POST-NATIONALIST TURBULENCE, LATE 1970S ONWARD

The second half of the 1970s, a period that led up to the restoration of civilian government after thirteen years of military rule, marked a decisive watershed in the history of Nigeria after independence. Religion came onto the political agenda as a factor in its own right, not just as an additional aspect of communal or regional difference. This first showed itself in the dispute in the constitutional assembly in 1977–78 about whether there should be a federal Sharia court of appeal. Yoruba Muslim opinion was divided but in general came down against it, fearing its potential to divide the community.[67] (Of this I will say more in chapter 8, below.) About the same time, there emerged onto the public stage new and more strenuous forms of devotion on both sides: Islamist reform movements and charismatic or born-again Christianity. In both cases the new movements had global or international links, and these tended to weaken those local attachments that had done so much to restrain religious conflict in Yoruba communities.

When we consider the articulation of religious identity and Yoruba ethnicity, the so-called Second Republic (1979–83) brought about a paradoxical double effect. On the one hand, the Unity Party of Nigeria (UPN), led by Chief Awolowo, won a much larger overall share of the Yoruba vote than its Action Group predecessor had done, even though it was defeated at the national level by its main rival, the NPN, led by a Muslim Northerner, Shehu Shagari.[68] Yet at the same time Muslims became a more distinct and assertive political force within the Yoruba arena. There were several reasons for this: the Sharia debate of 1977–78 had raised the Islamic consciousness of the most active; the dominance of Nigeria's government by Muslims (which continued after the return of the military in 1983) offered a political resource to be exploited; and Muslims' level of education had increased, so that they were less prepared to look to Christians to provide political leadership. In Oyo State, with its capital at Ibadan, the NPN picked up the threads of the old anti–Action Group tradition, now with a more strongly Muslim flavor. The state's UPN governor, Chief Bola Ige, was the particular target of Muslim criticism for pro-Christian bias in his appointments and educational policies, with the Muslim Students Society (which had recently become much more radical) taking a highly militant stand against him. A new role was played by a group of wealthy Muslims, most notably the *Baba Adinni* M. K. O. Abiola, who made alliance with the Northern Muslim establishment the cornerstone of his politics. Abiola, famously satirized in the 1970s for his corrupt business practices,[69] and well known for his lavish, philandering lifestyle, the very epitome of the Yoruba big man, used his business links with Northern politicians to good advantage for Muslims (though it must be said that non-Muslims also benefitted from his largesse). Federal contracts and funds came their way, as well as Saudi money for approved projects; and Abiola used his *National Concord* newspaper to support the cause of Sharia.

In 1985 there erupted the highest-profile public confrontation between Muslims and Christians that the Yoruba had known: the Ibadan-cross controversy. It was triggered by a reckless speech given by Abiola at the opening of a large new mosque—largely funded with Saudi money—on the University of Ibadan campus. About two hundred yards away from the mosque and in clear view from it, there had stood since 1954 a large, white, monumental cross, at a crossroads close to the Catholic chapel. Abiola took it into his head, possibly without premeditation, to demand that the cross be demolished. Other issues of Muslim grievance—essentially arising from their diffuse sense of their marginalization in an institution whose staff and students were overwhelmingly and often assertively Christian[70]—came into the dispute, which deepened when the Muslim side invoked the intervention of the federal commissioner for education, a Northern Muslim. The dispute ran on for many months but ended in a compromise: the cross stayed, but a concrete screen and a suitable Muslim emblem were erected nearer the mosque.[71] When the dispute was eventually settled, there was a great sense of relief at having pulled back from the brink of something very nasty and un-Yoruba—the more because of the intermittent outbreaks of serious religious violence that were by then occurring widely in Northern Nigeria.

At the end of the 1980s, the military head of state, General Ibrahim Babangida, a Northern Muslim, announced a program for a return to civilian rule: two parties were set up, with carefully vetted candidates. M. K. O. Abiola was approved as the candidate of the SDP, no doubt regarded (in view of his recent record) as a safe choice. But as the campaign got under way, an unexpected turnaround occurred. Because his opponent in the contest for the presidency, also a Muslim, was a Northerner, Abiola became the candidate of the South in the 1993 elections, and particularly the vessel of Christians' hopes to see the overthrow of the Northern-Muslim-military complex (to which they had come to apply the sobriquet "the Caliphate"). If ever a politician was defined by the hopes vested in him by his supporters rather than by the force of his own political convictions, it was Abiola. The military took fright at Abiola's victory and annulled the election.

There was an interim period before yet another Northern Muslim general, Sani Abacha, seized power, and Abiola (after a year of dithering) was imprisoned. So this most un-Awolowolike of politicians found the mantle of Awolowo placed around his shoulders and assumed the role of another Yoruba victim of Northern oppression—a role for which the Christian template of the suffering servant of his people was well suited. From having been a force to accentuate the Yoruba religious divide in the 1980s, in the 1990s Abiola became—virtually in spite of himself—a bridge across it. In some quarters this erstwhile advocate of Sharia even became seen as a kind of honorary Christian. While in Nigeria in 1994, I was once astounded to see a newspaper headline MKO BORN-AGAIN? The wish was surely father to that thought. Yet the born-again rhetoric of breaking with the past and receiving fresh empowerment in the spirit aptly expressed the yearning of many Yoruba of both religions for a fresh political start. Conversely, this was a difficult time for Yoruba Muslims, since their loyalties could not be quite so undivided. Alhaji Arisekola Alao, the *Arẹ Musulumi*, was nearly lynched by students in 1995 on an ill-advised visit to the University of Ibadan campus, on account of his friendship with Abacha. Even so, in general Yoruba Muslims were as strongly committed to Yoruba interests and the democratic cause as Christians were. Kudirat, Abiola's senior wife, was assassinated at Abacha's behest, and his most persistent legal opponent, the radical lawyer Gani Fawehinmi, was a Muslim from Ondo. The issue of Abiola's imprisonment put a very severe strain on relations between Yoruba and Northern members of the Nigerian Supreme Council for Islamic Affairs.[72]

By the time that both Abiola and Abacha died, in 1998, religious tension had subsided from the high levels of the 1980s, as Muslims and Christians again found common Yoruba ground in their opposition to the North. An ugly side of this was the anti-Hausa violence of the Oodua Peoples Congress, a vigilantist organization that emerged in the late 1990s, particularly active in and around Lagos.[73] The election of Olusegun Obasanjo in 1999 as president of Nigeria—the first Yoruba to hold the office that Awolowo had wanted so much—had a complicating effect on the religious alignments of Yoruba politics. Though a Christian himself, he had never stood close to the pro-Awolowo political mainstream; this was one thing that recommended him to the elders of the PDP, which stood roughly in the lineage of the Northern-led coalitions of earlier years. In fact, most Yoruba cordially detested Obasanjo,[74] and in the 1999 election they showed their fidelity to the Awoist tradition by supporting the AD (later AC), though this support was later eroded by the PDP's exercise of power. Significantly the PDP first broke through in Oyo State, the mainly Muslim heartland of earlier resistance to the Yoruba political mainstream, from Adelabu to the NPN, whose exemplary figure was Ibadan's notorious political godfather, Alhaji Lamidi Adedibu.[75] But this did not last: after 2011, in disgust at PDP misgovernment (and, more than that, in growing disaffection with the Nigerian national project), the five Yoruba States of the southwest returned to Awoist parties. The key element here was Lagos State, which alone had rejected the PDP massively and consistently since 1999. The ironical outcome here was that a political tradition that at its outset in the 1950s had been so largely dominated by Christians now had as its main standard bearers the Muslim politicians who for decades had controlled Lagos.[76]

The master theme of this chapter has been the evolving patterns of Yoruba community over the past century. Community, we may say, emerges from the continuous interplay between two spheres of human action: an external or political sphere, concerned with defending (and defining) the community against other entities of like kind; and an internal or social sphere, constituted by the associational activity of community members in pursuit of their various life goals. The original and primary focus of Yoruba community, the *ìlú* (city-state or town), has been subjected to two distinct but connected forces of change. As a result of incorporation into the Nigerian state, it has been extended outward to higher-order levels of community, to the Yoruba as an ethnic group and to Nigeria as a nation. But what has concerned us more here is how the *ìlú* has had to accommodate the new identities brought by the world religions, each intent on enlarging its constituency and realizing its own conceptions of community. The Yoruba have succeeded remarkably in domesticating them, to the extent that they are well suffused with Yoruba criteria of value, such as religious tolerance and the expectation that they deliver this-world benefits, whether for individuals or for the community. Yet Yoruba community, as configured by religion, is always historically provisional, never finally realized. At present, its political and its sociocultural aspects stand in a state of potential tension. On the one hand, as the foregoing narrative has suggested, Yoruba Muslims seem at last incorporated in a common political project with their Christian compatriots. On the other hand, currents within the religious sphere, principally but not exclusively on the Muslim side, are working to differentiate Muslims and Christians culturally more sharply than in the past. This differentiation is the theme of the next chapter.

8

Yoruba Ethnogenesis and the Trajectory of Islam

There has been a reciprocal and long-sustained relationship between the making of the Yoruba and the efforts of the world religions to plant themselves at home in Yoruba society. For more than a century, Christianity has been at the forefront of this, through the CMS adoption of "Yoruba" as an ethnic designation and the creation of a Standard Yoruba form of language for use in church and school, which became the main vehicle for the modern Yoruba identity. Both culturally and politically, Yoruba ethnogenesis has had its high moments, of which the most notable were the efflorescence of cultural nationalism in the 1890s[1] and the articulation of a political program by the Action Group in the 1950s, in both of which Christians played the leading part.

Yet those Christians who defined Yoruba language and history, such as Bishop S. A. Crowther and the Rev. Samuel Johnson, were ready to adopt and adapt Muslim materials, including the very name "Yoruba" itself, which passed from its distant Arabic origins through the Islamic polities of the savannah to designate the people of the Oyo Kingdom. The very first specific reference to them comes from Mali, by Ahmad Baba of Timbuktu (d. 1627),[2] and only later from Hausaland. It is an irony that Muslim Yoruba later adopted a tradition of having migrated from the Islamic east, when their Islam actually first came from the west, along the trade corridor provided by the river Niger. A trace of that origin survived in the common Yoruba name for Muslims, *Imale,* even though the memory of what it had once signified was lost. A deposit of vocabulary is also owed to these Malian roots, some of it denoting specifically Islamic items, some of it joining the religiously unmarked general lexicon of Yoruba.[3] One of these words, *bọrọkinni* (gentleman, respected man of comfortable means), came to connote a Yoruba cultural ideal, as indicated by its adoption in proverbial expressions.[4]

It is unlikely that at the beginning of the nineteenth century Islam had been adopted by more than a small minority of the Oyo-Yoruba and hardly at all by non-Oyo. For a long time its spread was so slow and gentle, unforced by violence and uncomplicated by dogma, that an easy cultural intimacy, involving influences running both ways, grew up between Islam and the (Oyo) Yoruba, sometimes so unobtrusive as almost to escape notice:

> One morning in 2008, I call to visit an imam and find him counseling a young couple engaged to be married. At the end of the session, the man hands the imam a 100-naira note (a trifling sum, less than the cost of a newspaper) with his thanks. The imam replies, *Ọlọrun gba* (God receives). The donation is technically a *saraa*, a word derived from the Arabic *sadaqa* (alms), but in Yoruba contexts often rendered as "sacrifice."[5] The verbal formula derives from what was said when kola was thrown, in the simplest of all Yoruba forms of divination, after a sacrifice to an *orisa* to determine if it was acceptable: *orisa gba* (The deity receives).

So far as I can see, this benign little ritual contains no idolatrous implications, though it would surely be condemned by today's Salafists as being without explicit authorization in the *sunna* of the Prophet. What is tacitly carried forward from *orisa* religion to Islam is an identification of the imam, as a man of God, with his God, just as an *orisa* priest, when he receives a donation for his services, receives it as the *orisa*'s representative. But the continuity in the form of the ritual goes with an emptying out of its content; and as with all such traces of the past, it is hard to tell if its origins mean anything (still less, are even known as such) to the participants.

By such mutual exchanges, Islam quietly made itself at home in Yorubaland, and the Yoruba absorbed elements of Islamic culture without any requirement of conversion. When, in the second half of the nineteenth century, through Christian agency, the term "Yoruba" began to be adopted by non-Oyo, and when, in an independent movement over roughly the same period, Islam began to spread from its Oyo heartland into non-Oyo areas, Islamic traits were easily adopted into the habitus of non-Oyo, thus coming to be seen as generically Yoruba. This process has continued, with Muslims continuing to contribute to the stock of items that serve to mark out what it is to be distinctively Yoruba, in such areas as language, dress, and music. So alongside Juju music, played mainly by Christians and greatly indebted to hymns, choruses, and the Afro-Christian music of independent churches, there is the Muslim-derived Fuji, whose chief source is the accompanied vocal music called *were,* sung to wake people up for the predawn meal (*sari*) during Ramadan. The enjoyment of either style of music is no longer religion-specific.[6] Fuji and Juju, when taken together, are unmistakable markers of modern Yoruba culture, in contrast to the musical styles popular among, say, Ghanaians, Igbo, or Congolese.

The three entities here—one ethnic culture and two world religions as locally realized—are all in continuous transformation and impact on one another in complex three-way interactions. Yoruba society has welcomed Islam and Christianity, and proved subtly capable of bending them to its ethos—up to a point. For while they compete vigorously with each other, they have had to do so under Yoruba rules—which have the tendency not only to domesticate them directly but to draw them into a process of mutual emulation that further enhances their shared Yoruba features (as I will explore in detail in the next chapter). Yet, being the kind of entities they are—global faith communities, conversionary and exclusivist, anchored in scriptures that constantly serve to remind their adherents of how imperfectly they are practiced—they cannot find this situation entirely to their liking. They are compelled by their own traditions to try to realize their own distinctive visions.

So how have Christianity and Islam sought to position themselves in relation to Yoruba culture and society? In the early days—around the 1870s, let us say—Christians were widely seen as standing right apart from it; and Muslims, as much more at home in it. The guiding question I want to ask, which for the sake of argument I state in a strong form, is this: Has it come about, over the past century and a quarter, that as Christians have found ways to reconcile themselves with Yoruba culture, Muslims (or at least the most Islamically self-conscious among them) have sought to distance themselves from it? Can we even say that a kind of reversal has come about, such that now it is Christians who are Yoruba undifferenced, whereas it is Muslims who are Yoruba marked by religious difference? The contrasting trajectories of the two faiths, it would seem, are in accord with their respective cultural logics: both have been true to themselves in the histories they have produced.

CHRISTIANITY: INDIGENIZATION AND CULTURAL NATIONALISM

A good place to start is with some comments by Edward Blyden, the West Indian–born pioneer of African nationalism, adopted citizen of Liberia, critic of the missions, and admirer of Islam's cultural achievements in West Africa. In *Christianity, Islam and the Negro Race* (1887), Blyden compared Christianity unfavorably with Islam as regards its local adaptation, which he linked to the continuing enthrallment of Christian converts to their missionary mentors. Whereas with Islam, he argued, "the Arabic superstructure has been superimposed on a permanent indigenous substructure, so that what really took place, when the Arab met the Negro in his own home, was a healthy amalgamation, and not an absorption or an undue repression . . . ," the local Christians remained mere imitators, who "try to force their outward appearance into, as near as possible, a resemblance to Europeans."[7] Despite this, he felt that they challenged heathenism less effectively than Muslims—Blyden was no primitivist—and failed to bring about real cultural change. This severe indictment was actually shared by some in the missions, notably the Rev. James Johnson, pastor of Breadfruit Church in Lagos, as fiery a nationalist as he was an evangelical and an evangelist. "Christians," he wrote in 1874, "are regarded as a people separate from [the mass of Lagosians], as identifying with a foreign people, and the dress they assume has become a mark of distinction."[8] Johnson responded by putting strong pressure on his parishioners to wear African dress and insisted on giving Yoruba names in baptism. In the wave of cultural nationalism in the 1890s, the adoption of Yoruba names and dress was a sign of commitment to the cause. Names and dress, the key personal markers of social identity, are themes I will return to later.

It was both paradoxical and painful for Christianity, a religion that had put provision of God's Word in the language of the people at the very heart of its evangelistic strategy, to find itself treated as alien compared with its rival, which had insisted on keeping its Word in the language in which it had first been delivered, a language incomprehensible to all but a handful of Yoruba Muslims. Even the imam's *khutba* or sermon was ideally first given in Arabic and afterward rendered into Yoruba. Since the missionaries—including radicals like James Johnson—were neither ready nor able to do much to modify the content of the Christian message to the Yoruba (e.g., as regards polygamy, the provision of charms, or domestic slavery), there were only two things to be done: to hope that with cultural change under colonial conditions Christianity would come to be positively valued and lose its aura of strangeness; and to find ways to persuade the Yoruba that, despite its strangeness, Christianity was actually the fulfillment of their historical destiny and the realization of the best potential in their old religion. The framework within which such potential was eventually achieved was the new extended category Yoruba—that is, the Yoruba as we know them today, including all the non-Oyo groups—which the Church Missionary Society first conceived. This was built on a combination of two values—the richness of their traditional culture and their modern enlightenment—that might once have been thought of as opposed or incompatible.

To this project, works on religion and on history were critical: religion because that was where Yoruba culture was at its most distinctive, and history as the medium through which the relations between tradition and modernity needed to be articulated. As to history, all other early historical writing by Christian clergy or laymen pales into insignificance besides the scale and scope of the Rev. Samuel Johnson's *The History of the Yorubas*. (See chapter 2, above.) The Christian literature on Yoruba religion is more varied and sustained but contains no single work of the caliber of Johnson's *History*.[9] Yoruba religion, qua discursive construct, was something devised by Christian evangelists to further their project of conversion. It served to throw a single concept round a body of practices that had not previously been so unified by those who engaged in them; and it treated as a single pan-Yoruba phenomenon what was in reality a spread of local-cult complexes. (See chapter 3, above.) However conceived, Yoruba religion was complex, but undoubtedly the *orișa* cults were its centerpiece: they above all were what converts had to renounce, handing over their images for destruction. The greatest such staging of conversion was the mass iconoclasm at the Aladura revival at Ilesha in 1930–31, where the abandonment of *oriṣa* was linked with the renunciation of other works of evil—witchcraft, bad medicines, charms or "juju"—in a grand demonization of past ritual practice.[10] But since the old religion had met real and continuing needs, this dramatic rupture at the phenomenal level had to be combined with functional alternatives at the existential level, through the Aladura prophets—like Muslim *alfa* before them—providing their own means of healing, guidance, and protection against enemies.

But demonization, however leavened with practical substitutes, could not generate pride in tradition. For that other strategies were needed. One was desacralization, where items of heathenism were rendered inoffensive by being taken out of the category of religion. This was first attempted with the Ogboni society—in its religious aspect a cult of the earth—which was argued to be none other than African freemasonry; and then (since many were not persuaded by this) became further refined into the Reformed Ogboni Fraternity, the brainchild of that interesting man Archdeacon T. A. J. Ogunbiyi. Then a homegrown euhemerism allowed *oriṣa* to be reconfigured as kings, heroes, and great men of old who had been deified after their deaths. This enabled them to be honored by Christians as ancestors and founding fathers. In recent decades, as already noted, a highly reified concept of culture has proved very serviceable, allowing the annual rituals of the patronal deities of the community to be promoted as cultural festivals pure and simple (though again, as we'll see, not everyone is happy to go along with this redefinition).[11]

Of all the traditional cults, that of Orunmila, the *oriṣa* of the Ifa divination cult, stood in a class of its own. Its priests, the *babalawo,* were treated with a unique degree of respect by the Yoruba clergy.[12] Ifa was reinterpreted in two ways. First, following the desacralization strategy, its corpus of oracular verses (the *Odu* of Ifa) was seen as containing Yoruba philosophy, a body of ancestral wisdom, a cultural archive. Ifa was, wrote the Rev. D. O. Epega, "the embodiment of the soul of the Yoruba nation, and the repository of their knowledge, religious, historical and medical."[13] This outlook continues strongly in the work of Yoruba scholars working in various cultural fields down to today. And second, its sacred character was allowed but treated as an anticipation, even a partial prerevelation, of Jesus Christ. The Rev. E. M. Lijadu, in particular, glossed the name Orunmila as "It is heaven that knows reconciliation" and saw it as pointing to Christ as his fulfillment. The culminating work in this tradition was a remarkable Ph.D. thesis—unfortunately never published—completed in 1976 by the Rev. E. A. A. Adegbola, "Ifa and Christianity among the Yoruba: A Study in Symbiosis and the Development of Yoruba Christology."[14] But this was always a tricky line-call for clergy of a cultural-nationalist inclination to make, since they ran the risk of valorizing Orunmila to such an extent that he, rather than Christ, came to be seen as Africa's savior and redeemer. In fact, this was what some people came to think. A short-lived

Ethiopian Church, founded by a Prophet Adeniran in Lagos in 1918, argued that each people had its own savior: Jesus for the Europeans, Mohammed for the Arabs, and Orunmila for the Africans.[15] There followed an Ijo Orunmila (Church of Orunmila), modeled on a Christian church but with an *Iwe Odu Mimọ* (Book of the Holy Odu) in place of the Bible, founded in 1934, which continues to exist, a minor current within the broad stream of Yoruba religiosity.[16] Professor Wande Abimbola's contemporary promotion of Ifa as itself a potential world religion belongs to the same tradition[17]—though nowadays the main audience for such views is in America rather than Nigeria. (See chapter 11, below.)

So Yoruba Christianity's efforts to reconcile itself with Yoruba history and culture, when set alongside institutional developments such as the emergence of the African and Aladura churches and the Africanization of the mainline mission-founded churches, especially after 1945, ran parallel to the general narrative of nationalism. Indeed the political nationalism of the period 1945–60 is better seen as following rather than leading developments in the religious field.[18] The symbolic apogee of nationalism was surely FESTAC, the Second World Festival of Black and African Arts and Culture, which took place in Lagos in 1977: a grand cultural jamboree sponsored by the Nigerian state, then flush with new oil revenues, which was intended to mold its diverse traditional cultures into a national culture and to proclaim Nigeria's standing among all people of African descent.[19]

Yet this event evoked protests, not merely for its extravagance and the corruption that it gave rise to but on religious grounds also, from both Muslim and Christian groups angry that the promotion of African culture should be the occasion for putting on performances that (as they argued) served to showcase idolatry.[20] That some Muslims were not happy with this is not surprising (for reasons shortly to be explored). What is more striking is the new indication of Christian estrangement from the cultural-nationalist project that mainstream clergy had had such a large part in shaping. This reaction against the trajectory of nearly a century was headed by the emerging Neo-Pentecostals: it was in protest against FESTAC that Pastor E. A. Adeboye's Christ the Redeemer Ministry—now a core agency of RCCG—was born.[21] This was the first public showing of not so much a new attitude as the revival of the old strategy of demonizing, rather than desacralizing, what was left of the old religion. Thus it came about that the new movements in both Christianity and Islam found common cause in a postnationalist cultural agenda, though their prescriptions for what should replace it were deeply at variance with each other.

ISLAM: FROM THE LOCAL TO THE UNIVERSAL

So what had meanwhile been going on in Yoruba Islam? The first thing to note is how relatively unengaged it was either with colonialism or with the nationalist reaction to it. Although colonialism had created conditions for the massive expansion of Yoruba Islam in the early decades of the twentieth century, it was never symbolically associated with it in the way that Christianity was, as the religion of the *oyinbo* (white man). But neither was it intrinsically hostile to it, as much Muslim opinion in Northern Nigeria was. That is not surprising, since there the British had overthrown an Islamic state and, as many saw it, subjected Muslims to the shameful and unnatural condition of being ruled by *Nasarawa* (Christians).[22] As a result, radical nationalists in the North, like Sa'adu Zungur, critical of the way the British had co-opted the emirate structure, were well able to ground both their socialism and their nationalism in their Islam.[23] It is illuminating to draw a contrast here between Sa'adu Zungur and Adegoke Adelabu of Ibadan: both Muslims, both professed socialists, and both affiliated to the NCNC in opposition to the dominant parties in their own respective regions. But Adelabu, though his populist Mabolaje Grand Alliance had its core support from Muslims and took on a certain local Muslim style, made no connection between his religion and his politics. In fact, in his robust exposition of his political credo, *Africa in Ebullition* (1952), he referred to his own Muslim identity as being "by chance," even as something he "deprecate[d] . . . more so when you import it into the political arena."[24] As Northern Muslims had a religious motive for nationalism that Yoruba Muslims lacked, so Yoruba Muslims did not have the motive for Africanizing their religion that Yoruba Christians did. We may even argue that if Africanization is parallel to nationalism, the dominant trend in Yoruba Islam was counternationalist since it was a movement away from the Africa-specific toward a more universalizing Islam. This trend had begun haltingly in the 1930s but accelerated in the late colonial period, and so the apparent step-change at the end of the 1970s did not come from nowhere.

A telling episode in this process occurred in the mid-1950s. It had become customary for the senior *alfa* of Ibadan to visit the *Olubadan* and chiefs annually on the tenth day of the month Muharram—Ileya, as the Yoruba call it—to pray for their welfare and to divine for the coming year. Rituals would be performed to help realize good predictions and avert bad ones; and afterward *saraa* would be given to the *alfa* to make a feast for their people. This was known as Gbigbohun-Tira (Listening to the Voice of Scripture).[25] Both in form and in function, it closely followed the model of a rite called Odifa-Odun (Casting Ifa for the New Year), which *babalawo* had used to perform. Controversy had raged among Muslim clerics since the 1930s about the legitimacy of this practice: Was it an idolatrous abuse of the sacred text of the Koran, or a justified expedient to replace Ifa with something more Islamic and to give a more Muslim face to public authority in Ibadan? The person who saved the *ulama* from further argument by abolishing the custom altogether was the first Christian to be elected *Olubadan* (1955–64), the ascetic I. B. Akinyele, who was also head of the Christ Apostolic Church. The irony of the situation was not lost on Shaykh Murtada, who celebrated his triumph in an Arabic poem he circulated to his colleagues: "You abused the book of Allah by taking it to a place filled with filth on all sides. . . . When the Christian among you ascended the throne, he removed from Islam some of its evils by saying, 'I don't want your book, my Christianity rejects it.' What sort of wonder [is this]?" His opponent, Ahmad al-Rufai, had cited a *hadith* in which the Prophet had backed some of his companions who had taken a sheep in payment for having given magicospiritual help to a pagan Arab chief: a once-cogent precedent that no longer had such force.

One thing that this episode highlights, when we set it alongside the treatment of Ifa in the Africanizing theology of this period, is how differently Islam and Christianity related themselves to this unique feature of Yoruba religion. Islam and Ifa went back a long time together in Yoruba history: indeed, I am persuaded by Louis Brenner's suggestion that Ifa actually arose as a Yoruba response to the stimulus of Islam, possibly as far back as the sixteenth century.[26] Thereafter, Ifa and Islamic divination existed in parallel; by the nineteenth century, their respective practitioners could actually cooperate with one another on difficult cases.[27] Christianity, of course, encountered Ifa only in the 1840s. The cognitive bridges that the two world religions respectively built between themselves and Ifa were very different. A Muslim legend of the origin of Ifa attributes it to one Setilu, who can be identified with Satih, a magician of pre-Islamic Arabia.[28] Ifa was thus set fully within an Arab-Islamic genealogy that carried the implication that it, like other works of pagan *jahiliyya,* must in due time be set aside for Islamic truth. By contrast, the Christian theology of Ifa, as proposed by a cultural nationalist like Lijadu (who actually went to the trouble of taking instruction from a *babalawo*), saw it as a partial revelation of God to the Yoruba, which could therefore serve as a *praeparatio evangelica,* a springboard into a distinctively Yoruba Christianity. This Christian invention of a continuity with something with which it had no prior historical links stands in contrast to Islam's insistence in principle on rupture from something with which it had a long historical relationship.

So some more Islamically self-conscious elements struggled—against the inclination of most ordinary Muslims, one has to say—to disown aspects of their own local past, to cast aside some of those syncretistic practices that had earlier given Islam an entry into Yoruba society. Increasingly the Middle East is looked to as a source of best practice, particularly by those of Salafist views. Among these, A.-R. Shittu drew an interesting contrast for me between the ways in which the two world religions had come to the Yoruba.[29] Christianity, he suggested, had come in a fairly pure form directly from its centers in places like Rome and Canterbury, but Islam had come through many African intermediaries, picking up a lot of *bid'a* (innovation) along the way.[30] Shittu's view of the history of Christianity is no doubt too generous, but it entails a characteristically Muslim perspective: that the movement away from the Arabian point of origin, which was equally temporal and spatial, unavoidably carried a declination from primordial truth. (We may note in passing how different Shittu's assessment of African Islam is from Blyden's, whose praise for Islam presupposed a quintessentially Christian view of the proper relationship between religion and culture.) So there is a logic to his argument, against mainstream Muslims who accuse him of wanting to import Saudi customs, that the Islam of its heartland in Saudi Arabia must be considered more nearly pure, less subject to *bid'a,* than the Islam of its spatial periphery.[31] This perspective was no doubt encouraged in the experience of Yoruba undertaking the *hajj,* whose numbers boomed in the 1950s, and again in the 1970s.[32]

The Middle East may be said to have first intervened directly and decisively in Yoruba Muslim affairs in the early 1970s. In 1970, the World Muslim League formally declared Ahmadiyya to be a non-Muslim organization, on the grounds that its founder, Ghulam Ahmad, had made claims about his inspired status that contradicted Mohammed's unique position as *Khatam an-Nabiyyin* (Seal of the Prophets).[33] This fed through to Nigeria by 1974, after the Saudi Arabian embassy announced it would no longer grant visas to Ahmadis wishing to undertake the *hajj.*[34] The Sultan of Sokoto—ever keen to burnish his credentials with the Saudi royal family and more than ready to fall in behind the Saudi initiative—called on all Nigerian Muslims to dissociate themselves from the Ahmadis. The impact of this fell almost exclusively on Yoruba Muslims, since Ahmadiyya's membership was virtually limited to Yorubaland. The most dramatic casualty was Professor I. A. B. Balogun—the doyen of Yoruba Arabists (with a doctorate from SOAS), imam of the UI mosque and an Ahmadi for forty years—who recanted after much soul searching. This caused consternation in Ahmadiyya ranks, since he took many others with him.[35] A large group seceded, calling themselves Anwar ul-Islam; nearly all the schools Ahmadiyya had founded were eventually lost to it; and though it has since been reorganized from its headquarters in Pakistan,[36] the moment has surely passed when Ahmadiyya made its most important contribution to the development of Yoruba Islam. Taken together, the pressure on local syncretisms like Gbigbohun-Tira and the expulsion of Ahmadiyya amount to a kind of pincer movement on the distinctively Yoruba expression of Islam, squeezing it at both the traditional and the modern end of its range in such a way as to move it overall closer to the orthodox Sunni mainstream and to reduce the differences between it and the Islam of Northern Nigeria. Ahmadiyya had been at the forefront of Yoruba Muslim modernity, but it had become by now rather an old-fashioned kind of modernity, once symbolized in the kind of formal dress that Ahmadi leaders had favored: a double-breasted suit with a red fez. Non-Ahmadi Muslims also resented a certain exclusiveness in Ahmadis, expressed in the feeling that they preferred to pray behind an Ahmadi imam. They also had a definite feel of the colonial period about them: politically they had been pro-British and strongly opposed to violent Islamic militancy. The *takfir* against them allowed other conceptions of Muslim modernity to come forward: more militant and assertive, and more in tune with contemporary currents in the wider world of Islam.

No Muslim organization registered these changes over the course of the 1970s so closely as the Muslim Students Society (MSS).[37] This had been founded in 1953 by a group of students attending various secondary schools in Lagos, led by a pupil at King's College, Abdul-Lateef Adegbite.[38] In its early years MSS—whose base would soon move to the universities—was mainly concerned with giving social support and promoting fellowship among Muslim students in institutions where they were massively outnumbered by Christians; but over time its focus shifted more toward the intersection of religion and politics. It changed its motto twice in its first twenty-five years: from its original "Peace, Love, and Community" to "Peace, Faith, and Brotherhood," and finally to the Kalimah itself, "There is no god but Allah. . . ." That sequence tells its own story: the development of a more defined and self-consciously orthodox Muslim identity. In 1969, over half the area chairmen of MSS had been Ahmadis (which is not at all surprising, granted their high level of education);[39] and one effect of the *takfir* had been to clear the way for a much more radically inclined leadership to take over. In the early 1980s, some MSS activists actually received paramilitary training in Libya—itself a token more of militancy than of orthodoxy.

This sharpening of Islamic identity went with a desire both to pull apart from some institutions in which Yoruba Muslims had joined with Christians (such as Boy Scouts and Girl Guides) and to establish closer ties with their Northern coreligionists. MSS, as a body originating in the Yoruba South, was at first regarded with reserve by Northern Muslims, though it made a point of appointing some emirs as patrons; and eventually it did establish itself firmly on Northern campuses. At a higher level, MSS's founder, by now Dr. Adegbite, was active in setting up the first all-Nigerian Muslim body, the Nigerian Supreme Council of Islamic Affairs (NSCIA).[40] This was triggered by the embarrassment felt by Nigerian Muslims at a conference in Libya in 1973, when there was no single national voice to speak for them. Dr. Adegbite took discreet soundings with the Sultan of Sokoto, who first suggested that Yoruba Muslims should simply join Jama'atu Nasril Islam (JNI: "Society for the Victory of Islam"), which had been set up in 1962 in the context of the Sardauna's Islamization campaigns in the North. Adegbite advised against this: he must have known very well how it would have played in places like Ikorodu and Ijebu-jesha. Even as it was, the sultan became president of the NSCIA and an official of JNI; his close relative Ibrahim Dasuki (later sultan himself) became its secretary-general, and Adegbite had to settle for the post of legal advisor. This was undoubtedly humiliating, and it amply confirmed suspicions that Northern Muslims regarded the Yoruba as very much their junior partners. It meshed with the stereotype, still widely current today though denied by some senior figures, that Hausa or Fulani Muslims are reluctant to pray behind a Yoruba imam.

Though Yoruba Muslims sometimes find the existence of their fellow Muslims in the North a useful counterweight to the influence of Yoruba Christians, their relationship with them is very ambivalent. It has surely worked toward a more uniform and presumptively more orthodox practice of Islam throughout Nigeria—though here Yoruba Muslims have sometimes been able to outflank the supposedly more correct Northerners. A perennially vexed issue has been over the fixing of the dates for key Islamic festivals—such as Ileya or Id al-Adha, the day of sacrifice at the end of the *hajj*—when the very strong normative ideal is that the whole *umma* should celebrate in unison.[41] Tradition dictates that the exact date should be fixed by sighting the new moon, and the sultan had a procedure that settled it for the Sokoto Caliphate—but it sometimes led to a celebration one day out from other parts of the Muslim world. Many Yoruba Muslims have argued for following the lead of the grand mufti of Mecca, thus enabling them to claim they are more universalist as Muslims than the Hausa-Fulani are. Some bold spirits, such as Professor Amidu Sanni, imam of the Lagos State University mosque, have gone so far as to argue that the sultan's claim to be regarded as the spiritual leader of Nigerian Muslims is un-Islamic because it depends on hereditary succession, which has no legitimacy in Sunni Islam.[42] This is rather an adroit strategy of Yoruba self-positioning as more Sunni than thou.

THE DIFFERENTIATION OF MUSLIM IDENTITY

The search of Yoruba Islam for a greater religious authenticity, which has led it over several decades both to sever itself from some of its distinctive local forms and to associate itself more closely with currents in the wider Islamic world, has made many individual Muslims want to present themselves more distinctly as Muslims within the community through the two main social indicators of personal status: dress and names. (These were, of course, precisely the same markers that James Johnson chose in the 1870s when he wanted Christian converts to show that they were Africans and not black Europeans.) This self-differentiation seems linked to other kinds of differentiation, actual or wished-for, that must tend to reduce the amount of symbolic commonality hitherto existing between Yoruba Muslims and Christians.

Dress. A generation ago, it was virtually impossible to distinguish people by religion in a Yoruba crowd, whether in a market or on a campus. Now it is much more common to be able to identify some people as Muslims, particularly women. Women in full black purdah (called *ẹlẹha* in Yoruba) are more often seen now, especially in the back quarters of towns like Ibadan. Once associated with traditionalist groups—such as Bamidele and Lanase's followers—that adopted it from pious circles in Ilorin or Hausaland, purdah is now encouraged by newer groups of Salafi or Deobandi views like Ahl us-Sunna or the fast growing Tablighi Jama'at, from Pakistan.[43] There is strong criticism of purdah from within the mainstream *ulama*, who in general are firmly opposed to it, for making Islam look alien and for impeding the activity of Yoruba women as traders, but it seems to be growing.

More novel is the wearing of indicative dress—*hijab* or full-length *jilbab*—by some Muslim women students on campus. A large notice-board authorized by the MSS outside the UI mosque proclaims: "O children of Adam! We have bestowed raiment upon you to cover the whole of your body and as an adornment and the raiment of righteousness" (Q. 7:26). Women so dressed, at least at the University of Lagos, are (or were) liable to have *Sharia!* shouted derisively at them by male students.[44] The comportment of women students can be controversial within the Muslim community: a few years ago, some particularly ardent female Salafists at UI adopted the practice of sitting sideways at their desks during lectures so as to avoid making eye contact with their male professors—and were robustly criticized for so doing by the then–university imam, Dr. D. A. Tijani, in a Friday sermon. Whether such displays are due to a desire to follow Sharia strictly or to a more general wish to declare Muslim identity in public is a moot point. Certainly the adoption of *hijab* as part of the school uniform for girls in Islamic primary schools, which is quite common, has to be seen as the latter, since the Sharia is concerned only with what adult or adolescent women should wear.

As regards male dress, there were always some discreet indicators of Muslim identity, such as the wearing of white embroidered caps, and recent changes in appearance (such as the untrimmed beards sported by some Ahl us-Sunna members) have been less conspicuous than in the case of women. A couple of high-profile instances are more notable for what they tell us about Christian attitudes toward Muslims' wearing un-Yoruba dress. As early as the 1950s, Awolowo is said to have rebuked the *Alafin* of Oyo for attending a meeting of *ọba*s wearing an Arab headdress—he had just returned from Mecca as an *alhaji*—rather than the customary beaded cap. A rather similar incident occurred between Awo's political son, Bola Ige, and the then-leader of the MSS, K. K. Oloso, at a stormy meeting in 1981 over alleged pro-Christian bias in the Oyo state governor's educational policies. Ige insultingly called Oloso an *ọmọ-ale* (bastard) for wearing a long Arab gown; to this Oloso smartly retorted, "Who is more of a bastard?" pointing out, to the cheers of his followers, that Ige was wearing a smart French suit.[45]

There are complex and interesting questions about the evolution of Yoruba dress to be considered here. Many if not most kinds of dress that Yoruba now wear were introduced through distinctively Muslim or Christian channels and were likely at first to be seen as religious identity markers, though this was not inevitably the case. What is now regarded as *the* Yoruba man's dress—the gown with voluminous open sleeves (*agbada*), usually hitched up onto the shoulders, embroidered at the neck, worn with a long-sleeved blouse (*buba*), loose trousers (*ṣokoto*), and some kind of cap—is essentially of Northern Muslim origin. As late as the 1880s, it was not worn by local people in southeastern areas like Ondo, where Islam had no presence. A European missionary at Abeokuta may have been referring to its adoption when he wrote in 1847 that "Mahomedan costume is become very fashionable with the young and gay," adding that it "is by no means put on as a religious peculiarity."[46] Like many other items or concepts introduced from the Muslim North, this costume rapidly lost what connotations of Islam it originally possessed and passed into the religiously unmarked cultural repertoire of the Yoruba. The same happened with the European dress—shirts and trousers; suits for the wealthier—that once proclaimed Christians as such (and that James Johnson excoriated as culturally alien).[47] From our present perspective, two broad distinctions have emerged in how the Yoruba classify dress: between African or traditional and international or modern styles; and between dress that expresses religious identity and whatever is religiously unmarked. As regards the first, the two dress styles have virtually lost all the religious connotations, respectively Muslim and Christian, that they once had: Muslim bankers wear suits and ties like other bankers, whereas traditional dress is obligatory at weddings and funerals (and, since nationalism, for politicians at public events)—as well as for *ọba*s and chiefs. In general, educational settings require religiously unmarked modern dress, especially for the young, though (as noted above) some Muslim women now advertise their faith by their dress. As regards the second style, apart from the professional dress of clergymen, nearly all religiously marked dress is worn by Muslims, whereas Christians appear as Yoruba unmarked by religious difference (with, I think, the single exception of White-garment Aladuras on their way to church, when they actually look a bit like some Muslims).

It must be stressed that these distinctions are flexible and contested as regards their specific content: the value or meaning attached to a particular item of dress may change. So in the Ige-Oloso confrontation referred to above, Oloso surely intended a strong statement of his Muslim identity by wearing the Arab-style gown, just as the *Alafin* meant to express his pride as a new *alhaji*—though here I presume with no combative intention—by wearing an Arab headdress at the meeting of traditional rulers with Awolowo. Yet something like the gown seen as Islamic when worn by Oloso in 1981—a straight, long-sleeved gown or caftan, reaching down to just above the ankles, worn with trousers underneath (sometimes known by the Hausa name *dandogo*) has since then come into fairly general use and may be worn instead of the *agbada* for occasions like going to church. Thus, it has lost its religious marking and become traditional or African, whereas other items—like the Arab headdress and the turban—have retained their Islamic character. In effect, then, it seems to have been Christians whose decision to adopt an originally Islamic dress item as theirs too makes it generically Yoruba. As in other spheres, they have fallen into the role of being the principal arbiters of what counts as general Yoruba culture. No doubt this is what lay behind Awolowo's reprimand of the *Alafin:* an *ọba,* of all people, should be the complete embodiment of Yoruba tradition and not express a religiously partisan identity at an official meeting.

Names. The choice of personal names—between European and Yoruba—was the other key focus of cultural self-reproach by Christian radicals in the 1870s. Who could consider somebody called Thomas Babington Macaulay or Joseph Pythagoras Haastrup to be a proper African?[48] The pressure among Christians for Yoruba names to be given in baptism built up over many decades to the point that today, in any list of names (e.g., a student class list or an electoral register), the religiously unmarked (i.e., purely Yoruba) names will in the great majority of cases be those of Christians. Virtually all Muslims have a distinctively Muslim name (though most have Yoruba surnames) and are more likely to be known by it. A Muslim woman friend of mine now in her forties—let me call her Sidikat—told me that while she was a student she was more than once asked (often with a note of reproach) by Christian fellow students why she didn't use a Yoruba name like Aduke or Funmi. It is not surprising that Muslim politicians often prefer to use a Yoruba forename rather than a Muslim one—for example, Bola, rather than Ahmed, Tinubu—as they must appeal to a cross-religious public; and to use Yoruba versions of Muslim names (e.g., Lamidi or even just Lam for Abdul-Hamid; Lasisi for Abdul-Aziz). These differences—with Christians more likely to present themselves as plain Yoruba, whereas Muslims are more likely to advertise their religion in their preferred names—do not indicate any difference in the intensity of personal belief but are the outcomes of the cultural logics of the two faiths.

Religious language. Here we find the same logic at work as with dress and personal names, with the Christian adoption of a great deal of the religious terminology of Arabic derivation already in use among Muslims. Some of this had already lost its religious marking by the nineteenth century: words such as *alafia* (peace, well-being) or *anu* (mercy). Some other words with a more definite religious content, like *alufa* (pastor, priest), *adura* (prayer), *woli* (prophet), *iwasu* (sermon) were soon naturalized as Christian terms, chiefly at the instance of Bishop Crowther, the principal translator of the Yoruba Bible. It seems reasonable to assume that the orthography he adopted in writing these terms comes close to expressing their actual phonetic values in nineteenth-century Yoruba speech—for example, as regards the insertion of the *u* in *alufa,* or the *r* in *adura.* Of the various names and epithets of God that were current in the nineteenth century, *Ọlọrun* (Lord of Heaven) was by far the preferred vernacular term among Muslims and was adopted without question by Christians, thus providing a common linguistic reference point for people of all faiths.

Subsequently there has been some movement of linguistic self-differentiation in Yoruba Islam. An interesting case is the use of *waasi* instead of *iwasu* for "sermon," which is a shift to a Hausa form from the ancient and original Malian or Songhai-derived word (both deriving from the Arabic *wa'z*).[49] It seems most likely that this occurred as a spontaneous effect of the growing links between Yoruba and Hausa Muslims that occurred in the late nineteenth and the early twentieth century rather than as a conscious attempt to differentiate Islam from Christianity. However that may be, its effect was to leave the old Muslim word as a Christian word. For "Muslim cleric," *alfa* (or sometimes phonetically closer to popular speech, *afaa*) has long been the preferred usage, thus differentiated from *alufa,* "Christian clergyman."

Two other shifts can be pinpointed more exactly to a new translation of the Koran published in 1977 under the auspices of the World Muslim League—made by a committee of senior *ulama* including Shaykh Adam al-Ilori—that has become in effect the "authorized version" for Yoruba Muslims.[50] One is a very slight shift toward Arabic usage: for example, *adua* rather than *adura* for "prayer." The other is equally slight phonetically but more telling in intention and potentially more momentous in effect: the substitution of *Ọlọhun* for *Ọlọrun* as the preferred Muslim rendition of "God." This hardly registers in speech at all, since *h* is barely aspirated and *r* is rolled only lightly in Yoruba—both forms sound pretty much like *Ọlọ'un*—but in a text, like the *Nasfat Prayer Book,* the difference strikes the eye. A brief explanation of the change is given in the preface of the 1977 translation. *Ọlọrun* is said to be unacceptable because it literally means "the one who owns heaven only but [by implication] not the earth" (*ẹniti o ni ọrun nikan ko si ni aiye*). *Ọlọhun* is glossed as *ẹniti o ni ọhun lori ẹnikẹni* (the one who has *ọhun* over anyone), which is claimed to be the equivalent of the Arabic Allahu or Allahuma (O God!). But what does *ọhun* mean?[51] Not a word in very common use, it connotes "taboo" or "forbidden thing," as in the phrase *o ti j'ọhun* ("he has done something he shouldn't" or "he has incurred a penalty"). Evidently al-Ilori, as the leading translator, meant to convey by *Ọlọhun* something like "the one who has the right to possession or obedience." Abubakre thinks it possible that *ọhun* may also have some of the connotations of the Arabic concept of *haram* (forbidden, but with the sense "holy" or "revered" when applied to God, like *sacer* in Latin) but still concludes that *Ọlọhun* is "a rare and difficult word formation" in Yoruba. Despite the semiofficial status of the translation proposed by al-Ilori, many Yoruba Muslims—whether literate in Arabic or not—still use *Ọlọrun* or else are inclined to provide their own etymologies for the difficult neologism. I once heard a preacher at a NASFAT Asalatu service explain *Ọlọhun* by deriving it from *olohun-gbogbo* (owner of all things), which he claimed to be the equivalent of the Arabic phrase *Rabi'l-'alamin* (Lord of all created beings) at Q. 1:2. This may be theologically sound, but it makes no etymological sense in Yoruba.

But perhaps more significant than this small step away from the religious lexicon common to Yoruba of all faiths is the decision that al-Ilori and his fellow translators did *not* take: to decline to translate *Allah* at all and instead to introduce the Arabic name of God into the Yoruba text. In fact, two other Muslim translations have done just this: one brought out by Ahmadiyya in 1976, and one published by Professor Y. A. Quadri in 1997.[52] In principle, that might have been the first step toward naturalizing *Allah* as the Yoruba name for the Supreme Being among Muslims, as has happened in Hausa, Fulfulde, Mande, and the languages of other peoples long established as Muslim (but notably not in Swahili), though that outcome is now effectively ruled out by the fact that so many Yoruba are Christian. The name *Allah* (in phonetic Yoruba form *Aala*) was not novel in Yoruba oral texts: it occurs not only in the popular Muslim devotional songs called *waka* but even in some Ifa divination verses.[53] Granted this background, the decision not to use the word *Allah* for God has to be seen as highly deliberate. It is as if al-Ilori (who was always concerned to balance his Islamic with his Yoruba loyalties) wanted to set a limit to how far Yoruba Islam should distance itself from what was common, established, and characteristic in Yoruba culture. There was a danger in allowing Christians to take exclusive possession of the name that Yoruba had always applied to God. So I interpret the adoption of *Ọlọhun,* which sounds less different from *Ọlọrun* than it looks, as a carefully calibrated way of correcting but yet retaining the age-old Yoruba designation of God.

SHARIA AND COMMUNITY

Potentially the farthest-reaching instance of the Muslim assertion of difference from common Yorubaness lies in the demand for Sharia. When the issue of Sharia came up in the constitutional assembly in 1977–78, Yoruba Muslims had had very limited experience of it, since the British had squashed the few incipient moves toward it early in the colonial period and required Yoruba of all faiths to live together under the same native law and custom.[54] The issue was reignited in 1999–2000, when twelve Northern States decided to adopt Sharia for criminal as well as civil cases.[55] What first became clear in 1977 and has continued to be the case ever since is that whereas most of the formal Muslim leadership, whether lay intellectuals like Adegbite or Shittu, or Muslim titleholders like Arisekola, or leading members of the *ulama,* profess themselves to be strongly in favor of Sharia, the mass of ordinary lay Muslims (including those who are traditional rulers or politicians) are far from enthusiastic about it. It is not hard to see why. The introduction of full Sharia in the North, although it generated much tension and (in some places, like Kaduna) violence, was at least in a region where religious and ethnic differences already tended to coincide, so that what Sharia implied was a deeper Islamization of groups that were already Muslim, leaving non-Islamic groups to their own legal devices (at least in theory). In Yorubaland, however, where not just all communities but also many families are mixed in religion, the notion of a separate law for Muslims must have an ominous potential to divide the community at all levels. I simply cannot see Sharia being generally implemented in Yorubaland in the foreseeable future, and I suspect that most of its advocates do not either.

Yet there is a substantial continuing literature—petitions, articles, books—in which the themes of the late 1970s are reiterated three decades later.[56] It is passionate but little focused on what the implementation of Sharia would mean concretely in the Yoruba situation, on such issues as exactly how far Sharia law would extend, what its effects would be on the integration of local communities, how a law supposed to apply only to Muslims could be made work for religiously mixed families, how to reconcile the Christian population to its introduction, and perhaps even more important, how to deal with the reservations of reluctant Muslims, some of whose freedoms would be curtailed by it. The arguments for it are typically very general, pitched at the level of high religious principle:[57]

> Sharia is such a concomitant of Islam that to deny access to it is to infringe on [a Muslim's] right to freedom of worship. This is because Islam is not just a set of rituals but a complete way of life. . . . Unlike other faiths, Islam provides for its adherents' guidance in all aspects of human behaviour and obliges them to strictly follow that guidance. . . . Sharia is to a Muslim like a soul to a body.

This view is couched in such a way as to make it hard for Muslims to oppose the implementation of Sharia without opening themselves to the danger of *takfir*, of being declared not to be real Muslims—or of being, as one Ahl us-Sunna activist put it to me, referring scornfully to a leading Muslim politician in Lagos State, half Muslim and half Christian, which in his view was no Muslim at all. In fact, this kind of Sharia advocacy has little to do with Christianity and everything to do with trying to enlist the help of the state in the continuing campaign by rigorist Muslims, both lay and clerical, to put pressure on their more easygoing coreligionists to adopt a more complete and (as they see it) correct practice of Islam.

The notion of Islam as a complete way of life presents a fundamental challenge to the way that most ordinary Yoruba Muslims have viewed the relationship between their religion and their culture. There are many popular sayings along the lines of:[58]

> I will practice my traditional rites [*oro ile mi,* literally "the custom of my house"]. Christianity will not stop me, Islam will not stop me, from practicing my traditional rites;

or

> When a Muslim is not hungry, he says he won't eat monkey flesh [a Muslim dietary taboo]. When Sule is hungry, he'll eat colobus monkey.

Since such attitudes, however much they obtain in practice, are not easy for Muslims to assert as the basis for open opposition to Sharia, there is instead much dissembling and foot-dragging. As the strongly pro-Sharia author of a Ph.D. thesis ruefully commented on the respondents in a survey he had conducted:[59]

> Some Muslims were hypocritical in their opinions. They seemed to be sceptical . . . on [the] re-establishment of Sharia in southern part of Nigeria. Although they hypocritically supported its re-establishment, it seemed they cherished and professed the Western system, but pretended to us . . .

In the absence of any articulated opposition to the implementation of Sharia on Muslim grounds—if that were possible—especially by recognized Muslim leaders, we find two ways of reconciling commitment in principle with the recognition of practical impossibility. One is to treat it simply as a very long-term objective, as I found in talking to a group of MSS activists, all vehement supporters of what had been done in Northern Nigeria. For the shorter term, they also had ideas about trying it out on a small scale, by doing a sort of *hijra* and establishing small-scale communities where Muslims might realize the ideal of a common life lived according to Sharia.[60] Another, more concrete but strictly limited experiment is the Islamic court set up under the auspices of the League of Imams and Alfas at Ibadan Central Mosque, where on a voluntary basis Muslims may submit cases for adjudication under Sharia, mostly concerning domestic issues.

The other approach is to argue that what is needed and can be realized in Southern Nigeria is a Sharia of the soul. This was expounded to me by Alhaji Abdullahi Akinbode, the Chief Missioner of NASFAT:[61]

> If there is no institutionalized Sharia, [there can still be] personalized Sharia. If men are good, there is no need for the state to intervene. Let us make ourselves perfect. . . . You can be policeman of your own soul . . . we concentrate on the soul . . . [and seek to build] a disciplined personality rather than the disciplined state.

This would seem to fit well with the experience of NASFAT's core constituency, educated Muslims who work alongside Christian colleagues in the modern commercial sector, who can appreciate the sheer unviability of having a separate legal sphere for Muslim Yoruba. The ideal of personal piety expressed here also seems to have a definite affinity with the outlook of many born-again Christians, especially those of a holiness tendency.

So Muslims' attitudes on the proper relation between their religion and Yoruba culture cover a wide spectrum, as can be seen from the views of two prominent figures who stand at either end of it. They are Chief Lanrewaju Adepoju, a famous poet in the Yoruba language and now a Muslim of strongly Salafist views, and the *Alafin* of Oyo, the most senior-ranking *oba* to be a Muslim. They used to be friends but are now bitter enemies over this very issue.

Adepoju is an entirely self-taught man who achieved renown in the 1960s for his practice of a kind of satirical poetry called *ewi*.[62] He had his own radio program for many years and earned the sobriquet *ọjọgbọn elewi* ("professor" or "the wisest" of *ewi* poets). He was born a Muslim to poor parents in one of Ibadan's farm villages but had no Koranic education and was not religiously observant. For a number of years, indeed, he became a sort of freethinking Christian and was drawn into some cultic activities that he later strongly repudiated. Eventually, after reading a biography of the Prophet Mohammed that he came across in an Islamic bookshop in London,[63] he returned to Islam, espousing a rigorously Salafist position and founding the Universal Muslim Brotherhood, which is part of the Ahl us-Sunna grouping. In his compound in Ibadan he has built a tiny mosque, complete with a minaret, next to his recording studio; his wives now go about as black-veiled *ẹlẹha;* and in his study he has many works of *tafsir* and entire sets of *hadith.* Adepoju insists that there is much more to Islam than just the Five Pillars, since it also requires "complete adherence to the Sunna of the Prophet" as evidenced in the *hadith.* Since for him Islam "is a complete way of life and itself a culture," even the question of a relationship with Yoruba culture seems to be theoretically precluded: it is simply a question of Yoruba Muslims' adopting the supposedly complete culture of Islam. So in interview I did not find it easy to get Adepoju to specify how Yoruba values might contribute positively to a Yoruba expression of Islam—"respect for elders," he eventually conceded. Instead, he was entirely concerned to stress how he had "broken from his ugly past" (sounding for a moment a bit like a born-again Christian). So he was vehement about what he called the "ugly aspects of Yoruba culture," such as its funeral customs and cult practices, and denounced those whom he regarded as nominal and syncretistic Muslims, such as charm-making *alfa* and Tijaniyya adherents. In 1995, after a confrontation between Muslims and traditionalists over the conduct of the Oro festival at Oyo, Adepoju circulated an *ewi* on audio cassette that abused the *Alafin* by calling him *ọba keferi* (pagan king).[64]

Now, *ọba*s are at the center of these culture wars, for they are the embodied symbols of the unity and integrity of their communities and are thus expected, whatever their personal beliefs, to sponsor and patronize all forms of locally recognized religion as contributing to the welfare of the town. This norm has been somewhat eroded since the 1950s, both through *ọba*s' refusing to take part in rituals they personally find offensive and through pressure on them from religiously motivated outsiders. This has come from both Christians and Muslims, such as on the one side *Olubadan* Akinyele, who (before he discontinued Gbigbohun-Tira) had upon promotion to the title of *Balogun* refused to propitiate the war staff with the usual blood sacrifices, or on the other, the *Awujalẹ* of Ijebu, the Muslim Sikiru Adetona, who from early in his long reign, in the 1960s, has refused to participate in the annual Agemo festival, the major integrative ritual of the Ijebu Kingdom.[65] There has even come into existence an Association of Born-Again Christian Obas, which functions as a pressure and support group for rulers who want to pick and choose what rituals they engage in, sometimes against the wishes of their subjects.[66] Another Muslim *ọba,* the *Ataọja* of Oshogbo (where the famous riverside shrine of the goddess Osun now has the status of a UNESCO World Heritage Site and is a potential tourist attraction), complains about the persistent nagging of the late Dr. Lateef Adegbite, who was "always in palaces . . . challenging the souls of rulers . . . he would want me to move 100% towards Islam . . . he [was] always saying, *Kabiyesi, ṣẹ̀ gbọ mi na o?* [Your majesty, are you *really* listening to me?]."[67] Yet, he adds, "it is not easy to divorce ourselves from our tradition, anyone who tries it will run into trouble." So the old expectations about *ọbas* have by no means lost all their power, and nowhere more than at Oyo, for all that it is now a predominantly Muslim town.

Alhaji Lamidi Adeyemi III, the *Alafin* of Oyo, is a genial and widely respected *ọba*, and at least a third-generation Muslim (in fact the son of that *Alafin* whom Chief Awolowo reprimanded for his lack of royal dress sense).[68] He is also regarded as the earthly successor to Sango, the thunder god, whose cult is central to Oyo kingship. Well practiced in expounding Oyo history and culture to visitors, he was not at all fazed or embarrassed when I asked him how he reconciled the discharge of his traditional duties with his personal identity as a Muslim. He did it by means of an ingenious two-way assimilation between Islam and Yoruba culture. First, he read Islam a long way back into Oyo history, maintaining that even Sango, deified after his death for his magical powers, had been a Muslim and was actually given the epithet *Akewugbẹru* (One given a slave for reciting the Koran).[69] At the same time, he interpreted Islamic conversion as an expedient policy of self-protection against the Fulani jihadists that at the same time allowed it to be subordinated to Yoruba values: "The Yoruba never allowed other religions to destroy their identity." The *Alafin*'s vision of Yoruba history, in fact, has more in common with the Rev. Samuel Johnson's than with Shaykh Adam al-Ilori's, and his response to my question on the Sharia issue was robust and indignant:

> Is [Sharia] practical? Is it fair? . . . [Its effect on the Yoruba would be] to enslave their mentality, to bar their values and make them lose their identity. Yoruba is a nation, not a tribe, a nation!

Of Dr. Adegbite he was frankly dismissive, and as for Chief Adepoju, when I gingerly brought up his name, "he is like a bat [an ambiguous, ill-omened animal] dangling between two cultures." The *Alafin*'s old-fashioned view as to the religious obligations of an *ọba* may be under pressure from the assertiveness of the new movements in Islam and Christianity, but it still has widespread popular support.

IMALE *NO LONGER?*

There is now a widespread sentiment among Yoruba Muslims that the term *Imale* should be abandoned and replaced by *Musulumi*. *Imale* was a designation given them early in their history by the mass of non-Muslim Yoruba, who chose to identify them by where the bearers of their religion had come from. Islam is a religion that was first proudly named as such by itself (or by its Prophet)—unlike Christianity, whose adherents were first named "Christians" by critical outsiders.[70] The motive of Yoruba Muslims for wanting to change the name by which they have been commonly known for centuries is understandable. They want to declare their identification with the worldwide *umma* of Muslims, not to bear a name that seems to tie them into a local and particular history. Yet it is surely to be hoped, particularly at the present juncture in relations between Islam and Christianity in Nigeria, that Yoruba Muslims do not at the same time abandon certain values associated with the "Imale tradition."

Here we may contrast two main ways in which Islam has sought to realize itself in West African history, each with its distinctive bearers, social forms, and doctrinal rationale. The first is jihadist, its prime instance being the movement led by a Fulani cleric, Usman dan Fodio, in the first decade of the nineteenth century, which led to the establishment of an Islamic state, the Sokoto Caliphate. There have been other such movements both before and since, but none was as enduring in its effects as this one, not least because of the co-optation of so much of it—its system of emirates with their attendant Islamic culture—by the British as the basis of their regime in Northern Nigeria. So it was that a baneful heritage—the use of violence in the name of Islam to establish a "just" social order, and the intimidation, subordination, enslavement, or exclusion of all sorts of religious other (the wrong kinds of Muslim, pagans, and Christians)—was perpetuated, thus bedeviling Nigerian politics down to the present.[71] Boko Haram, even though the vast majority of Muslims in Northern Nigeria no doubt disown it, is only the latest, most extreme outcome of this tradition. After all, its yearning for an exclusively Islamic political space under Sharia law is an ideal shared by many respectable Muslims, at least in the North; and though it is set apart from them by its readiness to use violence to achieve this end, it can still invoke the most irrefragable of precedents for that line of action in the jihad launched by Usman dan Fodio two centuries ago.

Very different is another kind of Islamic tradition, which has been termed Suwarian. As far as the name goes, it is a scholarly artifact and would not find any recognition as such in Nigeria, though it perfectly fits the outlook of the Yoruba *Imale*. Appropriately, the name comes from a Malian cleric of circa 1500, Al-Hajj Salim Suwari, who articulated a doctrinal rationale for a peaceable and non-hegemonic Islam. He argued that it was legitimate for Muslims to live under non-Muslim rule provided that they were not impeded in the practice of their faith and that it was by their moral example, not by violence, that they should promote it; for "it was not the responsibility of the faithful to decide when ignorance [*jahiliyya*] should give way to belief."[72] This tradition was originally associated with the social situation of Mande-speaking traders operating in non-Muslim areas, as was also the case with the *Imale*, who brought Islam to the Yoruba in the first place.

But the tradition has contemporary relevance in offering a model for the coexistence of Muslims with other faiths in religiously plural societies. Crucial to it is the presumption of a shared public sphere that is neutral, as between the competing world faiths, yet is also valued by each for providing sufficient conditions for its unimpeded practice. This was guaranteed in Yorubaland by the institution of *ọba*ship, the symbol of community values that were anterior to both world faiths; and this is what, at the national level, Nigeria has failed to develop after more than half a century of independence. Indeed, such a development was set back by the unilateral adoption of Sharia law in a third of its thirty-six states, spread across the high North, in 1999–2000. Behind this Islamization of the public sphere lies a yearning to realize as much as possible Usman dan Fodio's ideal of a *Dar al-Islam* or House of Islam, in which the adherents of other religions exist on the sufferance of a Muslim majority—in effect as a kind of *dhimmi* (protected non-Muslim).[73] The result is that Nigeria has gone a long way toward becoming two different countries within one inadequately functioning state: the one religiously plural within a secular framework (as Nigeria's constitution proclaims it to be), the other an Islamic country. Yorubaland is firmly ensconced in the former sphere, though Yoruba Muslims are in the peculiar position that in principle they can operate in either. It says much that in a Northern city like Kaduna, where a large measure of religious segregation came about as the result of the post-Sharia riots in 2000 and 2002, it is virtually only Yoruba Muslims who are able to live safely in either the Muslim or the Christian/mixed districts of the city.[74] Their primary identity marker is then respectively either Muslim in a context of religious homogeneity or Yoruba in one of ethnic diversity.

Though the great majority of Yoruba Muslims realize that they are better off, whether personally or collectively, in the religiously plural contexts that they know from their home towns, a vocal and articulate minority of them would like to see Sharia introduced for Muslims, as it has been in much of the high North. The main arguments put forward in support of it are twofold. First, it is claimed that Sharia is both a right and an obligation for Muslims, since Islam offers a complete way of life, for which Sharia provides the template. This is aimed to gain support from reluctant Muslims. Second, it is claimed that Sharia affects *only* Muslims, which is intended to defuse the opposition of alarmed Christians. But these claims contradict each other. For insofar as Sharia is taken to offer a complete system of social regulation for Muslims, it is bound to include within its remit relations between people of different religions; and in its classical forms it did so from the perspective of an absolute Muslim hegemony. In practice, even in the partial forms in which it has so far been implemented in the twelve states of the high North, the freedoms of Christians have been curtailed in several ways.[75] Yet the most problematic feature of Sharia is not any specific provision that it has but its implication that each confessional community should have its own law—in the case of Muslims, one that is divinely mandated rather than humanly decided—instead of them agreeing together upon the laws under which all citizens will live together as members of one political community.[76] It is the old traditions of the *Imale*, not those of Sokoto Caliphate, that can give a measure of cultural underpinning for Nigeria to become a religiously plural and democratic society.[77]

9

A Century of Interplay Between Islam and Christianity

In this chapter I go further into the complex and ever-evolving patterns of cooperation and conflict, of resemblance and difference, between Yoruba Christians and Muslims.[1] There is no fixed correspondence between these two pairs of terms such that resemblance must go with cooperation and difference with conflict. Chapter 7 explored the evolution of a situation wherein potential differences between Christians and Muslims were mainly overridden by resemblances grounded in the primordial values of community. If Émile Durkheim was our theoretical guide there, in chapter 8 it was Max Weber, since its focus was on how differences arising from within each religious tradition can work to challenge and disrupt communal amity, though how far this potential is realized depends on many contingent factors. The two movements described in those two chapters can be seen as working against each other, but they do not stand in a dialectical relationship such as we can see in the Yoruba reception of Christianity—missionary preaching (thesis), the "pagan" African response (antithesis), African Christianity (synthesis)—since all the time they run concurrently. So does the third movement to be explored in this chapter, continuously intersecting with the other two, so that all three must be taken together. The complex of forces of attraction and repulsion that is the Yoruba religious field may thus be viewed from three different angles. Each hinges on a particular key factor—community values, the ideological thrust of the world religions, the pragmatic values imposed on religions as they compete for popular favor—that sets limits to the historical working out of the other factors.

What concerns us now is resemblance arising from conflict rather than conflict arising from difference. There are many forms of sociation, to use Georg Simmel's useful term, in which processes of conflictual or competitive interaction can produce this effect.[2] One example would be systems of warring states, particularly those within a common cultural zone like those of ancient Greece or precolonial Yorubaland, where emulation leads to the adoption of ideas or practices from one's rivals because they appear more attractive or effective. Another would be markets, particularly as regards the competition between producers to command market share. There are ambiguities here, since at some times commercial competition has been seen as antithetical to military conflict, whereas at others it has been seen as itself a nonviolent kind of warfare.[3] The religious competition that concerns us here resembles market competition rather than the outright religious war that tends to occur during periods of general social crisis, since as a routine activity it is culturally framed. In the present case, the framing is provided by Yoruba rules (which we saw affecting the general practice of Yoruba religion in chapter 7, above.) Their most significant feature is that they require the world religions to pursue their conversionary ambitions peaceably, before the court of Yoruba opinion. Islam and Christianity thus have to engage in a paradoxical double struggle: against each other to win converts, a struggle that impels them to make compromises with the ambient religious culture of the Yoruba; and against that same culture, as they strive to realize their own distinctive religious ideals. (See chapter 8.) The paradox has become even more acute since the 1980s, with the emergence of radical Islamic reformism and neo-Pentecostalism—both because they are more anxious to realize their own distinctive visions and because they are more driven by the pressure of competition to borrow from each other in order to win Yoruba favor.

Competition within a common framework creates homologies between entities that were previously more different, as with the use of a charged language of the conquest/annexation of the public space of Nigeria by the more militant forms of Islam and Christianity, or with the pattern of recurrent religious violence involving revenge attacks, such as has occurred in (say) Plateau State.[4] But the form of competition that is most relevant to the Yoruba context is that between rival producers to supply a market. This idea carries these principal implications:

1. The overall situation is plural: that is, one with a number of religious suppliers who have to compete—not by the direct exercise of power or force on one another but by attracting the favor of the members of a religious public.
2. The members of the religious public are like consumers, disposed and able to choose between the various religious options that the suppliers make available to them.
3. Religion itself tends to be viewed instrumentally, as providing gratifications of particular kinds that the members of the religious public will judge for themselves rather than as a system of pregiven ends that obviate the need for making religious choices.

4. While the pressure of competition to meet the demands of a particular market tends to encourage convergences between the suppliers, there is also a countertendency to product differentiation, creating niches wherein general competition is reduced.[5]

As a model for the interaction of religions, the market is one that many religions will be uneasy with and that probably no religion will find entirely acceptable. It is perhaps not surprising that in Yorubaland neither Christians nor Muslims are entirely happy to acknowledge the extent of the resultant mutual borrowing that has occurred. But of all faiths, born-again Christianity is perhaps most likely to find the market congenial, since it is itself the product of the most demanding religious marketplace in the world, the USA, from which it has adopted many techniques of self-promotion. Conversely, Islam would seem likely to be more resistant to the idea of a religious market than almost any other religion, since in its heyday (and in some mainly Muslim countries to this day) Islam was able to impose a social framework for its coexistence with other faiths, which deployed the severest sanctions against Muslims' converting to them.[6] Conversion, in Islam, was seen as strictly a one-way street. The fact that under Yoruba conditions two-way conversion between Islam and one or another faith has been common, with the *alfa* proving themselves to be highly effective religious entrepreneurs, has not erased the idea from the minds of quite a few Muslims that this is not, Islamically speaking, how things ought to be.

The notion of a religious marketplace does not merely prove useful as a model but has some anchorage within Yoruba culture. *Aiye l'ọja, ọrun n'ile* (The world is a market; heaven is home) runs a well-known adage. But this also serves to remind us of the countertruth that the idea of the market cannot encompass all aspects of the religious situation. Since *ọrun* (heaven) is the source of the Yoruba word for God (*Ọlọrun*), the adage implies that Yoruba religion is not *just* a pragmatic search for benefits but is also a place to feel at home. There is the further implication that religions are not infinitely flexible in their capacity to respond to market pressures. They also have a built-in inclination to strive to be true to themselves, or (in other words) to be constrained by their own ideally conceived pasts, as chapter 8 showed.

EARLY TWENTIETH CENTURY: MUSLIM-TO-CHRISTIAN INFLUENCES

For the first half-century of their coexistence, from the 1840s, Islam and Christianity seem to have little influenced each other. Each projected itself in its distinctive way, though the mass of Yoruba people, still unattached to either one, started to make comparisons in terms of their own criteria of religious value, which would in due course shape the interplay between them. It was not until the first decades of colonial rule, as the two faiths came more closely into contact, especially in Lagos, that a two-way influence between them showed itself. What Islam then started to adopt from Christianity was more external: Western-style schooling (the better to counter Christianity's educational advantages), something of its organizational forms, even the imitation of its impressive church buildings. From the 1920s there emerged a distinctively Yoruba style of mosque architecture in which Muslim liturgical requirements were reconciled with Christian architectural forms, such as Gothic windows, twin western towers, pillared naves, Brazilian-style decorative features.[7] This lasted till the 1980s, when what may be called an international Islamic style took over. The two styles can be seen almost side by side in Nnamdi Azikiwe Street in central Lagos, in the vast Central Mosque built in the 1980s, with its four lofty minarets disposed around a domed prayer hall, and the little Alli Oloko mosque, completed in 1931, whose two square towers make it look like a church.

But the Christian borrowings were more to do with the religious essentials, particularly with what might be learned from Islam about making prayer more effective for personal needs. Already in the 1890s, in a circle around the Rev. James Johnson, a number of younger clergy had started to learn Arabic in order the better to understand and counter Islam.[8] The most active of these were M. S. Cole, who later made the first Yoruba translation of the Koran, and T. A. J. Ogunbiyi, who wrote a number of pamphlets and tracts aimed at Muslims in English, Yoruba, or Arabic.[9] As a Lagos indigene and the son of a chief, Ogunbiyi seems to have been more active in taking steps to counter the popular appeal of Islam than any of his contemporaries.[10] We may well suppose that the example of the *hajj,* though very few Yoruba Muslims had then made it, influenced his decision to make a pilgrimage to the Holy Land in 1912, which caused a great stir—thus anticipating the many Yoruba Christians who nowadays make pilgrimages to Jerusalem. In 1908 there was a formal motion at the Anglican synod expressing concern about Islam's recent advances and speculating about the reasons for it;[11] but the most effective responses came spontaneously from the grass roots. It is significant that their crucibles were Lagos, where most missions had their headquarters but whose indigenous population had become predominantly Muslim; and Ijebu, which in the wake of its conquest by the British was the scene of a strong competitive surge of the two faiths. Among the Christian responses two stand out:

Powerful names of God. These have an indigenous source in the *oriki* or praise names of the deities, enumerating their powerful attributes, which were invoked to elicit their favor and support.[12] In traditional practice, they were much more commonly addressed to the *orișa* than to God. But the most immediate precedent was the Ninety-Nine Beautiful Names of God long established in Muslim devotion. Beginning with Rev. S. M. Abiodun's *Akojọ Orukọ Ọlọrun* (Collection of the Names of God, 1919), there was a flurry of little pamphlets over the next decade or so, such as J. O. Shopekan's *The English-Yoruba Dictionary of the Names of God* (which gives no less than 209 names) or Victor White's *The Elementary Names of God.*[13] The names are given in Yoruba and Hebrew (or apparent Hebrew), such as El-Shaddai, Yavah-Shammah, Eloi-Magen; and there is a lot of semantic overlap between the Yoruba epithets and the Yoruba renditions of the Arabic names used in Muslim prayer pamphlets down to this day, as with *Ọba Alagbara* (Mighty King) for *al-Aziz,* or *Ọba Olupese* (God the Provider) for *ar-Razaq.*[14] Shopekan also provides a weekly schedule for using the names, each one to be said three times at three regular prayer times each day (which suggests the influence of Islam's five canonical daily prayers). The invocations found their way into the little booklets of prayers for personal use that also appeared about this time, such as Ogunbiyi's *Adura Tetedamilohun* (Prayers for Quick Answers) or *Awọn Adura Banusọ ati ti Ọfọ* (Prayers for Private Use and Incantation). Here a prayer *fun wahala ẹjọ* (for legal troubles) is addressed to JAH-SHAFAT (= *Oluwa Onidajọ,* Lord of Judgment), and one for *ipọnjukipọnju* (every kind of need) addresses JAH-RAHAM (= *Oluwa Alanu,* Merciful Lord), perhaps with an echo of the invocation of God as *al-Rahman, al-Rahim* (The Merciful, the Compassionate) in the opening verse of the Koran. A positively rococo elaboration of this phenomenon was the seal names, or powerful invocations of God revealed in visions, which were a speciality of Prophet Ositelu's Church of the Lord (Aladura) in the early 1930s. Here we find unmistakable phonetic allusions to Arabic, as with *Ollahhummumjarrar* (which evokes *Allahumma,* O God) or *Arrabalhabad* (cf. *al-Rabb,* the Lord).[15] What is also paralleled in Islam, and particularly in the ritual practices of the Sufi brotherhoods, is the notion that there is special power or virtue in verbal formulas of praise of God (*wird*) that have been revealed to the Sufi *wali* (saint).[16]

Night vigils. People nowadays, when they want to exemplify the influence of born-again Christianity on Islam, will sometimes point to the latter's adoption of vigils or watch-night services. But this is almost certainly a case of a debt being repaid. The historical question that no one has ever thought to ask is: Where did night vigils in Nigeria's churches come from, since they were not part of the parent evangelical missionary tradition? I feel the answer probably lies in the first major Aladura church, the Cherubim and Seraphim, founded in central Lagos in 1925.[17] When I first saw their *ile adura* (house of prayer) at Oke Seni, in Ibadan, in 1964, I was very struck that inside it felt more like a mosque than a church: no chairs, white robes, removal of shoes and washing of feet on entry, full obeisance to the floor in prayer. Regular congregational services did not take place there but only individual prayers, as well as the climactic service of the week, a watch-night service of several hours over Saturday–Sunday. All this was said to follow the pattern set by the original Seraphim Society in Lagos. Now although there was no mission precedent for the idea that nocturnal prayer is particularly powerful, a form of optional prayer at dead of night called *tahajjud*—quite distinct from the five canonical daily prayers—is ancient in Islam and is recommended in several *hadith* as highly efficacious. But *tahajjud* is an individual, not a communal, form of prayer, so is it likely to have served as a model? Here it is pertinent, as I learned from two Muslim informants, that the first major modernist Muslim group, Ahmadiyya (which was brought to Lagos by missionaries from the Punjab in 1916),[18] introduced an innovation: to help one another realize the benefits of *tahajjud*, Ahmadis would go round in a group to other members' houses to wake them up in time to say the prayer, thus giving it a communal dimension. The adoption of a modified form of *tahajjud* fits the pattern of other Islamic borrowings by the Seraphim.

Perhaps the most surprising of all the cases of Muslim influence on an Aladura group concerns the former village theocracy known as the Holy Apostles of Aiyetoro among the Ilaje on the coast of far southeastern Yorubaland.[19] Founded in 1947, this was an offshoot of the Cherubim and Seraphim, which had spread eastward from Lagos along the lagoon in the late 1920s and early 1930s, taking on in many places the character of an antiwitchcraft movement. Aiyetoro was exceptional in that it practiced community of goods and the abrogation of normal residential patterns under the Spirit-led rule of a sacred *ọba*, which brought it to a high level of material prosperity. By the 1980s it had largely abandoned its "communist" features, though most of its religious practices were retained. The church's prophets speak in a form of tongues known as *ede ẹmi* (language of the spirit), which phonetically has an Arabic ring to it, and which is even referred to sometimes as *kewu* (to recite the Koran). Children's names are given through the dictation of the Spirit and include a number of Muslim ones: Sanni, Sadiku, Tawakalitu, Awawu, and so on. One of the community's founding elders was actually known as Baba Lemomu (Father Imam). The white costumes of the community's apostles and prophets, complete with turbans, have a distinct resemblance to those commonly worn by *alfa*. Burial usage diverges from Yoruba Christian norms, being notably low-key and rather like what reformist Muslims press for: plain, unmarked graves with no elaborate mourning. Yet paradoxically, the Islamic provenance of these traits is not perceived as such by the Holy Apostles. In fact, Ilaje has perhaps a lower proportion of local Muslims than anywhere else in Yorubaland, so these "Islamic" practices can hardly be a local adaptation. It is more likely that they arise from an accentuation of traits carried from the Seraphim source in Lagos, possibly enhanced by their passage along the lagoon, whose middle stretch is dominated by the strongly Muslim town of Epe.

ALADURA AND THE SUFI BROTHERHOODS

From the mid-1930s, for several decades, there was little fresh influence of Islam and Christianity on each other. After the turbulence of the Aladura revivals, a fairly stable religious dispensation came into being, wherein new developments were incremental rather than radical and came from within each religious tradition. I need to run over these briefly if we are to understand the religious terrain on which the forces of the last thirty years have impacted.

The Aladura movement consists of a large number of churches, many of them quite small, distributed between two poles or tendencies that can be called the White-garment and the Apostolic or Old-Pentecostal. The first group, so named from the white prayer gowns that they wear to church, employ expressive rituals of a more eclectic and homegrown quality, with (as I have noted) a distinct Islamic influence. It includes the Cherubim and Seraphim, Josiah Ositelu's Church of the Lord (Aladura), and from the late 1940s, the Celestial Church of Christ, which originated in the French colony of Dahomey and is today the most widespread and typical instance of the White-garment group. The other tendency has been more continuously influenced by Euro-American sectarianism, beginning with the ascetic Faith Tabernacle in the 1920s, followed by the Apostolic Church in the 1930s, which first introduced specifically Pentecostal teaching. The Christ Apostolic Church (CAC) is now the largest church of this group. From the 1950s, successive waves of Pentecostal influence came in, increasingly from the USA, and in the 1970s this tradition melded with a new movement of interdenominational evangelical piety that had emerged on university campuses.[20] Thus neo-Pentecostalism or born-again Christianity was formed, growing rapidly in strength against the background of the crisis of the Nigerian state in the 1980s. Though born-again Christianity has important Aladura roots—its biggest single body, the Redeemed Christian Church of God, is actually a much-transformed breakaway from one of the oldest Seraphim congregations in Lagos[21]—it has also tended to define itself against the Aladura, especially the Celestial Church of Christ, criticizing them for having allowed themselves to be corrupted by demonic influences.

There was initially no direct Muslim equivalent or response to Aladura. It did not seem that there needed to be, since the *alfa* were already deemed effective providers of healing, protection, and guidance.[22] But there are some parallels to be drawn between Aladura and a major element in Yoruba Islam that grew strongly at the end of the colonial period and into early independence: the Sufi brotherhoods, especially Tijaniyya.[23] Though these had adherents among the *ulama* from the end of the nineteenth century and by the 1930s could claim some senior figures, they were still very much limited to respected *alfa* and elders. Sufi esoteric knowledge was judged just too powerful for the *hoi polloi* and the young: "If a young man joined the *tariqa* [brotherhood], he would be loved by God, and this would cause his early death."[24] Only in the 1950s did a modified form of Tijaniyya, promoted by Shaykh Ibrahim Niass, from Kaolack in Senegal, become a mass movement among the Yoruba. This followed developments in Northern Nigeria, where Reformed Tijaniyya started to take off in the late 1940s.

In Ibadan, a key vector was Shehu Usman Lanase (d. 1954), who had returned as a young man from the Hausa town of Zaria.[25] He was a controversial figure, who fell out with the elders at the central mosque and seceded with his followers to establish his own *jumat* mosque at Aremo quarter, where he encouraged the mass of his followers to adhere to Reformed Tijaniyya. But the first major charismatic figure in the Ibadan Tijaniyya was Alhaji Shehu Ahmed, of the Bere quarter, right in the center of town, who had spent many years at Kaolack and married a daughter of Ibrahim Niass. By the early 1960s his claim to wield esoteric powers had drawn many to him—like ants around a cup of sugar, according to one witness—but eventually he got so out of hand that that he lost credit altogether.[26] The next major Tijani charismatic was a Hausa from Kano named Sani Awwal, also a son-in-law of Niass, who came to Ibadan, first to the Hausa quarter of Sabo; but finding Tijanniyya already well established there, he eventually settled at Madina, on the southern edge of Ibadan, a complex established by Alhaji Adebolu, a wealthy trader and zealous Muslim, not an *alfa* but still with a reputation for powerful prayer. He became Awwal's material patron, supporter, and friend: their tombs are now to be seen in adjacent rooms at Madina.[27] Adebolu even built a house for Shaykh Ibrahim Niass, who declared him to be his representative in Ibadan. Niass died in 1975, and when Awwal and Adebolu followed him a few years later, Madina's influence faded, and Ibadan lost what for two decades or so had been a mini-Mecca (or at least mini-Kaolack). Tijanniyya too has perhaps passed its apogee, though it remains an important presence in Muslim life in Ibadan.[28]

Tijanniyya is not so much an organization as a loose network of initiates, spiritual clientages of individual *muqaddams* (initiating masters, otherwise styled shaykhs) who trace their authority back through a chain of initiators to the founder. Some of these have a *zawiya* (lodge) where the initiates meet for their spiritual exercises, but in most cases in Ibadan Tijaniyya initiates simply attend their local mosque and perform these exercises together after routine Friday or evening prayers. Tijaniyya has no regular head in any town, though a particular shaykh may enjoy exceptional prestige and influence, as happened with Sani Awwal at Madina in the 1960s and 1970s. The perennial irony of Sufism is that what began as a search for a closer relationship with God, through ascetic disciplines leading to esoteric knowledge, was converted under the pressure of popular demand into an attributed mystical power that was available for all the usual mundane objectives of Yoruba devotion. What had been a technique of spiritual empowerment largely confined to the *ulama* acquired a mass character—appropriate to the age of nationalist mobilization in which it occurred—as a flood of lay initiates looked for material benefits from their masters. When Ibrahim Niass visited Ibadan around 1971–72 and attended Friday prayers at the central mosque, people are said to have fought one another—non-Muslims as well as Muslims—to capture some of the water from his ablutions, as a medium of his *baraka*. The source of this demand lay much more in Yoruba than in Islamic culture. It recalls nothing so much as the power attributed to the water blessed by Prophet Babalola in the Aladura revival of 1930–31, known as *omi iye* (water of life)—or, going further back, to the water of the river Ogun at Abeokuta sanctified by the prophetess Akere in 1855–56, which attracted large crowds over many months.[29]

In the 1980s, the Sufi brotherhoods came under sustained attack as a corruption of Islam. The onslaught came from various groups of Salafist inclination that are now grouped in a body calling itself Ahl us-Sunna (People of the Way [of the Prophet]). The main influences came from the growing number of graduates returned from Saudi universities and from Izala, the Northern organization directed to the eradication of *bid'a* (innovation).[30] A great many *alfa* in Ibadan have been initiated into Tijaniyya and even when they are not active any more in its collective exercises, they still see value in it and may still recite the *dhikr* (pl. *adhkar:* the verbal formulas of remembrance that are the substance of the ritual) privately for their own spiritual benefit. Apart from the ritual innovations that attract vehement condemnation from Salafists,[31] even mainstream *ulama* have reservations about several features of Tijaniyya that have a definite resemblance to what can be found in Aladura churches: extraordinary claims to charisma by some of its shaykhs, the demand for efficacious prayer and the performance of miracles, and the attainment of ecstatic states through its rituals. One educated cleric, who had been an active Tijani in his youth, told me he became deeply worried by the trancelike condition that the repetitive chanting of the *dhikr* induced among initiates. For him, this kind of ecstasy did not sit well with a proper conception of Muslim worship.

The treatment of the Sufi brotherhoods by Yoruba Muslim scholars is ambivalent. On one side, they have misgivings about the impact of popular demand on them:[32]

> Many people accepted the Shaykh [Ibrahim Niass] because they wanted to know God . . . some others accepted [him] in order to acquire *sirr* (secrets) about God's name which they wanted for efficacious prayers . . . others because they thought they would become rich . . . [who] were eventually disappointed. . . . The Shaykh used to discourage his followers from praying to God for material needs and advised them to render a selfless service to God.

On the other side, they are aware that the permeation of the religious life of the brotherhoods by these pragmatic values has served to attach people to Islam:[33]

> The Qadiriyyah clerics contributed in no small scale to the conversion of mysticism to local traditional practices . . . [as a result] the high ambitions of the classical Sufis have been watered down to a large extent. It however serves as a means to retain within the fold of Islam some converts who if failed by the Muslim clergy would not hesitate to seek aid even from heathen priests and may get attracted to other religions.

The unidentified competition alluded to here must have been mainly the Aladura. They and the Sufis did not so much imitate each other as draw each on its own tradition's resources to meet the same popular demand. The born-agains would present a more direct and formidable challenge.

The shift in the religious climate, as seen from a Salafist Muslim perspective, can be gauged from the successive introductions to a best-selling Muslim prayer manual, Abdul-Raheem Shittu's *Muslim Prayers for Everyday Success.*[34] In the first edition (1985), he wrote (p. 10):

> There is no doubt that in the last fifty years or so, a great majority of Muslims have fallen victim to the devilish antics of non-muslim spiritualists and jujumen such as 'Aladuras', Celestial Churches, 'Babalawos' and other magicians in their quest to solve the myriads of social, economic, matrimonial, spiritual and other problems which inevitably confront man in everyday life.

The opposition here is still seen as a mixture of Aladura-Christian and traditionalist agencies. In the preface to the fourth edition (2007), Shittu makes two points that show the current of things in the intervening two decades (p. 41):

> In contemporary times, one observes the evolution of many so-called 'Muslim Prayer Groups' in the name of *Alasalatu* and so on. It is unfortunate that when you watch what goes on in some of these prayer-sessions, there is hardly any difference between them and Christian Revival Services with the peculiar characteristics of singing, dancing, free-mixing between males and females, improper and inadequate covering of the *awra* or beautiful parts of the female participants and so on. These are all *Bid'a* and/or sins as Muslims are not permitted to copy Christians in their mode of prayers and other acts of worship.

Shittu also apologizes for some *bid'a* of his own in the earlier editions that he has now removed, namely "the interpolation of the names of certain evil Jinns with those of Allaah and His Prophet . . . and certain prayer-methods objectionable to the true spirit of Islam" (p. 34). It is noteworthy that, although he clearly sees the problem posed by Christian initiatives, Shittu refuses to respond by slavishly imitating them. Rather, he sees the only way forward as being to cleave even more strictly to prayer texts that are explicitly authorized in the Koran or in *hadith.* These are given in the Arabic original, in a roman transliteration of the Arabic, and in an English translation, but not in Yoruba. Supplicants without a serious command of Arabic (i.e., nearly everyone, including Shittu himself) thus have to select the text that addresses their problem from the English and to use the Arabic transliteration in uttering the prayer.

Here market behavior is limited by constraints arising from within the religion itself. The idea of prayer handbooks for people's quotidian practical use, written in Yoruba or English, was pioneered by Christians, in the form of little pamphlets like those written by T. A. J. Ogunbiyi and others before 1920. Over the years, these got more elaborate and at some point started being emulated by Muslims. Shittu found a niche in the market waiting to be filled. With its successive editions, his *Muslim Prayers for Everyday Success* got longer and longer, and it is now (at 482 pages) the most substantial such handbook in either religion that I have come across. But Shittu's increasingly Salafist views have set limits on how far he is prepared to supply people with what they want. He told me that he had turned down the request of a woman who had wanted him to reprint an earlier edition that had included a prayer invoking some powerful jinns, which she had found highly efficacious. His decision to stick to scriptural prayer texts in Arabic may perhaps have a declining appeal in a market wherein the educated urban young, in particular, are attracted to the prayer styles of Pentecostalism.

MUSLIM ENTREPRENEURS OF THE SPIRIT

One can hardly exaggerate the variety of products on offer in the Yoruba religious marketplace,[35] adapted to a range of tastes and different contexts—though what is common to most of them is their concern to offer spiritual solutions to people's mundane needs. For the last thirty years the flow of influence has definitely been from Christianity to Islam—yet though this has coincided with the rise of born-again Christianity, Aladura models are still widely emulated. It appears that the former appeal more to a younger, better-educated constituency, whereas the latter speak more to older, more traditional-minded people, particularly women. This has apparently been accompanied by a significant net flow of converts from Islam to Christianity, to which Muslims have responded, both "through the introduction of Islamic alternatives"[36] and through the direct but selective appropriation of Christian idioms and practices.

At the top of a dusty side street in Ibadan, I used to pass a tiny mosque—barely more than a room—though at first I thought it was a church of some kind, since it had a board outside announcing its services, which *ratibi* mosques in Ibadan do not usually have:

> Below a line of Arabic script, it announces itself as *Jamuiyatu Qudiratu Lilhai Fidini Isilamu,* a rough transliteration adjusted to Yoruba pronunciation of Congregation of the Power of God through the Muslim Religion, and under that, in Yoruba, as *Ijọ Ṣehu Fatai Agbara Ọlọrun Oṣupa Imọlẹ* (Church of Shehu Fatayi of the Power of God, Moon of Muslims). Below is a heading *Eto Isin* (Order of Service), a phrase normally used in Christian contexts at the top of the program for a funeral or commemorative event but here used to refer to the weekly services held at the mosque, which are then listed. Over Saturday night is *Aisun Adura* (Prayer Watch night); on Sunday morning is *Asalatu* (Public Prayer); on Friday late afternoon is a prayer session for pregnant women, and at Thursday noon is one for those seeking employment, children, or the like. There is no mention of the canonical prayers of Islam. The format of the services is what one might find in any small Aladura church, and (with the exception of

> the word *Asalatu*) the terminology and spelling used are Christian throughout (e.g., *aisun* rather than *tahajjud* for "watch night"). The Christian idiom of it all is not surprising, granted that Fatayi, the leader of the group, is a young man whose spiritual mentor was a prophet of the Celestial Church of Christ. He encouraged Fatayi by telling him of a vision that his little building would one day become a *jumat* mosque.

The active Christian input here is perhaps unusual, though it surely indicates the sense of common objectives, pursued within shared assumptions about the world of spirit, that underlies the religious quest of all Yoruba.[37] It shows that many Yoruba people, of either world faith, are perfectly ready to see divine power as manifesting itself through practitioners of the other one.[38]

Elsewhere, the adoption by Muslims of Christian, especially Aladura, models arises more spontaneously—as if they have become parts of a common Yoruba stock, just as over a century ago a significant part of the Muslim religious lexicon was adopted by Christianity. Moreover, this is facilitated by the fact that underlying it are templates for religious action derived from *orișa* religion (though this is something that neither Muslims nor Christians are very ready to admit).

A case in point is the Fadilullah Muslim Mission, founded in Osogbo by Alhaja Sheidat Mujidat Adeoye in 1997.[39] She was twenty-seven when one day at work—trading in rice and beans—she became possessed. Her shouts and screams subsided into a recital of *Lahi lah illah 'llah* (There is no god but Allah), and after regaining normal consciousness she fasted and prayed for seven days. Mujidat interpreted her experience as a sign from God to leave her trade and instead to pray and prophesy for those who came to her for help: women more than men, Muslims and non-Muslims alike. Her following grew to the point that she and her husband built a mosque (able to accommodate two thousand people) and engaged an imam to lead Friday prayers. But many of Fadilullah's ritual activities strongly resemble those of an Aladura church. Petitionary prayer (*adura* rather than *salat*) is the keynote of what Mujidat offers, whether on an individual basis or at prayer services that have lively choruses or in sustained cycles of prayer lasting seven, twenty-one, or forty-one days. Whereas Fatayi calls his Sunday-morning service *asalatu,* Mujidat gives hers the very Aladura-sounding name of *Adura Ișẹgun* (Victory Prayer). Her assistants are called *afadurajagun* (prayer warriors), a term common in Aladura churches;[40] and as with the Aladura, water and olive oil—drunk, anointed, or bathed in—are used as physical media for the healing power of prayer.

Although Muslim women's praying societies (known as *ẹgbẹ alasalatu*) have existed for decades, and senior women were given titles at the mosque, female Muslim charismatics like Mujidat seem to have emerged only in the past two to three decades, mostly with small and local followings. A similar phenomenon emerged in Christianity much earlier: in Lagos in 1925 a fifteen-year-old girl, Abiodun Akinsowon, fell into a trance and had celestial visions that led to the founding of the Cherubim and Seraphim. The phenomenology of possession in Yoruba Christianity and Islam has clear precedents in *orịṣa* religion, where women were the main charismatics.[41] The irruption of charisma into the scriptural monotheisms always creates problems for them, the more so for Islam, because its absolute insistence that God spoke his last words to humanity through the Prophet Mohammed means that it cannot have prophets in the sense that Christianity still can. So how do Yoruba Muslims understand their own charismatics? The charismatic gifts may be regarded simply as talents or natural endowments, to be fortified by disciplines like fasting and prayer; and at the same time as signs (*ami*) of a divine commission. I have even been told by an educated *alfa* that women are by nature spiritually more powerful than men (which must be a carryover from pre-Islamic notions). Then a role may be claimed for the assistance of subdivine beings such as angels (*maleka*) or jinns (*anjọnu*), though this is treacherous, morally ambiguous ground, open to the charge of associating other beings with God, which is idolatry (*shirk*). Here the critique that Salafists (and indeed many mainstream educated *ulama*) direct against the practices of popular Yoruba Islam parallels that of some born-again Christians against White-garment Aladuras (notably the Celestial Church of Christ), for having spiritual truck with demonic forces.

The cross-pressures—the impulse of religious inspiration, popular thaumaturgical demand, social pressure to conform with orthodox norms—work themselves through to varying outcomes. They may be more intense because, as all these cases suggest, charismatic inspiration and Arabic learning are so often inversely related. In 1982 Shaykh Abdul-Hamid Olohungbemi set up what in born-again parlance may perhaps be called a ministry, Shamsuddin ul-Islamiyya, to preach the Oneness (*Tawhid*) of God. His target was the traditional *alfa*s of his home town, Ado-Odo, not far from Lagos, at whom he directed ferocious criticism for the *shirk* implicit in their healing and divinatory practices. So far, so orthodox; but Olohungbemi did acknowledge the support of visionary unseen helpers; and his own spiritual techniques sound as Aladura as Mujidat's, since he used holy water and castor oil for healing. He is a great preacher in Yoruba, but the "delivery of the sermon has striking resemblance of the method adopted by Christian preachers because everything is rendered in native indigenous language"—"usually spiced up with beautiful . . . hymns"—including portions of the Koran "with little or no recourse to the Arabic text." But he was persuaded by colleagues to moderate some of his procedures.[42]

More disconcerting to members of the mainstream *ulama* were the claims of another Muslim charismatic, Alhaji S. A. Olagoke. A lecturer in engineering with an Islamic background in Ibadan but with no formal Arabic education, he was inspired in 1983 to found a movement devoted substantially to healing, called Shafaudeen-in-Islam. Guided by visions and trances, in which he was directed to biblical as well as Koranic texts, he interpreted their source as the Holy Spirit. But the real problem was that he described himself as *Rasool* or Messenger—a title usually reserved for the Prophet Mohammed—as apparently revealed in a dream to one of his followers. When this became publicly known through the media, there were protests and questions from various Islamic parties ranging from the Muslim Students Society to the League of Imams and Alfas. Olagoke was called for questioning at the Ibadan central mosque. Anxious to retain Islamic respectability (and no doubt mindful of what had happened to Ahmadiyya), he toned down his claims: he was *Rasool-Shafau* (Messenger of Healing), thus prudently distinguishing himself from the Messenger of God. It must have helped that he is politically astute and an effective networker, even getting an endorsement for his book from the *Alafin* of Oyo, who is quoted as calling him an anointed man of God (a *very* born-again expression); and being appointed as a Justice of the Peace or lay magistrate. Shafaudeen-in-Islam now has a substantial mosque complex in Ibadan, the center of a network of more than a dozen branches and various social-development projects.[43]

Olohungbemi and Olagoke are both men of little Arabic learning, and their Christian point of reference is more Aladura than born-again. The next case involves an Arabic literate whose Christian bearings are toward the neo-Pentecostal surge of the last thirty years. This is Shaykh Rasheed Akinbile, who has led a Sufi group through many changes over more than two decades. I first became aware of him in 2002, when I saw the following proclamation on a banner advertising a meeting at the Ibadan University mosque:

> In the name of Allah, the Beneficient [*sic*], the Merciful. Caring and Sharing Sufi Centre (Inc.) Nigeria. Present *RAMADAN CELEBRATIONS* (30 Days of Spiritual Renewal and Manifestation of Miracles). Theme: OPEN THE FLOODGATES OF PROSPERITY.

This thoroughly born-again expression of what was evidently a Muslim undertaking had a complex history behind it. Akinbile is the son of an Ibadan imam; he had learned to recite the Koran by the age of nine and went on to some study of *hadith*. He was school imam at Ahmadiyya Grammar School, in Ibadan, and later a leader of the MSS at Obafemi Awolowo University, Ife, where he completed a B.A. in demography and statistics. His Muslim fellow students presented him with such problems as what prayers would help them to pass exams, and why did they lack "self-sufficiency in prayer," being unable to pray on their own, unlike their Christian compeers. His feeling that there "must be something deeper" than the "external part" of Islam (as he expressed it to me in interview) naturally pointed him in a Sufi direction, and he sought initiation into Tijaniyya (though he says he was also influenced by the writings of Inayat Khan, the Indian Sufi teacher, whose ten volumes he found in the university library). His own meditations on divine unity led to mystical experiences, and in 1989, the year he graduated from Ife, his followers urged him to form a group, which he called the Islamic Brotherhood of Sufism. During the 1990s he began to attract wider notice, at one point having his own TV program called *Fountain of Wisdom,* funded by a wealthy Muslim well-wisher.

Akinbile gradually came to feel that Sufism extended beyond Islam; he renamed his organization the International Brotherhood of Sufism, and he became active in interfaith dialogue. The activities of his group more and more came to echo born-again practices: meetings on Sundays, sitting on chairs, night vigils, men and women sitting together, testimonies and trances, the use of oil, water, handkerchiefs, and *tasbih* (Muslim rosary) as vehicles of power through prayer, a choir (wearing robes and accompanied by organ, guitar, and drums) singing songs such as these in Yoruba:[44]

> *Alasalatu, ki l'a gbojule? Lahila ilalahu l'a gbojule, t'o ba d'ọjọ ikẹhin o!*
> Praying people, who shall we depend on? It's "There is no god but Allah" we'll depend on at the last day.
>
> *Kurani mi ni ng o maa ke, oṣo o l'agbara lori rẹ, aje o l'agbara lori rẹ, eniyan o l'agbara lori rẹ, Kurani mi ee, Kurani ni ng o maa ke.*
> It's my Koran I'll recite, wizards have no power over it, witches have no power over it, evil people have no power over it, this is my Koran, it's my Koran I'll recite.

Or the following chorus in pidgin English:

> Winner o, winner, Allah you don win [have won] o, winner *patapata* [completely], you go
> [will continue to] win forever, winner.

For such things to be done in the name of Islam was just too much for the radical activists of MSS—the more so, perhaps, because Akinbile had once been one of them. They declared jihad against him and broke up an interfaith meeting at the University Conference Centre, where his Sufi singers were performing in the presence of the Oyo state governor and his wife, both Muslims. By then Akinbile's drift toward heterodoxy was causing concern among the Ibadan *ulama* at large, who surely were behind the personal plea of *Arẹ Musulumi* Arisekola, the wealthy lay chief of Ibadan's Muslims, for him to join the League of Imams and Alfas, their professional body. But he did not wish to be subject to the restraints of clerical collegiality that this would have brought. Finally he announced in a newspaper that he was neither a Muslim nor a Christian but just a Sufi. Much of his following fell away, but Akinbile has continued to offer what he now calls spiritual counseling.[45]

NASFAT: MUSLIM BORN-AGAINS?

Many of the factors that drove Akinbile's career are present in this final case, though they produced a very different outcome. This is an altogether more solid organization, in fact the most striking new movement to have emerged in Yoruba Islam during the last fifteen years: namely the Nasrul-Lahi-l-Fatih Society of Nigeria, always known by its acronym, NASFAT.[46] Sometimes (but superficially) referred to by outsiders as Muslim born-agains, it is probably the most effective response to the born-again phenomenon, from which it has consciously adopted many practices and strategies. More than any other Muslim body, NASFAT has a distinct class base: modern-educated, urban professionals. It was founded in 1995 by a group of lay Muslims working in the commercial sector in Lagos, the key figure being Alhaji Abdul-Lateef Olasupo, now retired from his post as a senior manager with one of Nigeria's largest banks but still chairman of NASFAT's Board of Trustees. Its chief missioner, Alhaji Abdullahi Akinbode, is the son of an imam at Ibadan and, like Akinbile, went to its Ahmadiyya Grammar School. The perspective of NASFAT's founders was that of the educated Muslim laity, lacking Arabic literacy, who felt that their own "[Islamic] knowledge was not so deep" and wanted a means to close the gap between "enlightened people and alfas."[47] The contrast between the two distinct status hierarchies, based on different kinds of knowledge, that divide the *umma* is very evident here. But Akinbode is ideally qualified to bridge that gap, since his credentials include both a B.A. in Arabic and an M.A. in international relations and diplomacy. In the 1980s he served on the Mission Board of MSS and—for he also has a fine singing voice—was the lead vocalist of its singing group, which released fourteen disks of what is somewhat incongruously known as Islamic gospel music.[48]

The challenge and example of the born-agains, while not averred as the primary stimulus for NASFAT,[49] are nevertheless very evident in much of what it does. Its main regular events are an *asalatu* (prayer) session on Sunday mornings from 8:30 to 12:30 and a *tahajjud* (night-vigil) session twice a month, between midnight and the dawn prayer. Their timing, length, and format are much more like the born-again Christians' than are the canonical *salat* prayers of Islam. While NASFAT's website speaks discreetly of the intention "to maximise favourably the leisure time that exists among Muslims who laze away Sunday mornings," the real problem was that this was when young Muslims were all too likely to go along with their Christian friends to the uplifting and entertaining services of the various born-again ministries. *asalatu* begins, as born-again services do, with praise worship: with praise of God and the invocation of blessings on the Prophet Mohammed, for which Arabic texts (in roman transliteration) from an official *NASFAT Prayer Book* are used, chanted in unison. Sometimes there may be a guided recitation of the Koran (known as *tankara*) and hymns in Yoruba. There is a sermon—an hour or more, which is much longer than the sermons given at the regular Friday prayers—often given by a visiting preacher, and proceedings conclude with an extended session of individual prayer requests. Similar elements occur in the nocturnal *tahajjud* service, though they are deployed less formally and there is a much more fervent and ecstatic quality to the prayers.

Many members of the *ulama* have severe misgivings about NASFAT's innovations, though they concede that they have done something to stem the appeal of rival religious attractions: "If they were not there, our people would flock to the mountain grounds and rivers," as one mainstream imam put it to me.[50] But for those who think that all forms of Muslim worship must be strictly authorized by the Koran or *hadith,* such as the members of Ahl us-Sunna, the NASFAT initiative is deeply problematic. Aware of this, NASFAT carefully justifies its activities as *mustahabb* (recommended but not compulsory, in terms of the Sharia's fivefold classification of actions) and as supererogatory, in that they do not—as its critics suspect—release their members from the obligation to perform the five daily prayers and the other pillars of Islam (all of which are set out clearly in its prayer book). NASFAT's aim, its leaders insist, is simply to make its members better Muslims without taking sides between Islam's various tendencies, from Tijaniyya to Ahl us-Sunna (though the supposed excesses of the former evoke stronger disapproval than what is thought of as the extremism of the latter). That is not surprising, since NASFAT and Ahl us-Sunna, despite their differences, both aim to modernize Yoruba Islam, whereas the popular devotional practices of Tijaniyya are seen as part of its unenlightened heritage. Even so, NASFAT's notably irenical tone toward radical Islamists is not much reciprocated by them, who sometimes disparage it as a ceremonial organization or charge its members with being mere social Muslims.

This conscientious Islamic orthodoxy is also combined with much use of a managerialist language that strongly recalls some of the larger born-again organizations. NASFAT's website offers both vision and mission statements, and refers to its stakeholders. Leaders spoke to me of "marketing our product . . . in line with Sharia," of the need to "strategize" their activities, of NASFAT "showcasing itself . . . as an enlightened Islamic organization" and of offering a "free market" to different Muslim groups; and even, in response to a question of mine about the prominence at the beginning of the *asalatu* service of the invocation of blessings on the Prophet Mohammed, of its "adding value" to their prayers.[51] A more extended instance of this blending of Islam with business values may be seen in a book entitled *Leadership Strategies of the Prophet Mohammad* by Mudathir Abdul-Ganiyu, a journalist and lecturer, with a foreword by NASFAT's chief missioner, Alhaji Akinbode.[52] It is difficult to tell how far such expressions arise directly from the jargon of the world of business, media, and administration, where so many leading NASFAT activists are employed, or whether they are partly mediated through born-again Christianity, which came from its American sources already well saturated with the idioms of corporate business.

The self-conscious modernity of NASFAT also shows in the wide range of its extraritual activities: visiting prisons, microfinance for small businesses, educational programs (including its Fountain University, at Oshogbo), empowerment schemes for women, vacation camps for students, guidance and counseling services for young people, medical outreach, a soft-drink manufacturing business,[53] and so on. Once more a born-again comparison is irresistible, especially with the Redeemed Christian Church of God (RCCG), whose parachurch activities are so extensive and well known that they must serve as a major point of reference. RCCG, like NASFAT, successfully projects itself as an organization that aims to attract an elite membership. In building up a portfolio of welfare and development activities that offer on a small scale what citizens tend to expect from an effective modern state—an ideal that Nigeria professes but conspicuously fails to live up to—NASFAT follows a trail that RCCG has blazed. A few miles down the Lagos-Ibadan expressway from RCCG's Redemption Camp, with its vast auditorium and many facilities, NASFAT now has a campground of its own, a Muslim facility rubbing shoulders with several Christian ones strung along the expressway.[54]

But the bottom-line commonality between NASFAT and RCCG is due not to the contingencies of recent history—the aspirations of the Yoruba professional class, the neoliberal context, NASFAT's need to pay attention to what the religious market leader is doing—but to the age-old Yoruba demand that religion provide them with answers to the practical problems of human existence, particularly sickness and poverty. Both bodies contrast their own ways of responding to this demand with what they see as the doctrinally compromised practices prevalent within their respective faiths. The self-conscious modernity of their critique is expressed in the insistence that the basis of healing practices must be scriptural, biblical or Koranic as the case may be, not corrupted with elements specific to the Yoruba cultural repertoire: the immediate past of Yoruba tradition is to be negated by the distant foundational past of a world religion. So the born-agains denounce the errors of the White-garment churches (*alasofunfun*)—as they disparage the Aladura, particularly the Celestial Church of Christ, and the myriad of small autonomous or breakaway *woli* or prophet—for adopting illicit means to supplement Christian prayer. An exactly analogous point is made in modernist Muslim criticism of the healing and divinatory practices of the mass of ill-educated but often popular *alfa*.[55]

In the tangled undergrowth of popular religion, where pragmatism outweighs doctrine, there is now so much borrowing between Muslim *alfa*, traditional *babalawo*, and Christian *woli*, all engaged in much the same task, that the boundaries between them become blurred. Yoruba Islam differs from Christianity in that it harbors both a more elaborate corpus of syncretistic practice and a broader set of guidelines, mainly to be found in the *hadith*, for a theologically correct Muslim system of healing. Mr. Mustapha Bello, until lately a senior administrator at NASFAT headquarters, has written a fascinating short book, part theological and part ethnographic, advocating reform to what he terms the practice of *jalbu*, defined as "the process of offering spiritual guidance and counselling to [a] distressed and troubled clientele on multifarious issues involving more than physical/medical attention."[56] Bello does not doubt that personal problems can have mystical (or, as he would have it, metaphysical) causes, which need mystical solutions, but he wants to see them tackled in ways that do not subvert the principle of *tahwid* or faith in the unity and all-sufficiency of God. At the same time, the born-again influence is discreetly yet unmistakably present, not just in the language of counseling and consultancy but in his concluding assertion (p. 87) that man needs "a personal relationship with God."

Yet just how significant is this partial adoption of a hegemonic discourse? For Bello has no sooner used this hallmark evangelical phrase—"personal relationship with God"—than his argument turns in quite another direction from where evangelical Christianity would have taken it, for he immediately speaks of it as requiring a "soul receptive and submissive to divine rules and regulations as enunciated in the Revealed Books and exemplified by His chosen Messengers." This contrast says much. The born-again ideal of a personal faith rests on the theology of an incarnate God who has offered Himself as a personal savior: "What a friend we have in Jesus," as the words of an old evangelical hymn put it. It is not easy to imagine Alhaji Akinbode addressing God in a NASFAT *asalatu* service as "Daddy," as Pastor Adeboye of RCCG does. This whole doctrinal and affective complex is radically alien to Islam. Yet the austerity of the orthodox Sunni ideal espoused by Bello—that it is obedience to His revealed rules and regulations that brings a Muslim personally close to God—has often proved too arid for individual Yoruba Muslims, who have sought something more emotionally vibrant. This is a source of the perennial appeal of Sufism (as witness the career of Shaykh Akinbile) and may perhaps underlie the fervency of the collective invocation of blessings on the Prophet that is such a striking feature of the *asalatu* session. Still, one's overriding impression of *asalatu*—the main congregation all men, sitting shoulder to shoulder in rows on the floor, wearing white gowns—is of a sober solidarity, of a characteristically Muslim aesthetic of worship.[57]

The individualism and free emotionalism of born-again Christianity not only contrasts systematically with the restrained and collective ethos of NASFAT's worship, as of Muslim prayer more generally, but seems to correlate with other, organizational, features. To be born again, with its main external token speaking in tongues, is understood as to receive a divine charisma; and charisma, qua the reception of extraordinary spiritual gifts, is the condition of leadership in the large born-again or neo-Pentecostal churches. Their founders and leaders—men like the late Benson Idahosa, E. A. Adeboye, W. F. Kumuyi, David Oyedepo, Matthew Asimolowo—are celebrities, variously credited with powers of healing, prophecy, deliverance, and so forth. In Muslim terms, they are more like great Sufi shaykhs than the leaders of an organization like NASFAT. Akinbode is a respected leader who can certainly give a forceful sermon, but as he says, he likes to work behind the scenes, as the chief clerical appointee of the board of trustees. NASFAT is set strongly against "hero worship"—whether more of the Sufi than of the born-again kind is not clear—an attitude that fits well with something common among Muslims, a particular distaste, alike for the noisy, ecstatic quality of Pentecostal worship and for the kind of personality cult that envelops prominent born-again pastors. Despite the much-remarked resemblances between NASFAT and neo-Pentecostal Christianity, the differences show the strength of what is distinctive of Islam. Indeed, if NASFAT realizes its founders' religious aims, its long-term impact should be to make those who attend its services more aware of the Islamic tradition and of the options available within it.

10

Pentecostalism and Salafism in Nigeria

Mirror Images?

There are certainly empirical grounds for drawing parallels between Christian Pentecostalism and Muslim Salafism—whether the frame for the comparison is Yorubaland, Nigeria, the West African region, or indeed the world at large. Since their members (and even more their leaders) are so strongly aware of themselves as belonging to worldwide fellowships of faith and sentiment, the movements themselves draw us outward from local to national, regional, and finally global frames for their comparison. But what has made the perception of parallels so compelling is less their empirical points of resemblance than the primary conceptual lens through which they have been viewed, namely fundamentalism. Rarely has a term moved so far from its original connotation: from being a term of positive self-description by a group of doctrinally conservative American Protestants, of small political import, to a pejorative label applied by outsiders to forms of religion deemed extremist—a designation that nowadays most often connotes radical political views within Islam.

Over time the use of the term "fundamentalism" has been subject to two counterpressures. On the one hand, attempts to develop it as an analytical concept have run into the problem that, as the range of empirical cases has been extended, with an ever-growing number of only partly shared and overlapping features, its explanatory power weakens.[1] On the other, its appeal continues to be linked with a perception of the world as subject to a dangerous clash of fundamentalisms,[2] regarded as entities at once homologous and hostile to each other. The closely cognate vision of Samuel P. Huntington, of world history as driven by a clash of civilizations,[3] is typically deplored by historians and anthropologists, on grounds both normative and empirical.[4] They are more inclined to look for the exchanges, links, and compromises between cultures, though in so doing they tend to discount the influence of precisely those religious agents who in fact *are* driven by something like what Huntington's view of the world imagines.

If the tone of the last three chapters was distinctly anti-Huntingtonian, this effect was due less to theoretical considerations than to the impress of the Yoruba context—though there was also the sense that forces of a more fundamentalist nature had grown stronger and needed to be fought off. But if we want to examine how far recent movements in the two faiths should be seen as homologous but opposed, as the notion of a clash of fundamentalisms implies, we ultimately need to move to a broader, looser context, defined less as a cultural community (like Yorubaland) than as a political arena (like Nigeria, or Northern Nigeria) or as merely a region where a range of common conditions prevails (like West Africa). A convenient starting point is an influential essay by Brian Larkin and Birgit Meyer that articulates the widely held view that the salient new forms of Islam and Christianity in contemporary West Africa—Pentecostalism and Salafism (or, as they term it, Islamism)[5]—should be seen as "doppelgangers, enemies whose actions mirror those of the other."[6]

Though Larkin and Meyer frame their comparison in terms of West Africa as a whole, most of their data are drawn from the two very different societies that they know from intensive fieldwork: southern Ghanaian in the case of Meyer, Northern Nigerian in the case of Larkin. Logically, this framework is less helpful than there would have resulted if they had used two societies with a similar religious profile or (even better) a single society wherein both movements were present. For southern Ghana is overwhelmingly Christian (with many Pentecostalists); its Muslim minority is little influenced by Salafism—in fact there are many Ahmadis—and there is no serious interfaith conflict. On the other hand, Northern Nigeria is a crucible of both Salafism and interfaith conflict, but although the Christian body is substantial and internally diverse, Pentecostalism is less influential than in Southern Nigeria and is less prominent in interfaith conflict than some other churches are. Though Larkin and Meyer are right to emphasize the need to study movements in the two religions in their interrelations,[7] they cannot do this properly, since Pentecostalists in southern Ghana and Salafists in Northern Nigeria are hardly in a position to interact with each other. So they have to fill out the empirical picture with material drawn from elsewhere, especially from Nigerian (largely Yoruba) Pentecostalism. This may sometimes be justified, granted the powerful influence of Nigerian evangelists and religious media throughout the region, but it does foreclose on the question—critical for understanding such a protean faith as Pentecostalism—of how such external influences are modified by the receiving context.[8]

So what Larkin and Meyer give us is a rather general picture, particularized by illustrative material selected to support the similarity thesis but without any very close analysis either of interaction between the movements or of the play of similarities and differences between them. They identify three basic commonalities between the two: they both mount a vehement attack on local religious and cultural traditions; both offer their adherents new ways and means of becoming modern; and both have a strong sense of their participation in global movements in their respective faiths. We can even go further and point to other, more concrete similarities: their social grounding in the experience especially of the educated, urban young and their extensive use of modern media to diffuse their messages (where Pentecostalism particularly has shown the way). In both cases, too, there is the paradox that their modernizing critiques of the immediate past are grounded in the invocation of an older normative past: thus they both see themselves as movements of revival or renewal of their respective faiths. Moreover, both promote more than personal agendas, since they also offer critiques, albeit in rather oblique and ambiguous ways and with large differences in content, of how state and society have developed in West Africa since independence.

All this is well as far as it goes, but the real issue is to do with what significance is to be attached to similarities *and differences*. There are at least two great areas of difference between the two movements evident even in Larkin and Meyer's account—indeed, they are far too conspicuous to be disavowed—but these are discounted in the authors' analysis. For shorthand reference, let me label them "Prosperity" and "Politics."

1. The authors' account of Pentecostalism naturally lays much emphasis on what has become one of its dominant emphases across Africa, the Gospel of Prosperity—and particularly so in some of the larger churches, such as Winners' Chapel or the Redeemed Christian Church of God in Nigeria or Action Chapel International in Ghana.[9] Prosperity is typically combined, in varying proportions in different churches, with other pragmatic concerns: healing, oracular guidance, deliverance from demons, and so on. While the theological expression of this orientation can be traced to an authoritative source in the so-called Faith Gospel, as propounded by such North American Pentecostalists as T. L. Osborn or Kenneth Hagin, it also meshes with the emphasis on powerful prayer that was prominent in the earlier wave of African independent churches (AICs).[10] In noting this, Larkin and Meyer implicitly modify their earlier comments on Pentecostalism's break with its cultural past.[11] But what is more striking is the apparently complete absence of any similar orientation in the Salafist movements that they invite us to see as mirroring Pentecostalism. On the contrary, their only reference to anything like Prosperity is to Izala's *opposition* to "the magical uses of Islamic knowledge for healing or prosperity."[12]
2. Larkin and Meyer's treatment of Islamism reads at times like an account of a religion with a radically different primary orientation from Pentecostalism,

despite their aim of making the most that can be made of the resemblances between them. In contrast to the extremely feeble velleities of some Ghanaian Pentecostal pastors toward the idea of a Christian state,[13] which they mention, such Nigerian Muslim activists as Abubakar Gumi and Ibrahim Al-Zakzaky[14] were fully engaged in the political conflicts of the region (such as between the traditional political elite or *sarauta* and its populist critics), propounding religious ideas that require command of the state to be properly implemented and ready to align themselves ideologically and materially with the main power blocs of the Muslim world—Saudi Arabia vs. Iran—in order to achieve them.[15]

II

In attempting to balance these differences against similarities in the comparison of Salafism and Pentecostalism, it should not escape notice that they are of a significantly different kind: the similarities are chiefly a matter of form, whereas the differences are chiefly ones of content or substance. The three key points of similarity, as proposed by Larkin and Meyer, all hinge on a contrast between tradition and modernity: both movements imagine themselves as bearers of modern values and set themselves in sharp opposition to cultural practices that they see as traditional. Now tradition and modernity, particularly as anthropologists view them, are notoriously empty categories: they tend to be filled situationally, with contents that shift from one context to another (and that may even, over time, shift from one category to the other), though always in antithesis to each other. The idea of a normative sacred past, relevant to both movements, is another such religious form, which is available to be filled with an indefinite number of possible contents as particular traditions may supply them.

Now, while religious forms undoubtedly have real historical effects, it is above all a religion's content that will mainly determine its substantive impact over time, since this is the matrix of the distinctive orientations to action that it engenders in its adherents. So in the present case, the sets of orientations that I have labeled Prosperity and Politics can be seen as contrasting ways in which believers are prompted to realize themselves and so to shape their worlds. In the light of that widespread African ontology of well-being that brackets health and prosperity together, let Prosperity be understood more broadly as what the Yoruba call *alafia*, that condition of all-round this-worldly being at ease (with health its main component) that sums up what individuals pray for and wish for one another. Two questions then occur. Why should this orientation be so salient in Christian rather than Muslim fundamentalism; and why should the contrasting political orientation apparently typify the Muslim rather than the Christian movement? Then do we interpret this contrast in the light of factors independently affecting the two religions, or in terms of some kind of overall unifying logic?

It can hardly be supposed that African Muslims are intrinsically less interested in health, welfare, security, and the like than African Christians are. In the Yoruba case Muslim clerics adapted so well to the popular demand for spiritual technologies to attain these objectives that it was long before the Christians could catch up; and indeed the term that encapsulates them, *alafia,* is a word of Arabic origin introduced through Muslim channels,[16] a word well naturalized in Yoruba by the nineteenth century. So how is it that it is Pentecostalism (like *oriṣa* religion and Aladura Christianity) that seems to have made the quest for *alafia* central to its project, whereas Salafism instead embraces a political agenda, which presents a much more radical challenge to the prevailing order of things?

That these agendas are not just different but to some extent alternative was suggested by Matthew Schoffeleers in relation to churches that practice ritual healing in southern Africa. He argued that they are strongly inclined to political acquiescence, not just as a matter of contingent fact but from an underlying logic. This is because, he suggests, "healing . . . individualizes and therefore depoliticizes the causes of sickness."[17] The same would go for those churches that focus on prosperity through prayer or the conquest of demons that impede the realization of personal success. The distinctiveness of Pentecostalism's healing agenda is further grounded by Murray Last, who brings the perspective of a medical anthropologist as well as a historian of Islam to the contrast between the two faiths.[18] He argues that, despite the existence of a distinct Islamic corpus of medicine,[19] healing (and the wider problem of suffering) has been much less central to Islam than to Christianity, a contrast that he traces back to the primary representation of Mohammed as the prophet of a divine law, not a worker of healing miracles like Christ.[20] In Last's view, the Sokoto jihad of the early nineteenth century involved "a deliberate project to take the experience of illness out of the religious sphere" as part of a campaign against the survival of pagan practices among Muslims.[21] This seems to have been strongly revived in contemporary Salafism.

All this implies that while there is, broadly speaking, a common set of social conditions that the two religions have to address (or that present them with opportunities), a good deal of free play or room for maneuver also exists between the demand arising from these conditions, and the supply offered by the religions. The first step in analysis must be to characterize the conditions of this demand; the second, to trace how it is shaped by what the religions are moved to supply. As to the former, Larkin and Meyer speak of a "reconfiguration of African states and the progressive disembedding of the African economies from the formal world market [that generate] . . . the unstable and often depressing flux of life in [contemporary] Africa."[22] In similar vein, Charles Piot typifies contemporary Togo as "a world of post-national sovereignty, of non-state-centric idioms of belonging, of horizontal networked forms of sociality, . . . of global immanence."[23] The conditions of what Piot calls the "neo-liberal moment" are not just a matter of political economy but are also (what is very important) of material culture, particularly the electronic media, which coincidentally came on stream in the 1990s and provided an essential condition if not for the initial emergence of Pentecostalism at least for its massive expansion. The chameleon character of Pentecostalism equips it particularly well able to respond to this situation, by fashioning subjectivities that enable individuals to make practical sense of the experiences of living under the exigencies of such a neoliberal order.[24]

Yet despite the elective affinity between the two, it is crucial not to merge them—as Piot comes close to doing when he shifts imperceptibly from speaking of "the neo-liberal moment" to "the charismatic moment."[25] For if the solution is thus virtually elided into the problem, the possibility of a dynamic interplay between social context and religious tradition all but disappears. Piot then confounds his binding of Togolese Pentecostalism into the present by simultaneously also tying it to the very distant past, tracing the genealogy of what he sees as its "instinctively anti-authoritarian" character back to the "the anti-imperial politics of the early Christian community [in the Roman Empire]."[26] But this, surely, is to overdetermine contemporary Pentecostalism by positing something like an egalitarian essence mysteriously replicating itself over a vast span of historical time. In any case, it ignores how in both Nigeria and Ghana Pentecostalism has also taken some highly authoritarian forms under miracle-working charismatic pastors. In the light of this, it is not surprising that Piot ends up confessing his uncertainty about the political import of Pentecostalism.

There is a crucial problem of method here. While Pentecostalism, like any other religious movement, is shaped both by its context and by its tradition, these have always to be analyzed as working interactively, not independently of each other. Neither context nor tradition is a fixed given to the other: both are to be seen as yielding possibilities, albeit constrained ones. And the cultural work by which a religion reassesses its history in the light of its predicament is reciprocally linked to how it is guided by its past as it seeks to realize itself in the present. This is why I will conclude this chapter by comparing two recent historical interpretations of their faiths by Nigerians, respectively a Pentecostalist and a Salafist.

These abstractions become concrete when we start to compare the responses of more than one religion to the neoliberal predicament. Islam faces it too, but the solutions it supplies are its own. Take the yearning for renewal, particularly among the young, which is common to movements in both faiths. Whereas the Pentecostal paradigm is for renewal to occur first in individuals, empowered by the Holy Spirit according to the sacred promise of Acts 2, and then to spread out to energize the whole Church, the classic pattern of Islamic renewal involves the paradigm of a *mujaddid* who appears every century to reform the *umma*.[27] Here the process of renewal proceeds in the reverse direction, for the *mujaddid* is called to reestablish the proper institutional framework for pious practice by individual Muslims, through implementing normative rules drawn from the Koran and the *hadith*. This is inherently a much more political project. It would seem that Salafism, though its appeal implies a real ability to meet the experiential needs of individual West African Muslims, offers a much more refracted response to the neoliberal predicament, one more heavily mediated through the layers of its tradition, than Pentecostalism does. The weight of normative tradition is much lighter in Pentecostalism, its charter precedent much more open and permissive—and this seems to have made it easier to meet the age-old local demand for healing and other forms of *alafia* with such Christian confidence.

But I must now qualify the thrust of my argument so far. For healing, a gift of the Holy Spirit, is not only significant in its literal sense for Pentecostalists in West Africa but is also taken by them as a potent metaphor for their wider claim to be able to make all things over anew. Such an open potential clearly undermines the sharp distinction between healing (in the literal sense) and politics (in the conventional sense) that I have been using, and so it requires us to probe more deeply the politics of Pentecostalism. Yorubaland provides an excellent place to start, since the relative time-depth of its Pentecostalism, and the fact of its being deeply rooted in earlier local forms of evangelical Christianity, enable us to view it in a historical perspective; while the copresence of Islam provides a check on any cause-effect relations that its history may suggest.

III

Looking back at more than thirty years of born-again Christianity from a vantage point in 2015, we are no longer tempted to see it simply as a grand ruptural moment, vital as this conception has been for numberless individuals swept up in it. No one has analyzed more profoundly the logic of Pentecostalism's redemptive promise in Nigeria, of its "will to found anew," than Ruth Marshall in her book *Political Spiritualities*. The book's very title, taken as it is from an essay by Foucault on the Iranian revolution of 1979, as well as her remark that "in many respects, the Born-Again and [Islamic] reformist projects are doppelgangers," suggest she too regards the two movements as fundamentally comparable and equally political projects.[28] The broad commonalities she sees between them fall under two main heads. First, they are both concerned to evoke in their members a broadly similar kind of religious subjectivity, one that involves "a work of the self on the self";[29] and second, they have both become hegemonic projects competing in Nigeria's public space but implying incompatible visions for the future development of Nigerian society. Pentecostalism, she insists, has a "highly political agenda."[30] But this is not an unnuanced judgment, since she also attributes to it "an ambivalent form of negative political theology"; and, though she regards it as rooted in many of the same aspirations as Salafism, she concedes that it displays "important historical, socio-political and theological differences."[31] So what are these differences?

The immediate origins of Yoruba neo-Pentecostalism lie in the early 1970s—the years just after the Nigerian Civil War, when a dramatic growth in oil revenues raised dizzy hopes for Nigeria's national development, though significant roots run back to contacts with American Pentecostals in the 1950s and 1960s, and even earlier through the Aladura movement in the 1920s. During Olusegun Obasanjo's first turn as head of state (1977–79), as leader of a military government, oil revenues permitted the vigorous pursuit of highly statist policies in health and education. There was a massive expansion of higher education, which facilitated neo-Pentecostalism's earliest constituency, the campus prayer fellowships where so many of its early leaders were formed.[32] Nigeria's ambition for itself as a leader in the struggle for black and African advancement across the world was lavishly staged in FESTAC in 1977. This was when a Pentecostal group first entered the public arena (alongside like-minded Muslims) to protest against what it saw as a showcasing of idolatrous culture in the name of national pride. Apart from that, Pentecostal concerns and activities were still essentially limited to individual and private spheres.

All changed in the 1980s, when Nigeria found itself in a prolonged economic crisis due to collapsed oil prices combined with chronic corruption and mismanagement by successive governments, first civilian and then again military. The state, while still a massive engine for private accumulation by the members of the political class, had progressively reneged on its promise to bring development to the mass of the people. Pentecostalism now moved off campus and, in the form of rapidly growing ministries under charismatic pastors, raised its public profile dramatically through all forms of media and by holding large, conspicuously advertised revival meetings across Nigeria. Shifts in the movement's orientation started to appear. The first was a shift from its strong initial focus on holiness—typically taking the form of a quest for personal sanctification through ascetic self-disciplines—to a greater emphasis on external, this-worldly objectives, including the conquest of demonic enemies. This may be seen both as a trajectory characteristic of movements of evangelical spirituality and as a substantial reversion to the default system of Yoruba religious culture.[33]

Accompanying this, and at some tension with it—recalling Schoffeleers' suggestion that healing and politics are essentially *alternative* orientations for religious movements—was the emergence of a new political relevance for born-again Christianity. What had begun as a redemptive promise of rebirth addressed to individuals, the more urgent through being set within a messianic end-time, came to provide a powerful idiom for collective renewal. This yearning grew through the 1980s against a backdrop of an ever-deepening economic and political crisis, which lasted through sixteen years of military rule under generals from the Muslim North. It reached its nadir in the mid-1990s, after the military had annulled the 1993 presidential election, ushering in the brutal dictatorship of General Sanni

Abacha. Islam now clearly eclipsed paganism as the grand imagined spiritual enemy for Christians, though under the Yoruba etiquette of public amity between the two faiths, hostility was usually expressed in somewhat muted forms, such as the use of the term "the Caliphate" to denote the forces of Northern oppression. This apocalyptic mood was readily articulated in born-again discourse, which was widely taken up to prefigure and presage redemptive change in the condition of Nigeria. E. A. Adeboye, the leader of the Redeemed Christian Church of God, was widely credited with having prophesied Abacha's sudden death in 1998.

But that was the high-water mark. With Obasanjo's second coming in 1999 as elected president of Nigeria, some limits of Pentecostal politics soon became evident. Even though he claimed to be born-again himself and gathered a coterie of Pentecostal pastors around him,[34] any promise of a redemptive politics was buried—or at least returned to its original sphere, the redemption of individual lives. If ever these pastors spoke truth to power, no significant effects were discernible, though some of them may have gained personal favors. Some individual pastors, such as Tunde Bakare, have persistently spoken out against the corruption of the political class,[35] but in general prevailing secular status hierarchies are fully accepted. Obviously, wealth per se is no embarrassment for celebrity pastors who preach the Gospel of Prosperity; and the RCCG, in particular, has developed a highly successful strategy to establish congregations among the well-heeled middle class with its so-called model parishes.[36] Tremendous energy and resources go into church expansion, not only in Nigeria but along the networks of the Nigerian diaspora in Europe and North America. Yet alongside their disgust at the state of secular politics in their country, many Nigerian Pentecostalists take great pride *as Nigerians* in this expansion. It is true that Pentecostalism in general has some strongly postnationalist features—for example, the marked universalism of its aspirations expressing disappointment at the failures of the nationalist political project—but in the case of Nigeria, it can also be seen as a form of nationalism displaced: a projection of the nation onto the world through the medium of Pentecostal Christianity.

IV

Optimal conditions for a contextual comparison of Salafism and Pentecostalism are not easily found. Although Yorubaland is an excellent place to compare diverse forms of both Islam and Christianity, the two fundamentalist movements are not on an even footing there. For while Pentecostalism has a strong place within Yoruba Christianity, with local roots going back over a hundred years,[37] enabling us to see it as a virtually endogenous movement, Salafism is not merely a minority (albeit growing) strand within Yoruba Islam but one that has only appeared within the last thirty-plus years. As argued in the last chapter, several other strands within Yoruba

Islam—Tijaniyya, NASFAT, and Tablighi Jama'at—have more obvious points of resemblance to Pentecostalism than Salafism does.[38] Though Yoruba Salafism—the grouping known as Ahl us-Sunna—owes its origins more to currents in the wider Islamic world than to the impact of the radical reformism of Northern Nigeria, it still draws inspiration from the latter and identifies with its major figures, such as Usman dan Fodio. So the most fruitful comparison for Yoruba Pentecostalism is in fact Salafism in Northern Nigeria. Though we lose the advantage of comparing the two movements in the same cultural context, we gain from being able to compare them at full expression in their respective home contexts.

Northern Nigeria offers a much looser context than Yorubaland. It is multicultural rather than monocultural, but with one culture historically hegemonic over a large part of it: the Hausa-speaking Islamic culture of the Sokoto Caliphate. Since the 1970s, it has seen a succession of radical Islamic or Salafist movements of the kind discussed by Larkin and Meyer, the latest being Boko Haram. Amid their diversity, two features have been salient: vehement hostility to the Sufi brotherhoods and pressure to implement Sharia law, both grounded in a Salafist vision of Islam. From the 1960s till his death in 1992, one man exercised a towering influence here, Alhaji Abubakar Gumi, the former grand khadi of the Northern States—there has been no remotely comparable figure in Nigerian Christianity.[39] Gumi was the guiding force of the best-known and most influential movement, known as Izala, an abbreviated Hausa form of its Arabic name, which means the Society for the Removal of Innovation (*Bid'a*) and the Restoration of the *Sunna*.[40]

To understand these movements, we need to relate them not just to the immediate past, which has directly bequeathed the situation Izala wants to reform, and the distant past of the credited founders of Islamic Salafism, which provide its normative exemplar, but to a middle-distance past that mediates these two temporal reference points. That is the Sokoto Caliphate, the Islamic state created through a jihad led by a Fulani cleric, Usman dan Fodio, in the first decade of the nineteenth century.[41] The British conquered it a century later but preserved the system of emirates (with their Fulani Muslim ruling elites) to make it the classic terrain of Lugardian indirect rule.[42] They greatly cut back the scope of Sharia law to the personal sphere, but Islam remained fundamental to the integration of Muslim society in Northern Nigeria and enjoyed a large demographic expansion. When nationalism arrived, fifty years later, it was intercepted by a scion of the ruling dynasty, Ahmadu Bello, the Sardauna of Sokoto, who promoted a form of conservative modernization drawing inspiration from his ancestor, Usman dan Fodio. The Sardauna was as much concerned with keeping out the corrosive influence of Southern politics as he was with securing independence from the colonial masters. Once independence came and lifted any need to reassure the British, he shifted quite quickly from a policy of One North, One People, in which Christians could feel they belonged as much as Muslims, to one of treating the North more as a

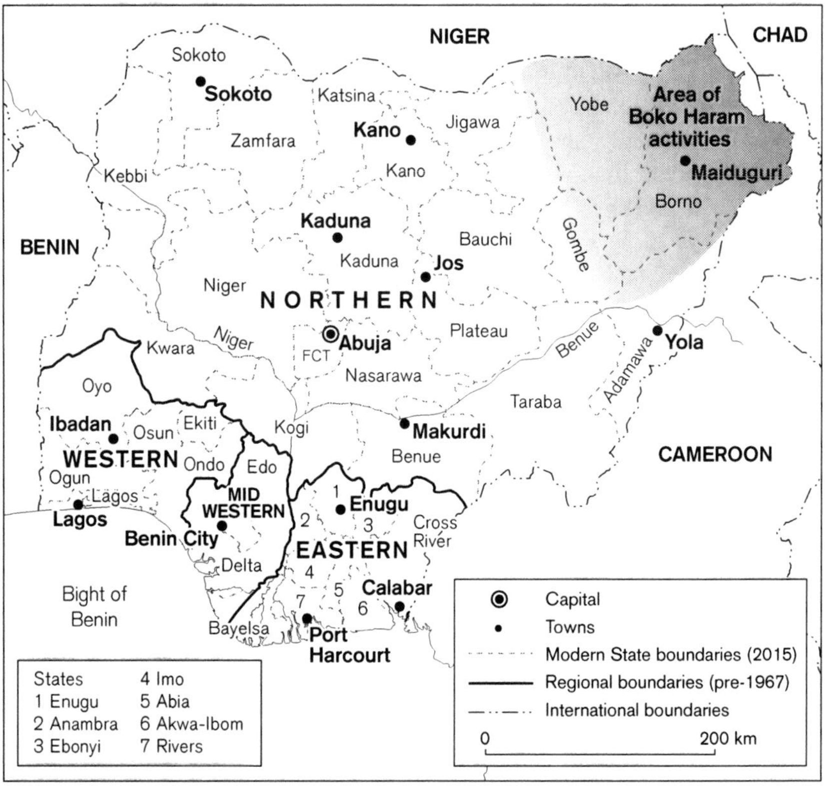

MAP 4. Nigeria: Regions and states.

successor state to the old Caliphate.[43] Seeing Islam as the only viable source of public morality and political cohesion, he sponsored highly controversial Islamization campaigns in the non-Muslim parts of the North.[44] Support for this came from a new organization, the *Jamaʿatu Nasril Islam* (Society for the Victory of Islam), founded in 1962 to foster unity among Muslims and to promote the cause of Islam, in which both the Sardauna and Abubakar Gumi took active roles.

The Sardauna also arranged for many of the works of dan Fodio to be published, in Arabic and Hausa. These covered such topics as the legal conditions for conducting jihad, the key question of just who is a Muslim, relations with non-Muslims, principles of government and law, and so on. They even include a text entitled "The Revival of the *Sunna* and the Removal of *Bidʿa*" (which closely anticipates the name that Izala chose for itself), more than half of which consists of quotations from the works of scholars across the Muslim world from the fourteenth to the seventeenth century.[45] One of the most important of these texts, the *Bayan*

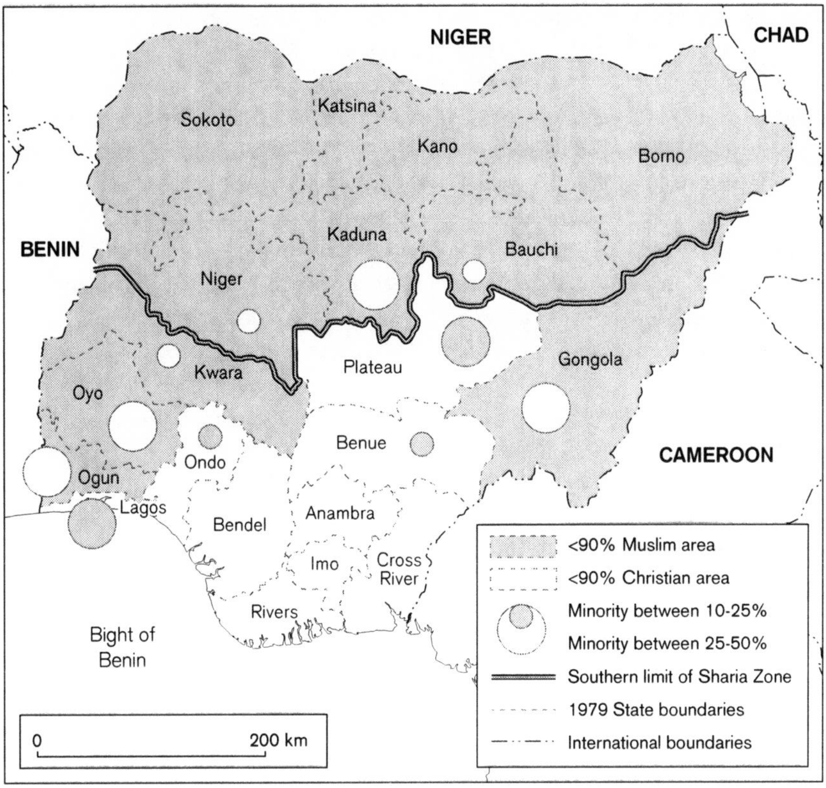

MAP 5. Nigeria: Religious distribution.

Wujub, was still circulating and actually being copied in Northern Nigeria in the 1960s.[46] Usman dan Fodio had belonged to the Qadiriyya, so it was only after the death of the Sardauna in 1966 that Gumi felt able to come out in outright condemnation of the brotherhoods for their *bid'a* (innovation) and *shirk* (idolatry).[47] So if (like Ousmane Kane) we want to emphasize the modernity of these movements, it is vital to see that their challenge to older ways arose from within a tradition that they reproduced as much as repudiated.

Izala's assault on Sufism was part of a more general drive for the renewal of Muslim society in Northern Nigeria. In striking at the charisma of Sufi shaykhs and the esoteric knowledge-claims of traditionalist clerics more generally, Izala had a rationalizing and egalitarian tenor, which appealed to the educated young and to traders. Its import for women was ambiguous—as Adeline Masquelier has shown in her fine study of a town in Niger[48]—since it both enforced their stricter seclusion and promoted their religious education. Even if there are some parallels here with the moral objectives of Pentecostal Christianity, where the Islamizing movements diverged radically from the Pentecostal ones was in that all their specific aspirations came together in the demand for Sharia, imagined as Allah's instructions for a just and well-ordered society. After two top-downward attempts to institute Sharia in the late 1970s and the 1980s, a bottom-upward movement finally led to its adoption in twelve states of the high North in 2000 and 2001.[49] One primary drive was the desire of ordinary Muslims to hold their elites to account in terms of the moral framework of Islam that they shared. It was also, argues Last, rooted in a diffuse sense of insecurity among the Muslims of Northern Nigeria, a sentiment arising not just from social conditions such as poverty and unemployment (important as these are) but also from specifically Islamic aspirations and anxieties. The young men (and some women) who enforce Sharia, the *hisba*, are often called vigilantes; but this is misleading, since though they take direct physical action against offenders, they act more like "concerned citizens" (as Last puts it), guided by the Koranic injunction to Muslims to "command right and forbid wrong."[50] We are dealing here not just with a discursive tradition but with institutional forms and precedents for action that have come down with it.[51]

V

The notion of different religious groups coming to resemble one another through a process of mirroring or directly copying one another has its most obvious application in situations of competition and conflict, as the last chapter explored in relation to the vigorous but peaceful rivalry between Islam and Christianity in Yorubaland. So how far has it occurred in the context of Northern Nigeria, where violence in the name of religion has become endemic? And has Pentecostalism proved to be the hard edge of Christianity in its confrontation with Islam? Certainly it is widely so regarded. A prominent Northern intellectual, Sanusi Lamido Sanusi, attributes interreligious violence in the region, which he characterizes as a recent phenomenon, to "the emergence of Pentecostal Christian and extremist Islamist groups"; and tendentiously invokes Ruth Marshall (whose remarks specifically concerned only Yorubaland) to the effect that "Pentecostals began aggressively proselytizing, demonizing Islam and thus fueling the rise of Islamic fundamentalism."[52] Although this certainly conveys the alarm that many Muslims in the North have felt at its religious impact, it is highly misleading to imply that Pentecostalism coincided with or even preceded the appearance of radical Islamism, and so could be even partly responsible for it. It arrived much later. Moreover, religious violence, though more sporadic in its incidence, long predates the arrival of Pentecostalism and was at first intra-Islamic in its character: in the Sokoto jihad itself, in fighting between the two Sufi brotherhoods, in Izala's challenge to them, and in the Maitatsine uprising, which erupted in Kano in 1980.[53] Apart from tit-for-tat episodes of violence at a community level, the clearest case of mirroring at an organizational level was the foundation of the Northern Christian Association in 1964 in response to the *Jamaʿatu Nasril Islam* in the context of the Sardauna's Islamization campaigns. Its members were drawn from the main Protestant churches active in the North (which did not then include Pentecostals).[54] This was the precursor of the enduring Christian Association of Nigeria (founded 1976).[55] But Pentecostalists did not make a significant public mark till the late 1980s, coming into an existing situation of tension between Muslims and Christians that had grown steadily since the early 1960s.[56] And if Adam Higazi's fine microstudy of conflict in Plateau State is anything to go by, Pentecostalists have been less active as militants than members of some mainline churches, especially those linked with local ethnonationalisms, like the Church of Christ in Nigeria.[57]

The prominent role of young men in acts of religious violence is commonly ascribed to their impoverishment and marginalization. But this is not the only possible response. For the chosen target may be an ethnic rather than a religious other and the vehicle of their anger ethnic militias rather than radical religious groups. Of course the different dimensions of otherness often stack up, as in confrontations between (say) Muslim Fulani pastoralists and Christian Berom farmers on the Jos Plateau, but still the dominant coding of the conflict, which is *not* reducible to socioeconomic causes, has telling effects. Here, religion has been salient in the North, whereas ethnicity has prevailed in the South of Nigeria; and it is not accidental that this correlates with the regional predominance of Islam and Christianity, respectively. The saliency of religion as a public identity marker in the North—that is, the politicization of faith—was strongly promoted by the jihadist Islam of the Sokoto Caliphate, continued through the colonial period, and was revived by the Sardauna after 1960.[58] Christianity's impact was more ambiguous, for although it certainly created a new supralocal religious identity, this was often undercut by denominational rivalries and offset by its role in valorizing or reshaping ethnic distinctions through promoting local languages in the context of Bible translation. What is undeniable is that in the most heavily Christian part of Nigeria, the Southeast, the anger of young men has typically not gone into religion but into ethnic militias and vigilante groups, which often make use of traditional masquerade forms and magical charms, which are offensive to Pentecostalists.[59]

Between the polar cases of the Southeast and the Muslim North, the cases of Yorubaland and the Northern Christians present some instructive variations. At its height in the early 2000s the main Yoruba ethnic militia, the Oodua People's Congress (OPC), had a broad membership across the religious spectrum, though in greater Lagos, where it was most active, it is likely that the mass of its activists (like their charismatic leader, Gani Adams) were young Muslims.[60] It is wholly consistent with the general pattern of Yoruba politics that, for the mass of Yoruba Muslims, ethnicity trumps religion as a political marker; nor is it surprising that the North has typically been their primary target, as in their past assaults on Hausa traders, and more recently their threat that any Boko Haram attacks in Yorubaland would meet with severe reprisals. One feature of the OPC's support is of especial note: the religious group *least* likely to be involved in it appears to be active Pentecostalists. This is because Pentecostalists strongly oppose the "revalidation of traditional spiritual practices,"[61] in the form of the fortifying charms and rituals provided by *alfa, babalawo,* and probably some Aladura *woli* for OPC activists. An analogous phenomenon is found among the mainly Christian Tarok in their confrontation with mainly Fulani Muslims in the lowland areas of Plateau State. Here, as in some vigilante groups in the Southeast, anti-Muslim activists employ the resources of their traditional culture, such as protective charms and masquerades associated with ancestral spirits.[62] Since much of this culture is still belittled by the churches, there is dismay among many Christians at the revival of paganism, even though the traditionalists and the COCIN leadership are de facto allies in the struggle against local Muslims. I think it can be presumed that Pentecostalists would be the most opposed to this aspect of the religious conflict in Plateau State, as they are to similar practices in the OPC.

VI

Islamic reformism and Pentecostalism are embedded in radically different ideological and institutional complexes. Pentecostalism, deeply marked by the voluntarism and individualism of its evangelical origins, only has, as Marshall put it, a "negative political theology."[63] But Islam was formed in the crucible of a process of statemaking reciprocally molded by its revelation—whether we think of the original Arab-Islamic Empire established by the Prophet and his successors in the seventh century or of the Sokoto Caliphate whose founders consciously modeled their actions on that precedent. Pentecostalism, by contrast, emerged in the USA and in northwestern Europe in the social space outside the state, yet within an order already guaranteed by it. The modes of political action adopted by Pentecostals in the public sphere are not in principle different from those of any other voluntary association in civil society: through converting individuals to their way of thinking, seeking to modify public opinion, acting as a pressure group on legislators and those who wield power, and so forth. It has nothing like a Sharia of its own to implement, and its tradition contains no models of direct political action of the kind that Muslims have deployed.

Both Muslims and Christians have very critical things to say about the Nigerian state, and at the individual level—to judge from many casual conversations with Yoruba people—I have hardly been able to distinguish between them. But when we consider the critique of religious groups, a distinct difference of emphasis is evident. This highlights the two general criteria that African states need to fulfill in order to be seen as legitimate by their populations: they must be seen as just, and they must be seen to bring development. The Nigerian state performs abysmally on both counts.

Muslim groups have been more concerned with what they see as the state's injustice. The demand for Sharia is of course the supreme expression of this. For attacks by radical groups on police stations, government facilities, the houses of corrupt politicians and traditional rulers, even churches—and in 2011 the wave of violent protest against what was seen widely in the North as an election stolen from them—are also fueled by an angry sense of injustice informed by Islamic ideals. So injustice tends to be linked to idolatry and unbelief (which especially means Christianity and its cultural concomitants). Again there is a precedent for such direct action in Usman dan Fodio's career: first a *hijra* or retreat of the faithful from the territory of corrupt so-called Muslim rulers, against whom *takfir* is declared; and then, at an opportune time, jihad to establish a Dar al-Islam, where justice will prevail.[64] Yet dan Fodio's work also contains ambiguities, notably his refusal to collapse injustice entirely into unbelief, as in the much-quoted conclusion of the *Bayan Wujub:* "A kingdom can endure with unbelief, but it cannot endure with injustice."[65]

Justice is preeminently a political virtue, and so it is not surprising that such an apolitical faith as Pentecostalism has little to say about it beyond the heartfelt though conventional criticisms that individual born-agains make of the behavior of Nigerian politicians. What, then, of their implicit critique of the Nigerian state, for failing to bring about development? It rests on the assumption that a key aim of religion is to bring about prosperity and the other good things of life. That makes the goal of development belong to the religious as much as the political sphere, and though it is pursued by distinct (that is, spiritual) means, these are felt to be quite complementary to secular, instrumental ones. At the same time, the larger Pentecostal churches have revived the missions' engagement in education and welfare projects, especially after state provision of these things faltered badly in the 1980s. The RCCG has built up a vast complex of facilities at its campground on the Lagos-Ibadan expressway: a veritable town (now known as Redemption City) with its own electricity and water supplies, banks and supermarkets, schools and university, media businesses, planned orderly housing, and all suchlike. It all amounts to what Asonzeh Ukah calls "an alternative society, properly equipped with all the necessary instruments of a functioning secular state."[66] It is an icon, or small-scale model, of the developed society that Nigerians aspire to. This was dramatically manifest at a Holy Ghost Night that I attended in 1994, when the church dedicated its new generator—that supreme index of the failure of the Nigerian state to guarantee a reliable power supply—which was switched on to joyous acclamations of *Let there be light, and there was light!* and scornful negative comparison with the public electricity supplier, NEPA.

Compared with the Islamist critique, the Pentecostal one is pragmatic as much as ethical: the ineptitude of Nigeria's rulers is condemned as much as their corruption. If this may seem rather contingent as a manifestation of Christianity, it does connect intimately with a core value of born-again Christianity in Nigeria: namely life or spirit. Pentecostalism in general rides on an ever-shifting balance between *Logos* (Word) and *Pneuma* (Spirit). Whereas its *Logos* derives from the parent evangelical tradition, its emphasis on *Pneuma* is both original and distinctive, for it is this that empowers individuals when they are born again. Now, Spirit was translated into Yoruba as *Ẹmi*, a noun derived from the verb *mi*, meaning "to breathe," and always carries connotations of life force, of what makes the difference between things living and things dead.[67] This enabled Pentecostalism to connect with indigenous ideas about life and well-being. Here it is worth noting that the main charge that the born-agains bring against the older mainline churches is not for their moral failings but for their being dead. This value had already found expression in Yoruba politics in the Gospel-derived motto of its dominant party, the Action Group (AG): "Life More Abundant."[68] The Yoruba name for the AG was *Afẹnifẹre*, Lovers of Good Things, which expresses the same idea more explicitly from an indigenous viewpoint.[69] This expression of development objectives in language fusing Christian and Yoruba values, made possible by a century of cultural Africanization, was ready-made for incorporation into Pentecostal criticism of the Nigerian state. Once again it shows that continuities, whether acknowledged or not, are as essential to the appeal of Pentecostalism as its claims of radical rupture from the past.

VII

Since the stories that religions tell about themselves play such an integral role in their self-realization, there is hardly a better way to bring out the contrasting thrusts of Salafism and Pentecostalism, political and cultural, than through two accounts of them written by engaged insiders, both recently published in Nigeria. These are *Islam in Nigeria: One Crescent, Many Voices* (2007), by Abdul-Fattah Olayiwola, and *A Heritage of Faith: A History of Christianity in Nigeria* (2009), by Ayodeji Abodunde.[70] Though both authors are Yoruba, each offers a Nigeriawide perspective on his religion. Neither one is a professional historian: Abodunde has a degree in science—engineering—and runs his own media company in Ibadan; Olayiwola teaches Arabic and Islamic studies at the University of Maiduguri. That is significant, since his views are much more characteristic of Northern than of Yoruba Islam.

Abodunde's book takes a more conventional, narrative form, with six parts running from the nineteenth-century missions through Nigerian Christianity's successive phases up to the present. His own commitment is not explicitly elaborated, though it is well evident in his overall conception of Nigeria's Christian history and in the much greater space and detail he devotes to its later Pentecostal stages. Against all that has been said about Pentecostal rupture, Abodunde presents this history as a continuous work of the Holy Spirit moving through various individuals and churches in which a growing Christian heritage of faith is built upon. So he treats non-Pentecostals in a very ecumenical spirit, and even the religious eccentricities of men such as the Aladura prophet Josiah Ositelu are treated gently.

Olayiwola, by contrast, does not offer a sequential narrative as such but rather a Salafist interpretation of the history of Islam in Nigeria. His book is polemical where Abodunde is irenical and is thus in an immediate sense a politically more engaged work. A question not to be avoided is whether these highly individual works may also be taken to represent broader bodies of opinion. Olayiwola's clearly stated antipathies—to the mixing Islam targeted by Usman dan Fodio, to the Sufi brotherhoods, to Ahmadiyya—show him to be a characteristic and consistent advocate of a Salafist viewpoint.[71] By contrast, while Abodunde's book is strongly Pentecostal in its sympathies, it is not the only kind of history that a Pentecostalist might have written. One can easily imagine a history with a much more negative treatment of non-Pentecostal churches or of some tendencies within Pentecostalism, though a person subscribing to such notions would perhaps have been unlikely to want to write a history at all.

The most revealing differences between the worldviews implicit in the two books lie in how each author articulates his core religious subject matter with such adjacent themes as culture, nation, state, and politics. Where Abodunde treats Christian history as occupying a space alongside but distinct from the secular or political history of Nigeria,[72] despite the points of interaction between them, Olayiwola gives no space to the secular: for him, Islam's history in Nigeria has to be understood *as* a political history. The reason is clearly stated:[73]

> Islam is a faith and a state. . . . Sovereignty belongs only to Allah . . . so any earthly ruler of Muslims must . . . rule them strictly in accordance with the injunctions of Allah as provided in the Holy Quran and the Prophetic Hadith. Justice is uncompromisable.

There is no doubt a weak politics running though church history of any kind, but it is the strong politics of Olayiwola's kind of Islamic history that explains the prominence in it of two salient themes—violence and *takfir*—that have no presence or parallels in Abodunde's Christian history.

Violence is precisely where Olayiwola's narrative begins, more particularly Muslim-on-Muslim violence, the kind involved in the setting up of Islamic states and the correction of deviance in them. He traces the genesis of his work back to Jos in 1981, where he[74]

> witnessed the first conflict between Muslims on account of differences of conviction of faith. The conflict between Tariqah [Sufi brotherhoods] and Izalah [anti-Sufi

> activists] was so elaborate that lives were lost. . . . Back home in Yorubaland, remonstrance between scholars . . . never took that form. . . . it has never been allowed to degenerate to the midst of followers on the street. [He refers to his] shock and dismay when [he] found [himself] among Muslims, who according to the Qur'an are supposed to be brethren, killing one another [even] within the premises of mosques.

Anyone other than a Salafist may perhaps draw an obvious inference from this contrast between peaceful Yorubaland and the violent North that it probably has something to do with the Yoruba culture of religious tolerance, grounded in the outlook of their pre-Islamic *jahiliyya,* in contrast to the tradition of jihadist state-formation in Northern Nigeria. But these are possibilities that Olayiwola cannot allow himself to entertain. For him, the only conceivable basis of Islamic unity, the social counterpart of divine unity (*tawhid*), is a rightly guided regime in accord with the Prophet's revelation. It follows that responsibility for violence can never be laid at the door of those who promote this ideal but only of those who, in opposing it, are *justly* taken as the enemies of God and to be treated accordingly.

This gives Olayiwola his doctrinal key for the interpretation of the history of Nigerian Islam, namely *takfir,* the anathematization as non-Muslim of certain groups who falsely present themselves as Muslim and thus undermine the true unity of Islam. *Takfir* is equally a religious and a political act, since it is concerned with defining the boundaries of the *umma.* Its first major use in Nigerian history was by Usman dan Fodio, in order to challenge the legitimacy of the Hausa kingdoms (then Muslim in their own eyes for several centuries) against which he launched his jihad and to justify his stance against his most formidable Muslim rival, al-Kanemi of Borno.[75] *Takfir* changes the status under Islamic law of those so anathematized, for it redefines them as apostates and so legitimates the use of violence against them. Olayiwola wholeheartedly endorses dan Fodio's position and without cavil or qualification declares that "no ideal Islamic community . . . has ever been built in history without Jihad."[76]

The ideal of the *umma* as a political community, the framework for the collective life of Muslims, is at the center of Olayiwola's thinking. Now, since he also happens to be Nigerian, the question cannot be avoided of how this may relate to the two other frameworks offered by Nigerian history: state and nation. These concepts are not of the same order, since the state is a definite material reality but the nation is an "imagined community."[77] A supposed merit of *nation*-states, as against any other kind of state, is that the moral and cultural attachments rooted in belonging to a nation may be harnessed to create the basis for state citizenship. Since the *umma* is also an imagined community (and as such provided the moral basis for the early Islamic Empire and many later Islamic states), it has potential rivals in any nation based on different principles, such as language, ethnicity, race or descent, shared historical experiences, territorial logic, and so on, though historic compromises have often been found between them.[78]

Nigeria figures in Olayiwola's account in two contrasting guises. First, it is an imaginary Muslim country, but one that was never allowed to come to fruition. This Nigeria "could have been united on the basis of Islam," but the "unifying revolution . . . as commenced by Shaykh Uthman bn Fudi" was choked off by British colonial intervention.[79] Then there is the real Nigeria, the one that was created by the British in 1914, a century after dan Fodio's death, which Olayiwola represents as a country where "people who were brothers and sisters in Islam before the incursion of the West have been reduced to warring parties over what the colonialists have indoctrinated them to . . . Nationalism and Patriotism."[80] Thus he objects to Muslims' adopting communal identities and getting caught up in local conflicts, since it results in them "[ceasing] to see one another as Muslims first and foremost." The idea of Nigeria as a nation is thus a chimerical distraction from the only identification that has value for him, that of the Muslim *umma,* whereas Nigeria as a state is a mere political space that he would like to see entirely filled with the Islamic content of Sharia.

If I have given more space to Olayiwola's book than to Abodunde's, it is because (although less rich as a history of religion) it is so much more revealing as a political document. That the Pentecostalist literature is so devoid of a religiously theorized politics of any kind is itself an indication of just how different the two movements are in this respect. Yet whereas Olayiwola is much concerned about the establishment of an Islamic state but has no time for nationalism, Abodunde is a nationalist who has almost nothing to say about the state. One may think his nationalism surprising, granted that the rise of born-again Christianity was linked to a loss of faith in the secular project of Nigerian nationalism. But here the sense of national destiny is restored through pride in what Nigerians are doing in the world, whether through the dynamic and innovatory forms of Christian faith that they have taken to other lands or their fidelity to the traditions brought by the Gospel pioneers. The fitting heroes of Abodunde's last chapter are thus Pastor Sunday Adelaja, founder of the Embassy of God in the Ukraine,[81] and Archbishop Peter Akinola, the staunch defender of traditional teaching on sexuality in the Anglican Communion. There is no contradiction here between Abodunde's sense of Pentecostalism being a global movement and his proud conviction that "history has placed in our [Nigerian] hands the baton in this hour."[82]

The contrasting attitudes to nationalism between the two movements also express attitudes toward culture more generally that are deeply rooted in their parent religious traditions. The main focus of Pentecostalism's hostility to the culture of African nationalism was where the latter was felt to promote idolatry (as in the anti-FESTAC protests). But Pentecostalists are not in principle opposed to cultural specificities, and they have often taken trouble to adapt and preserve the cultural markers of ethnic distinction, provided that they are free (or can be purged) of any idolatrous taint.[83] The Babel of linguistic diversity, as a fact of human history—the

"Parthians and Medes and Elamites . . . Cretes and Arabians" of Acts 2—is *not* there simply to be erased. Rather, it has provided the occasion for two complementary responses: transcendence though the Pentecostal gift of tongues and translation of the Bible into vernacular languages.[84] The latter, famously, has worked powerfully to valorize the nations that are the bearers of those languages. We can see a strong modern evocation of this conjunction of the universal and the particular in that favored mise-en-scène of big Pentecostal revival services, where the back of the stage, behind the preacher's rostrum, is adorned with a row of national flags.[85] The message is implicit but clear: the Gospel is for all nations, since Christ is less the source of any one culture than the redeemer of all.[86]

Salafists, by contrast, are very uneasy about cultural diversity because of their conviction that Islam offers a complete way of life[87] This notion, if taken literally, would obviate any discussion of the relationship *between* Islam and particular cultures, since it leaves no space for true Muslims to have any culture except what is derived from Islam. Even Olayiwola has to recognize that this is fantastical, and he concedes that "Islam permits the incorporation of people's customs into the framework of Shari'ah."[88] The trouble is that in Nigeria, as he delicately puts it, "this concession . . . seems to have been overutilized," so that Muslims from one part of the country are not able to recognize as Islam what they find Muslims practicing in the name of that same religion in another part. Without uniformity, he feels, the ideal of unity is always at risk, and so Nigerian Islam needs to be restored as closely as possible to that pristine form of social cohesion that Émile Durkheim called mechanical solidarity: "All should understand that our ability to remain united depends on how closely alike we are. The culture of Islam [is] good enough for any people [in] any age. The more tenaciously we hold to it—devoid of admixture—the more united we shall be."[89]

VIII

On the surface, these two narratives may just seem to be very different; but they also harbor deep incompatibilities: not primarily as regards the faith and practice of individuals but as to how the two religions should connect with the political community. Salafism tends to come with explicit views of the kind of Islamic state that it aspires to, but Pentecostalism shrinks from any statement of its own politics, save for the oblique criticism of the Nigerian state for its failure to bring about development and the expression of disgust at political corruption that is common among individual Pentecostalists (as among Nigerians in general). But is the apolitical character of Pentecostalism simply to be taken at face value? It is surely not helpful to regard all religions as equally political in principle, as a thoroughgoing disciple of Foucault may be inclined to do, on the grounds that the play of power is all-pervasive in social life, and that power implies politics. Yet even on the narrower view that the political is what relates to the *polis* or state, the most apolitical of movements may have important political consequences, whether from how the state responds to them (as Jehovah's Witnesses have often found to their cost)[90] or through the mobilizing and empowering effects that they may have in the sphere of civil society. It is also quite possible that any group of Pentecostalists may take up an active political position and feel empowered by their faith in so doing, but in that case they will need to get their political script from some source other than Pentecostalism.

The key point here is how far the political messages of a religion in any particular situation are to be seen as integral or contingent to it. What is striking here is how much more historically contingent are the messages carried by Nigerian Pentecostalism—it may be better to say "Pentecostalists"—than those of Salafism, such as its articulation of resistance to the Abacha tyranny in the mid-1990s or the various affinities that it has established with other social forces (such as the Life More Abundant theme of the Awoist political tradition in Yorubaland). It is precisely this protean character of Pentecostalism that has enabled it to flourish in such diverse social contexts. Putting the point another way, we may say that Pentecostalism, as far as politics goes, offers a much more empty or open religious disposition, one whose content is less constrained by its traditions, than Salafism does. There are certainly forms of Pentecostalism that enjoin strict codes of behavior, but in general the Holy Spirit is a vastly more flexible guide, one far more open to what the contingencies of history may bring, than the Koran and *hadith* are. Whereas Pentecostalists, existing as they do in many varieties, presume (and therefore also tend to promote) an open, plural, and level religious field, Salafists strive to reinstitute the religiopolitical regime that they believe Allah revealed to mankind through his Prophet. To that extent, the two movements offer Nigeria radically incompatible blueprints for the placement of religion in society.

11

The Three Circles of Yoruba Religion

Once in 2008 I was flying back from East Africa and had to take a night's stopover in Addis Ababa. The driver sent to collect me spoke such good English that I asked him if he had spent time outside Ethiopia, thinking he might have been a student in the United States or Britain. He replied that he had been to Lagos, where the headquarters of his church was. This turned out to be Winners' Chapel, led by the charismatic Bishop David Oyedepo. Two years later I came across Oyedepo's confidently smiling features on a weather-faded poster in a small town in the interior of western Liberia, advertising a power summit at his church's national headquarters in Monrovia. The Yoruba have exported their brand of neo-Pentecostalism all over sub-Saharan Africa, especially to major cities like Nairobi and Johannesburg. And to Europe too, whether to serve mainly their own diaspora or to light the Pentecostal fire in a native white population (as with the Embassy of God in Ukraine). In the New World, the picture is more complicated, since Yoruba religion takes two forms: the *orịṣa* religion, which came more than 150 years ago with those forcibly transported there as slaves, chiefly to Brazil and Cuba, or later diffused from there since 1950; and the faiths that Yoruba migrants have taken with them in recent decades.

But what are we calling "Yoruba religion" here? I think the term may be legitimately used in either of two ways: as whatever religion is actually practiced by Yoruba people or as a religion of distinctively Yoruba origins and character. These two criteria do not need to coincide in theory and may not substantially do so in practice. Putting them together, we may today distinguish three main concrete realizations or circles of Yoruba religion over the past century or so, which I may characterize as follows:

1. Yoruba religion practiced by Yoruba in their homeland, or what is conventionally called Yoruba traditional religion (YTR), to which the cult of *orịṣa* was central.

2. Religion practiced by the overwhelming majority of Yoruba people today, not of Yoruba origin but consisting of various forms of Islam and Christianity.
3. Religion of Yoruba origin practiced in the world today, overwhelmingly outside Africa by people who are not Yoruba.[1]

Though the three circles are linked through the historical experiences of the Yoruba over recent centuries and in the trajectories of the various religions implicated in them, this connectedness has not been adequately matched in scholarship, which has been fragmented. The classic work of Pierre Verger was exemplary in bridging Circles 1 and 3[2] and has been followed in several recent collections on particular *orișa:* Ogun, Osun, Sango.[3] The relationship between Circles 1 and 2 is central to all studies of religious conversion in Yorubaland, though it has to be said that, since the perspective and documentation comes mainly from the side of the world religions, that usually receives much more detailed coverage than the "pagan" side. (I don't exempt my own work from that criticism.) But the gulf between Circles 2 and 3, though they have a common point of reference in Circle 1, has been enormous. (The main exception has been the work of J. Lorand Matory, though he has relatively little to say about the place of Christianity in the Atlantic nexus.)[4] Circle 1 is now increasingly of residual importance and hence attracts less original study; it is Circles 2 and 3 where the serious contemporary action is, both as regards religious practice and in its scholarly study.

My contention here is that the gulf between Circles 2 and 3 needs to be closed if we are to answer a glaring question prompted by their comparison. How can we explain that *orișa* cults have fared so badly in their homeland—where they have shrunk to a pale shadow of their former importance (many cults, indeed, have died out altogether) and become subject to attack from dominant Muslim and Christian groups as demonic—while they have flourished and expanded outside it, not merely among African-descended populations but attracting many people not of African descent? Since my own primary research has been limited to Nigeria (Circles 1 and 2), my remarks about the situation of Circle 3 are both secondary and speculative.[5] Although I do not have an answer to the question that I have posed, I hope that the comparisons I make in this chapter will do something to clear the way toward it. A further implication of this inquiry, with its Yoruba subject matter, is that the partition that has tended to exist between students of *orișa* religion, wherever practiced, and of Christianity and Islam needs to be broken down.

CIRCLE 1

We must begin from the so-called YTR—or, less tendentiously, *orișa* religion—since it was the baseline for the two trajectories of Yoruba religious development, in the homeland and in the New World. I begin here from a paradox: that in several ways the very term "Yoruba traditional religion" gives a misleading picture of its historical reality. As with Voltaire's famous quip about the Holy Roman Empire—that it was so called because it was neither holy nor Roman nor an empire—there are things that are problematic about each of its three terms.

"Yoruba" is a Hausa name of Arabic origin, originally applied just to the Oyo, adopted by the (Anglican) Church Missionary Society in the 1840s as their name for the people they proposed to evangelize and extended by them over succeeding decades to many other cognate peoples (the Egba, Ijesha, Ijebu, et al.). There were many close resemblances of language and culture between these peoples, as well as traditions of common descent from Ile-Ife, and these resemblances explain why they were readily grouped under a common name in diasporic situations, where they stood against much more different cultural others: Nago in Brazil, Lucumi in Cuba, Aku in Sierra Leone. But the notion of a specifically *Yoruba* religion implies a content that is both common to all Yoruba and distinctive of them. Here the problem is less that important Yoruba *oriṣa* (e.g., Ifa, Ogun, Esu-Elegba) were widely found among neighboring non-Yoruba peoples than that the cults to be found in different Yoruba towns varied so much. For example, in the 1870s, the main public cults of Ibadan were considered to be Orisa Oko, Ogiyan, and Oke'badan, whereas in Ondo they were Ogun, Esu, Oramfe, and the royal ancestors.[6] Sango, who bulks so large in *oriṣa* religion in the New World, was an Oyo deity regarded as alien to the Yoruba East (Ondo, Ijesha, Ekiti). Oduduwa, understood as a male ancestral ruler of Ife in the Center-East, was considered the female consort of the creator god in the Southwest.[7] Of river deities, Yemoja belonged mainly to the West; Osun to the Center-East; and Oya, being linked with the Niger as well as the tornado, to the North. So what existed on the ground was less a single Yoruba religion than a spectrum of local-cult complexes that varied from town to town and from West to East. The more heavily forested East was remote from the control of Oyo as well as from the Islamic influences that came with it.

1. The great and persistent problem with the term "traditional" is that it is used to refer both to a state supposedly anterior to the cultural impact of colonialism and to a certain range of contemporary beliefs and practices, namely those that cannot be assigned to either Islam or Christianity. There is the typical implication that the traditional exists in a state of stability, handed down from previous generations. No doubt this was the ideal, but there is plenty of evidence that, even before the upheavals of the nineteenth century, the reality was dynamic and changing. This dynamism was fueled by two enduring features of Yoruba religion: the possibility of individuals moving between cults and the competitive, expansionist character of many of the cults themselves. Nineteenth-century evidence suggests that this was especially true of the cult of the thunder god Sango. It seems likely that it opened the way to conversion to Islam, which had been part of the

(Oyo-)Yoruba religious scene for at least four centuries, and started to make significant numbers of converts by the early nineteenth century. So the notion that Islam and the "traditional" belong to absolutely separate circles is untenable.

2. Finally we have to ask the most radical question of all: Is precolonial YTR strictly to be considered *a* "religion" at all? People had identities as members of their communities and (in many cases) as initiates of the cult groups of *particular* deities but not as adherents of a generalized religion. The word *ẹsin,* which means "religion" in modern Yoruba, was introduced by Christians and Muslims to refer exclusively to their own self-consciously held faiths.[8] It was not its adherents but missionaries who first discursively constructed YTR as such (initially under the rubric "Yoruba heathenism"). In so doing, they both delimited and expanded it: they cut it out from the wider field of practices by which Yoruba people sought to control the environment of their lives and they treated as a single pan-Yoruba entity—one corresponding to the Yoruba nation that they had also identified and named—the spectrum of local-cult complexes, which was what YTR was in reality.

But despite these reservations about the portrayal of them as a unified and bounded entity, unvarying across time and space, the religious practices of this large and diverse area undeniably have many strong and distinctive commonalities. The main components, of variable form, content, and local presence, are the *oriṣa* or deities, strongly personalized but at the same time expressive of natural forces (rivers, mountains, meteorological phenomena) or associated with human activities linked to them (farming, healing, ironworking); a supreme being, Olorun or Olodumare, the author of all existence but mainly active in human affairs through the *oriṣa;* ancestors, who were represented in various ways, such as the *egungun* masquerade cult among the Oyo or the Oro society among the Egba, whose voice was heard as the whirring sound of the bullroarer; other forms of power embodied in human form, such as witches and the cults directed against them, like Gelede; medicines (*oogun*), quasi-animate embodiments of power in material substances; and a wide range of divinatory techniques, of which the most complex and prestigious was Ifa.

At the heart of Yoruba religious action, whether undertaken by individuals or by communities, was the search for empowerment and protection through establishing relations with the unseen but personalized forces that controlled everything that occurred in the phenomenal world. Two principal modes of relationship linked human beings and the deities. One was possession, whereby divine power was made available through the *oriṣa* mounting (*gun*) or entering the body of a devotee.[9] This was limited to the minority who were priests or active initiates and were thus enabled to mediate the power of their *oriṣa* to the laity.

The other, sacrifice (*ẹbọ*), involved virtually everyone from time to time, whether on the many mundane occasions when individuals sought oracular advice, at the periodic festivals of *oriṣa* when cult activists and the community reaffirmed their links with their divine patrons, or when exceptional sacrifices were needed since it appeared that something had gone seriously wrong and the anger of an *oriṣa* needed appeasement. Sacrifice involved a kind of gift exchange between the sacrificer and the *oriṣa:* something of value—maximally the life of a living creature, even a human being, but also cowries or other items—was offered to the *oriṣa* in anticipation of life being given in return. The maintenance of life, keeping death in abeyance, was indeed the grand objective of YTR, and largely remains so in all the three circles of Yoruba religion.

Ifa has often been seen as the apex or centerpiece of YTR, and in a sense it was: it was arguably the most pan-Yoruba of all the cults, and it played a role in their overall articulation through the mytho-legendary material about them contained in its divinatory verses. Yet there were ambivalences in Ifa's relationship with the other *oriṣa* cults. Ifa had its own *oriṣa,* Orunmila, whom it represents as superior to the others, indeed as the coeval associate of Olodumare himself. Yet it also stands in contrast to the other cults. Ifa was a strongly male-oriented cult and did not possess the *babalawo.* By contrast, many, if not most, *oriṣa* priests were women, and so too were the great mass of active devotees. The greatest paradox about Ifa was that, despite its centrality to the *oriṣa* religion of Circle 1, it also provided a link to the world religions that would engender Circle 2. This seems to go back to the very origins of Ifa.

The sixteen-options basic form of Ifa shows it to belong to a family of divination systems of West Asian origin, whose vector in sub-Saharan Africa can only have been Islam. But its positively indigenous content suggests it is best regarded as a local response to the challenge of Islamic knowledge, the appropriation of one of its techniques to serve the cosmology that underpinned ancient Ife. Yet Ifa's emphasis on Olodumare as its ultimate source indicates an opening to monotheism unique within YTR, and many references to Islam within the Ifa corpus indicate a strong awareness of the activities of Muslim clerics; yet at the same time *babalawo* sometimes divined that the solution to a client's problem was for him to become a Muslim.[10] Ifa, for all that it retells precedents, has always played an important role in legitimating novel responses to new situations: it mediates between continuity and change. Its remarkable degree of openness and disinterestedness eventually extended to Christianity too, and in turn African mission agents gave *babalawo* a degree of respect that they accorded to representatives of no other *oriṣa.* The first local study of YTR by a Yoruba pastor, James Johnson's *Yoruba Heathenism* (1899), treated Ifa and the *oriṣa* in sharply contrasting ways: Ifa was seen as pointing toward Christianity, whereas the *oriṣa* were seen as the work of Satan. Johnson's chief informant was a figure from the nascent Circle 3, an Ijesha *babalawo* called Arije or Philip Jose Meffre, who converted from a nominal Catholicism to a committed evangelical Christianity when he returned from Brazil in 1862.

CIRCLE 2

The roots of Circle 2 run back to the arrival of Islam in Yorubaland, perhaps four centuries ago, but only in the twentieth century has it been fully realized, during the colonial and postcolonial periods. The process took place in three phases: first, a slow buildup during the nineteenth century, when Islam was joined (from the mid-1840s) by Christian missions; second, mass conversion during the colonial period from the 1890s onward, reaching a tipping point in the 1930s and continuing into the age of high nationalism up to the late 1970s; and third, the emergence within both world religions of new movements more stringently opposed to the surviving forms of *orişa* religion.

The crucial point about the competition between the world religions in the nineteenth century was that it took place under Yoruba rules. Except for an area of northern Yorubaland that fell under Fulani jihadist rule as the Emirate of Ilorin, in the 1830s, Yoruba Islam expanded by peaceful, decentralized means. It was chiefly spread by clerics (*alfa*) who operated as entrepreneurs, offering their magicospiritual services to chiefs and people: at the public level it was a matter of means to deal with fires and epidemics, and to bring success in war; to individuals, it was the same kind of guidance, healing, protection, and material benefits that the *orişa* cults offered. The chief Islamic means were a kind of sacrificial offering known as *saraa,* made through the *alfa,* and charms made from Koranic texts written on scraps of paper and sewn into leather amulets (*tira*). Thus Islam became part of the Yoruba system of religious provision, without any strong pressure to convert. If people did decide to convert, there was not much strong pressure on them for further cultural renunciation. Many Yoruba Muslims continued active in the worship of their family's *orişa* and ancestral cults: the *orişa* were often reconfigured Islamically as *maleka* (angels).

Initial expectations of Christianity ran along similar lines: seen as another cult of God above, like Islam, and a distinct source of empowerment, giving access to the white man's power. But in general and officially, the missions could not make this power available in the magicospiritual forms shared by *orişa* religion and local Islam, though popular Christian belief might tend this way (e.g., the ABD reading primer understood as a protective charm). Moreover, in their early days the missions made very heavy demands for cultural change (e.g., over polygamy, slaveholding, and participation in domestic rituals) and promoted ethical values that were strongly at variance with much of Yoruba life. The long course of instruction and catechizing that preceded baptism actually made it quite difficult to become a

Christian. Christian converts were often seen as a people apart and initially were mostly drawn from marginal social categories. Even in Lagos (annexed by the British in 1861) Islam won many more local converts than Christianity. It was here that radical Yoruba clergy first defined Christianity's problem as being culturally alien and too close to the European colonial presence.

Yet the British colonization of interior Yorubaland in the 1890s radically changed the conditions of conversion to both world religions, giving a particular fillip to Christianity on account of its association with the white man's knowledge and its virtual monopoly of Western education. Islam benefited too, especially in areas where it was already well established, but its educational weakness remained a major drawback. On the other hand, Christianity found ways to correct its two main weaknesses: its overall sense of estrangement from Yoruba culture and particularly its inability to address the popular demand for magicomedical services. So Africanization became a main item on its agenda for most of the twentieth century. A key breakthrough was achieved in the Aladura (Praying) movement, which burst on the scene in the 1920s and 1930s. This was led by charismatic prophets who developed Christian means of healing, guidance, protection against evil, and the relief of mundane needs, thus triggering mass movements of conversion, which led to the emergence of new churches that have flourished down to this day. The paradox of Aladura is that while it offered a Christianity well in line with the traditional values of Yoruba religion and incorporating some of its symbolic idioms, it was also much more vehemently hostile to Ifa and the *oriṣa* cults than the mainline churches were. In fact the Aladura revivals of 1930–31 brought a massive wave of iconoclasm directed against idols and the association of *oriṣa* with demons and other "powers of darkness."

The 1930s marked a watershed in the history of religion in Yorubaland, and by the early 1950s the world religions could claim a majority of nearly 90 percent, near equally divided between Islam and Christianity. Though *oriṣa* religion was in a process of steady contraction—many of the smaller, more local cults seem to have died out in the wake of Aladura activity—cult festivals of major civic importance continued to be celebrated; divinatory and magicomedical services remained in high demand, even among Muslims and Christians, and much of the old cosmological framework still informed the practice of the world religions (e.g., belief in witchcraft and the power of "juju"). The culture of *oriṣa* religion also sustained a social ethos of tolerant religious coexistence that served to domesticate the potential intolerance and exclusivism of the monotheisms.[11] By the late colonial period, Yoruba religion was conceived as like a stool with three legs, or a crossroads (*orita*) between three faith traditions.[12] This dispensation continued through the nationalist period of the 1940s and 1950s and for nearly twenty years after Nigeria became independent in 1960.

A marked change began to show itself in the late 1970s, with two new developments reaching across Nigeria as a whole. First, the world religions assumed a much greater saliency in the public sphere, as in the vehement debates about Sharia law that first erupted in 1977–78 during the debates that preceded the establishment of a new civilian constitution; and in the intermittent outbreaks of religious violence between Muslims and Christians, mostly in Northern Nigeria, which began in the early 1980s and have continued up to the present. Though the Yoruba continue as a beacon of religious amity, even here relations between Islam and Christianity are more tense than they used to be before 1980. This is linked to the second development, the rise of new and more strenuous forms of devotion within each faith: charismatic or neo-Pentecostal (born-again) Christianity on the one side, and more rigorous versions of Islamic reformism on the other, which have each gained millions of converts and stamped their assertive presence alike on urban space and the electronic media.

Despite their antagonism, these have several features in common: they are strongly aware of themselves as movements for reform and renewal within their own faith traditions and are aware of themselves as belonging to transnational movements. They are both intensely critical of many of the local adaptations made by their respective faiths and have redoubled their efforts to stigmatize and eliminate what remains of *orișa* religion. They promote universalizing rather than Africanizing idioms for the expression of their respective faiths: if the drive toward a more normative Middle Eastern style has been going on in Yoruba Islam for decades, the loss of momentum of the Africanizing impetus in Christianity is striking. Though the born-agains had important roots in the Aladura movement, it is common for them to attack such White-garment churches as the Celestial Church of Christ for having incorporated pagan practices. Nollywood movies often incorporate born-again perspectives in their hyperrealistic portrayals of witches and demons, thus serving to perpetuate a distorted simulacrum of traditional belief and practice, while Pentecostal literature attacks wealth-bringing female deities like Mami Wata, Yemoja, or Olokun.[13] Direct iconoclastic assault has in recent decades been more the work of Muslims, with such public displays as *egungun* masquerades their particular targets. Whilst at Oyo it is Islam that encroaches upon the royal rituals of Sango, at Ife the *Ọọni*, the very reincarnation of Oduduwa, gives ground to pressure from evangelical Christianity. *Ọọni* Sijuade has renounced his divine status and the title of *Alaye* (Ruler of the World) that expressed it, while his forceful senior wife, a zealot of the Christ Apostolic Church, has built her own chapel in the palace and sponsors a nativity play that stages the downfall and replacement of *orișa* religion.[14] It is an irony indeed that over a period when Ife has become a pilgrimage center for *orișa* devotees from the New World, its indigenous traditional priesthood experiences, as Jacob Olupona puts it, "despair and outrage, . . . gasping for air in a restricted space, occupied by . . . hostile forces."[15]

Yet *orișa* religion is so closely related to the glories of Yoruba culture, and to what makes the Yoruba distinctive as a people, that the demonization of it to which they have been led by their convictions as Christians or Muslims has never been their only response to it. Christians particularly have developed another strategy to make the *oriṣa* safe, which is to secularize them by taking them out of the category of religion altogether. This began with the euhemeristic interpretation of *oriṣa* by African pastors of the missions: they were seen as heroes, founder kings, ancestors, or great men deified after their deaths, thus enabling them to be treated with respect. In recent years, a highly reified concept of culture has been used to present the annual festivals of major patronal deities as cultural festivals, celebrations of the community and its history *rather than* as religion (though not everyone, including some *ọba*s themselves, has felt able to accept this redefinition). No part of YTR has been more important in this regard than Ifa; no group of indigenous religious specialists has won the same kind of respect from Christian pastors and Muslim *alfa* as did the *babalawo.* The idea of Ifa as Yoruba philosophy or as a great cultural archive remains very influential among Yoruba intellectuals down to this day. Here we have a perspective among a minority of well-educated Yoruba, even at a time when the dominant movements in Islam and Christianity so strongly negate everything to do with traditional religion, that is able to connect with the flourishing practice of *oriṣa* religion in the Americas.

CIRCLE 3

Clearly *oriṣa* religion could not cross the Atlantic under the conditions that it did without major changes in its social bearings, its organization, and (most problematically) its content. It is the last of these that has most engaged scholars, concerned as they have been to celebrate the African achievement, under the most adverse circumstances, in saving such a large portion of their religious heritage and the values implicit in it. The extent to which this happened was variable, depending both on the culture and capacity of particular groups of slaves and on the institutional conditions into which they were received.

The distinctiveness of the Yoruba case can be pinpointed through two contrasts. First, although many different African groups succeeded in establishing something of their old religion in New World settings, the success of the Yoruba in so doing—above all in the shape of *Santería* in Cuba and *Candomblé* in Brazil—is outstanding. This seems due partly to the inherent durability yet adaptability of the forms, both cultural and institutional, by which *oriṣa* religion was carried and partly to the historical contingency of the numbers and timing of Yoruba slave imports to the Americas. While Yorubaland had supplied slaves to the Atlantic trade during the eighteenth century—it had been a major source of revenue for the Oyo Empire—the great surge in slaves of Yoruba origin came only from the 1810s and peaked as late as 1826–50.[16] That was due precisely to the collapse of Old Oyo, which created a regional power vacuum and decades of internecine warfare across the whole of Yoruba country. The resultant human debris fed the continuing demand for slaves, both local and international. Since both Great Britain and France had by the 1830s abolished slavery in their colonies and outlawed the slave trade, this late flood of Yoruba slaves passed by illicit channels into the Spanish and Portuguese colonies, where slavery was abolished much later (Cuba in 1886; Brazil in 1888).

The other condition for the survival of so much of *orịṣa* religion came from the side of the slaveowners, where the key factor was whether they were Catholic (especially Iberian) or Protestant. The contrast between the religious outcomes in Cuba, Brazil, and Haiti on the one hand, and Jamaica or the Anglo-American colonies (or states) on the other, with Trinidad (passing from Spanish through French to British control) an interesting hybrid case, is striking. The Catholic powers were prepared to recognize and accept the existence of African nations and to allow associations based on them a limited sphere of activity, which clearly worked to facilitate the survival of ethnic religious traditions, more than the Protestant powers were. This was further facilitated by the Catholic institution of the *cabildo* or religious fraternity. For the Yoruba in particular, the Catholic cult of saints was important in providing a framework within which *oriṣa* worship, first perhaps disguised and then genuinely synthesized with elements of Catholic devotion, could be continued. Most *oriṣa* devotees no doubt regarded themselves as Catholics too and participated in Catholic festivals. Nevertheless the Yoruba-derived ritual complexes did not simply maintain a sense of themselves as such but also developed organizationally, ritually, and theologically, as they responded to the challenges of the new contexts. This is not to be grasped within the terms of the model put forward by Melville J. Herskovits, in which a single continuum runs between poles labeled "most African" and "most acculturated to Euro-Catholic norms."[17] Rather, as David Brown has put it, "borrowed 'non-African' narratives may have helped recrystallize heterogeneous resources into a modern, theologically rationalized religion."[18]

Oriṣa religion has evolved as a belief system in the Americas in three principal ways:

1. The number of deities worshipped has been greatly reduced from the total that must have originally been taken across the Atlantic, still less the 401 (i.e., indefinitely numerous) *oriṣa* that are conventionally said to have existed in Circle 1.
2. The main survivors—Sango, Ogun, Yemoja, Esu-Elegba, Obatala (Orisanla in Brazil), Ososi, Osun, Oya, Sopona (Babaluaye)—are particularly characteristic of Oyo and the Center and northwest rather than of eastern Yorubaland. Among these Sango, the royal deity of Oyo, has risen to a position of such overall preeminence that in some regions his name has eclipsed all others (e.g., Shango in Trinidad, Xango in parts of Brazil).[19] On the other

hand there are the contrasting outcomes for Ifa (Orunmila), which virtually died out in Brazil but flourished greatly in Cuba. At first sight it seems surprising that it is this way round, since *far* more Yoruba people were taken as slaves to Bahia than to the Spanish Caribbean,[20] and there was also a great deal more flux and reflux between Yorubaland and Brazil than there was with Cuba. The names of some prominent *babalawo* are known.[21] By comparison it seems due to contingent (or at least not fully explained) circumstances that Ifa became so solidly established in Havana in the late nineteenth century through the efforts of five Yoruba-born *babalawo* who are recognized as the founders of the main branches of the entire *Regla de Ifa* in Cuba and the Cuban diaspora down to today, with far-reaching consequences.[22]

A further point may perhaps be made about the varying fortunes of Yoruba *oriṣa* in these new settings. Although I strongly incline to a creolist overall perspective in the interpretation of Cuban or Brazilian phenomena—that is, one that fully accepts their authenticity as such rather than evaluating them primarily as more or less effective vehicles for the transmission of pregiven African traits—it is important to stress that some New World developments seem also to be extensions of cultural dynamics already evident in nineteenth-century Yorubaland. Two examples come to mind. First, the same features of the Sango cult that fueled its expansion from its Oyo heartland into areas to the east and south during the Age of Confusion after the collapse of the Oyo Empire continued overseas as occasions presented themselves, whether in Brazil or the Caribbean.[23] Second, the way in which Lucumi religion in Cuba became bifurcated between what Brown calls "Ifa-centric" and "Ocha-centric" ritual fields,[24] the former male-oriented and the latter female-oriented, while it has to be seen as a distinctly Cuban development, is still also the further working out of a cultural logic that was already evident (and noted by our first contemporary witnesses, native CMS agents) in mid-nineteenth-century Yorubaland.[25]

3. *Oriṣa* religion has become markedly more "pantheonized," in David Brown's term, or rationalized as a unified, hierarchical system. Not surprisingly, in Cuba this was mainly the work of *babalawo,* though an analogous process occurred more spontaneously in Brazil. Although it is now common for scholars of Yoruba religion in Nigeria to speak of a "pantheon" of deities—by analogy with Greco-Roman religion—this is quite misleading, at least for the nineteenth century, for a reason already indicated: What existed in concrete reality was less a single Yoruba religion than a range of distinct cult complexes that varied from one town and region to another. In Yorubaland the different *oriṣa* did not share temples or festivals as they did in the New World—in fact there was a lot of rivalry between them[26]—though the

festivals of the *orișa* found in one town would usually be coordinated with one another in that town's unique ritual calendar. But the Sango, Osun, or Orisa Oko festivals were not synchronized with one another across different towns: there was no pan-Yoruba equivalent of saints' days.

Again, individuals or compounds might have collections of *orișa,* which could all be brought out together on special occasions, but these were contingent accumulations, not "pantheons."[27] Ifa verses *do* tell many stories about the relations between *orișa,* and can be used to construct a systematized pantheon, but Ifa does not really go very far in that direction itself. Since Ifa contains a vast collection of mostly quite short narratives dealing with a particular subject—primordial episodes of oracular consultation—it is in itself much less "pantheonic" than such grand mythological narratives as the Hindu *Mahabharata* or Hesiod's *Theogony.* Yet the *babalawo,* intellectuals as they were, were certainly adept at rationalizations that pointed in a pantheonic direction. So when *babalawo* in Ibadan in 1854 wanted to justify *orișa* worship to critical missionaries, they argued that the relationship of the *orișa* to God was analogous to that between the junior titleholders and the *Balẹ* of the town, both acting as intermediaries between ordinary folk and the supreme power.[28] Other Cuban developments—the reduced number of *orișa,* the notion of a single Lucumi religion, the bringing together of different *orișa* in one temple, the acquisition by a new initiate of several *orișa* at the same time[29]—must all have encouraged the *babalawo* to realize more fully the pantheon potential latent in circle-1 *orișa* religion. Here it is hard to resist the conclusion that, just as it was missionary outsiders in Yorubaland who first discursively fashioned Yoruba heathenism (YTR), so it was practitioners in the outside of the Americas who first created the reality of a single Yoruba religion.

The Yoruba religion of Circle 3 has been in continuous development. Perhaps we may discern three main stages of this: its initial formation from existing materials and traditions carried directly from West Africa in the nineteenth century; a period of consolidation and relative stability in the first half of the twentieth century (when it first became the object of positive academic study by scholars like Fernando Ortiz, R. Nina Rodrigues, Melville J. Herskovits, Roger Bastide, Ruth Landes, and others); and the later twentieth century, which has brought not only further internal development but also a dramatic expansion, particularly into North America. The background conditions of this last phase are diverse, but include a new national consciousness in many Latin American countries, such that indigenous and African traditions, long despised by their white *criollo* elites, came to be valorized; the impact of the Cuban revolution, ranging from the vicissitudes of its cultural policies toward religion (or religions) at home, to the growth in the USA of a large Cuban exile community that carried *Santería* with it; and a new cultural politics of race in the USA that led growing numbers of African-Americans to recover or recreate what they regarded as more authentically African forms of religion.

The tension between re-Africanization and universalist outreach is perhaps the crucial dilemma faced by the Yoruba religion of Circle 3 today. There are important differences between its two main forms: Yoruba reversionism, as found among African-Americans, and *Yorubización* among Cubans and Cuban-Americans. For the former, the primary impetus to re-Africanization has been a search for racial integrity, of which the archetypal product is Oyotunji (Oyo Revived) village in South Carolina. In this reinvented Yoruba community, a whole ritual cycle of festivals of major *orịṣa* has been instituted, and a roots divination introduced to provide clients with a Yoruba ancestry. The career of *Ọba* Adefunmi, Oyotunji's founder, exemplifies the tensions in the relations between black American Yoruba reversionists and the Cuban *Santeros* who introduced *orịṣa* religion to the United States from the late 1940s. Adefunmi (or Walter S. King, as he then was) had been led from a more eclectically African phase (with Akan and Dahomean elements) to a more specifically Yoruba one through the influence of a *Santero,* Cristóbal Oliana, from 1959 onward. A decade later, he had moved into black-nationalist politics and broke his previous ties with *Santería.* The idea of receiving a black religion from practitioners who included whites was unacceptable, and Adefunmi turned toward a more thorough and deliberate reinvention of Yoruba religious practice, including getting direct legitimation from the *Ọọni* of Ife.[30] Here the ironies really start to pile up, for as we have seen the *Ọọni* is a Christian subject to strong Pentecostal influence, while the Nigerians saw Adefunmi and his people as *oyinbo* (Europeans).

But re-Africanization and universalist outreach do not have to be so sharply opposed. As Stephan Palmié has shown, in contrast to how race has been culturally constructed in Anglo-America, where blackness and Africanity were mutually indexical, in Cuba "'Africanity' and 'blackness' just did not match up against up against each other."[31] This made it much more likely for Africanity to offer values of universal human relevance, so that *orịṣa* religion could at least aspire to be a world religion. The prime motive of re-Africanization or *Yorubización* then becomes the conviction that the purest, most authentic, most effective forms of ritual and doctrine are to be sought at their point of origin.[32] Although this notion is found in very many religions, its precise emphasis varies: in *orịṣa* religion it is on geographical origin (specifically on Ile-Ife as the site of the cosmogony); in Christianity and Islam it is more on temporal origin, on the age when divine incarnation or revelation occurred.

Whatever the primary motive, the impetus to re-Africanize has led to a search for authoritative or (what might be called) truly traditional knowledge about *orịṣa* religion in its homeland, for application in the diaspora. Partly this has been sought from the large body of academic and quasi-academic literature on the Yoruba—by scholars of religion, anthropologists, art historians, experts in oral (especially Ifa) literature, and so on—and partly it has come from personal contact with Yoruba priests, *babalawo,* herbalists, drummers, and other specialists. *Orișa* devotees have traveled from the New World to be initiated by and to learn from religious authorities in Nigeria, while Yoruba specialists have gone the other way, to offer their services and to build up followings or spiritual clientages across the Atlantic.[33] With the deep decline of *orișa* devotion in Yorubaland, these emerging markets for authentic ritual knowledge in the New World are an enticing opportunity for those with the relevant expertise. The most prestigious of these traveling experts or *episcopi vagantes* is surely Professor Wande Abimbola, who bears the title (conferred on him by the *Ọọni* of Ife) of *Awișẹ ni Agbaye* (Spokesperson for Ifa throughout the World).[34] He has been active in the World Orișa Conferences held periodically since 1981, which have tended to promote Nigerian Yoruba practice as normative—and significantly won more support in Brazil than in Cuba, with its own distinctive and strongly instituted *Regla de Ifa.*

A paradoxical reversal lurks in these moves toward re-Africanization, insofar as these can be justified as a kind of desyncretization: the removal of Catholic accretions to bring *orișa* religion back to its pure, primordial form.[35] For in most writing about modern African religion, the term "syncretism" has been used to express this concern when directed the other way: the anxiety of Christians and Muslims of the mainline traditions that distinctively African manifestations of those faiths (e.g., healing practices in Aladura churches, Sufi devotional rituals) have become corrupted by "pagan" elements.[36] As I argued above, the dominant movements in contemporary Nigeria, both Muslim and Christian, are run strongly against such "contamination" of their own traditions. So a war against syncretism appears to be the *ordre du jour* across the whole religious field. But while a notion of syncretism as spiritual danger seems to sit easily with doctrinally grounded faiths addressed to a single, jealous God "of Abraham, Isaac, and Jacob," it is hard to see how it can be applied plausibly or coherently to *orișa* religion, which was both undogmatic and accommodative to new cults joining its ensemble. Moreover, it appears that a certain spirit of mix-and-match arising from within American culture is producing fresh syncretisms, whether with various forms of "Afrikan" Protestant Christianity, with New Age spiritualities, or with other Afrocentric traditions. Where more likely than New Jersey to find an Egbe Sankofa Kingdom of the Gods of Afrika?[37]

Ifa has always been a critical interface between *orișa* religion and the scriptural monotheisms. Early on, these latter were often seen in terms of Ifa—for example, as where their scriptures were seen as analogous to the signs made in the dust on the diviner's tray and treated as a vehicle of predictive prophecy—but later, as Islam and Christianity acquired a general hegemony over the Yoruba religious field, the assimilation has tended to go the other way. The Church of Orunmila, which appeared in the 1920s, modeled its services upon those of Protestant churches;[38] and although this appealed to only a small minority, it has become common for educated Yoruba to read Ifa in a fundamentalist fashion, similarly to how Muslims regard the text of the Koran or evangelical Christians conceive of the Bible: as an inerrant, unchanging, pristine transcript of God's Word, set in a primordial Ile-Ife.[39] When this perspective is applied to Ifa in other, non-Yoruba settings, as in early twentieth-century Dahomey (as recorded by Bernard Maupoil for the Fon diviner Gedegbe)[40] or in the *Regla de Ifa* in Cuba, any variations in its content will have to be seen as deviations from or corruptions of its pristine character. That this is false to the historical reality of how Ifa has been produced, as an evolving and ever self-adapting system of practical oracular wisdom, is cogently shown by Noel Amherd in his study of Ifa in Ijebu Remo.[41]

In recent years the question has been raised of "*oriṣa* devotion as world religion," as in the title of an edited volume based on the papers of a large conference on Yoruba religion held in Miami in 1999.[42] Does the evident globalization of a religion so far strongly identified with its ethnolinguistic origins indicate that it has the potential truly to become "a world religion," as the volume editors suggest? Certainly "Yoruba" religion is a very different case from the sort of "glocalized" religious phenomenon represented by, say, Mouridism among Senegalese migrants in Paris or New York or the Deobandi-derived Tablighi Jamaat among Pakistani migrants and their descendants in London, in that Yoruba are not now its primary vectors but people from the Hispanic Caribbean or African-Americans. When Nigerian Yoruba go to the U.K. or the USA, they are overwhelmingly more likely to set up branches of the Redeemed Christian Church of God or of NASFAT than congregations of *oloriṣa.* Yet some Yoruba cultural entrepreneurs, including a few converts to the *oriṣa* from Christianity, have made contact with African-Americans and produced forms of *oriṣa* worship that incorporate a declamatory, testifying style like what is found in North American Protestantism.[43] Ironically, that same style, taken eastward across the Atlantic by Pentecostal evangelists (more white than black) over recent decades, has become naturalized in born-again Christianity in Nigeria. The outcomes of this cross-play of religious forces—in North America between Nigerian Yoruba migrants and visitors, African-Americans, and Latino *orichá* devotees—on both sides of the Atlantic remain wide open.

Despite the positive appeal of re-Africanization for many of those drawn to *oriṣa* religion today, whether for racial or religious reasons, the strains between it and global outreach can only grow. Religions can only become world religions if they are able to loosen their links with their racial and linguistic origins and adjust their distinctive forms to a wide range of new situational demands. Classic *Santería* and *Candomblé* were successful in doing this, but syncretism—in Bengt Sundkler's sense of "new wine [i.e., meeting religious demand from non-Yoruba in non-African settings] in old wineskins [i.e., Yoruba cultural forms]"—*was* integral to it. Even the monotheistic world religions, for all their inherent suspicion of syncretism, have in their expansion depended on employing a good deal of it in practice, though their adherents are prone to disavow it. What is certain is that these cultural struggles of *orișa* religion within Circle 3 can be resolved only there, despite the importance of cultural resources from Circle 1 (especially when conveyed by ritual experts from Nigeria). For granted the strength of anti-*orișa* sentiment in Circle 2, the cultural resource-base for Nigerian intervention in *orișa* religion outside Africa can be expected only to erode further in years to come. If this happens, it may even come about—and not for the first time, as witness the Amish or the Shakers—that a religion of Old World origins makes its primary home in the New.

. . .

I have treated Circle 1 as the baseline for two divergent lines of historical development: The first is a story of *orișa* religion's contraction in situ, where many contextual features remain in place, whereas the second is a story of expansion in radically new contexts of the diaspora, which have resulted in a push-and-pull between adaptation to new demands and struggles to maintain or recover the tradition. This contrast poses a general issue so far not addressed. Are we merely dealing with two different histories with a common starting point but driven each by its own contingencies? The comparison may have usefully pinpointed some of these, but can we also derive from it a theoretical understanding of the differences that they have produced? To do this, we need to be able to typify the two religious outcomes—the Abrahamic faiths as practiced by Nigerian Yoruba in Circle 2 and the *orișa* religion of Circle 3—in such a way as to be able to match them with a fitting general characterization of the circumstances in which they exist.

What first comes to mind here is Robin Horton's contrast between a cultic focus on a host of subordinate deities as against a High God or Supreme Being, correlating respectively with the local community (microcosm) and a world of wider social relations (macrocosm). But this contrast does not allow us to place Circle 3 in a coherent or persuasive way, since its cosmology of multiple deities does not correspond to a sociology of localized relations. Rather, the deities transited from their original microcosm(s), proving themselves equally serviceable to their devotees in the relative macrocosm of the plantations and towns of Cuba and Brazil with their populations of heterogeneous origins; and then onward to the greater macrocosm of the cities of eastern North America. On the way they took on a further macrocosmic dimension not embraced within Horton's theory: they attracted fresh devotees of diverse origins, many of non-Yoruba or even non-African origin. So it is hard to see that the worship of *orichás* in Havana, Miami, or New York, or of *orixás* in Bahia or Rio de Janeiro, is functionally either more or less microcosmic or macrocosmic than the Islam or Christianity practiced in Lagos or Ibadan.

Another dimension of religious difference seems more promising: How far, or in what respects, is any religion, or religion as such, to be seen as an instrumental or an expressive phenomenon—that is, as providing its adherents with a set of adaptive instruments or of intrinsic satisfactions? Most religions have something of both, but Christianity in the modern West has relinquished most of its erstwhile instrumental functions to science-based technology and medicine, leaving itself largely an expressive phenomenon. The instrumental and expressive aspects of religion may each take various forms, some more intrinsic and some more contingent, but for present purposes the two most pertinent are, first, where religion is an instrument for the "explanation, prediction and control" (in Horton's phrase) of this-worldly phenomena, and second, where it becomes the vehicle for the expression of an ethnic or racial identity. A strongly instrumental attitude toward the sacred was largely transferred from Circle 1, through the experience of conversion, into the Yoruba Christianity (and Islam) of Circle 2. Those who carried the *orișa* with them in their hearts across the Atlantic into the nascent Circle 3 no doubt fully shared this orientation too, initially with no sense of their expressing thereby a racial or ethnic identity but merely one of devotion to their own *orișa* or Ifa as their personal guardian and helper. For the *orișa* of Circle 1, where it all began, were not at that stage marked as Yoruba, still less as black or as part of a system that some others called idolatry. But under the conditions of Circle 3, where slaves (and later freedmen) of Yoruba origin mingled with many different ethnic others, as well as with a white racial other, some kind of ethnoracial marking became inevitable. So in Cuba a Lucumi religion came into being—in Brazil, Nago—which was probably the first time that the practitioners (as against the missionary opponents) of *orișa* religion came to see it as a single, overall entity, as *a* religion.

What did *not* happen in Cuba was that it became marked as a black religion, as happened later in the USA. Is it possible to say why Cubans who were phenotypically white not only joined *Santería* but sometimes became deep experts in its African knowledge? At this point, Palmié's argument seems to shift into a different epistemological register, for he turns to explain this through the agency of the *orișa* themselves: it was not the white initiates who chose their *orișa* but the *orișa* who chose them. Thus it becomes irrelevant to ask about the motives of the white Cubans who joined *Santería*. That certainly accords with what he describes as the "racially unmarked theology of recruitment" of Afro-Cuban religion, which surely has roots in the open recruitment patterns of some *orișa* in the Yoruba homeland.[44] But whenever was theology a sufficient condition for the religious choices of human beings? Granted the racial barriers of Cuban society in the nineteenth and the early twentieth century, it seems probable that it was instrumental concerns—"to improve their health or to reverse streaks of bad luck"[45]—rather than expressive ones that first drew whites to the *orișa*, with the expressive satisfactions of cult membership coming later; but it seems unlikely that we can ever really know. Walter S. King (later *Ọba* Adefunmi), by contrast, seems to have been drawn first to the expressive aspects of *orișa* religion and later to the instrumental uses of Ifa divination. So neither does the instrumental/expressive distinction serve to explain the difference between the paths taken by Circle 2 and Circle 3. So our quest comes to an end in contingency, indeterminacy, and the unpredictability accorded to the *orișa* themselves.

THE CONCLUSION, IN WHICH NOTHING IS CONCLUDED

"It was now the time of the inundation of the Nile. A few days after their visit to the catacombs the river began to rise. [Rasselas and his companions] were confined to their house. The whole region being under water gave them no invitations to any excursions, and, being well supplied with materials for talk, they diverted themselves with comparisons of the different forms of life, which they had observed, and with various schemes of happiness, which each of them had formed."[46]

In his poised and lambent prose, Samuel Johnson—the other one!—takes us back to where the comparative method began, in the social thought of the Enlightenment. The Grand Cham of English letters was not a systematic theorist, still less a writer whom we consider a founding father of social anthropology, yet in *The History of Rasselas, Prince of Abissinia,* he shows how fully he shared its cognitive and moral assumptions. More an extended philosophical fable than a novel, *Rasselas* drew its empirical inspiration from the account of Ethiopia written by a Portuguese Jesuit, Fr. Jerónimo Lobo, of which Johnson had published an abridged translation. His own immersion in the comparativism of the age is well evident in how he commends the credibility of Lobo's account: "Here are no Hottentots without religion, polity or articulate language, no Chinese perfectly polite and completely skilled in all the sciences";[47] or in how he makes his characters in *Rasselas* turn to ethnographic comparison as they play with the central question of the book—to which Johnson refuses a definite answer—What is the path to human happiness?

Rasselas first appeared in 1759, that *annus mirabilis* for the emergent British Empire, when the Atlantic slave trade was close to its height yet the abolitionist movement was starting to gain momentum. Johnson was well known for his passionate opposition to slavery, as well as for his personal sympathy for black people.[48] His book gained a large readership on both sides of the Atlantic, but it seems to have resonated particularly with the experience and aspiration of some of the black victims of the slave trade. It makes sense that Rasselas was a name not uncommonly given to (or taken by) by liberated slaves, like the Rasselas Belfield (d. 1822) who lies under a handsome gravestone in the churchyard of Bowness-on-Windermere in the English Lake District. For Rasselas was an African prince, and in identifying with him these former slaves were asserting an ancestral dignity, thus mildly anticipating the African-Americans who adopt Yoruba names through the roots divination offered at Oyotunji village. More than that, Johnson's book gave a significant boost toward that image of Abyssinia or Ethiopia as an idealized African homeland or the focus of an authentic spiritual life for people of African descent, from the Rastafarians to the Ethiopian Church that Adeniran Oke proclaimed to his fellow Yoruba in the aftermath of the influenza pandemic of 1918. Of course, all this goes much further than what Johnson intended—but that is the way with potent stories. *Rasselas* has often been compared with Voltaire's *Candide,* but the archetype of the Happy Valley from which Rasselas escaped in search of knowledge of the world's diversity is surely the Eden of Milton's *Paradise Lost.* An essential feature of both stories—in contrast to the various attempts to reverse history by a returning to a primordial Ife or Mecca, places where the lineaments of the good life are divinely fixed—is that the principal actors are not able to return to the paradisal state but have to go forth to make an original history through their choices:

> The world was all before them, where to choose
> Their place of rest, and Providence their guide.
> They, hand in hand, with wandering steps and slow,
> Through Eden took their solitary way.

GLOSSARY OF YORUBA AND ARABIC TERMS APPEARING IN THE TEXT AND NOTES

YORUBA

adua	prayer (Muslim) [Tones: low, high, low]
adura	prayer (Christian) [Tones: low, high, low]
afin	palace [Tones: low, mid]
agbada	man's gown [Tones: mid, high, high]
aiye	age, world, time [Tones: mid, high]
alasalatu	member of women's Muslim prayer group [Tones: mid, high, low, high, low]
alfa	Muslim cleric [Tones: low, high]
alufa	Christian clergyman [Tones: low, low, high]
babalawo	diviner, priest of Ifa [Tones: third syllable high, others mid]
balogun	war chief, warlord [Tones: mid, high, mid]
Baṣọrun	Oyo's main subroyal chief [Tones: mid, low, mid]
ẹgbẹ	club, society, association [Tones: mid, high]
ẹṣin	religion (especially world religion) [Tones: low, low]
ìlú	town, community [Tones: low, high]
Imale	Muslim [Tones: low, unmarked middle, low]
itan	story, historical narrative [Tones: low, low]
Lẹmọmu	imam [Tones: low, high, low]
mọgaji	Ibadan lineage head [Tones: high, low, high]
Nọibi	deputy to imam [Tones: high, -, high]

ọba	king, ruler [Tones: mid, mid]
odu	sacred division of Ifa verses [Tones: mid, low]
ọlaju	enlightened person [Tones: low, high, high]
ologun	warrior, war leader [Tones: mid, high, mid]
oogun	medicine [Tones: mid, low, low]
oriki	praise name [Tones: mid, then high and low on each *-i-*]
oriṣa	traditional deity [Tones: low, low, low]
oyinbo	white man, Westerner [Tones: low, low, high]
ratibi	minor local mosque, from "stipend" in Arabic [Tones: low, mid, low]
saraa	sacrifice, alms, religious feast [Tones: low, high, high]
waka	Islamic song, specially heard in Ramadan [Tones: high, low]
woli	Christian prophet [Tones: low, high-low]

ARABIC

alhaji	pilgrim to Mecca
bid'a	heresy
dhimmi	protected non-Muslim
hadith	recognized traditions of the Prophet's sayings
hajj	annual pilgrimage to Mecca
hijab	women's head scarf
hijra	emigration (esp. of the Prophet from Mecca to Medina)
jahiliyya	pre-Islamic supposed disorder
jumat	Friday prayers
mujaddid	centennial revivalist of the Islamic faith
muqaddam	facilitator, especially in Sufi rituals
salaf	ancestor, Muslim of the early generations
shirk	idolatry
sunna	the way of the Prophet
tafsir	interpretation, exegesis
tahajjud	voluntary night prayer
takfir	excommunication, expulsion from Islam
tariqa	a Sufi order or fellowship
tawhid	unity (of God)
ulama	Muslim clerics (sing. *alim*)
umma	the Muslim community at large

NOTES

INTRODUCTION

1. E.g., V. Lanternari, *Religions of the Oppressed: A Study of Modern Messianic Cults* (London: McGibbon and Kee, 1963); T. Hodgkin, *Nationalism in Colonial Africa* (London: Frederick Muller, 1956), chapter 3.

2. R. Horton, "African Conversion," *Africa* 41 (1971), 85–108.

3. J. D. Y. Peel, "Religious Change among the Yoruba," *Africa* 37 (1967), 292–306, and "Conversion and Tradition in Two African Societies: Ijebu and Buganda," *Past and Present* 77 (1977), 108–41.

4. J. D. Y. Peel, *Religious Encounter and the Making of the Yoruba* (Bloomington: Indiana University Press, 2000).

5. See H. Whitehouse, *Arguments and Icons: Divergent Modes of Religiosity* (Oxford: Oxford University Press, 2000); and H. Whitehouse and J. Laidlaw, eds., *Ritual and Memory: Toward a Comparative Anthropology of Religion* (Walnut Creek: AltaMira Press, 2004).

6. M. Pelkmans, ed., *Conversion after Socialism: Disruptions, Modernisms and Technologies of Faith in the Former Soviet Union* (New York: Berghahn, 2009), being selected papers from a conference held at the Max Planck Institute Halle in April 2005.

7. T. G. Gbadamosi, *The Growth of Islam among the Yoruba, 1841–1908* (London: Longman, 1978). It is worth noting that, though Gbadamosi is a Muslim himself, his study is bookended in Christian terms, since its start and end dates have no Muslim relevance but derive from mission activity and documentation.

8. See Rosalind I. J. Hackett, "The Academic Study of Religion in Nigeria," *Religion* 18 (1988), 37–46.

9. For a recent work that usefully spans its trajectory up to the present, see Jens Kreinath, ed., *The Anthropology of Islam Reader* (London: Routledge, 2012).

10. See especially D. N. Gellner, *The Anthropology of Buddhism and Hinduism: Weberian Themes* (New Delhi: Oxford University Press, 2001).

11. See further Aram A. Yengoyan, *Modes of Comparison: Theory and Practice* (Ann Arbor: University of Michigan Press, 2006).

12. On which see Ladislav Holy, *Comparative Anthropology* (Oxford: Blackwell, 1987), especially the chapter by Hobart, Parkin, and Overing.

13. On which see Abdul Raufu Mustapha, ed., *Sects and Social Disorder: Muslim Identities and Conflict in Northern Nigeria* (Woodbridge: James Currey, 2014), covering the manifestations of intra-Islamic violence from the Sokoto Caliphate to Boko Haram.

14. I happen to be writing this the week after the Islamist violence in Paris of 7–9 January 2015. It was noticeable that both President François Hollande and David Cameron, the U.K. prime minister, in referring to the atrocities, declared that the violence was against the true spirit of Islam. The well-known authority on Islam Mr. Tony Blair has also expressed this view. While one appreciates that it was statesmanlike for them to say so, it is hard to see what entitlement any non-Muslim has to say what "true" Islam is.

15. M. Cook, *Ancient Religions, Modern Politics: The Islamic Case in Comparative Perspective* (Princeton: Princeton University Press, 2014).

16. For example, Q.2, 190–93, which justifies retaliatory violence against persecutors; or Q.9, 5, the so-called "sword verse," which sanctions the killing of polytheists. Against this there is the "No compulsion in religion" verse at Q.2, 256.

17. Cook, *Ancient Religions*, 248.

1. HISTORY, CULTURE, AND THE COMPARATIVE METHOD: A WEST AFRICAN PUZZLE

1. An earlier version of this chapter was published in Ladislav Holy, ed., *Comparative Anthropology* (Oxford: Blackwell, 1987), 88–119.

2. J. S. Mill, *A System of Logic* (Toronto: University of Toronto Press, 1973 [1843]), book 6. See too W. G. Runciman, A *Treatise on Social Theory*, vol. 1 (Cambridge: Cambridge University Press, 1983), 193–98.

3. R. Horton, "African Conversion," *Africa* 41 (1971), 85–108, and "On the Rationality of Conversion," *Africa* 45 (1975), 219–35, 373–99.

4. See further below, chapter 7.

5. M. J. Field, *Search for Security: An Ethnopsychiatric Study of Rural Ghana* (London: Faber, 1960); T. C. McCaskie. "Anti-Witchcraft Cults in Asante," *History in Africa* 8 (1981), 125–54, J. Allman and J. Parker, *Tongnaab: The History of a West African God* (Bloomington: Indiana University Press, 2005).

6. As E. A. Hammel, "The Comparative Method in Anthropological Perspective," *Comparative Studies in Society and History* 22 (1980), 145–55.

7. M. Ginsberg, "The Comparative Method," in *Evolution and Progress* (London: Heinemann, 1961); E. E. Evans-Pritchard, *The Comparative Method in Social Anthropology* (London: Athlone Press, 1963).

8. R. L. Meek, *Social Science and the Ignoble Savage* (Cambridge: Cambridge University Press, 1976).

9. Adam Ferguson, *An Essay on the History of Civil Society* (Edinburgh: Edinburgh University Press, 1966 [1767]), 80.

10. L. T. Hobhouse, G. C. Wheeler and M. Ginsberg, *The Material Culture and Social Institutions of the Simpler Peoples* (London: Routledge and Kegan Paul, 1965 [1915]); A. M. Hocart, *Kings and Councillors* (Chicago: University of Chicago Press, 1970 [1936]).

11. M. G. Smith, *Government in Zazzau* (London: Oxford University Press, 1960); R. Horton, "From Fishing Village to City-State: A Social History of New Calabar," in M. Douglas and P. Kaberry, eds., *Man in Africa* (London: Tavistock Press, 1969).

12. Luc de Heusch, *Rois nés d'un cœur de vache* (Paris: Gallimard, 1982).

13. C. S. Littleton, *The New Comparative Mythology*, 3rd ed. (Berkeley and Los Angeles: University of California Press, 1982).

14. Examples in *Herbert Spencer on Social Evolution*, ed. J. D. Y. Peel (Chicago: University of Chicago Press, 1972), chapter 10.

15. F. W. Maitland, "The Body Politic," in *Selected Essays* (Cambridge: Cambridge University Press, 1936 [1899]), 249.

16. E.g., I. M. Lewis, ed., *History and Social Anthropology* (London: Tavistock, 1968), xv.

17. M. Weber, *Economy and Society*, ed. G. Roth and C. Wittich, 2 vols. (Berkeley and Los Angeles: University of California Press, 1968), 4–24.

18. F. Boas, "The Limitations of the Comparative Method of Anthropology," *Science* 4 (1896), 901–8.

19. R. Naroll, "Galton's Problem," in R. Naroll and R. Cohen, eds., *A Handbook of Method in Cultural Anthropology* (New York: Columbia University Press, 1973); Hammel, "Comparative Method" (above, n. 6), 146–47.

20. E. B. Tylor, "On a Method of Investigating the Development of Institutions Applied to Laws of Marriage and Descent," *Journal of the Royal Anthropological Institute* 18 (1889), 245–56, 261–69. For a full discussion see G. W. Stocking, Jr., *After Tylor: British Social Anthropology 1888–1951* (London: Athlone Press, 1996), 10–12.

21. A. R. Radcliffe-Brown, "The Comparative Method in Social Anthropology," *Journal of the Royal Anthropological Institute* 81 (1951), 15–22.

22. M. Fortes, *Oedipus and Job in West African Religion* (Cambridge: Cambridge University Press, 1959), p. 10 and chapter 3.

23. M. Fortes, "Pietas in Ancestor Worship," in *Time and Social Structure* (London: Athlone Press. 1970).

24. A. C. Edwards, "On the Non-Existence of an Ancestor Cult among the Tiv," *Anthropos* 79 (1984), 77–112.

25. A. R. Radcliffe-Brown, foreword to M. Fortes and E. E. Evans-Pritchard, eds., *African Political Systems* (London: Oxford University Press, 1940), xi.

26. R. Needham, *Exemplars* (Berkeley and Los Angeles: University of California Press, 1985), 72–74, 146, 150, 151, 184.

27. S. F. Nadel, *The Foundations of Social Anthropology* (London: Cohen and West, 1951), especially chapters 8 and 9.

28. S. F. Nadel, "Witchcraft in Four African Societies: An Essay in Comparison," *American Anthropologist* 54 (1952), 18–29.

29. S. F. Nadel, "Two Nuba Religions: An Essay in Comparison," *American Anthropologist* 57 (1955), 661–79.

30. Ibid. 676.

31. I. Schapera, "Some Comments on Comparative Method in Social Anthropology," *American Anthropologist* 55 (1953), 353–62; F. Eggan, "Social Anthropology and the Method of Controlled Comparison," *American Anthropologist* 56 (1954), 743–63.

32. A. Kuper, *Wives for Cattle* (London: Routledge and Kegan Paul, 1982).

33. R. Fardon, "Sisters, Wards, Wives and Daughters: A Transformational Analysis of the Political Organization of the Tiv and Their Neighbours," *Africa* 54 (1984), 2–21, and 55 (1985), 77–91.

34. Fortes and Evans-Pritchard, *African Political Systems* (above, n. 25), 3.

35. I. M. Lewis, *Ecstatic Religion* (Harmondsworth: Penguin, 1971), 12.

36. Fortes, *Oedipus and Job* (above, n. 22), 66.

37. For example, M. Wilson, "Witch Beliefs and Social Structure," *American Journal of Sociology* 56 (1951), 307–13; essays in J. Middleton and E. H. Winter, eds., *Witchcraft and Sorcery in East Africa* (London: Routledge and Kegan Paul, 1963); M. Douglas, "Witch Beliefs in Central Africa," *Africa* 37 (1967), 72–80; J. D. McKnight, "Extra Descent-Group Ancestors in African Societies," Africa 37 (1967), 1–21; I. Kopytoff, "Ancestors as Elders in Africa," *Africa* 41 (1971), 129–42.

38. R. E. Bradbury and Peter Morton-Williams, *Benin Studies* (London: Oxford University Press, 1973), 230.

39. Middleton and Winter, *Witchcraft and Sorcery* (above, n. 37), 5–6.

40. M. Gluckman, "Kinship and Marriage among the Lozi . . . and the Zulu," in A. R. Radcliffe-Brown and C. D. Forde, eds., *African Systems of Kinship and Marriage* (London: Oxford University Press, 1950), 166–206.

41. In P. J. Bohannan and G. Dalton, eds., *Markets in Africa* (Evanston: Northwestern University Press, 1962).

42. E. E. Evans-Pritchard, *Anthropology and History* (Manchester: Manchester University Press, 1961).

43. E. E. Evans-Pritchard, "Fifty Years of British Anthropology," *Times Literary Supplement*, 6 July 1973, 764.

44. E. E. Evans-Pritchard, *Theories of Primitive Religion* (Oxford: Clarendon Press, 1965).

45. M. G. Smith, "History and Social Anthropology," *Journal of the Royal Anthropological Institute* 92 (1962), 73–85; I. Schapera, "Should Anthropologists Be Historians?" *Journal of the Royal Anthropological Institute* 92 (1962), 143–56.

46. M. G. Smith, *Government in Zazzau, 1800–1950* (London: Oxford University Press for the International African Institute, 1960); G. I. Jones, *The Trading States of the Oil Rivers: A Study of Political Development in Eastern Nigeria* (London: Oxford University Press, 1963); P. C. Lloyd, *The Political Development of Yoruba Kingdoms in the Eighteenth and Nineteenth Centuries* (London: Royal Anthropological Institute, 1971).

47. D. Forde and P. M. Kaberry, eds., *West African Kingdoms in the Nineteenth Century* (London: Oxford University Press, 1967); Lewis, *History and Social Anthropology* (above, n. 16).

48. P. C. Lloyd, "Conflict Theory and Yoruba Kingdoms," in Lewis, *History and Social Anthropology* (above, n. 16), 25–82.

49. P. Morton-Williams, "The Fulani Penetration into Nupe and Yoruba in the Nineteenth Century," in Lewis, *History and Social Anthropology* (above, n. 16), 1–24.

50. M.G. Smith, *The Affairs of Daura* (Berkeley and Los Angeles: University of California Press, 1978), 12–13.

51. On Ibadan history, for example, see J.D.Y. Peel, *Ijeshas and Nigerians: The Incorporation of a Yoruba Kingdom, 1890s–1970s* (Cambridge: Cambridge University Press, 1983), 11–13.

52. Such as Forde and Kaberry's *West African Kingdoms in the Nineteenth Century* (above, n. 47) or *Systèmes étatiques africains,* special issue of *Cahiers d'Études Africaines,* 87–88 (1982).

53. E.g., Lloyd, "Political Structure of African Kingdoms" (below, n. 55), and *Political Development of Yoruba Kingdoms* (above, n. 46), 1–8.

54. Thus R.E. Bradbury, "The Historical Uses of Comparative Ethnography, with Special References to Benin and the Yoruba" (1964), reprinted in Bradbury and Morton-Williams, *Benin Studies* (above, n. 38), 3–14; and P. Morton-Williams, "The Influence of Habitat and Trade on the Politics of Oyo and Ashanti," in M. Douglas and P.M. Kaberry, eds., *Man in Africa* (London: Tavistock Press, 1969), 79–98.

55. P.C. Lloyd, "The Political Structure of African Kingdoms," in M. Banton, ed., *Political Systems and the Distribution of Power* (London: Tavistock, 1965), 63–112.

56. J. Goody, *Technology, Tradition and the State in Africa* (London: Oxford University Press, 1971).

57. R. Law, "Horses, Firearms and Political Power in Pre-Colonial West Africa," *Past and Present* 72 (1976), 112–32.

58. M. Fortes, "Strangers," in M. Fortes and S. Patterson, eds., *Studies in Social Anthropology* (London: Academic Press, 1975), 229–53.

59. As Goody, *Technology, Tradition and the State* (above, n. 56).

60. I. Wilks, "Ashanti Government," in Forde and Kaberry, *West African Kingdoms in the Nineteenth Century* (above, n. 47), 206–39; and at greater length in *Asante in the Nineteenth Century: The Structure and Evolution of a Political Order* (Cambridge: Cambridge University Press, 1975).

61. Ibid. 446–55.

62. R.S. Rattray, *Ashanti* (Oxford: Clarendon Press, 1923); M. Fortes, "Kinship and Marriage among the Ashanti," in Radcliffe-Brown and Forde, *African Systems of Kinship and Marriage* (above, n. 40), 252–84.

63. M.J. Herskovits, *Dahomey: An Ancient West African Kingdom* (New York: J.J. Augustin, 1938), vol. 1, 194.

64. P.C. Lloyd, "Sacred Kingship and Government among the Yoruba," *Africa* 30 (1960), 221–38; and R. Law, *The Oyo Empire, c. 1600–c. 1836: A West African Imperialism in the Era of the Atlantic Slave Trade* (Oxford: Clarendon Press, 1977), 72.

65. J.D.Y. Peel, "Kings, Titles and Quarters: A Conjectural History of Ilesha, Part II, Institutional Growth," *History in Africa* 7 (1980), 225–57; and R. Law, "Making Sense of a Traditional Narrative: Political Disintegration in the Kingdom of Oyo," *Cahiers d'Études Africaines* 87–88 (1982), 395–96.

66. Lloyd, *Political Development of Yoruba Kingdoms* (above, n. 46), 70.

67. O. Otite, *Autonomy and Independence: The Urhoho Kingdom of Okpe* (London: Hurst, 1973), 14–18.

68. Peel, "Kings, Titles and Quarters" (above, n. 65), 249, taking further Bradbury and Morton-Williams, *Benin Studies* (above, n. 38), 11–12 n. 9.

69. M. Johnson, "The Economic Basis of an Islamic Theocracy: Masina," *Journal of African History* 17 (1976), 481–95.

70. D. Northrup, *Trade without Rulers: Pre-Colonial Economic Development in South-Eastern Nigeria* (Oxford: Clarendon Press, 1978).

71. Law, *Oyo Empire* (above, n. 64), 312.

72. Goody, *Technology, Tradition and State* (above, n. 56), 57–72.

73. Ibid.

74. Johnson, "Economic Basis of an Islamic Theocracy" (above, n. 69), 490.

75. C. Geertz, "Religion as a Cultural System," in M. Banton, ed., *Anthropological Approaches to the Study of Religion* (London: Tavistock, 1966), 1–46.

76. Wilks, "Ashanti Government" (above, n. 60), 227.

77. Herskovits, *Dahomey* (above, n. 63), vol. 2, 104; B. Maupoil, *La géomancie de l'ancienne Côte des Esclaves* (Paris: Institut d'Ethnologie, 1943), chapter 2.

78. R.F. Burton, *A Mission to Gelele, King of Dahome,* ed. C.W. Newbury (London: Routledge and Kegan Paul, 1966 [1864]), chapters 11–19; T.C. McCaskie, *State and Society in Pre-Colonial Asante* (Cambridge: Cambridge University Press, 1995), especially chapter 4.

79. T.C. McCaskie, "Time and Calendar in C.19 Asante: An Exploratory Essay," *History in Africa* 7 (1980), 179–200.

80. Cf. appendix to K.A. Busia, *The Position of the Chief in the Modern Political System of Ashanti* (London: Oxford University Press, 1951).

81. J. Middleton, "One Hundred and Fifty Years of Christianity in a Ghanaian Town," *Africa* 53 (1983), 2–18.

82. Wilks, *Asante in the Nineteenth Century* (above, n. 60), 127.

83. Herskovits, *Dahomey* (above, n. 63), vol. 2, 138.

84. T.C. McCaskie, "Accumulation, Wealth and Belief in Asante History," *Africa* 53 (1983), 23–24.

85. T.G.O. Gbadamosi, "*Odu Imale:* Islam in Ifa Divination and the Case of Predestined Muslims," *Journal of the Historical Society of Nigeria* 8 (1977), 88–92.

86. T. Shaw, *Nigeria: Its Archaeology and Early History* (London: Thames and Hudson, 1978), chapter 8.

87. I.A. Akinjogbin, *The Cradle of a Race: Ife from the Beginning to 1980* (Port Harcourt: Sunray Publications, 1992); J.K. Olupona, *City of 201 Gods: Ile-Ife in Time, Space, and the Imagination* (Berkeley and Los Angeles: University of California Press, 2011).

88. W.R. Bascom, *Ifa Divination: Communication between Gods and Men in West Africa* (Bloomington: Indiana University Press, 1969); W. Abimbola, *Ifa: An Exposition of Ifa Literary Corpus* (Ibadan: Oxford University Press, 1976).

89. Maupoil, *Géomancie* (above, n. 77), 34.

2. TWO PASTORS AND THEIR HISTORIES: SAMUEL JOHNSON AND C. C. REINDORF

1. An earlier version of this chapter was first presented at a seminar to celebrate the work of C.C. Reindorf at Basel in 1995 and published in Paul Jenkins, ed., *The Recovery of*

the West African Past: African Pastors and African History in the Nineteenth Century (Basel: Basler Afrika Bibliographien, 1998), chapter 4.

2. As argued in J. D. Y. Peel, "The Cultural Work of Yoruba Ethnogenesis," in E. Tonkin, M. McDonald, and M. Chapman, eds., *History and Ethnicity* (London: Routledge, 1989), chapter 13.

3. Hayden White, *Metahistory: The Historical Imagination in Nineteenth-Century Europe* (Baltimore: The Johns Hopkins University Press, 1973).

4. For a full and sound survey, see Robin Law, "Early Yoruba Historiography," *History in Africa* 3 (1976), 69–89, also reprinted in Toyin Falola, ed., *African Historiography: Essays in Honour of Jacob Ade Ajayi* (Harlow: Longman, 1993), 9–25; and also his "Local Amateur Scholarship in the Construction of Yoruba Ethnicity, 1880–1914," paper presented at the conference "Ethnicity in Africa," University of Edinburgh, May 1995.

5. Strikingly evident to anyone who looks at the footnotes of Robin Law's *The Oyo Empire, c. 1600–1836* (Oxford: Clarendon Press, 1977), the major work of modern scholarship on early Yoruba history.

6. This use of a prayer to conclude a narrative is a very common stylistic device in the daily entries in the journal extracts that all CMS missionaries were required to send in, usually every three months.

7. Bühler to Venn, 3 May 1862 (CA2/O/24/16), describing his disagreement with Townsend, who (he said) wanted as agents "good Christians only who can just read such portions of the Bible as are translated and nothing else." Cf. Townsend to Venn, 6 June 1862 (CA2/O/85/83), disapproving of T. B. Macaulay's approach at the Grammar School in Lagos and quoting a Lagos chief's refusal to send his children as it was too literary, "which unfits them for the practical duties of life." See further J. F. Ade Ajayi, *Christian Missions in Nigeria* (Longman: London, 1965), 150–52.

8. On Johnson's education, see M. R. Doortmont, "Recapturing the Past: Samuel Johnson and the Construction of Yoruba History" (Ph.D. thesis, Erasmus University, Rotterdam, 1994), 66–71.

9. Such as his comparison of the English and the Yoruba ("what the one is among the whites the other is among the blacks": *HY*, xxii) and his very positive account of the British conquest of Ijebu (chap. 33, #9) and of the establishment of the protectorate (chaps. 34 and 35).

10. Quotation from *HGCA*, iv. The closest Yoruba CMS parallel to this is provided by Daniel Olubi, Hinderer's successor as pastor of the Ibadan church and the man under whom Johnson started his career as teacher and preacher. At the death of his mother, a priestess of Igun at Abeokuta, he recalled his childhood role as her assistant, "called early into the service of the Lord, like Samuel" (Journal, 6 Feb. 1867, in CA2/O/49/19).

11. Which anticipates the distinction between centralized and segmentary polities made by E. E. Evans-Pritchard and M. Fortes, eds., *African Political Systems* (London: Oxford University Press, 1940).

12. I use the term in White's sense, which derives from the Canadian critic Northrop Frye: "Romance is fundamentally a drama of self-identification symbolized by the hero's transcendence of the world of experience, his victory over it, and his final liberation from it—the sort of drama associated with the Grail legend or the story of the resurrection of Christ in Christian mythology. It is a drama of the triumph of good over evil, of virtue

over vice, of light over darkness." (*Metahistory* [above, n. 3], 8–9). It is the only one of White's four modes of emplotment—the others being comedy, tragedy, and satire—that has a Christian rather than a classical source. Missionaries are manifestly among the great practitioners of romance.

13. Doortmont, "Recapturing the Past" (above, n. 8), 10–12, 71–76.

14. E.g., his remark in the preface that "Educated natives of Yoruba are well acquainted with the history of England and with that of Rome and Greece, but of the history of their own country they know nothing whatever!" (*HY*, vii), his use of the proverbial phrase "When Greek meets Greek" for the title of chap. 18 #3, dealing with the climax of the Ijaye War, or his comparison of the *arokin* of Oyo with the Homeric rhapsodists (*HY*, 125), and of the role of a debt distrainer as "a veritable Thersites" (*HY*, 131).

15. G. F. Buhler, Half-yearly Report of the Training Institution, April 1859 (CA2/O/24/43).

16. D. Olubi to Parent Committee, CMS, 7 Dec. 1870 (CA2/O/75/39).

17. S. Johnson, Journal Extracts 1870–73, n.d. (CA2/O/58/1). He says it was destroyed 70 or 80 years before, but in fact this happened less than forty years earlier (Law, *Oyo Empire* [above, n. 5], 290–91). The *Onikoyi* in Ibadan had died five years earlier and seems not to have been replaced.

18. S. Johnson, Journal, 29 Feb. 1875 (CA2/O/58/4), which is used nearly verbatim in *HY*, 28–29.

19. S. Johnson, journals for the half-years ending Dec. 1874, June 1877, and Dec. 1877 (CA2/O/58/3, 8, 9), which must have been primary sources for the published versions in *HY*, 391–94, 407–12, 417–19.

20. S. Johnson, Journal, 4 July 1879 (G3 A2/O/1880/160). The Agberi are otherwise unknown to me and do not appear elsewhere in *HY*.

21. S. Johnson, journals for the half-years ending Dec. 1874, June 1877, and Dec. 1877 (CA2/O/58/3, 8, 9), which must have been primary sources for the published versions in *HY*, 391–94, 407–12, 417–19.

22. S. Johnson, Journal, 8 March 1880 (G3 A2/O/1880/161). A very similar view of the Ikale had been earlier expressed by D. Olubi, who added to their backward traits that they had no markets and that their women farmed like the men (Journal, 11 Dec. 1879, in G3 A2/O/1880/125). For a valuable appreciation of the context of Ikale cultural forms, see Paul Richards, "Landscape of Dissent: Ikale and Ilaje Country, 1870–1950," in J. F. Ade Ajayi and J. D. Y. Peel, eds., *People and Empires in African History: Essays in Memory of Michael Crowder* (London: Longman, 1992), 161–84.

23. S. Johnson, Journal, 16 April 1882 (G3 A2/O/1883/101).

24. S. Johnson, Journal, 9 Nov. 1882 (ibid.).

25. S. Johnson, Journal, 16 Nov. 1882 (ibid.).

26. E.g., on Abiodun, C. Phillips, Sr., Journal, 22 March 1855 (CA2/O/77/11), at Ijaye; S. W. Doherty, Journal, 20 May 1876 (CA2/O/35/11), at Okewere in Oke Ogun; on Afonja, W. S. Allen, Journals, 13 March 1872, 27 Jan. 1878 (CA2/O/19/13,18), both in Ibadan. See too the account of Afonja's role in the English missionary V. Faulkner's six-page "A True Story of the Yoruba Country," dated 11–12 July 1874 (CA2/O/37/71), which he must have derived purely from Yoruba informants.

27. S. Johnson, Journal, 24 Dec. 1876 (CA2/O/58/7). The date of 1800 is no more than a rough approximation. The reference to Mungo Park (who never got to Old Oyo) is curious.

As far as we know, the first Europeans to visit Old Oyo were Clapperton and Lander in 1826, long after Abiodun's death (which on Law's dating was in 1789). What Johnson appears to have done, knowing that a European visited Old Oyo, is to have made it the most famous of European explorers of West Africa and the most famous *Alafin*. This did not get into *HY*, but it underscores how very different Johnson's cognitive situation was from Reindorf's, that events at so late a date were subject to this kind of mythologization.

28. D. Olubi, Journal, 8 July 1883 (G3 A2/O/1884/100). If correct, this would have taken her back to *Alafin* Abiodun's predecessor Majeogbe (sometime before 1774).

29. D. Hinderer, Journal, 15 Dec. 1854 (CA2/O/49/110).

30. S. Johnson, Journal, 18 June 1878 (CA2/O/58/10).

31. S. Johnson, Journal, 29 Sept. to 1 Oct. 1883 (G3 A2/O/1883/101). A history of Sango, highlighting the legend that as *Alafin* he hanged himself, was published in one of the CMS reading books. Johnson reports how an intelligent slave boy, reading this, commented that the people must have been deceived about Sango; and himself replied "that all the other idols have a similar history": Journal, 18 April 1881 (G3 A2/O/1882/23). This euhemeristic strategy against the *orișa* became widely known. A Brazilian historian, Nina Rodrigues (d. 1906), wrote: "another version [of Sango traditions] I find in Bahia, mostly among the Blacks who were under the influence of English missionaries in Lagos, . . . gives Sango a totally euhemeristic origin. In general, our Blacks attribute it to the Protestant missionaries, who have an interest in removing from Sango his *orișa* qualities": *Os Africanos no Brasil*, 2nd ed. (Sao Paulo, 1935), 333. I am grateful to Paulo de Moraes Farias for this reference.

32. Tugwell to Baylis, CMS secretary, 5 Feb. 1898 (G3 A2/O/1899/32).

33. S. Johnson, Journal, 5 April 1876 (CA2/O/58/6).

34. Informant D. Olubi, Journal, 14 Jan. 1884 (G3 A2/O/1886/38).

35. Ibid. One of the houses delivered was that of the patriarch of Johnson's congregation of Aremo, David Kukomi, Johnson's prime informant for the wars earlier in the century. Although the Christians generally received respect and protection from the chiefs, especially from the *Arẹ* Latosisa, the army's acute shortages in the Ekitiparapo War led the chiefs in the Kiriji camp to sanction their war boys to pressgang recruits and to commandeer supplies by any means.

36. S. Johnson, Journal, especially 10 July 1874; cf. *HY*, 391–94.

37. S. Johnson, Journal, 7 Aug. 1875 and 23 July 1876 (CA2/O/58/5, 7).

38. J. Barber to H. Venn, CMS. secretary, 23 Dec. 1856 (CA2/O/21/22).

39. D. Olubi to H. Wright, CMS. secretary, 22 April 1878 (CA2/O/75/37).

40. For a view of Reindorf that does just this, see Kwame Bediako, *Christianity in Africa: The Renewal of a Non-Western Religion* (Edinburgh: Edinburgh University Press, 1995), 39–48.

3. OGUN IN PRECOLONIAL YORUBALAND: A COMPARATIVE ANALYSIS

1. An earlier version of this chapter first appeared in Sandra T. Barnes, ed., *Africa's Ogun: Old World and New*, 2nd ed. (Bloomington: Indiana University Press, 1997), 263–89. In preparing this paper I have been much helped by discussions with Karin Barber, Sandra Barnes, Tom McCaskie, Peter Morton-Williams, Bayo Ogundijo, Akin Oyetade, and John Picton, and by several of those who attended the Tenth Satterthwaite Colloquium on African Religion and Ritual, April 1994.

While working on CMS papers, I incurred a debt of gratitude to their then custodians at Birmingham University Library, notably Dr. B. S. Benedikz and Miss Christine Penney. The documents I have cited are all from the Yoruba Mission, series o (incoming papers), classified before 1880 under the heading CA 2 (by author) and from 1880 under G3 A2 (by year).

2. Thus the title of the first study of Yoruba traditional religion by a Yoruba, the Rev. James Johnson: *Yoruba Heathenism* (Exeter: James Townsend, 1899).

3. R. I. Ibigbami, "Ogun Festival in Ire-Ekiti," *Nigeria Magazine* 126–27 (1978), 44–59.

4. J. K. Olupona, *City of 201 Gods: Ile-Ife in Time, Space and the Imagination* (Berkeley and Los Angeles: University of California Press, 2011). Because Ife was deserted as a result of the wars and so hosted no missionaries for most of the second half of the nineteenth century, we have virtually no eyewitnesses of its religion until after 1900.

5. Charles Phillips, Jr., Journal, 16 Sept. 1883; E. M. Lijadu, Journal, 21 Aug. 1891. On Ogun in Ondo, J. K. Olupona, *Kingship, Religion and Rituals in a Nigerian Community: A Phenomenological Study of Ondo Yoruba Festival* (Stockholm: Almqvist and Wiksell, 1991).

6. M. J. Luke, Journal, June 1889.

7. J. D. Y. Peel, *Ijeshas and Nigerians: The Incorporation of a Yoruba Kingdom, 1890s-1970s.* (Cambridge: Cambridge University Press, 1983), 269, 326–27.

8. We can, however, be sure that Sango was not so new to the southwest as to Ondo and the southeast, since his cult would have accompanied Oyo control of the trade corridor through Egbado to the coast since the early eighteenth century: P. Morton-Williams, "The Oyo Yoruba and the Atlantic Trade, 1670–1830," *Journal of the Historical Society of Nigeria* 3 (1964), 25–45; A. I. Asiwaju, *Western Yorubaland under European Rule, 1889–1945: A Comparative Analysis of French and British Colonialism* (London: Longman, 1976).

9. Thus F. L. Akiele, letter to T. Harding, 6 May 1902, referring to a large sacrifice to Ogun by the chiefs of a village near Ogbomosho.

10. The Abeokuta church elders consulted by Harding expressly stated that no images were made of Ogun but that anvil stones might be worshipped; they didn't even think it needed to be said that *any* iron could serve as Ogun (Harding to Merensky, 19 Nov. 1888). Kevin Carroll's judgment (*Yoruba Religious Carving* [London: Geoffrey Chapman, 1976], 64) that "Yoruba people do not identify any spirit with an image; nor can it be said that they believe the spirits come to dwell in the images" would seem not quite to apply to Ogun, since iron, though the object to which the actions of Ogun worship are addressed, is not equivalent to an image that is thought to represent an *orịṣa.*

11. J. Barber, Journal, 14 Jan. 1856.

12. C. Phillips, Jr., Journal, 4 Dec. 1877.

13. E. W. George, Journal, 5 June 1890.

14. T. B. Wright, Journal, 21 Jan. 1867.

15. J. A. Maser, Journal, 2 Oct. 1864. A house of Ogun might range in type from a thatched roof on four posts, only a few feet high, covering an old anvil stone or some iron implements, to a proper temple big enough for worshippers to enter. We may surmise from the time interval between the two occasions that the oracular consultation was to determine a propitious day for the *ọdun.*

16. M. J. Luke, Journal, 27 Apr. 1877. Palma, near Leki on the lagoon, had a very mixed population, many inhabitants being escaped slaves.

17. J. White, Journal, 4 Aug. 1870.

18. E.W. George, Journal, 29 Jan. 1877. On iron cult objects of other *orịṣa*, see R.F. Thompson, *Black Gods and Kings: Yoruba Art at UCLA* (Bloomington: Indiana University Press, 1976), chaps. 7–11.

19. M.J. Luke, Journal, 27 May 1889, met one who supported his preaching at Okemesi. In Ilesha, tradition holds that when a new quarter was founded, a blacksmith (*agbẹdẹ*) was always included among the first settlers.

20. J. White, Journal, 30 April 1857, at Ota.

21. W.S. Allen, Journal, 24 Sept. 1872, at Ibadan.

22. See D. Hinderer, Journal, 24 Sept. 1849, at Abeokuta; W.S. Allen, Journal, 7 July 1869, at Ibadan.

23. Women wove on upright looms, which were set up in the courtyard or on the veranda of the house; whereas men's weaving involved long horizontal looms, set up in sheds or under awnings in public places.

24. G.J. Afolabi Ojo, *Yoruba Culture: A Geographical Analysis* (London: University of London Press, 1966), 96, 171. On smelting in Ilobi and Imeko (Egbado), see Asiwaju, *Western Yorubaland* (above, n. 8), 23. Ibadan itself should surely be included: one of its ironworking quarters, Eleta, was named after the ironstone (*ẹta*) found there: Toyin Falola, *The Political Economy of a Pre-Colonial African State: Ibadan, 1830–1900* (Ile-Ife: University of Ife Press, 1984), 96–98. Ilorin's name is often linked to the "grinding" of iron (*lọ* + *irin*), as by R.C. Abraham, *Dictionary of Modern Yoruba* (London: University of London Press, 1958), s.v. "Ilorin," but this does not seem to imply smelting. At Ile Bandele in Ilorin, a large stone is shown where this is said to have been done (Professor Stefan Reichmuth, pers. comm.).

25. Eugenia W. Herbert, *Iron, Gender and Power: Rituals of Transformation in African Societies* (Bloomington: Indiana University Press, 1993), 12–14, 160–61, chap. 5 passim: "Smith and forge [are] much more integrated into the life of the community than the smelting furnace, and the smithy becomes simultaneously a place of asylum and an adjunct to political power." The sort of specialized smelting settlement that existed in central Yorubaland, such as Isundunrin near Ejigbo—see C.V. Bellamy, "A West African Smelting House," *Journal of the Iron and Steel Institute* 66 (1904), 99–126—or the various villages called Iponrin, fits her thesis better. But smelting was clearly not limited to such places.

26. Ilesha tradition, for example, recalls that smelted iron was imported from the Ejigbo area (Peel, *Ijeshas and Nigerians* [above, n. 7], 22).

27. This is consistent with Denis Williams's linkage of West Africa's "iron hunger" with the ritualization of the metal, though he does not extend his persuasive argument to intra-Yoruba variations in Ogun/iron: *Icon and Image: A Study of Sacred and Secular Forms of African Classical Art* (London: Allen Lane, 1974), 67–86.

28. See further Peel, *Ijeshas and Nigerians* (above, n. 7), 22–24, 27.

29. For eyewitness accounts of this at the Ogun festival in nineteenth-century Ondo, see Charles Phillips, Jr., Journal, 23 Sept. 1877, and E.M. Lijadu, Journal, 21 Aug. 1891. For a certain shift in the character of the modern festival there, see Olupona, *Kingship, Religion and Rituals* (above, n. 5), chap. 5, and further discussion in J.D.Y. Peel, "Historicity and Pluralism in Some Recent Studies of Yoruba Religion," *Africa* 64 (1994), 159–60.

30. P. Verger, *Notes sur le culte des orisa et vodun à Bahia, le Baie de Tous les Saints, au Brésil, et à l'ancienne Côte des Esclaves en Afrique* (Dakar: Institut Français de l'Afrique Noire,

1957), 150–53; Margaret J. Drewal, *Yoruba Ritual: Performers, Play, Agency* (Bloomington: Indiana University Press, 1992), 183–84.

31. E. M. Lijadu, Journal, 11 Nov. 1892.

32. See the *oriki* (praise name) to "Aje Onire Ogungunniso," collected at Kuta near Iwo by Belasco, who speaks of "the theme of interpenetrated trade and war, the inextricable unity of Ogun and Aje": B. I. Belasco, *The Entrepreneur as Culture Hero: Preadaptions in Nigerian Economic Development* (New York: Praeger, 1980), 140–42.

33. On Ori, see Karin Barber, "Money, Self-realization and the Person in Yoruba Texts," in Jane Guyer, ed., *Money Matters* (New York: Heinemann, 1994), 204–44; and as particularly a women's cult of personal protection, see J. D. Y. Peel, "Gender in Yoruba Religious Change," *Journal of Religion in Africa* 32 (2002), 150–51.

34. Charles Phillips, Sr., Journal, 26 Oct. 1855.

35. J. White, Journal, 31 May 1855.

36. For a full analysis of the practice and its meaning as sacrifice, see J. D. Y. Peel, "Poverty and Sacrifice in Nineteenth-Century Yorubaland," *Journal of African History* 32 (1994), 465–84.

37. T. King, Journal, 9 March 1852.

38. R. S. Oyebode, Journal, 22 Oct. 1889.

39. F. L. Akiele, Journal, 10 Sept. 1890.

40. J. F. T. Halligey, "The Yoruba Country, Abeokuta and Lagos," *Journal of the Manchester Geographical Society* 9 (1893), 39–40. He does not in fact *say* she was a devotee of Ogun, but I can't see what else she would be. The Yoruba do not have snake charmers as such.

41. Letter from Mrs. Ernest Fry, no. 25 (printed), 5 July 1911.

42. P. Amaury Talbot, *The Peoples of Southern Nigeria*, vol. 2 (London: Oxford University Press, 1926), 88.

Margaret Drewal, "Dancing for Ogun in Yorubaland and in Brazil," in Barnes, *Africa's Ogun* (above, n. 1), 204, refers to a small black-and-red snake called *agbaadu* as a symbol of Ogun, but the point of the symbolism—that it is "quick, vicious and deadly"—seems to put it in quite a separate case from the placid *mọna-mọna.*

43. T. Harding to A. Merensky, 19 Nov. 1888.

44. Charles Phillips, Jr., Journal, 19–20 Aug. 1878.

45. As Verger, *Notes sur le culte des orisa* (above, n. 30), 511–22, observes, of all West African cults Dangbe's was one of those most commonly described by European visitors. See, for example, R. F. Burton, *A Mission to Gelele, King of Dahome* (London: Routledge and Kegan Paul, 1966 [1864]), 73–76. For CMS reports of "Idagbe" (as they call it in Yoruba style) at Badagry, see the journals of S. A. Crowther and of H. Townsend for the three months ending 25 June 1846, and of S. Pearse, 5 Oct. 1861.

46. Verger, *Notes sur le culte des orisa* (above, n. 30), 233–38; M. J. Herskovits, *Dahomey: An Ancient West African Kingdom,* vol.2 (New York: Augustin, 1938), chap. 32, "The Cult of the Serpent."

47. Such as Ede and Iseyin. At Ede, Ogun was originally the principal *orịṣa* of the town, only later displaced by Sango, but is still linked with the New Yam, Oranyan, and the royal ancestors: U. Beier, *A Year of Sacred Festivals in One Yoruba Town* (Lagos: Nigeria Magazine, 1959), 42. At Iseyin, the Oro festival (of collective ancestors) began with the worship of

Ogun, attended by the king in the marketplace (S. Johnson, Journal, 12 Aug. 1882). R.E. Dennett, *Nigerian Studies; or, the Religious and Political System of the Yoruba* (London: Frank Cass, 1968 [1910]), 123–24, briefly describes the court in the palace at Iseyin where the king heard cases: an iron chain was stretched across it, which as Ogun received sacrifices.

48. Peter Morton-Williams, personal communication, 1994.

49. For a review of the main listings of *orișa* in a pantheon, arguing that "the variations in the hierarchical ordering make the lists untenable," see J.R.O. Ojo, "The Hierarchy of Yoruba Gods: An Aspect of Yoruba Cosmology," unpublished seminar paper, Department of African Languages and Literatures, University of Ife, 1978.

50. Karin Barber, "How Man Makes God in West Africa," *Africa* 51 (1981), 724–45, is illuminating on the social mechanisms involved here.

51. See Marc Schiltz, "Yoruba Thunder Deities and Sovereignty: Ara versus Sango," *Anthropos* 80 (1985), 67–84, on how at Ketu and Sabe, Sango is considered to be the senior wife of Ara, the locally established thunder god.

52. T. King, Journal, 23 June 1861. This entry gives a remarkable account of the Orisa Oko cult, triggered by a devotee's renunciation of the cult to become a Christian. This was considered very unusual, granted the strong devotion of this *orișa*'s followers. See too H. Townsend, "Journal of a Journey from Abbeokuta to Ijaye, Shaki and Isein," 16 Jan. 1855. The best modern study is J. R. O. Ojo, "Orisa Oko, the Deity of 'the Farm and Agriculture' among the Ekiti," *African Notes* 7 (1973), 25–61, though the case is rather atypical since it relates to a village in Ekiti where the cult was an introduction from the Oyo area. Also useful is Thompson, *Black Gods and Kings* (above, n. 18), chap. 10, especially on the staves.

53. On the special status of Orisa Oko devotees, see further James Johnson, annual report for 1879; T. King, Journal, 2 April 1852.

54. S. Crowther, Jr., Journal, June 1855.

55. As the Rev. S.A. Crowther put it, writing from Abeokuta but referring to the Yoruba in general, " there is an established religion connected with government, which is the worship of the dead or their deceased ancestor" (letter to T.J. Hutchinson, 10 Sept. 1856).

56. D. Olubi, Annual Letter to Fenn, 28 Dec. 1875. Olubi was an Egba who first came to Ibadan as a servant to David Hinderer in 1851 and took over as leader of the Ibadan church in 1869. No outsider was in a better position to make this judgment.

57. W.S. Allen, Journal, 13 Aug. 1883.

58. Ojo, "Orisa Oko" (above, n. 52), 58.

59. John Pemberton, "A Cluster of Sacred Symbols: Orisa Worship among the Igbomina Yoruba of Ila-Orangun," *History of Religions* 17 (1977), 1–28, and "The Dreadful God and the Divine King," in Barnes, *Africa's Ogun* (above, n. 1), 105–46.

60. A selection of New Yam deities: Obalufon at some households at Ibadan (J. Barber, Journal, 3 Aug. 1856) and as god of yams at Akure (E.M. Lijadu, Journal, 1896); the Oro ancestors at Iseyin (A. Mann, Journal, 2 Aug. 1856); Ifa in at least one household at Ilesha (M.J. Luke, Journal, 20 Aug. 1889); Oramfe as god of yam at Ondo (E.M. Lijadu, July 1895); Sango at Ijaye (H. Townsend, 6 June 1857).

61. J.L. Matory, *Sex and the Empire That Is No More* (Minneapolis: University of Minnesota Press, 1994), chap. 1.

62. Compare William Rea's observation on Ogun in contemporary Ikole-Ekiti: "The [Ogun] festival is the major 'civic' (as opposed to 'religious') event of the year. As a festival it

transcends the division between town and palace. . . . [It] is about Ikole as a unified town": W. R. Rea, "No Event, No History: Masquerading in Ikole-Ekiti" (unpublished Ph.D. thesis, University of East Anglia, 1994), 42.

63. Such as chiefs *Ogboni, Sajowa* (head blacksmith), and *Salotun* (in front of whose house the mock battle between town and palace chiefs takes place during the Ogun festival): see J. D. Y. Peel, "Kings, Titles and Quarters: A Conjectural History of Ilesha, Part II: Institutional Growth," *History in Africa* 7 (1980), 225–57.

64. J. F. Ade Ajayi and R. S. Smith, *Yoruba Warfare in the Nineteenth Century* (Cambridge: Cambridge University Press, 1964); Bolanle Awe, "Militarism and Economic Development in Nineteenth-Century Yoruba Country," *Journal of African History* 14 (1973), 65–77; Toyin Falola and Dare Oguntomisin, *The Military in Nineteenth Century Yoruba Politics* (Ile-Ife: University of Ife Press, 1984).

65. J. Barber, Journal, 14 Jan. 1855.

66. S. Johnson, Journal, 29 Feb. 1875.

67. In an incident in March 1881, a woman had a fit during a flash of lightning, and another woman told her husband it was Sango's vengeance. In panic he and the other residents ran away. The Sango cultists came and barred the entrance to the house. Next day, she was feeding her chickens when the Sango people returned to plunder the house, and she tried to stop them. They clubbed her to death, saying she was Sango's victim (S. Johnson, Journal, 23–24 March 1881).

68. Cf. again Rea, "No Event, No History" (above, n. 62), 43, on Ikole-Ekiti: "If asked about the personality of Ogun as an individuated deity . . . people would suggest Ogun was all around: wherever there was iron there was Ogun. There is no Ogun 'cult' per se in Ikole, and no 'priest' or *aworo* of Ogun."

69. For example, if lightning struck while the Ibadan army was in the field, "the [war chiefs were] forbidden by custom to offer battle or fight until Sango [was] propitiated (S. Johnson, Journal, 30 Sept. 1882).

70. M. J. Luke, Journal, 24 May 1889. It concerned a "confinement"—an obligation to stay indoors—imposed on the town by the Sango cult in the king's name, like those imposed by Oro in times of crisis at Abeokuta. The circumstances at Ilesha are not described.

71. G. A. Vincent, Journal, 15 April 1885. Vincent, himself Ijesha-born, quotes a woman as saying that the Ijesha "hated those thunder worshippers by their doings."

72. Charles Phillips, Jr., letter to Fenn, 23 Nov. 1977: Journal, 1 Sept. 1879.

73. Charles Phillips, Jr., Journal, 17 July 1879; C. N. Young, Journal, 13 Feb. 1880. The disease continued to break out for several years, until, in 1884, the chiefs turned against both the Sopona and the Sango cults and banned them.

74. Charles Phillips, Sr., journals, 3 Nov. 1853, 20 Oct. 1856.

75. E. Buko, Journal, 16 Feb. 1883: a young man executed for murdering his master, to whom he been a bondsman (*iwofa*).

76. D. Hinderer, Journal, 1 Oct. 1851.

77. J. B. Wood, letter to Lang, 18 Sept. 1884.

78. Charles Phillips, Sr., Journal, 9 June 1853, at Ijaye.

79. S. A. Akintoye, *Revolution and Power Politics in Yorubaland, 1840–1893* (London: Longman, 1971), 135.

80. J. Barber, Journal, 26 Feb. 1854; J. Okuseinde, Journal, 21 Jan. 1873. In both these reports, Oranyan (or Oranmiyan) is called god of war.

81. J. B. Wood, letter to Lang, 18 Jan. 1884.

82. On Owode, the wife who ran off to Lagos: S. Doherty, Journal, 6 Apr. 1882; V. Faulkner to J. B. Wood, 18 Apr. 1882; Wood to CMS secretaries, 21 Apr. 1882. A later incident: Wood to Lang, 12 Nov. 1885.

83. J. B. Wood, letters to Lang, 10 and 18 Aug. 1887.

84. Halligey, "The Yoruba Country" (above, n. 40), 33. This meeting with Ogundipe took place in 1887, a few months before his death. Notable chiefs often had their own distinctive staff (*ọpa*), which their messenger would carry as a mark of authorization.

85. On which see Olatunde Olatunji, "The Poetry of J. S. Sowande, Alias Sobo Arobiodu," in Wande Abimbola, ed., *Yoruba Oral Tradition,* Ife African Languages and Literatures Series, no. 1 (Ile-Ife: Department of African Languages and Literatures, 1975), 973–1029.

86. See Oyin Ogunba, "The Performance of Yoruba Oral Poetry," in Abimbola, *Yoruba Oral Tradition* (above, n. 85), esp. 807–76, on *oriki* addressed to Ogun, who like Ogundipe "is intensely self-conscious, [and] enjoys . . . flattery, for it is man's admission of Ogun's preeminence and a way of keeping him at a distance."

87. Wood to Lang, 18 Aug. 1887.

88. E. O. O. Moore, *History of Abeokuta* (London and Bungay: Richard Clay 1916), 92.

89. W. Moore (an Egba and the only Anglican pastor left in Abeokuta after the "Outbreak," or general expulsion of missionaries in 1867) to CMS Parent Committee, 27 June 1868. The name of the river Ògùn has no connection with the name of the god Ògún: different tones.

90. As a well-known *oriki* of Ogun puts it: *Ogun alada meji, o nfi okan sa oko, o nfi okan ye ọna* (Ogun with two cutlasses: you use one to clear the farm; you use the other to clear the road).

91. Whether it should be considered as strictly a title or more like an informal sobriquet is unclear. The Egba historian Olympus Moore (A. K. Ajisafe) writes both "Ogudipe Alatise of Ikija" and "Ogudipe Alatise": E. O. O. Moore, *History of Abeokuta* (London and Bungay: Richard Clay 1916), 77.

92. The full proverb is *Alatise ni mo atise ara re* (The one whose task it is to do something knows he has to do it himself). I am indebted to my colleague Dr. Akin Oyetade on this.

93. Halligey, "The Yoruba Country" (above, n. 40), 28–44, says he took the *Alatunṣe* title after declining the Alakeship for himself. E. O. O. Moore (above, n. 91: 89–90), who calls him merely Alatise, describes him as the most powerful man in Abeokuta during the interregnum of 1881–84 and in particular as the main kingmaker during that period.

94. Cf. the anonymous greeting to Hinderer (half-yearly report ending Sept. 1859) while he was traveling in Ijesha country: *O ku tọnṣe aiye* (Greetings to you, working to restore the world); or the prophecy of Christian "light and restoration" (*atunṣe*) quoted by Samuel Johnson and Obadiah Johnson, *History of the Yorubas: From the Earliest Times to the Beginning of the British Protectorate* (Lagos: CMS Bookshops, 1921), 296.

95. Wole Soyinka, *Myth, Literature and the African World* (Cambridge: Cambridge University Press, 1976), 27–32, 140–60. See too the picture of Ogun given by Toyin Falola, *Counting the Tiger's Teeth* (Ann Arbor: University of Michigan Press, 2014), chap. 1, "Ogun's

Gift": an autobiographical account of the author's participation in the Agbekoya peasant uprising of 1968–69.

96. T. Harding to A. Merensky, 19 Nov. 1888.

4. DIVERGENT MODES OF RELIGIOSITY IN WEST AFRICA

1. An earlier version of this chapter appeared in Harvey Whitehouse and James Laidlaw, eds., *Ritual and Memory: Toward a Comparative Anthropology of Religion* (Walnut Creek: AltaMira Press, 2004), 13–30.

2. H. Whitehouse, *Arguments and Icons: Divergent Modes of Religiosity* (Oxford: Oxford University Press, 2000).

3. Roy A. Rappaport, *Ritual and Religion in the Making of Humanity* (Cambridge: Cambridge University Press, 1999); Pascal Boyer, *Religion Explained: The Human Instincts That Fashion Gods, Spirits and Ancestors* (London: William Heinemann, 2001).

4. Whitehouse, *Arguments and Icons* (above, n. 2), 3–4.

5. B. R. Wilson, *Magic and the Millennium: A Sociological Study of Religious Movements of Protest among Tribal and Third-World Peoples* (London: Heinemann, 1973).

6. Whitehouse, *Arguments and Icons* (above, n. 2), 5.

7. E. Durkheim, *The Division of Labour in Society* (New York: Free Press, 1964 [1892]).

8. Robin Horton, "On the Rationality of Conversion," *Africa* 45 (1975), 219–35, 373–99.

9. Igor Kopytoff, "Ancestors as Elders in Africa," *Africa* 41 (1971), 129–41.

10. J. D. Y. Peel, *Religious Encounter and the Making of the Yoruba* (Bloomington: Indiana University Press, 2000), 93–97.

11. Karin Barber, "How Man Makes God in West Africa: Yoruba Attitudes towards the *Orisa*," *Africa* 51 (1981), 497–518, Margaret T. Drewal, *Yoruba Ritual: Performers, Play, Agency* (Bloomington: Indiana University Press, 1992).

12. Willy De Craemer, Jan Vansina, and Renee C. Fox, "Religious Movements in Central Africa: A Theoretical Study," *Comparative Studies in Society and History* 18 (1976), 458–75; Wyatt McGaffey, *Modern Kongo Prophets* (Bloomington: Indiana University Press, 1983).

13. J. D. Y. Peel, "The Pastor and the *Babalawo:* The Encounter of Religions in Nineteenth-Century Yorubaland," *Africa* 60 (1990), 338–69.

14. Wim van Binsbergen, "Regional and Historical Connections of Four-Tablet Divination in Southern Africa," *Journal of Religion in Africa* 26 (1996), 2–29; Louis Brenner, *Histories of Religion in Africa: An Inaugural Lecture* (London: School of Oriental and African Studies, 2000).

15. Bernard Maupoil, *La géomancie a 'l'ancienne Côte des Esclaves* (Paris: Institut d'Ethnologie, 1943).

16. H. W. Turner, "A Typology for African Religious Movements," *Journal of Religion in Africa* 1 (1967), 1–34.

17. B. G. M. Sundkler, *Bantu Prophets in South Africa* (London: Oxford University Press for the International African Institute, 1961 [1949]); and J. B. Webster, *The African Churches among the Yoruba, 1888–1922* (Oxford: Clarendon Press, 1964).

18. James W. Fernandez, "African Religious Movements: Types and Dynamics," *Journal of Modern African Studies* 2 (1964), 531–49.

19. James W. Fernandez, "African Religious Movements," *Annual Review of Anthropology* 7 (1978), 194–234.

20. Hermione Harris, *Yoruba in Diaspora: An African Church in London* (New York: Palgrave Macmillan, 2006), chapter 8.

21. Such as Georges Balandier, *Sociology of Black Africa: Social Dynamics of Black Africa* (London: Andre Deutsch (1970 [1955]); Vittorio Lanternari, *The Religions of the Oppressed: A Study of Modern Messianic Cults* (London: MacGibbon and Kee (1963 [1960]); Peter Worsley, *The Trumpet Shall Sound: A Study of 'Cargo' Cults in Melanesia* (London: MacGibbon and Kee (1968 [1957]).

22. J.D.Y. Peel, *Aladura: A Religious Movement among the Yoruba* (London: Oxford University Press for the International African Institute, 1968), 287–88.

23. Fernandez, "African Religious Movements" (above, n. 18).

24. James W. Fernandez, *Bwiti: An Ethnography of the Religious Imagination in Africa* (Princeton: Princeton University Press, 1982).

25. Ibid. 512–13.

26. Whitehouse, *Arguments and Icons* (above, n. 2), 15.

27. See further below, chapter 10.

28. Whitehouse, *Arguments and Icons* (above, n. 2), 150–55.

29. Ibid. 140–46.

30. Max Weber, *The Protestant Ethic and the Spirit of Capitalism* (London: Allen and Unwin, 1930 [1904–5]), 175.

31. Peel, *Religious Encounter* (above, n. 10), 250–53.

32. J.C. Pollock, *The Keswick Story* (London: Hodder and Stoughton, 1964).

33. David Hempton and Myrtle Hill, *Evangelical Protestantism in Ulster Society, 1740–1890* (London: Routledge, 1992), 145–58.

34. Robert L. M'Keown, *Twenty-Five Years in Qua Iboe: A Missionary Effort In Nigeria* (London: Morgan and Scott, 1912), 157.

35. Eva Stuart Watt, *The Quest of Souls in Qua Iboe,* (London: Marshall, Morgan and Scott, 1951), 94.

36. For the Anang example, I am deeply indebted to the work of David Pratten. See further his splendid *The Man-Leopard Murders: History and Society in Colonial Nigeria* (Edinburgh: Edinburgh University Press for the International Institute, 2007), esp. chapter 3.

37. Karla Poewe, ed., *Charismatic Christianity and Global Culture* (Columbia: University of South Carolina Press, 1994); Harvey Cox, *Fire from Heaven: The Rise of Pentecostal Spirituality and the Reshaping of Religion in the Twenty-First Century* (New York: Addison Wesley, 1994); Andre Corten and Ruth Fratani, eds., *Between Babel and Pentecost: Transnational Pentecostalism in Africa and Latin America* (London: Hurst, 2001); David Martin, *Pentecostalism: The World Their Parish* (Oxford: Blackwell, 2002).

38. Peel, *Religious Encounter* (above, n. 10), 127, 152–54.

39. Peel, *Aladura* (above, n. 22), 83–91.

40. Matthews Ojo, *The End-Time Army: Charismatic Movements in Modern Nigeria* (Trenton: Africa World Press, 2006), chapter 2.

41. Asonzeh Ukah, *A New Paradigm of Pentecostal Power: A Study of the Redeemed Christian Church of God in Nigeria* (Trenton: Africa World Press, 2008); Paul Gifford,

Christianity, Development and Modernity in Africa (London: Hurst, 2015), chapters 2 and 3 on Winner's Chapel.

5. POSTSOCIALISM, POSTCOLONIALISM, PENTECOSTALISM

1. An earlier version of this chapter appeared in Mathijs Pelkmans, ed., *Conversion after Socialism: Disruptions, Modernisms and Technologies of Faith in the Former Soviet Union* (New York: Berghahn, 2009), 183–99. Its chapters are based on selected papers from a conference held at the Max Planck Institute for Social Anthropology held at Halle in April 2005.

2. C. Wanner, "Conversion and the Mobile Self: Evangelicalism as 'Travelling Culture,'" in Pelkmans, *Conversion after Socialism* (above, n. 1), 174.

3. J. D. Y. Peel, "Conversion and Tradition in Two African Societies: Ijebu and Buganda," *Past and Present* 77 (1977), 108–41; E. A. Ayandele, *The Ijebu of Yorubaland, 1850–1950: Politics, Economy and Society* (Ibadan: Heinemann, 1992), chapter 2.

4. J. D. Y. Peel, *Aladura: A Religious Movement among the Yoruba* (London: Oxford University Press for the International African Institute, 1968), 87–111.

5. J. D. Y. Peel, "Religious Change in Yorubaland," *Africa* 37 (1967), 292–306.

6. Toyin Falola, *Violence in Nigeria: The Crisis of Religious Politics and Secular Ideologies* (Rochester: University of Rochester Press, 1998).

7. C. Verdery, "Whither Postsocialism?' in C. Hann, ed., *Postsocialism: Ideals, Ideologies and Practices in Eurasia* (London: Routledge, 2002), 15–19.

8. See, for example, Marx's letter to Engels of 23 May 1851, in which he condemns the Poles as a "doomed nation, to be used as a means until Russia itself is swept by the agrarian revolution," but praises the capacity of Russian rule—despite "all its nastiness, . . . all its Slavonic filth"—to homogenize its diverse incorporated cultures: S. Avineri, *Karl Marx on Colonialism and Modernization* (Garden City: Doubleday, 1969), 447. A similar robust readiness to treat the morally odious as historically progressive marks his assessment of British rule in India: "actuated only by the vilest interests . . . [but] the unconscious tool of history" (ibid. 94).

9. J.-F. Bayart, *The State in Africa: The Politics of the Belly* (London: Longman, 1993); F. Cooper, *Africa since 1940: The Past of the Present* (Cambridge: Cambridge University Press, 2002).

10. As argued by S. Ellis and G. ter Haar, *Worlds of Power: Religious Thought and Political Practice in Africa* (London: Hurst, 2004).

11. C. Strandsbjerg, "Kérékou, God and the Ancestors: Religion and the Conception of Political Power in Benin," *African Affairs* 99 (2000), 395–414.

12. R. Banégas, *La démocratie à pas de caméléon: Transition et imaginaires politiques au Benin* (Paris: Karthala. 2003).

13. C. Meyrargue, "The Expansion of Pentecostalism in Benin: Rationales and Transnational Dynamics," in A. Corten and R. Marshall-Fratani, eds., *Between Babel and Pentecost: Transnational Pentecostalism in Africa and Latin America* (London: Hurst, 2001), 274–92.

14. P. Claffey, *Christian Churches in Dahomey-Benin: A Study of their Socio-Political Role.* (Leiden: Brill, 2007).

15. E. Morier-Genoud, "Of God and Caesar: The Relation between Christian Churches and the State in Post-Colonial Mozambique," *Le Fait Missionaire*, cahier no. 3 (1996).

16. P. Freston, "The Universal Church of the Kingdom of God: A Brazilian Church Finds Success in Southern Africa," *Journal of Religion in Africa* 35 (2005): 33–65; and Ilana van Wyk, *The Universal Church of God in South Africa: A Church of Strangers* (New York: Cambridge University Press for the International African Institute, 2014).

17. J. Goody, *Technology, Tradition and the State in Africa* (London: Oxford University Press, 1971).

18. D. Donham, *Marxist Modern: An Ethnographic History of the Ethiopian Revolution* (Berkeley and Los Angeles: University of California Press, 1999).

19. See chapters 3 and 4, by V. Vate and L. Vallikivi, respectively, in Pelkmans, *Conversion after Socialism* (above, n. 1).

20. Donham, *Marxist Modern* (above, n. 18), 144–45. See too O.M. Eide, *Religion and Revolution in Ethiopia, 1874–85* (Oxford: James Currey, 2000).

21. J. Haustein, "Pentecostal and Charismatic Churches in Ethiopia" and "A Brief History of Pentecostalism in Ethiopia," both on www.glopent (2007), and *Writing Religious History: The Historiography of Ethiopian Pentecostalism* (Wiesbaden: Harrassowitz, 2011).

22. On its origins, A. Mohr, "Out of Zion into Philadelphia and West Africa: Faith Tabernacle Congregations, 1897–1925", *Pneuma* 32 (2010), 56–79. For an overview of (neo)-Pentecostalism's later development, see B. Meyer, "Christianity in Africa: From African Independent to Pentecostal-Charismatic Churches," *Annual Review of Anthropology* 33 (2004), 447–74.

23. For this formulation I am indebted to Patricia Crone and Michael Cook's brilliant *Hagarism: The Making of the Islamic World* (Cambridge: Cambridge University Press, 1977), especially chapter 12.

24. On the relations between early Pentecostalism and its American background, see Harvey Cox, *Fire from Heaven: The Rise of Pentecostal Spirituality and the Reshaping of Religion in the Twenty-First Century* (New York: Addison-Wesley, 1994), parts I and II; G. Wacker, *Heaven Below: Early Pentecostals and American Culture* (Cambridge, Mass.: Harvard University Press, 2004). Every student of Pentecostalism in the wider world is greatly indebted to the work of David Martin, especially *Tongues of Fire: The Explosion of Pentecostalism in Latin America* (Oxford: Blackwell, 1990) and *Pentecostalism: The World Their Parish* (Oxford: Blackwell, 2002).

25. Cf. H. Bloom, *The American Religion: The Emergence of the Post-Christian Nation* (New York: Simon and Schuster, 1992).

26. A phrase that I think I have borrowed from David Martin, but neither he nor I can place its exact source.

27. S. Brouwer, P. Gifford, and S. Rose, *Exporting the American Gospel: Global Christian Fundamentalism* (New York: Routledge, 1996).

28. The major studies include M. Ojo, *The End-Time Army: Charismatic Movements in Modern Nigeria* (Trenton: Africa World Press, 2006); D. Maxwell, *African Gifts of the Spirit: Pentecostalism and the Rise of a Zimbabwean Transnational Religious Movement* (London: James Currey, 2006); A. Ukah, *A New Paradigm of Pentecostal Power: A Study of the Redeemed Christian Church of God in Nigeria* (Trenton: Africa World Press, 2008); R. Marshall, *Political Spiritualities: The Pentecostal Revolution in Nigeria* (Chicago: University of Chicago Press, 2009).

29. B. Meyer, "Make a Complete Break with the Past: Memory and Postcolonial Modernity in Ghanaian Pentecostalism," in R. Werbner, ed., *Memory and the Postcolony* (London: Zed Books, 1998), 182–208.

30. As P. Gifford, *Ghana's New Christianity: Pentecostalism in a Globalising African Economy* (London: Hurst, 2004).

31. The balance between rupture and continuity has recently become the focus of considerable debate within anthropology: see Joel Robbins "Continuity Thinking and the Problem of Christian Culture: Belief, Time and the Anthropology of Christianity," *Current Anthropology* 48 (2007), 5–38, and the ensuing comments debate.

32. Notably Pastor Matthew Asimolowo's Kingsway International Christian Centre, on which see H. Harris, *Yoruba in Diaspora: An African Church in London* (New York: Palgrave Macmillan, 2006), 218–38.

33. L. Vallikivi, "Christianization of Words and Selves: Nenets Reindeer Herders Joining the State through Conversion," in Pelkmans, *Conversion after Socialism* (above, n. 1), chapter 4.

34. This is echoed in Mathijs Pelkmans's judgment about Kyrgyz: "Remarkable similarities between the worldview promoted by the [Pentecostal] Church of Jesus Christ and indigenous notions about spirits, as well as between Christian faith-healing and traditional Muslim healing": "Temporary Conversions: Encounters with Pentecostalism in Muslim Kyrgyzstan," in Pelkmans, *Conversion after Socialism* (above, n. 1), 155.

35. L. Broz, "Conversion to Religion? Negotiating Continuity and Discontinuity in Contemporary Altai," in Pelkmans, *Conversion after Socialism* (above, n. 1), chapter 2.

36. J. Ries, "'I Must Love Them with All My Heart': Pentecostal Mission and the Romani Other," *Anthropology of East Europe Review* 2 (2007).

37. C. Tripp, *Islam and the Moral Economy: The Challenge of Capitalism* (Cambridge: Cambridge University Press, 2006).

6. CONTEXT, TRADITION, AND THE ANTHROPOLOGY OF WORLD RELIGIONS

1. Thus Robert W. Hefner, *Conversion to Christianity: Historical and Anthropological Perspectives on a Great Transformation* (Berkeley and Los Angeles: University of California Press, 1993), 3.

2. The idea of transvaluation originates with Nietzsche—see *On The Genealogy of Morals* (Oxford University Press, 1996), 17–20—from whom it passed to Weber. For an application of it to the encounter between missionary Christianity and a nontransvaluatory religion, see J. D. Y. Peel, *Religious Encounter and the Making of the Yoruba* (Bloomington: Indiana University Press, 2000), 162–67.

3. Fernand Braudel, cited by Wendy James and D. H. Johnson, *Vernacular Christianity: Essays in Honour of Godfrey Lienhardt* (Oxford: JASO, 1988), 5.

4. R. W. Bulliet, *Islam: The View from the Edge* (New York: Columbia University Press, 1994).

5. The locus classicus being B. Sundkler, *Bantu Prophets in South Africa,* 2nd ed. (London: Oxford University Press, 1961), chapter 7. See further C. Stewart and R. Shaw, eds., *Syncretism/Anti-Syncretism: The Politics of Religious Synthesis* (London: Routledge, 1994).

6. N. Cohn, *The Pursuit of the Millennium* (London, 1957). For a twentieth-century African case, see, for example, Wyatt MacGaffey, *Modern Kongo Prophets* (Bloomington: Indiana University Press, 1983), esp. chapter 7; and more generally S. Hunt, ed., *Christian Millenarianism: From the Early Church to Waco* (London: Hurst, 2001).

7. See, for example, T.O. Ranger, "Religious Movements and Politics in Sub-Saharan Africa," *African Studies Review* 29 (1986), 1–69.

8. See Peter Worsley, *The Trumpet Shall Sound: A Study of Cargo Cults in Melanesia*, 2nd ed. (London: MacGibbon and Kee, 1968).

9. See the symposium "What Is a Christian? Notes towards an Anthropology of Christianity," *Religion* 33 (2003), 191–99, especially papers by Joel Robbins, "On the Paradoxes of Global Pentecostalism and the Perils of Continuity Thinking," 221–31; and Tamar Frankiel, "The Cross-Cultural Study of Christianity: An Historian's View," 281–89. Also, M. Engelke and M. Tomlinson, eds., *The Limits of Meaning: Case Studies in the Anthropology of Christianity* (New York: Berghahn, 2006); J. Robbins, "Continuity Thinking and the Problem of Christian Culture: Belief, Time and the Anthropology of Christianity," *Current Anthropology* 48 (2007), and following comments, 5–39; F. Cannell, ed., *The Anthropology of Christianity* (Durham: Duke University Press, 2007); and more skeptically, C. Hann, "The Anthropology of Christianity *per Se*," *European Journal of Sociology* 48 (2007), 383–430.

10. Cannell, *Anthropology of Christianity* (above, n. 9), 39.

11. It is perhaps worth noting here that virtually all the contributions to Cannell's *Anthropology of Christianity* (above, n. 9) deal with the "old" or sphere-one popular Christianities rather than the "new" (recent-mission) sphere-two ones, such as those of Africa and the Pacific.

12. T. Asad, *Genealogies of Religion: Discipline and Reasons of Power in Christianity and Islam* (Baltimore: The Johns Hopkins University Press, 1993), chapter 1.

13. D. Gellner, *The Anthropology of Buddhism and Hinduism: Weberian Themes* (New Delhi: Oxford University Press, 2001), chapter 2, esp. 49–52.

14. As John R. Bowen puts it for Islam, "This tacking forth between conflicting visions is, if anything, the historical essence of Muslim ritual life": "On Scriptural Essentialism and Ritual Variation: Muslim Sacrifice in Morocco and Sumatra," *American Ethnologist* 19 (1992), 656–71.

15. Chrislam is a characteristically Yoruba phenomenon, a self-avowed composite of Islam and Christianity. See further below, chapter 9.

16. Thus Daniel Varisco, *Islam Obscured: The Rhetoric of Anthropological Representation* (New York: Palgrave Macmillan, 2005). See too Gabriele Marranci, *The Anthropology of Islam* (London: Berg, 2008).

17. Varisco, *Islam Obscured* (above, n. 16), 162.

18. Cf. W.G. Runciman's discrimination between the two spheres, but from the other side: "Although beliefs may be sociologically *explained* in categories foreign to the subjects themselves, they can only be identified in the subjects' own terms," *Sociology in Its Place* (Cambridge: Cambridge University Press, 1970), 60.

19. For an up-to-date and comprehensive review, see Jens Kreinath, ed., *The Anthropology of Islam Reader* (London: Routledge, 2012).

20. T. Asad, *The Idea of an Anthropology of Islam* (Washington, D.C.: Center for Contemporary Arab Studies, Georgetown University, 1986), 3. There is a common form of

fallacious argument here—one that Durkheim was very prone to—the thesis that he brushes aside is simply not the thesis that Ernest Gellner put forward. Anyone inclined to follow Asad on this point would benefit from looking at Michael Cook, *Ancient Religions, Modern Politics: The Islamic Case in Comparative Perspective* (Princeton: Princeton University Press, 2014).

21. Asad, *Idea* (above, n. 20), 3–4.

22. For examples, see B. Meyer, "'Make a Complete Break with the Past': Memory and Post-Colonial Modernity in Ghanaian Pentecostal Discourse," in R. Werbner, ed., *Memory and the Post-Colony* (London: Zed Books, 1998), 182–208; R. Marshall, *Political Spiritualities: The Pentecostal Revolution in Nigeria* (Chicago: University of Chicago Press, 2009), chapter 2, "Rupture, Redemption and the History of the Present"; or Robbins, "On the Paradoxes" (above, n. 9).

23. See C. F. Robinson, *Islamic Historiography* (Cambridge: Cambridge University Press, 2003).

24. Asad, *Idea* (above, n. 20), 15.

25. Perhaps it is just possible. Parallels were drawn in early Islam between the asceticism of monks and of *mujahidun* ("monks by night, horsemen by day"), in both cases regarded as the "hard edge" of their community: T. Sizgorich, *Violence and Belief in late Antiquity: Militant Devotion in Christianity and Islam* (Philadelphia: University of Pennsylvania Press, 2009), 158–67.

26. Thus Roy Dilley, ed., *The Problem of Context* (New York: Berghahn, 1999), 1.

27. M. Sahlins, *Islands of History* (Chicago: University of Chicago Press, 1985), 155.

28. My thoughts on this balance (and indeed on all other aspects of tradition) are greatly influenced by Edward Shils's wise (and sadly neglected) book *Tradition* (London: Faber, 1981).

29. Rodney Needham, "Polythetic Classification: Convergence and Consequences," *Man* 10 (1975), 349–69.

30. W. G. Runciman, *The Theory of Cultural and Social Selection* (Cambridge: Cambridge University Press, 2009).

31. B. Malinowski, "Myth in Primitive Psychology," in *Magic, Science and Religion and Other Essays* (Garden City: Doubleday, 1948 [1926]), 96–126.

32. This issue is a problem for Harvey Whitehouse's *Arguments and Icons: Divergent Modes of Religiosity* (Oxford: Oxford University Press, 2000) insofar as his argument focuses on how religions *do* succeed in reproducing themselves. The sheer diversity of local religions in PNG does, I feel, argue for memory failure playing a significant role in their differentiation, as Frederik Barth argued in *Ritual and Knowledge among the Baktaman of New Guinea* (New Haven: Yale University Press, 1975), 106–7.

33. Western and Muslim scholars tend to disagree in their judgment as to the extent of such invention, with the former much more skeptical and the latter arguing for a substantial deposit of genuine tradition preserved in the classic *hadith* collections by Bukhari and others. But the very labors of these scholars indicated that they clearly recognized the circulation of enormous numbers of forged or invented *hadith*—for whose detection they developed a methodology by assessing their alleged chains of transmission. See J. A. C. Brown, *Hadith: Muhammad's Legacy in the Medieval and Modern World* (Oxford: Oneworld, 2009); M. Z. Siddiqi, *Hadith Literature: Its Origin, Development and Special Features* (Cambridge:

Islamic Texts Society, 1993); and, for a close study of the best-known classical collector of *ahadith*, G. Abdul-Jabbar, *Bukhari* (London, I. B. Tauris, 2007).

34. For a brief but suggestive view, in relation to Christianity, see Rowan Williams, *Why Study the Past: The Quest for the Historical Church* (London: Darton, Longman & Todd, 2005), esp. chapter 1, "Making History: What Do We Expect from the Past?"

35. On Englishmen "turning Turk" in Barbary (North Africa), see Linda Colley, *Captives: Britain, the Empire and the World, 1600–1850* (London: Cape, 2002).

36. See Philip Burnham, *The Politics of Cultural Difference in Northern Cameroon* (Edinburgh: Edinburgh University Press for the International African Institute, 1996), 48: "Islam may be seen [locally] as a peculiarly Fulbe cultural property."

37. Think of those thirteenth-century clerics Antony Bek, bishop of Durham, who donned full armor to lead his feudal levies against the Scots, or Arnald-Amaury, abbot of Citeaux, leader of the crusading host against the Albigensian heretics, who also played a key role in the crushing defeat of the Moors at Navas de la Tolosa in 1209. This militarization of Christianity had many cultural obstacles to surmount and took centuries to mature. A key stage in this process was the campaigns of Charlemagne against the Saxons in the eighth century, which were followed by forced conversions. See Richard Fletcher, *The Conversion of Europe: From Paganism to Christianity, 371–1386 AD* (London: Fontana, 1998), chapters 6 and 7; and G. R. Murphy, *The Saxon Savior: The Germanic Transformation of the Gospel in the Ninth-Century Heliand* (New York: Oxford University Press, 1989), which analyzes an epic poem in which Christ and the apostles are configured as a lord and his warrior companions.

38. The close association of mission and empire has become such a banality that more nuanced views are badly needed: see especially Andrew Porter, *Religion versus Empire? British Protestant Missionaries and Overseas Expansion, 1710–1914* (Manchester: Manchester University Press, 2004), and his edited conference volume *The Imperial Horizons of British Protestant Missions, 1880–1914* (Grand Rapids: Eerdmans, 2003).

39. See especially Patricia Crone, *God's Rule: Government and Islam* (New York: Columbia University Press, 2004), esp. 10–15, and chapter 3 on the Umayyads, arguing that they still saw the caliphal role as combining political and religious functions, even though a certain differentiation of the religious and the political had begun to emerge with the rise of the *ulama* (42–44 and chapter 11); also Jonathan P. Berkey, *The Formation of Islam: Religion and Society in the Near East, 600–1800* (Cambridge: Cambridge University Press, 2003), chapter 13.

40. See S. J. Tambiah's *World Renouncer and World Conqueror: A Study of Buddhism and Polity in Thailand against a Historical Background* (Cambridge: Cambridge University Press, 1976), esp. part. 1. But he also notes (pp. 6–8) that within the resemblance there is an important difference, in that the church internally adopted much more from the secular hierarchy of society than the Buddhist *sangha* did. This I would put down in large measure to Christianity's being a congregational religion, which meant that it had to include "all sorts and conditions" of men.

41. For English examples, see W. A. Chaney, *The Cult of Kingship in Anglo-Saxon England: The Transition from Paganism to Christianity* (Manchester: Manchester University Press, 1970); and N. J. Higham, *The Convert Kings: Power and Religious Affiliation in Early Anglo-Saxon England* (Manchester: Manchester University Press, 1997), esp. chapter 4.

42. Michael Carrithers, "Jainism and Buddhism as Enduring Historical Streams," *Journal of the Anthropological Society of Oxford* 21 (1990), 141–63, esp. 149.

43. See Berkey, *Formation of Islam* (above, n. 39), chapter 15, "The Formation of Sunni Traditionalism."

44. As argued persuasively by J. M. Abun-Nasr, *Muslim Communities of Grace: The Sufi Brotherhoods in Islamic Religious Life* (London: Hurst, 2007).

45. Olivier Roy, *Globalised Islam: The Search for a New Ummah* (London: Hurst, 2004), pp. 111–47.

46. Tzvetan Todorov, *The Conquest of America: The Question of the Other* (New York: HarperPerennial, 1984), pp. 108–9, citing the Spanish missionary sources.

47. See Stephen Robinson, "Trouble in the 'Hood," www.standard.co.uk, 18 February 2011.

48. A typical recent example: the columnist Nick Cohen, writing in the British Sunday newspaper *The Observer,* 19 September 2012: "As there is no great difference between Christian and Muslim extremists, why not intervene in this clash of fundamentalisms?"

49. See chapter 10 below.

50. Cf. the recent revival of interest in Karl Jaspers's idea of "the Axial Age": for example, R. N. Bellah, "What Is Axial about the Axial Age?" *Archives Européenes de Sociologie* 46 (2005), 69–89; and Charles Taylor, "What Was the Axial Revolution?" in R. N. Bellah and H. Joas, eds., *The Axial Age and Its Consequences* (Cambridge, Mass: Belknap Press, 2012), 30–46.

51. M. Weber, *The Sociology of Religion,* trans. E. Fischoff (London: Methuen, 1965), chapter 6.

52. Thus R. Gombrich and G. Obeyesekere, *Buddhism Transformed: Religious Change in Sri Lanka* (Princeton: Princeton University Press, 1988), esp. chapter 6. It is significant that this was not a purely endogenous development but in good measure a response to the critique of evangelical missionaries.

53. See S. J. Tambiah, *Buddhism and the Spirit Cults in North-east Thailand* (Cambridge: Cambridge University Press, 1970). For a brilliant short analysis of an analogous phenomenon in Japan, the complementary coexistence of Buddhism and Shinto, the former standing for other-worldly renunciation and the latter for this-worldly life affirmation, see Maurice Bloch, *Prey into Hunter: The Politics of Religious Experience* (Cambridge: Cambridge University Press, 1992), 51–62.

54. For an example, see Peter R. Mackenzie's *Hail Orisha! A Phenomenology of West African Religion in the Mid-Nineteenth Century* (Leiden: Brill, 1997), which employs the phenomenological categories of Friedrich Heiler. Or virtually the entire oeuvre of Mircea Eliade.

55. John Bowker, *The Problem of Suffering in the Religions of the World* (Cambridge: Cambridge University Press, 1970).

56. Nevertheless, the fecundity of Weber's insights is amply demonstrated in David Gellner's application of them in his *Anthropology of Buddhism* (above, n. 13).

57. C. Geertz, *Islam Observed: Religious Development in Morocco and Indonesia* (Chicago: University of Chicago Press, 1968).

58. It is instructive to compare Geertz's procedure ibid. with his account of Ruth Benedict's expository method in his *Works and Lives: The Anthropologist as Author*

(Cambridge: Polity Press, 1988), chapter 5. What could be more Benedictine than this: "On the Indonesian side, inwardness, imperturbability, patience, poise, sensibility, aestheticism, elitism, and an almost obsessive self-effacement, the radical dissolution of individuality; on the Moroccan side, activism, fervor, impetuosity, nerve, toughness, moralism, populism, and an almost obsessive self-assertion, the radical intensification of individuality" (*Islam Observed* [above, n. 57], 54)?

59. These were/are what he calls "the classical styles": ibid. chapter 2, 21–55.

60. Ibid. 70.

61. Ibid. 62.

62. Ibid. 65.

63. *The Economist,* 29 September 2012.

64. I am grateful to Bishop Fearon for discussing with me his efforts toward religious amity, which many other Christians (such as the local leadership of the Christian Association of Nigeria) view with some reserve: interview, 13 March 2008.

65. *Culturalisme* in French takes in the idea of essentialism that is current among anthropologists. Its critique, however, is part of a broader philosophical project: the secular, universalist vision that underlies French *laïcité.* For a systematic onslaught on *culturalisme,* see J.-F. Bayart's *The Illusion of Cultural Identity* (London: Hurst, 2005), especially part 1. Bayart takes this outlook to its extreme in his *L'Islam republicaine: Ankara, Teheran, Dakar* (Paris: Albin Michel, 2010), where he maintains (p. 225) that "Islam does not exist historically or sociologically."

66. Roy, *Globalised Islam* (above, n. 45), 9–10.

67. Ibid. 6.

68. Ibid. 26.

69. Ibid. 10.

70. Richard Dawkins, *The God Delusion* (London: Bantam Press, 2006); Christopher Hitchens, *God Is Not Great* (London: Atlantic, 2007).

71. Susan Bayly, *Saints, Goddesses and Kings: Muslims and Christians in South Indian Society, 1700–1900* (Cambridge: Cambridge University Press, 1989).

7. CONVERSION AND COMMUNITY IN YORUBALAND

1. This was my friend Salahuddeen Busairi, imam of the Alhaji Yekini Adeoyo Mosque, to whom I am grateful for many conversations about all aspects of Islam in Yorubaland. Though he pronounced it just as a born-again pastor might, he later justified his use of the phrase to me in terms of the Arabic meaning he attributed to it, namely as *Hu-a-i-lu,* a contraction of *Lahuala wala quwata ilabillah,* "There is no authority and power except through Allah": interview, 5 May 2009.

2. Imam H. A. Oluwakemi at Akabiako Mosque. My guides were Mrs. Funmi Akosile and her friend Mrs. Samuel, to whom many thanks.

3. On the Yoruba concept of *ìlú* in relation to "community," see J. D. Y. Peel, "Yoruba as a City-State Culture," in M. H. Hansen, ed., *A Comparative Study of Thirty City-State Cultures* (Copenhagen: Royal Danish Academy of Sciences and Letters, 2000), 507–18; and *Ijeshas and Nigerians: The Incorporation of a Yoruba Kingdom, 1890s–1970s* (Cambridge: Cambridge University Press, 1983), 221–25.

4. For details of the survey and the results as regards the course and explanation of religious change see ibid. 164–74.

5. Robin Horton, "African Conversion," *Africa* 41 (1971), 85–108; and a more elaborate version, "On the Rationality of Conversion," parts 1 and 2, *Africa* 45 (1975), 219–35 and 373–99, formulated in response to H. J. Fisher's critique, "Conversion Reconsidered," *Africa* 43 (1973), 27–40.

6. E.g., E. A. Ayandele, *The Missionary Impact on Modern Nigeria, 1842–1914* (London: Longman, 1966), 68, on the Ijebu conversion movement that followed a few years after the British conquest, as an attempt to acquire "the secret of the white man's power."

7. For an earlier version of this argument, which was not framed within the terms of Horton's theory, see J. D. Y. Peel, "Religious Change in Yorubaland," *Africa* 37 (1967), 292–306. This presents the detailed religious statistics, drawn from the 1952 Census of Western Nigeria.

8. See H. O. Danmole, "The Frontier Emirate: A History of Islam in Ilorin" (unpublished Ph.D. thesis, University of Birmingham, 1980), and Ann O'Hear, *Power Relations in Nigeria: Ilorin Slaves and Their Successors* (Rochester: University of Rochester Press, 1997).

9. For an overall account of the history of Islam, T. G. O. Gbadamosi, *The Growth of Islam among the Yoruba, 1841–1908* (London: Longman, 1978). See too G. O. Gbadamosi, "Patterns and Developments in Lagos Religious History," in A. B. Aderibigbe, ed., *Lagos: The Development of an African City* (Lagos: Longman Nigeria, 1975), 173–96. (Gbadamosi is a Muslim by birth who became a Christian but later returned to his original faith, evidently between these two works.)

10. For a picture of Muslims in the Northern and Western areas from the mid-nineteenth century onwards, see J. D. Y. Peel, *Religious Encounter and the Making of the Yoruba* (Bloomington: Indiana University Press, 2000), chapter 7.

11. On the acceleration of conversion from the 1890s, ibid. 242–47.

12. J. D. Y. Peel, *Aladura: A Religious Movement among the Yoruba* (London: Oxford University Press for the International African Institute, 1968), chapter 3.

13. See Aribidesi Usman, *The Yoruba Frontier: A Regional History of Community Formation, Experiences and Changes in West Africa* (Durham: Carolina Academic Press, 2012), chapters 5 and 6, on the variable religious outcomes along Yorubaland's northern marches: in the 1950s Ilorin Division had Muslims 64 percent, Christians 8 percent, whereas Kabba Division had Muslims 12 percent, Christians 62 percent.

14. I say this on the basis of casual observation, since I know of no census or survey statistics that distinguish the indigenous Ife and Modakeke areas. The first local Muslim, Kasumu Adeosun, was a Modakeke with an Ife mother, converted in Lagos. In fact, the Christians too got their first foothold in Modakeke but expanded more rapidly in indigenous Ife from the 1920s: see D. Laitin, *Hegemony and Culture: Politics and Religious Change among the Yoruba* (Chicago: University of Chicago Press, 1986), 51–55, and E. D. Adelowo, "Islam and Christianity in Ile-Ife," in I. A. Akinjogbin, ed., *The Cradle of a Race: Ife from the Beginning to 1980* (Port Harcourt: Sunray Publications, 1992), chapter 17.

15. This section largely draws on J. D. Y. Peel, "Conversion and Confusion: Religious Change in Ijebu and Buganda," *Past and Present* 77 (1977), 108–41.

16. Quoted by Peel, *Religious Encounter* (above, n. 10), 148–49.

17. On the spatial structure of the Ijebu kingdom , see P.C. Lloyd, *Yoruba Land Law* (Oxford: Oxford University Press, 1962), chapter 6. An excellent ethnography of the western part of Ijebu (Remo) is Insa Nolte, *Obafemi Awolowo and the Making of Remo* (Edinburgh: Edinburgh University Press for International African Institute, 2009).

18. See the Adelaja genealogy in chapter 5 above.

19. As argued strongly by Caroline Ifeka-Moller in relation to Eastern Nigeria, "White Power: Social Structural Factors in Conversion to Christianity in Eastern Nigeria, 1921–66," *Canadian Journal of African Studies* 8 (1974), 55–72.

20. Such as the future historian and vice-chancellor Saburi Biobaku, who came from a well-established Muslim family in Abeokuta. His grandfather Alfa Bisiriyu Giwa (ca. 1860–1937) held a title in *Ẹgbẹ Killa*, the popular Muslim society, and he received a solid Koranic education, as well as attending church primary schools. The crunch came when he won a scholarship to Government College Ibadan—not a mission school—but "my grandfather listened to me patiently and approved my going . . . but made one condition, that on no account should I permit myself to be converted to Christianity": S.O. Biobaku, *When We Were Young* (Ibadan: University Press PLC, 1992), 41. Such a decision must have come more easily in a family whose Muslim identity was already strong. Biobaku's pious grandmother had prayed that Almighty Allah would grant him to pass the exam "if He felt it would be good for me" and later had a confirmatory dream "that I was going somewhere far away from her."

21. Thus the *Apena* (spokesman) of the Osugbo society at Iperu, in Ijebu Remo, as quoted by Rev. James Johnson to CMS Secretary, 21 June 1878, CMS Papers (University of Birmingham), CA2/O56. The reference to slaves as Sango worshippers is evidence for the recentness of Sango worship in Ijebu and its Oyo origins.

22. This was sung around Osogbo and the Odo Otin area. For this, I am indebted to Dr. Sola Ajibade of Osun State University.

23. On nineteenth-century persecution, see Peel, *Religious Encounter* (above, n. 10), 191–92 (of Muslims), 235–38 (of Christians). For an early colonial case, in the small Ijesha town of Ibokun—no doubt typical of many—see F.A. Ajayi, *In Our Days: An Autobiography* (Lagos: West African Book Publishers, 2005), 55. Dr. Ajayi's father, a Christian pioneer, was among those thrown into a dungeon pit used for criminals, where they were kept without food for hours or days at a time: "Their persecutors genuinely believed that Christianity with the attendant abandonment of the worship of the ancient deities would result in an ancestral annoyance whereby the whole community would suffer from untold pestilence and tribulation."

24. LaRay Denzer, *Folayegbe M. Akintunde-Ighodalo: A Public Life* (Ibadan: Sam Bookman, 2001), 5–11. Okeigbo had its origins in the nineteenth century as a heterogeneous settlement ruled by an Ife prince who had been enslaved to Ibadan, where he learned the art of war: in sum, it came close to being a microcosm of the Yoruba world.

25. Biyi Afonja, *In His Hands: The Autobiography of a Nigerian Village Boy* (Ibadan: STATCO Publishers, 2005), 29–31.

26. For an example, see Margaret Drewal, *Yoruba Ritual: Performance, Play, Agency* (Bloomington: Indiana University Press, 1992), chapter 9, on the rural Ijebu town of Imewuro. Local elites devised a week-long festival of events, incorporating *orișa* celebrations—but taken out of their original contexts—along with a torchlight parade, prayers in the mosque

on Friday, a football match, a grand Saturday-night social dance, the launching of a local electricity project, all culminating with thanksgiving in the Anglican church on Sunday. See too Nolte, *Obafemi Awolowo* (above, n. 17), chapter 8.

27. *Ọlaju* refers to both enlightenment and to enlightened people (otherwise elites, in the peculiar Nigerian sense of the word). For a fuller explication of the concept, see J. D. Y. Peel "*Ọlaju:* A Yoruba Concept of Development," *Journal of Development Studies* 14 (1978), 135–65.

28. Thus John Laoye as *Timi* of Ede (1946–75), Samuel Abimbola as *Oluwo* of Iwo, Samuel Adenle as *Ataoja* of Osogbo (1944–75).

29. See, for example, Edmund M. Hogan, *Cross and Scalpel: Jean-Marie Coquard among the Egba of Yorubaland* (Ibadan: HEBN Publishers, 2012), a biography of the founder of the Sacred Heart Hospital at Abeokuta.

30. He was the grandson of David Kukomi, the most prominent of David Hinderer's converts, who (as of 1969) was the ancestor of no less than twelve Anglican clergymen: see T. A. Adebiyi, *The Beloved Bishop: A Biography of Bishop A. B. Akinyele* (Ibadan: Daystar Press, 1969), and on the nineteenth-century antecedents Peel, *Religious Encounter* (above, n. 10), 232–33, 273–74.

31. Two of the most substantial I have come across are J. O. Soriyan, *A Comprehensive History of St Saviour's (Anglican) Church, Ikenne-Remo, 1898–1986* (published by the church, 1986?), 271 pages, and (no author named) *A Century of St. Paul's (Ang.) Church, Yemetu, Ibadan, 1894–1994* (Ibadan: Mabambu Publishers, 1994), 224 pages. Sadly, there is no comparable literature produced by Muslims.

32. Wole Soyinka, *Aké: The Years of Childhood* (London: Collings, 1981), and *Ìsarà: A Voyage around "Essay"* (London: Methuen, 1990). On the latter see Insa Nolte, "Cultural Politics and Nationalist History: A Background to Wole Soyinka's *Ìsarà*," in Toyin Falola, ed., *Christianity and Social Change in Africa* (Durham: Carolina Academic Press, 2005), chapter 10.

33. For examples, the progressive circle round the *Ẹgbẹ Agbaotan* at Ibadan as described by Ruth Watson, *'Civil Disorder Is the Disease of Ibadan': Chieftaincy and Civic Culture in a Yoruba City* (Oxford: James Currey, 2003); or for Ilesha, Peel, *Ijeshas and Nigerians* (above, n. 3), s.v. *Ẹgbẹ Atunluṣe;* and M. A. Ifaturoti and O. I. Orolugbagbe, *The History of Egba Atunluṣe of Ile Ijesa* (Lagos, 1992).

34. The landmark study remains J. B. Webster, *The African Churches among the Yoruba, 1888–1922* (Oxford: Clarendon Press, 1964).

35. The main studies are H. W. Turner, *African Independent Church,* 2 vols. (Oxford: Clarendon Press, 1967); Peel, *Aladura* (above, n. 12); J. A. Omoyajowo, *Cherubim and Seraphim: The History of an African Church* (New York: Nok Publishers, 1982), C. O. Oshun, "Christ Apostolic Church of Nigeria" (unpublished Ph.D. thesis, University of Exeter, 1981). Many studies continue to come out of Nigeria, such as M. O. Idowu, *The Great Revival of 1930: The Origin of Modern-day Pentecostalism in Nigeria* (Ikeja: Divine Artillery Publications, 2007).

36. Thus Patrick J. Ryan, *Imale: Yoruba Participation in the Muslim Tradition* (Missoula: Scholars Press, 1978), 180, a pioneering study of Yoruba Islam, which puts the *alfa* at the center of its account.

37. E.g., by making amulets containing Koranic texts or esoteric formulas in Arabic script (*tiraa*) or potions from the inky water washed from slates on which sacred texts had been written (*hantu*).

38. See H.J. Fisher, *Ahmadiyyah: A Study in Contemporary Islam on the West African Coast* (London: Oxford University Press, 1963). Interestingly, it came about through a friendship between a Christian, Dr. Oguntola Sapara, and an educated Muslim of Brazilian background, L.B. Agusto. Sapara passed to his friend some Ahmadiyya literature he had come across on a visit to London.

39. On AUD, see A.D. Amoo, "Non-formal Education Programmes of the Ansar-ud-Deen Society of Nigeria in South-West Nigeria" (Ph.D. thesis, University of Ibadan, 2001). He notes the influence of Blyden on its formation. By 1960, AUD had 200 primary schools, 18 modern schools, 3 grammar schools, and 3 teacher-training colleges.

40. A.R.I Doi, "The Bamidele Movement in Yorubaland," *Orita: Ibadan Journal of Religious Studies* 3 (1969), 101–10; and Lateef M. Adetona, "The Metamorphosis of the Bamidele Movement," in Toyin Falola and Ann Genova, eds., *The Yoruba in Transition: History, Values, and Modernity* (Durham: Carolina Academic Press, 2006), 85–98.

41. See E.A. Ayandele, *The Ijebu of Yorubaland, 1850–1950: Politics, Economy and Society* (Ibadan: Heinemann, 1992), 270, 278.

42. Details of this and the varying succession practices in other Yoruba towns in L.O. Abbas, "Imamship in Islam: Its Concept and Practice among the Yoruba of Oyo and Osun States" (unpublished Ph.D. thesis, University of Ibadan, 2003), 163–215.

43. Ibid. 144–55.

44. R.O. Ojelade, "The Emergence, Doctrines and Practices of Alalukurani Group of Lagos Muslims" (unpublished Ph.D. thesis, University of Ibadan, 1990). The Alalukurani split further in 1919, and one section allied itself with Ahmadiyya for some years (1921–34). They retain their independence down to the present.

45. See P.D. Cole, *Modern and Traditional Elites in the Politics of Lagos* (Cambridge: Cambridge University Press, 1975), 98–104; Gbadamosi, "Patterns and Developments" (above, n. 9), 186–88.

46. The liaison group between the Jama'at and the leading Christian activists was known as the Ilu Committee, on which see Kunle Lawal, "The Role of the Ilu Committee in the Politics of Lagos," *Odu*, n.s., 4 (1989). The Yoruba term *ìlú* (town, city-state, polity) does not mean the same as the Arabic *jama'at* (congregation, society), but there is a semantic overlap between them, which centers on something like "community."

47. Ayandele, *The Ijebu of Yorubaland* (above, n. 41), 40–42, 273–75.

48. T.A. Odutola had in fact been born a Muslim, as his brother Jimoh (also a noted trader) remained.

49. Ayandele, *Ijebu of Yorubaland* (above, n. 41), chapters 4 and 6; and M.O.A. Abdul, "Islam in Ijebu-Ode" (unpublished M.A. thesis, McGill University, 1967), 29–30, 39.

50. Still useful is W.A.O. Nasiru, "Islamic Literacy among the Yoruba, 1896–1963" (unpublished Ph.D. thesis, University of Ibadan, 1977), esp. chapter 3, on the synthesis of Western and Islamic systems of education. Nasiru's has formed the basis for several later Ibadan Ph.D. theses focused more on the content of this Yoruba Arabic scholarship, the bulk of which addressed topics of religious debate among the *ulama*. See M.O. Abdul-Rahmon, "A Thematic and Stylistic Study of Arabic Poetry in Ibadan, 1986–1976" (1989); F.O. Jamiu, "A Study of the Contents and Structural Patterns of the Didactic Arabic Poetry of Yoruba Ulama, 1885–1995" (2004); and I.A. Jimoh, "Arguments and Counter-Arguments in Selected Works in Arabic in Nigerian [*de facto* Yoruba] Authors" (2005).

51. P.F. de Moraes Farias's "Yoruba Origins Revisited by Muslims: An Interview with the *Arokin* of Oyo and a Reading of the *Asl Qaba'il Yuruba* of *Al-Hajj* Adam al-Iluri," in P.F. de Moraes Farias and K. Barber, *Self-Assertion and Brokerage: Early Cultural Nationalism in West Africa* (Birmingham: Centre of West African Studies, 1990), esp. 128–47, is still almost the only treatment of his ideas that is widely available. More recent and of great value, but yet little known outside Nigeria, is R.D. Abubakre, *The Interplay of Arabic and Yoruba Cultures in South-Western Nigeria* (Iwo: Daru 'l-Ilm Publishers, 2004), chapter 4. Two unpublished Ibadan M.A. theses I have also found helpful: T.A. Yekini's "Shaykh Adam Abdullah al-Ilori in the Eyes of Selected Elegists" (2004) and L.A. Tadese's "Annotated Translation of Shaykh Adam Abdullah al-Ilori's *Tawjih al-Da'wah wa al-Du'at fi Nayjiriya wa Gharb Afriqiya*" (2002). In the theses cited in n. 50 above, there are discussions of aspects of al-Ilori's work in Jimoh (chap. 5) and Jamiu (chap. 2). I am also indebted to the late Professor I.A. Ogunbiyi for giving me a copy of his draft translation of al-Ilori's *Al-Islam al-yawm wa ghadan fi Naijiriya* (Cairo, 1985). A book-length study of al-Ilori's work in its totality is much needed.

52. On whom see further below, chapter 10.

53. Interview with Professor D.O.S. Noibi, executive secretary of MUSWEN, at its headquarters, Arisekola's Mosque, Iwo Road, Ibadan, 8 April 2009. As an academic and former imam of the university mosque, Professor Noibi himself fully bridges the two status hierarchies.

54. Interview with Alhaji Arisekola Alao, 26 March 2008.

55. The strength of Arisekola's identity as an Ibadan man came over strongly in our interview—though it was triggered by my companion, Wale Adebanwi, who rather mischievously introduced me as the author of a book on the Ijesha! As the Ijesha and the Ibadans were historical enemies, Arisekola plunged with gusto into tales of Ibadan's past military prowess against the Ijesha.

56. For a fascinating detailed study, see H.A. Akintoye, "Islam and Chieftaincy Titles in Lagos Island since 1775" (M.A.thesis, Lagos State University, ca. 2005). He traces back to the mid-nineteenth century the granting of mosque-level titles, such as *Osupa Adinni* (Moon of Religion) or *Iya Sunna* (Mother of the Way, an equivalent of the Christian *Iya Ijo*). The wealthy merchant Alli Balogun (1836–1933), who founded *Ẹgbẹ Killa*, a noted Muslim social club, and built the Wasimi Jamiu Mosque, seems to have been the first to have received a higher-level title, that of *Seriki Adinni* (Captain of Religion) of Lagos Muslims. I am grateful to Professor Amidu Sanni for allowing me access to this and other unpublished LASU theses.

57. For details, see R.L. Sklar, *Nigerian Political Parties* (Princeton: Princeton University Press, 1963), 247–51; and K.W.J. Post and G.D. Jenkins, *The Price of Liberty: Personality and Politics in Colonial Nigeria* (Cambridge: Cambridge University Press, 1973), 396–97.

58. The name, meaning "Don't let the honor [of the town] spoil," harks back to the glory days of nineteenth-century Ibadan. For the full complexity of Ibadan politics, see again Sklar, *Nigerian Political Parties* (above, n. 57), 284–320.

59. See Post and Jenkins, *Price of Liberty* (above, n. 57), the classic political biography of Adelabu.

60. As astutely noted by Sklar, *Nigerian Political Parties* (above, n. 57), 294. The same paradox occurred elsewhere in late colonial Africa: see D.R. Peterson, *Ethnic Patriotism and the East African Revival: A History of Dissent, c. 1935–1972* (Cambridge: Cambridge University Press, 2012), 281–83.

61. Muili's critics are said to have protested *O gbe aja wọ si mọṣalaṣi!* (He has brought a dog into the mosque!).

62. Thus Sklar, *Nigerian Political Parties* (above, n. 57), 55.

63. Pauline H. Baker, *Urbanization and Political Change: The Politics of Lagos, 1917–1967* (Berkeley and Los Angeles: University of California Press, 1974), esp. chapters 5 and 8 (on the power of the market women), is sound and detailed on the religious dimension of the AG takeover. But for the essential irrelevance of religion to the routine business of patron-client relations within the system, Sandra T. Barnes's anthropological study of outer Lagos, *Patrons and Power: Creating a Political Community in Metropolitan Lagos* (Manchester: Manchester University Press for the International African Institute, 1986) is without equal.

64. See Lai Olurode, *The Life and Times of LKJ* (Lagos: Rebonik Publications, 2005), an instructive short biography of Jakande, who edited the AG newspaper (the *Daily Service*) in the1950s and 1960s, shared Awolowo's imprisonment for alleged sedition in 1962–66, served as UPN governor of Lagos State, 1979–83, and was seen by some as his true political successor after 1987. Jakande was deeply rooted in the culture of Lagos Islam. His great-grandfather was the *Oluwo* (chief *babalawo*) of *Ọba* Kosoko, as were his grandfather and father (who were also Muslims), while his mother was a daughter of the chief imam of the Alalukurani Muslims.

65. Here the definitive study is Wale Adebanwi, *Yoruba Elites and Ethnic Politics in Nigeria: Obafemi Awolowo and Corporate Agency* (Cambridge: Cambridge University Press, 2014).

66. D. Laitin, *Hegemony and Culture* (above, n. 14).

67. D. Laitin, "The Sharia Debate and the Origins of Nigeria's Second Republic," *Journal of Modern African Studies* 20 (1982), 411–30.

68. In the federal election of 1959, the AG got 49.5 percent of the vote in the Western region (and only 43.8 percent in Lagos), whereas in 1979 the UPN share of the vote in the four Yoruba states ranged between 82.3 percent in Lagos and 94.5 percent in Ondo: Sklar, *Nigerian Political Parties* (above, n. 57), 36; and R.A. Joseph, *Democracy and Prebendal Politics in Nigeria* (Cambridge: Cambridge University Press, 1987), 127.

69. He was famously the butt of Fela Anikulapo-Kuti's 1979 song ITT (International Thief Thief), a parodic allusion to International Telephone and Telegraph, the U.S. company of which Abiola was the local representative, the archetypal comprador businessman: see T. Olaniyan, *Arrest the Music! Fela and His Rebel Art and Politics* (Bloomington: Indiana University Press, 2004), 145–50.

70. P.L. Van den Berghe, *Power and Privilege at an African University* (London: Routledge and Kegan Paul, 1973).

71. Sources: the account by the vice-chancellor, Professor Ayo Banjo, *In the Saddle: A Vice-Chancellor's Story* (Ibadan: Spectrum Books, 1997), 69–76; interview with Professor D.O.S. Noibi (who was imam of the university mosque at the time), 8 April 2009.

72. Yoruba delegates went to seek support from Northern *ulama* to approach Abacha for Abiola's release, which they were reluctant to give, saying it was a political and not a religious issue. A furious argument took place between some of the emirs present and the fearless and forceful Dr. Oloso (a former MSS president): interview with K.K. Oloso, 9 May 2009.

73. See below, chapter 10.

74. John Iliffe, *Obasanjo: Nigeria and the World* (Woodbridge: James Brewer, 2011), while very informative about Obasanjo's career, fails to get the measure of this. But see Adebanwi, (above, n. 65), chapter 6, "How (Not) to Be a Proper Yoruba."

75. Even so, Adedibu's long career illustrates shows the crossovers that abound in Yoruba politics. Born in 1927, he entered politics in 1951 as a follower of the Rev. E. A. Alayande (a convert from Islam) in the Ibadan Peoples Party, which merged into the Action Group. By 1979 he had switched over to the other side and was active in the NPN, which seems more natural for a populist Ibadan Muslim. The Third Republic found him for Abiola and the SDP. After 1999, he was the local power broker who finally delivered Ibadan to the anti-Awoist PDP and was almost certainly behind the mysterious destruction on the night of 29 May 2003 of the statue of Chief Awolowo that stood in front of Government House in Ibadan. See ibid. chapter 2.

76. Ibid. 227–39, particularly his analysis of the politics of Bola Tinubu.

8. YORUBA ETHNOGENESIS AND THE TRAJECTORY OF ISLAM

1. On which see E. A. Ayandele, *The Missionary Impact on Modern Nigeria, 1842–1914* (London: Longman, 1966), chapters 6–8; and P. F. de Moraes Farias and Karin Barber, eds., *Self-Assertion and Brokerage: Early Cultural Nationalism in West Africa* (Birmingham: Centre of West African Studies, 1990).

2. In a work published in 1615–16, Ahmad Baba included the Yoruba in a list of pagan peoples whom Muslims were entitled to enslave: Robin Law, *The Oyo Empire, c.1600–c.1836* (Oxford: Clarendon Press, 1977), 14. Law also notes a lost Arabic work of 1667 entitled *A Reply to the Learned Men of Yoruba.* Does this imply there was already then a core of Yoruba *ulama?*

3. See Stefan Reichmuth, "Songhay-Lehnwörter im Yoruba und ihr historischer Kontext," *Sprache und Geschichte in Afrika* 9 (1988), 269–99.

4. See R. C. Abraham, *Dictionary of Modern Yoruba* (London: University of London Press, 1958), s.v. *bọọkinni,* which quotes two of the proverbs. *Bọrọkinni* has the same root as appears in the name of the country Burkina Faso, said to mean "Country of Honest Men."

5. The term *saraa,* deriving (like cognate terms in many other West African languages) from Arabic (*sadaqa,* "alms"), most commonly means a payment made to *alfa* and other religious specialists for their services. From this core meaning, there has been a semantic spread in two directions: sometimes (and particularly in nineteenth-century missionary reports) it comes close to being a synonym for "sacrifice," qua offering made in anticipation of divine favor; and elsewhere (particularly in twentieth-century usage) something more like "ritual feast," where the alms or offering is recycled for shared consumption within the community. See further discussion in J. D. Y. Peel, *Religious Encounter and the Making of the Yoruba* (Bloomington: Indiana University Press, 2000), 200–202, and "Christianity and the Logic of Nationalist Assertion in Wole Soyinka's *Ìsarà,*" in D. Maxwell, ed., *Christianity and the African Imagination: Essays in Honour of Adrian Hastings* (Leiden: Brill, 2002), 141–44.

6. C. J. Waterman, *Juju: A Social History and Ethnography of an African Popular Music* (Chicago: University of Chicago Press, 1990), 231, refers to professional rivalry between Juju and Fuji musicians in the early 1980s. While still especially patronized by Muslims, Fuji was then rapidly growing in popularity among Christians too. On Fuji more generally, see Bode

Omojola, *Yoruba Music in the Twentieth Century* (Rochester: University of Rochester Press, 2012), chapter 8; and Debra Klein, "Fuji," an unpublished article to appear in *Bloomsbury Encyclopedia of Popular Music*, volume 6.

7. E.W. Blyden, *Christianity, Islam and the Negro Race* (Edinburgh, Edinburgh University Press, 1967 [1887]), 14, 43.

8. Quoted in Peel, *Religious Encounter* (above, n. 5), 205. On Johnson more generally, see E. A. Ayandele, *Holy Johnson: Pioneer of African Nationalism* (London: Cass, 1970).

9. The main item was Rev. James Johnson's *Yoruba Heathenism* (Exeter: Townsend, 1899): drawing much on the experience of Rev. E.M. Lijadu's researches on Ifa, the latter title led to two pamphlets, *Ifa* (1899) and *Orunmla!* (1908), on which see further J. D. Y. Peel, "Between Crowther and Ajayi: The Religious Origins of the Modern Yoruba Intelligentsia," in Toyin Falola, *African Historiography: Essays in Honour of Jacob Ade Ajayi* (Harlow: Longman, 1993), 64–79. Later came Ven. J. Olumide Lucas, *The Religion of the Yorubas* (Lagos: CMS Bookshop, 1948), though that was largely driven by the perverse aim of showing that the Yoruba language derived from ancient Egyptian.

10. J.D.Y. Peel, *Aladura: A Religious Movement among the Yoruba* (London: Oxford University Press for the International African Institute, 1968), 91–105.

11. Margaret T. Drewal, *Yoruba Ritual: Performers, Play, Agency* (Bloomington: Indiana University Press, 1992), chapter 8; I. Nolte, *Obafemi Awolowo and the Making of Remo* (Edinburgh: Edinburgh University Press for the International African Institute), 214–28.

12. J. D. Y. Peel, "The Pastor and the *Babalawo*," *Africa* 60 (1990), 157–70.

13. D.Ọ. Epega, *The Mystery of Yoruba Gods* (Ode Remo: Imole Oluwa Institute, 1932). Epega, from Ode Remo, was a pastor of one of the African churches.

14. Unpublished Ph.D. thesis, University of Bristol, 1976. For a full appreciation, see J. D. Y. Peel "Yoruba Religion: Seeing It in History, Seeing It Whole," Third Bishop Adegbola Memorial Lecture, *Orita: Ibadan Journal of Religious Studies* 40 (2008), 1–24.

15. S. Adeniran, *The Ethiopian Church: A National Necessity* (1918). Adeniran is a shadowy figure. As S.A. Oke, he had been a pastor in the United African Native Church and seems to have been radicalized by the collective trauma of the great influenza pandemic of 1918.

16. Karin Barber, "Discursive Strategies in the Texts of Ifa and in the 'Holy Book of Odu' in the African Church of Orunmila," in Farias and Barber, *Self-Assertion and Cultural Brokerage* (above, n. 1), 196–224.

17. 'Wande Abimbola, with Ivor Miller, *Ifá Will Mend Our Broken World: Thoughts on Yoruba Religion and Culture in Africa and the Diaspora* (Roxbury: Aim Books, 1997).

18. As was argued by Thomas Hodgkin in his little classic *Nationalism in Colonial Africa* (London: Frederick Muller, 1956), chapter 5, "Prophets and Priests." Hodgkin was misled by his Marxism into believing that the religious movement was merely a precursor to the political one rather than one with its own autonomous dynamic.

19. A. Apter, *The Pan-African Nation: Oil and the Spectacle of Culture in Nigeria* (Chicago: University of Chicago Press, 2005).

20. As Apter notes without elaboration in his last sentence: ibid. 284.

21. Asonzeh Ukah, *A New Paradigm of Pentecostal Power: A Study of the Redeemed Christian Church of God in Nigeria* (Trenton: Africa World Press, 2008), 119.

22. On the perception of British colonialism as rule by Christians, see texts cited in J. N. Paden, *Religion and Political Culture in Kano* (Berkeley and Los Angeles: University of California Press, 1973), 53–54, and particularly in M. S. Umar, *Islam and Colonialism: Intellectual Responses of Muslims of Northern Nigeria to British Colonial Rule* (Leiden: Brill, 2006), chapters 4 and 5.

23. A. M. Yakubu, *Sa'adu Zungur: An Anthology of the Social and Political Writings of a Nigerian Nationalist* (Kaduna: Nigerian Defence Academy Press, 1999). Sa'adu was an accomplished poet in Hausa, two of his best known poems being *Waƙar Bidi'a* (Against Heresy) and *Mulkin Nasara* (European Colonialism). In the latter, Yakubu's translation fudges the literal meaning, which is "Christian Rule."

24. *Africa in Ebullition* (Ibadan: Board Publications, 2008 [1952]), 63.

25. For a detailed account, see I. A. Jimoh, "Arguments and Counter-Arguments in Selected Works in Arabic by Nigerian Authors," unpublished Ph.D. thesis, University of Ibadan, 2005.

26. L. Brenner, "Muslim Divination and the History of Religion in Sub-Saharan Africa," in J. Pemberton, ed., *Insight and Artistry: A Cross Cultural Study of Divination in Central and West Africa* (Washington, D.C.: Smithsonian Institution Press, 2000), 45–59. Islamic divination is known as sand writing (*Yanrin Titẹ*) in Yoruba, or *khatt ar-raml* in Arabic. The name Orunmila has been widely construed by Yoruba Christians (from Lijadu onward) as a contracted form of some such phrase as *Ọrun l'o mọ ilaja* (It is Heaven that knows reconciliation) or *Ọrun l'o mọ ẹniti yio la* (Heaven knows who will be saved). Edifying as such etymologies may be, it seems to me equally possible (and perhaps phonetically more likely), that it simply derives from *ar-raml*, with vowels added to fit the patterns of Yoruba speech.

27. As reported by a missionary in Abeokuta in 1877: see Peel, *Religious Encounter* (above, n. 5), 115.

28. For Samuel Johnson and Obadiah Johnson, *History of the Yorubas from the Earliest Times to the Beginning of the British Protectorate* (Cambridge: Cambridge University Press, 2010 [1957]), 32–33, Setilu was taken to be a Nupe, expelled from his home by Muslims. See further P. F. de Moraes Farias, "Yoruba Origins Revisited by Muslims: An Interview with the Arókin of Oyo and a Reading of the Asl Qabā'il Yūrubā of Al-Hājj Adam al-Ilūri," in Farias and Barber, *Self-Assertion and Brokerage* (above, n. 1), 109–47, esp. 123–25 on Setilu's origin as Satih bin Rabi'a.

29. Abdul-Raheem Shittu (b. 1953) is a lay Muslim intellectual and qualified lawyer, former MSS activist, who represented his home town, Shaki, in the Oyo State Assembly (1979–83) and was for a while attorney general. He traces his Salafist views to reading the works of the South African Ahmad Deedat and the Indian Mawlana Mawdudi, distributed by the MSS. Though not an Arabic scholar—which is why some educated *ulama* look askance at his work—he is a prolific author of polemical books and serves as legal advisor to the Salafist Ahl us-Sunna group of Muslim organizations (interview, 5 April, 2009).

30. Ibid.

31. A.-R. Shittu, *What Is Sunnah? What Is Bid'ah?* (Shaki: al-Fur'qaan Publishers, 1996), 32, inveighing against many Muslims' attachment to Yoruba funeral practices: "It is in Saudi Arabia, Kuwait and other Islamic and Muslim countries that unalloyed commitment to [Islam] is culturally entrenched and governmentally enforced. One can say . . . that such communities would be better standard-bearers of pristine Islam than most other

communities where legacies of atheistic [he means 'polytheistic'] and other un-Islamic cultural traditions are umbilically attached to Islamic norms."

32. K.K. Oloso, "Hajj and Its Operations in Nigeria, 1854–1880," Ph.D. thesis, University of Ibadan, 1984.

33. This is known as *takfir,* the declaration of a person or group of Muslims as *kafir,* "unbelievers." New to the tolerant Yoruba, it was a standard tactic of political conflict among Muslims in the precolonial North, since it changed the status under Sharia law of those it so stigmatized. (E.g., it allowed them to be enslaved.) It was used by Usman dan Fodio to legitimate his uprising against the Muslim rulers of pre-jihad Hausaland, and was mutually employed by him and the Shehu of Borno in their diplomatic skirmishing: see L. Brenner, "The Jihad Debate between Sokoto and Borno: An Historical Analysis of Islamic Political Discourse in Nigeria," in J.F.A. Ajayi and J.D.Y. Peel, eds., *People and Empires in African History: Essays in Memory of Michael Crowder* (London: Longman, 1992), 21–44.

34. For a brief account of the Ahmadiyya crisis, see A.R.I. Doi, "Islam in Nigeria: Changes since Independence," in E. Fashole-Like, R. Gray, A. Hastings, and G. Tasie, eds., *Christianity in Independent Africa* (London: Rex Collings, 1978), 350–53.

35. There resulted a bitter exchange of articles in the Lagos press putting forward the pro- and anti-Ahmadi arguments, which Balogun later arranged to be reprinted: I.A.B. Balogun, *Islam versus Ahmadiyya in Nigeria* (Lahore: Sh. Muhammad Ashraf, 1977). I am grateful to Dr. L.O. Abbas for procuring a copy of this work for me.

36. Officially known as Ahmadiyya Muslim Jama'at Nigeria. Alhaji Abdul-Gani Sobambi, a senior missioner of Ahmadiyya, kindly provided details (interview, 4 April 2009).

37. For the early history of the MSS see K.K. Oloso, "The Contribution of the Muslim Students Society of Nigeria to the Islamic Resurgence in Southern Nigeria, 1954–1980" (M.A. thesis, University of Ibadan, 1981). Also interview with Dr. Oloso (who was MSS president in 1980–81), 9 May 2009. For Adegbite's role in it see M.A. Adedayo, *Abdul-Lateef Adegbite: A Life for the People* (Lagos: WEPCOM Publishers, 2006), 131–37.

38. Born at Abeokuta, Adegbite (1933–2014) was the half-brother of the historian S.O. Biobaku—same mother, different father—and later went on, following a Ph.D. in law at SOAS, to a distinguished career as a lawyer and administrator.

39. P.B. Clarke and I. Linden, *Islam in Modern Nigeria: A Study of a Muslim Community in a Post-Independence State, 1960–1983* (Grunewald: Kaiser, 1984), 50.

40. Adedayo, *Abdul-Lateef Adegbite* (above, n. 37), 140–45.

41. See pamphlet by a lecturer at Lagos State University, Shaykh Luqman Jimoh, *Moon Sighting: An Essential Manual* (Lagos: Jam'iyyat Junud Dinil-Islamiyyah, 2000), with foreword by Dr. Lateef Adegbite. It refers to a clutch of previous articles and books on the subject.

42. A.M. Sanni, "Eid controversy in Nigeria and the problem of legitimation: The Sultan and his opponents," personal e-mail communication.

43. L.F. Oladimeji, "*Da'wah* Trend in Islam: A Case Study of the *Jama't ut-Tabligh* in Nigeria" (Ph.D. thesis, University of Ilorin, 2004).

44. E.A. Adedun, *Slang as a "Dialect": A Study of the Use of Language among Undergraduates of the University of Lagos,* Faculty of Arts Monograph Series, no. 8 (Lagos: University of Lagos, 2008), 27.

45. Dr. K. K. Oloso, interview, 8 April 2009.

46. H. Townsend in 1847, cited Peel, *Religious Encounter* (above, n. 5), 194.

47. T. A. J. Ogunbiyi, visiting Ikale country in 1908, commented on "a mania among the converts for English clothes," whose effects he sometimes found ridiculous but yet thought "who will dare blame them for this when it is known that the very putting on of an English dress is an ensign . . . that Christ is reigning within them?": "Report of a Mission Tour to the Eastern District of Lagos," CMS Papers, G3A2, 1909, no. 34.

48. Macaulay was the principal of the CMS Grammar School, the son-in-law of Bishop Crowther and the father of Herbert Macaulay. There is an indirect link with his namesake, Lord Macaulay, since his surname derived from Governor Macaulay of Sierra Leone, who shared an ancestor with the historian in the person of Zachary Macaulay, a prominent member of the Clapham Sect, some of whose members were involved in the project that led to the settlement of Freetown. J. P. Haastrup was a prominent Lagos auctioneer, Methodist lay preacher and pioneer of Yoruba hymnody. He got his unusual Danish surname from having lived in the house of a prominent Ijesha merchant called Frederick Kumokun Haastrup, who in turn got it from a Danish CMS missionary who baptized him in Sierra Leone in the 1840s. Pythagoras must just have sounded splendid and impressive. Swept up in the wave of cultural nationalism in the 1890s, he later dropped J. P. for Ademuyiwa, to back up his claim to be a prince of Remo.

49. See Reichmuth, "Songhay-Lehnwörter" (above, n. 3).

50. *Al-Kurani ti a tumo si Ede Yoruba* [The Koran as Translated into the Yoruba Language] (Beirut: Dar al-Arabia, 1977).

51. Here I am greatly indebted to R. 'Deremi Abubakre, *Linguistic and Non-Linguistic Aspects of Qur'an Translating to Yoruba* (Hildesheim: Georg Olms Verlag, 1986), esp. 67–79, supplemented with interviews with Professors Amidu Sanni, 27 April 2009, and D. O. S. Noibi, 30 April 2009.

52. *Alkurani Mimo ni Ede Yoruba ati Larubawa* [The Holy Koran in the Yoruba Language and Arabic] (Lagos: Ahmadiyya Mission in Islam, 1976). This translation had been envisaged for decades, with part completed by Alhaji H. O. Sanyaolu as far back as 1957, but actually appeared only after the crisis of Ahmadiyya in the mid-1970s. *Al-Kur'anu Alaponle: Itumo si Ede Yoruba* [The Glorious Koran: Its Meaning in the Yoruba Language] (Ijebu-Ode: Shebiotimo Press, 1997). Quadri was the son of the proprietor of the Shebiotimo Press, one of the longest-established publishers of Islamic literature.

53. See examples cited in R. 'Deremi Abubakre, *The Interplay of Arabic and Yoruba Cultures in South-Western Nigeria* (Okeọla: Dāru 'l-'Ilm Publishers, 2004), 211. A long section of that study, pages 210–40, gives many illuminating examples of literary genres in which languages switch between Yoruba and Arabic, thus potentially serving to ease the passage of names like *Allah/Aala* into Yoruba.

54. For the text of the 1894 petition of Lagos Muslims for Islamic courts, see T. G. O Gbadamosi, *The Growth of Islam among the Yoruba, 1841–1908* (London: Longman, 1978), 233–34. See too A.-F. Kola Makinde, "The Institution of Shari'ah in Oyo and Osun States, Nigeria, 1890–2005" (Ph.D. thesis, University of Ibadan, 2007), chapter 2. In addition to various requests for official Sharia courts to be set up, some degree of Sharia had been administered informally in pious Muslim circles in several towns, such as Iwo, Ikirun, and Ede, and among the members of strict sects like the Bamidele of Ibadan.

55. For overall views, see P. Ostien, J.M. Nasir, and F. Kogelmann, eds., *Comparative Perspectives on Shari'ah in Nigeria* (Ibadan: Spectrum Books, 2005); Rotimi Suberu, "Sharia and the Travails of Federalism in Nigeria," Research Report submitted to the French Institute for Research in Africa (IFRA) (Ibadan, 2007); and J. Harnischfeger, *Democratization and Islamic Law: The Sharia Conflict in Nigeria* (Frankfurt: Campus Verlag, 2008).

56. For example Is-Haq Akintola, *Shari'ah in Nigeria: An Eschatological Desideratum* (Ijebu-Ode: Shebiotimo Publications, 2001); A.D. Ajijola, *What Is Shariah?* (Kaduna: Straight Path Publishers, n.d.); Abdulkadir Orire, *Shari'a: A Misunderstood Legal System* (Zaria: Sankore Publishers, 2007). Akintola is a lecturer at LASU and director of a Muslim human-rights NGO; Ajijola, a legal practitioner; Orire, the former grand khadi of Kwara State.

57. Thus D.O.S. Noibi and S.T. Malik, "Memorandum to Members of the Constituent Assembly on the Shari'ah in the Draft Constitution in 1978." Much of this was recycled in the "Memorandum to Osun State House of Assembly on the Review of 1999 Constitution," presented by the League of Imams and Alfas, December 1999. Both documents are reproduced as appendixes 1 and 2 in Makinde, "Institution of Shari'ah" (above, n. 54).

58. Quoted in J.S. Adekoya, "The Role of Music in Promoting Islam in Yorubaland" (Ph.D. thesis, University of Ibadan, 2005), chapter 1.

59. Makinde, "Institution of Shari'ah" (above, n. 54), 30.

60. As advocated, for example, by A.-F. Olayiwola, *Islam in Nigeria: One Crescent, Many Focuses* (Lagos: Sakirabe Press, 2007), 281, a work that I discuss at greater length below in chapter 10. I heard the same idea from MSS members studying Arabic at the University of Ibadan.

61. Interview, 17 April 2008.

62. Interview, 27 March 2008. For a full account of Adepoju as poet and intellectual, see Oyeniyi Okunoye, "Lanrewaju Adepoju and the Making of Modern Yoruba Poetry," *Africa* 81 (2011), 175–203.

63. It is adjacent to Finsbury Park Station, but has no direct connection with the nearby mosque, which became notorious as a hotbed of radical Islamism in the 1990s.

64. H.O. Danmole, "Religious Encounter in Southwestern Nigeria: The Domestication of Islam among the Yoruba," in J.K. Olupona and T. Rey, eds., *Òrìṣà Devotion as World Religion* (Madison: University of Wisconsin Press, 2008), 202–21, esp. 215.

65. Margaret J. Drewal, *Yoruba Ritual: Performers, Play, Agency* (Bloomington: Indiana University Press, 1992), 151.

66. Olufunke Adeboye, "The 'Born-Again' Oba: Pentecostalism and Traditional Chieftaincy in Yorubaland," *Lagos Historical Review* 7 (2007), 1–20.

67. Adedayo, *Abdul-Lateef Adegbite* (above, n. 37), 151–52. On the cultural conflicts at Oshogbo, see Peter Probst, *Osogbo and the Art of Heritage: Monuments, Deities and Money* (Bloomington: Indiana University Press, 2011).

68. Interview, 21 April 2008. Warm thanks to Wale Adebanwi for setting up these interviews with the *Alafin* and Chief Adepoju.

69. J.L. Matory, "Rival Empires: Islam and the Religions of Spirit Possession among the Oyo-Yoruba," *American Ethnologist* 21 (1994), 495–515, further documents—from fieldwork conducted in the northern Oyo town of Igboho in the late 1980s—the local understanding of Sango as a Muslim, even at a time when conflict between Muslims and traditionalists was

considerable. He even witnessed (n. 34) a denunciation of *orișa* worship from Adepoju, visiting to attend the opening of a new mosque. This aspect of Sango is altogether omitted from the collection of essays edited by Joel E. Tishken, Toyin Falola, and Akintunde Akinyemi, *Ṣàngó in Africa and the African Diaspora* (Bloomington: Indiana University Press, 2009).

70. See Stephen Sykes, *The Identity of Christianity* (London: SPCK, 1984), 11–12. According to Acts 11:26, Christians were first so called in Antioch.

71. For a telling indictment of the malign long-term consequences of the Sokoto jihad, see Murray Last, "Muslims and Christians in Nigeria: An Economy of Moral Panic," *Round Table* 96 (2007), 605–16. It is a sad irony that, written against Huntington's thesis of a clash of civilizations but shortly before the rise of Boko Haram, Last's exhortation to optimism has (at least for the time being) been brutally invalidated by a group of Muslims who emphatically *do* believe in the clash of civilizations.

72. For this summary of Suwarian doctrine, see David Robinson, *Muslim Societies in African History* (Cambridge: Cambridge University Press, 2004), 56. For a full elaboration of the Suwarian tradition and its context, see Ivor Wilks, "The Juula and the Expansion of Islam into the Forest," in N. Levtzion and R. L. Pouwels, eds., *The History of Islam in Africa* (Athens, Ohio: Ohio University Press, 2000), 93–116. For an impassioned contemporary advocacy of what amounts to Suwarian Islam, see Lansine Kaba, *Allahou akbar—Islam, terrorisme et tolerance: Une perspective africaine* (Paris: Presence Africaine, 2010).

73. The Rt. Rev. J. I. Fearon, the Anglican Bishop of Kaduna (a Nupe from Lokoja who grew up in Kaduna) told me that when, during an M.A. in Islamic Studies, which he took at Selly Oak Colleges in Birmingham, he was asked to present a paper on the status of the *dhimmi* in Islam, he broke down in class, and (when the lecturer asked what the matter was) he said it was just how it felt like being a Christian in Northern Nigeria. His reaction in 1999 was "I've lived as a *dhimmi* all these years, and now they've reintroduced *hudud* [the punishments stipulated by Sharia criminal law]" (interview, 13 March 2008).

74. This I was able to see for myself on a conducted tour of Kaduna on 19 March 2008, for which many thanks to my knowledgeable guide, Mr. Samuel Aruwan. It was most striking to compare what is now the vast, homogeneously Muslim quarter of Rigasa, where there were once a dozen churches and a Catholic secondary school, with the nearby Kabala West, which is Christian/mixed and where you could see small mosques and evidently Yoruba Muslims as well as many churches. Samuel asked me about the Ibadan Cross incident and admired the way it had been resolved: "They [the Yoruba] love themselves [i.e., one another]; they put religion aside. They bear more affinity to themselves [as an ethnic group or community] than to religion,"

75. This is variable as between states, since it depends on the policies of state governors, but gender segregation on public transport, bans on the sale of alcohol, pressure on Christian schools to observe Muslim dress codes, even the levying of special taxes on churches have all been reported. For a short case study of Kano State, see Insa Nolte, with N. Danjibo and A. Oladeji, "Religion, Politics and Governance in Nigeria" (Religions and Development Research Programme, University of Birmingham, Working paper 39, 2009), chapter 3; and on the complexities of implementing Sharia, see Alexander Thurston, "Muslim Politics and Shari'a in Kano State, Northern Nigeria," *African Affairs* 114 (2015), 28–51.

76. See here Abdullahi Ahmed An-Na'im, *African Constitutionalism and the Role of Islam* (Philadelphia: University of Pennsylvania Press, 2006), esp. chapter 4, arguing that while Sharia

is not acceptable as the basis of a constitutional order under modern conditions (because of its discrimination against women and non-Muslims, and its divinely given character), nevertheless a viable constitutional order in any largely Muslim society (such as Nigeria) has to come to terms with Islamic values. That precisely is the circle that Nigeria needs to square.

77. As trenchantly argued by Harnischfeger, *Democratization and Islamic Law* (above, n. 55), esp. chapter 5.

9. A CENTURY OF INTERPLAY BETWEEN CHRISTIANITY AND ISLAM

1. An earlier version of this paper was published as "Un siècle d'interactions entre Islam et Christianisme dans l'espace Yoruba," *Politique Africaine* 123 (2011), 27–50.

2. G. Simmel, *Conflict and the Web of Group Affiliations*, trans. K. H. Wolff (New York: Free Press of Glencoe, 1955), 14–55 and chapter 2, "Competition."

3. This was a was regular topos of nineteenth-century social thought, especially among advocates of the newly emergent industrial order, such as Andrew Ure, Harriet Martineau, and Herbert Spencer: see J. D. Y. Peel, *Herbert Spencer: The Evolution of a Sociologist* (London: Heinemann, 1971), chapter 8, esp. 195–96.

4. On which see Adam Higazi, "Political Histories of Conflict: Power, Authority and Collective Violence in Plateau State, Nigeria" (unpublished D.Phil. thesis, University of Oxford, 2011).

5. On the balance between competition and coexistence between cults in plural situations, the excellent study by Meera Venkatachalam on the Ewe of southeastern Ghana is very illuminating: *Slavery, Memory and Religion in Southeastern Ghana, c. 1850–Present* (New York: Cambridge University Press for the International African Institute, 2015).

6. See Wael B. Hallaq, *Shari'a: Theory, Practice, Transformation* (Cambridge: University Press, 2009), s.v. *ridda* (apostasy), esp. 319–20.

7. T. A. O. Oladimeji, "Islamic Architecture in Ijebuland, 1926–1994: A Historical Study of Forms" (unpublished Ph.D. thesis, University of Ibadan, 2001).

8. T. G. O. Gbadamosi, *The Growth of Islam among the Yoruba, 1841–1908* (London: Longman, 1978), 129–30. Their teacher, Idris Animasaun, was teacher at the Government Muslim school set up by Blyden.

9. M. S. Cole, *Alkorani ni Ede Yoruba* (Lagos: CMS Bookshop, 1925), a reprint of the original published in 1906: Gbadamosi, *Growth of Islam* (above, n. 8), 149–50. For Ogunbiyi's pamphlet writing, ibid. 130. His short *Itan Anabi Momodu* (History of the Prophet Mohammed) was reprinted in two successive issues of the CMS monthly magazine *In Leisure Hours*, vol. 2, nos. 9 and 10, contained in CMS Papers G3/A2/o (1911), 35 and 38. Professor Amidu Sanni (personal communication) has drawn my attention to a pamphlet *Awon Ọrọ Ọlọrun li ede Larubawa ati Yoruba* [The Words of God in Arabic and Yoruba: i.e., the Ten Commandments] (Lagos: CMS Bookshop, 1911), written by one Alhaji Alimi Ogunbiyi, which I think must be a playful self-reference by T. A. J. Ogunbiyi.

10. Ogunbiyi was the son of Chief Jacob Ogunbiyi and when later installed as pastor of Holy Trinity, Ebute Ero—the most "downtown" of all the Lagos CMS churches—was described as having been "one of those wild Isale Eko boys rescued from his evil ways by the Rev. James Johnson" (*Lagos Standard*, 4 March 1903). He later became archdeacon of Lagos and the principal founder of the Reformed Ogboni Fraternity (1918)

11. Gbadamosi, *Growth of Islam* (above, n. 8), 230–32.

12. On *oriki* in general, see Karin Barber, *I Could Speak until Tomorrow* (Edinburgh University Press for the International African Institute, 1991).

13. I came across these pamphlets in the papers of Herbert Macaulay (Kenneth Dike Library, University of Ibadan), who must have been sent them as complimentary copies. The grandson of Bishop Crowther, Macaulay was an Anglican but also eclectically interested in all sorts of mysticism.

14. Such as the listing in the *Nasfat* (see below) *Prayer Book* (Ikeja, 2006), 32–38.

15. See H.W. Turner, *African Independent Church* (Oxford: Clarendon Press, 1967). Further on Aladura-Muslim parallels, see H.J. Fisher, "Independency and Islam: The Nigerian Aladuras and Some Muslim Comparisons," *Journal of African History* 11 (1970), 269–77.

16. Here we may note that the term *woli,* used for "prophet" in the Bible and applied to the leading Aladura prophets like Babalola (CAC) and Ositelu (Church of the Lord), is etymologically a variant of *wali.*

17. J.D.Y. Peel, *Aladura: A Religious Movement among the Yoruba* (London: Oxford University Press, 1968).

18. See H.J. Fisher, *Ahmadiyya: A Study of Contemporary Islam on the West African Coast* (London: Oxford University Press, 1963).

19. For the information in this paragraph I am entirely indebted to Dr. B.O. Ololajulo of the University of Ibadan, himself an Ilaje man who has written on the local impact of oil. For a general account of Aiyetoro at its height, see S.R. Barrett, *The Rise and Fall of an African Utopia: A Wealthy Theocracy in Comparative Perspective* (Waterloo, Ont.: Wilfred Laurier University Press, 1977), though he says little about these Islamic influences.

20. For an authoritative account, M.A. Ojo, *The End-Time Army: Charismatic Movements in Modern Nigeria* (Trenton: African World Press, 2006).

21. A. Ukah, *A New Paradigm of Pentecostal Power: A Study of the Redeemed Christian Church of God in Nigeria* (Trenton: Africa World Press, 2008), esp. chapters 2 and 3.

22. On the central role of the *alfa* in the history of Yoruba Islam see Patrick J. Ryan, *Imale: Yoruba Participation in the Muslim Tradition, a Study of Clerical Piety* (Missoula: Scholars Press, 1978).

23. This paragraph and the next are much indebted to two Ph.D. theses of the University of Ibadan: Y.A. Quadri, "The Tijaniyyah in Nigeria: A Case Study" (1981), and A.F. Ahmad, "The Qadiriyyah and Its Impact in Nigeria" (1986). On Tijaniyya's history more generally, see J.M. Abun Nasr, *The Tijaniyya: A Sufi Order in the Modern World* (London: Oxford University Press, 1965).

24. Quadri, "Tijaniyyah" (above, n. 23), 100. He notes that this view was expressed by many of his informants.

25. Interview with Mr. Habeeb Usman Lanase, the grandson of Shehu Lanase, 4 May 2009. Lanase promoted other "un-Yoruba" practices, such as purdah for women and hostility to lavish funerals, but it was his secession and his support for Reformed Tijaniyya—both of which challenged the influence of the established Ibadan *ulama*—that most upset the older generation.

26. According to Imam Salahuddeen Busairi (interview, 13 May 2009), Shehu Ahmed had taken to calling himself *Aseda,* which might be understood literally as "Creator"

or more loosely as "One Who Can Do and Undo." Imam Busairi had joined Reformed Tijaniyya as a young man in the 1950s, having been introduced to it by a Hausa friend and colleague while working at Sapele, in today's Delta State.

27. Interview with Alhaji Abdussalam Adebolu, at Madina, 12 May 2009. I am indebted to Dr. K. K. Oloso for his introduction and to Imam Salahuddeen Busairi for further background and elucidation.

28. The clear evidence of close interaction between Yoruba and Hausa adepts of Tijaniyya must call into question a widely cited argument in Abner Cohen's classic study of Sabo, the Hausa settlement in Ibadan, *Custom and Government in Urban Africa* (London: Routledge and Kegan Paul, 1969). Cohen maintains that "the Hausa [of Sabo] adopted Tijaniyya in the 1950s because [it] provided solutions to some of the political problems they faced as a result of the coming of party politics" (p. 152). Specifically, he argues, it enabled them to set up a cultural barrier between themselves and the Yoruba, since it led to a "localization" of ritual in Sabo, separating them from their Yoruba fellow Muslims. There are several problems with this view, apart from its brazen reductionism. (1) It is too locally specific, granted that the move toward Tijaniyya at this time was so widespread among the Hausa, both at home and in their diaspora. (2) It ignores the nearly simultaneous and massive turn of Yoruba Muslims to Tijaniyya. This Cohen relegates to a one-line endnote: "Some Yoruba became Tijanis but because of the localization of ritual under local mukaddams no interaction with Tijani Hausa could take place" (227 n. 1). But (3), as I have shown, such interaction not only took place but played a significant role in the rise of Tijaniyya among the Yoruba. Finally (4), the "localization of ritual" that Cohen emphasizes was due not to the rise of Tijaniyya but to a decision of the Hausa in 1952 to stop attending Friday prayers at the Ibadan central mosque and pray separately in their own mosque in Sabo. The *Olubadan*, the chief imam, and the elders of the central mosque reacted as angrily to this secession as they had to the secession of Lanase and his followers to a separate *jumat* mosque, which occurred around the same time. Cohen conflates the Hausa turn to Tijaniyya and their decision to have their own *jumat* mosque. But these were distinct: Tijani devotion can take place in any mosque, whereas the Hausa withdrawal from weekly association with their Yoruba coreligionists at Friday prayers was a political decision of their own.

29. On which see J. D. Y. Peel, *Religious Encounter and the Making of the Yoruba* (Bloomington: Indiana University Press, 2000), 20–21.

30. On Izala in Northern Nigeria see R. Loimeier, *Islamic Reform and Political Change in Northern Nigeria* (Evanston: Northwestern University Press, 1997), and Ousmane Kane, *Muslim Modernity in Postcolonial Nigeria* (Leiden: Brill, 2003); and more generally D. Westerlund and Eva E. Rosander, eds., *African Islam and Islam in Africa: Encounters between Sufis and Islamists* (London: Hurst, 1997).

31. Notably a prayer called *al-Salat al-Fatih,* revealed to the founder Ahmad al-Tijani (d. 1815), and the use of a white sheet, placed in the center of the group during the rituals of praise. A very forceful attack on Tijanniya for *bid'a* is to be found in a book by A.-R. Shittu, *A Critique of Dr Adekilekun Tijani's Handbook on the Tijanniyah* (Shaki: al-Furqaan Publishers, 1999). This is a riposte to Dr. D. A. Adekilekun Tijani's *A Handbook on the Doctrines and Rites of the Tijanniyah in Question and Answer Form* (Ede: Moyanjuola Islamic Publications, 1997). Dr. Tijani was a scion of an old *ulama* family from Ede and the imam of the University of Ibadan mosque.

32. Quadri, "Tijaniyyah" (above, n. 23), 202.

33. Ahmad, "Qadiriyyah" (above, n. 23), 315.

34. On Mr. Shittu's background, see above, chapter 8 n. 29.

35. One of the most extraordinary, and distinctively Yoruba, is Chrislam, a mélange of Islam and Christianity: see Marloes Janson "Unity through Diversity: Chrislam's Proliferation in Lagos" (unpublished paper, 2014). Janson describes two Chrislamic groups, both created by people from a Muslim background but assuming the character of small churches, which differ in whether their Christian elements are more of Aladura or of born-again inspiration.

36. See A. O. Sanni, "Conversion and Reversion in the Power Accession Narratives of Muslim Prayer Groups in Nigeria," *Journal of Oriental and African Studies* 21 (2012), 157–66

37. It also has an Islamic precedent, of which it is very unlikely that either Fatayi or his Celestial mentor were aware, in the tradition that one of the earliest attestations to the genuineness of Mohammed's revelation came from a Christian charismatic, the monk Bahira: see T. Sizgorich, *Violence and Belief in Late Antiquity: Militant Devotion in Christianity and Islam* (Philadelphia: University of Pennsylvania Press, 2009), 156–58.

38. As Sanni observes ("Conversion and Reversion" [above, n. 36], 162): "Membership of [Muslim] prayer groups is not denomination specific, and there are even reports of non-Muslims partaking in the prayer sessions of the Muslim prayer groups from time to time, as long as they believe in the efficacy of prayer, whatever the source or agency."

39. Details in D. O. Ogungbile, "Religious Experience and Women Leadership in Yoruba Islam," *Gender and Behaviour* 2 (2004), 117–39. The name is a contraction of a phrase meaning "This is a sign from God," based on Q. 6:124.

40. Cf. the *Ẹgbẹ Afadurajagun*—rendered as "Praying Battalion"—in the Christ Apostolic Church in Ibadan, described in Peel, *Aladura* (above, n. 17), 168–71.

41. On women's religious roles see Oyeronke Olajubu, *Women in the Yoruba Religious Sphere* (Albany: State University of New York Press, 2003) and Deidre H. Crumbley, *Spirit, Structure and Flesh: Gendered Experiences in African Instituted Churches among the Yoruba of Nigeria* (Madison; University of Wisconsin Press, 2008).

42. The term "moderate" was used to me by M. A. Bello, whose valuable M.A. thesis I draw upon here: "Shaykh Abdul-Hamid Olohungbemi and His Da'wah Activities in Ado-Odo (Ogun State) and Its Environs, 1982–2002" (Lagos State University, 2004). Mr. Bello was at the time a senior official of NASFAT.

43. See S. A. Olagoke, *Shafaudeen at 21: The Story So Far* (Ibadan: SAO Multi Ventures, c. 2004), esp. chapter 8, "The Rasool Controversy."

44. These details from a fascinating thesis by J. S. Adekoya, "The Role of Music in Promoting Islam in Yorubaland" (Ph.D. thesis, University of Ibadan, 2005), which devotes several pages (98–100) to Akinbile. I am grateful to Dr. Adekoya for introducing me to Akinbile. I have myself heard an almost identical version of the second of these choruses—with *Bibeli* instead of *Kurani*—sung in Aladura churches.

45. Shaykh R. Akinbile, interview, 1 April 2008.

46. The official rendition of the Arabic is "There Is No Help Except from Allaah." See too see B. Soares, "An Islamic Social Movement in Contemporary West Africa: NASFAT of Nigeria," in S. Ellis and I. van Kessel, eds., *Movers and Shakers: Social Movements in Africa* (Leiden: Brill, 2009).

47. Thus NASFAT members, Samonda, Ibadan, interview, 2 March 2008.

48. For a full account and many examples of song texts, see Adekoya, "Role of Music" (above, n. 44).

49. In the brief accounts of its origins and programs on the NASFAT Web site, there is no mention of the born-again opposition except indirectly in a reference to "organizing guzlu [ritual bath] for Muslim women reverts." A revert is a Muslim who has returned to Islam after converting to Christianity.

50. He was thinking of the favored location of Aladura and born-again prayer grounds on the tops of hills (*ori oke*) or of streams as venues for rituals of healing and purification. There are several on the wooded ridge that is the spine of Ibadan, near Bower Tower. There is also a prominent Ibadan-based Pentecostal church called Mountain of Fire and Miracles.

51. All these expressions come from my notes from interviews with three or four figures at NASFAT's Lagos headquarters, 17 April 2008.

52. Headlined "Timeless Wisdom for Modern Managers" (183 pp.; Ibadan: Emgee Books, 2006), I bought it from a bookstall outside the Lagos State Secretariat Mosque during a Sunday *Asalatu* service. What is very characteristic of the NASFAT outlook is the wide spread of its Muslim references: dedicated to the governor of Zamfara State who introduced Sharia law in 1999, it also has messages of support from Prince Bola Ajibola (a distinguished lawyer, founder of Crescent University), Professor I. A. B. Balogun (the late doyen of Arabic studies in the Yoruba academic world), and at least one academic of Ahl us-Sunna affiliation.

53. Its main product is Nasmalt, which closely resembles Maltina, a nonalcoholic drink like a sweet dark beer popular at elite born-again social events.

54. For an attractive photo essay bringing out the resemblances between the campsites of NASFAT and Mountain of Fire and Miracles, see *The Spiritual Highway: Religious World Making in Metropolitan Lagos*, pamphlet to accompany an exhibition at the Brunei Gallery, SOAS (April–June, 2014): photographer Akintunde Akinleye; curator Marloes Janson.

55. A very useful case study—written with the clear and characteristic intention of "analysing and correcting the anomalies and bringing to focus the pristine Islamic way of doing things"—is M. A. Balogun, "Religious Syncretism in Epeland through the Practice of Magic and Divination among Muslim *Alfas* (Clerics)" (M.A. thesis, Lagos State University, 2002). Epe, an Ijebu town on the lagoon that hosted ex-king Kosoko of Lagos and his followers in the 1850s and 1860s, became a strong early center of Islam in the Yoruba South. I am grateful to Professor Amidu Sanni of LASU for allowing me access to this thesis.

56. M. A. Bello, *Meeting Heart Desires: A Concise Discourse on Faith and Spiritual Consultancy* (Lagos, 2007), p. 39. He explains that the word *jalbu* originally meant "acquiring" in Arabic. Its practitioners may be called *onijalibi* in Yoruba.

57. This aesthetic dimension is important: NASFAT's Web site states it as a primary aim "to project the beauty of Islam in words and deeds."

10. PENTECOSTALISM AND SALAFISM IN NIGERIA: MIRROR IMAGES?

1. From a large literature, see Steve Bruce, *Fundamentalism* (Cambridge: Polity Press, 2000), Malise Ruthven, *Fundamentalism: A Very Short Introduction* (Oxford: Oxford University Press, 2004).

2. Thus Tariq Ali, *The Clash of Fundamentalisms: Crusades, Jihads and Modernity* (London: Verso Press, 2002).

3. Samuel P. Huntington, "The Clash of Civilizations," *Foreign Affairs* 72/3 (1993), 22–49, and *The Clash of Civilizations and the Remaking of World Order* (New York: Simon and Schuster, 1996).

4. For example, Richard Bonney, *False Prophets: The 'Clash of Civilizations' and the Global War on Terror* (Oxford: Peter Lang, 2008).

5. I use the term "Salafism"—literally "following the [religious practice of] the ancestors or forebears [*salaf*]"—since the notion of Islamism, while often Salafist too, suggests a project to establish an Islamic state or politics, which does not apply to all Salafists. Salafism may be seen as a contemporary or farther-reaching version of what has often just been called reformism, a term applied to movements in West African Islam going back to the eighteenth century. For an overview of Salafism, which brings out its many tensions and tendencies, see Roel Meijer, ed., *Global Salafism: Islam's New Religious Movement* (London: Hurst, 2009).

6. B. Larkin and B. Meyer, "Pentecostalism, Islam and Culture: New Religious Movements in West Africa," in E. K. Akyeampong, ed., *Themes in West Africa's History* (Oxford: James Currey, 2006), 287.

7. Ibid. 286.

8. A questionable inference arising from such assumptions is that the yearning of some Ghanaian Pentecostal leaders for a Christian state (whatever exactly that means) is due to their links with Nigerian Pentecostals "who seem to mirror Islamic reform movements' appropriation of a number of federal states in Northern Nigeria" (ibid. 298).

9. The literature is growing quickly, but the leading studies for Nigeria are Matthews A. Ojo, *The End-Time Army: Charismatic Movements in Modern Nigeria* (Trenton: Africa World Press, 2006), which is strong on the origins and the holiness tendency; Asonzeh Ukah, *A New Paradigm of Pentecostal Power* (Trenton: Africa World Press, 2008), a detailed study of the Redeemed Christian Church of God (RCCG); Ruth Marshall, *Political Spiritualities: The Pentecostal Revolution in Nigeria* (Chicago: University of Chicago Press, 2009); and Ayodeji Abodunde, *A Heritage of Faith: A History of Christianity in Nigeria* (Ibadan: PierceWatershed, 2009), chapters 17–22 and 24–26, which gives the broadest overview. On Ghana, Paul Gifford, *Ghana's New Christianity* (London: Hurst, 2004).

10. See Paul Gifford, "The Complex Provenance of Some Elements of African Pentecostal Theology," in A. Corten and Ruth Marshall-Fratani, eds., *Between Babel and Pentecost: Transnational Pentecostalism in Africa and Latin America* (London: Hurst, 2001), 62–79. But an imported theological idiom can express a thoroughly indigenous orientation, as Gifford acknowledges (ibid. 64), against the thrust of his earlier "Prosperity: A New and Foreign Element in African Christianity," *Religion* 20 (1990), 373–88.

11. Larkin and Meyer, "Pentecostalism, Islam and Culture" (above, n. 6), 290, 287.

12. Ibid. 304.

13. The nearest such a notion ever came to realization in Africa (outside pre-1974 Ethiopia) was President Chiluba's declaration of Zambia as a Christian nation in 1991, to the joy of many Pentecostalists. This proved to be a wholly vacuous initiative, which had no discernible impact on the quality of governance: see Paul Gifford, *African Christianity: Its Public Role* (London: Hurst, 1998), 197–219.

14. Al-Zakzaky, a former MSS activist, founded the Islamic Movement in Nigeria in the early 1980s with support from Iran and is often described as a Shi'ite. He was jailed for

sedition several times in the 1980s and 1990s. For a sound recent review of the varieties of political Islam in Northern Nigeria, see Abdul Raufu Mustapha, ed., *Sects and Social Disorder: Muslim Identities and Conflict in Northern Nigeria* (Woodbridge: James Currey, 2014), esp. chapters 1 and 3.

15. On Northern Nigeria, see J.N. Paden, *Religion and Political Culture in Kano* (Berkeley and Los Angeles: University of California Press, 1973); M.H. Kukah, *Religion, Politics and Power in Northern Nigeria* (Ibadan: Spectrum, 1993); Roman Loimeier, *Islamic Reform and Political Change in Northern Nigeria* (Evanston: Northwestern University Press, 1997); Ousmane Kane, *Muslim Modernity in Postcolonial Nigeria: A Study of the Society for the Removal of Innovation and Reinstatement of Tradition* [Izala] (Leiden: Brill, 2003).

16. Cf. *lafiya*, Hausa for "health," though the Yoruba form probably came through Songhai rather than Hausaland.

17. Matthew Schoffeleers, "Ritual Healing and Political Acquiescence: The Case of the Zionist Churches in Southern Africa," *Africa* 61 (1991), 1–25.

18. M. Last, "Religion and Healing in Hausaland," in Toyin Falola, ed., *Christianity and Social Change in Africa: Essays in Honor of J. D. Y. Peel* (Durham: Carolina Academic Press, 2005), 549–62.

19. Known as *tibb al-Nabi* (medicine of the Prophet), it was the subject of numerous books, often compilations going back to medieval sources, such as those written by Muhammad Bello, the son of Usman dan Fodio. (See Last, "Religion and Healing" [above, n. 18], 556.)

20. Which is sometimes directly picked up by African Christians—see again M. Schoffeleers, "Folk Christology in Africa: The Dialectics of the *Nganga* [Healer] Paradigm," *Journal of Religion in Africa* 19 (1989), 157–83.

21. Last, "Religion and Healing" (above, n. 18), 556–60. In practice, the success of this project to drive healing out of religion is limited. As is shown by J. A. McIntyre, "A Cultural Given and a Hidden Influence: Koranic Teachers in Kano," in D. Parkin, L. Caplan, and H. Fisher, eds., *The Politics of Cultural Performance* (Providence: Berghahn, 1996), 257–74, medicospiritual activities remain as much part of the stock-in-trade of Muslim clerics in Hausaland as they are for Yoruba *alfa*. Even so, in accordance with Last's point, they tend to be practiced furtively.

22. Larkin and Meyer, "Pentecostalism, Islam and Culture" (above, n. 6), 287.

23. C. Piot, *Nostalgia for the Future: West Africa after the Cold War* (Chicago: University of Chicago Press, 2009), 75.

24. See above, chapter 5.

25. Piot, *Nostalgia* (above, n. 23), 66, 69–70.

26. Ibid. 75.

27. For a view of Usman dan Fodio, the source of the Salafist tradition in Nigeria, as a *mujaddid* see I. A. B. Balogun, "Uthman dan Fodio: The Mujaddid of West Africa," in Y. B. Usman, ed., *Studies in the History of the Sokoto Caliphate* (Zaria: Ahmadu Bello University for Sokoto State History Bureau, 1979), 473–92.

28. Marshall, *Political Spiritualities* (above, n. 9), 222.

29. See Ruth Marshall and D. Peclard, "La religion du sujet en Afrique," and other essays in *Les sujets de Dieu*, special issue of *Politique Africaine*, 87 (2002), 5–20.

30. Marshall, *Political Spiritualities* (above, n. 9), 204.

31. Ibid. 206, 222.

32. On which see Ojo, *End-Time Army* (above, n. 9), chapter 2.

33. Marshall herself is against the latter interpretation, sometimes described as a revenge of paganism or the return of the *génie sorcier,* arguing that it treats the demonic as external to Pentecostal discourse—whereas in fact it serves as a witness to its internal incoherence. That itself is a fair point; but these interpretations are not alternatives that we have to choose between.

34. See Ebenezer Obadare, "Pentecostal Presidency? The Lagos-Ibadan 'Theocratic Class' and the Muslim 'Other,'" *Review of African Political Economy* 110 (2006), 665–78.

35. Tunde Bakare is rather a stormy petrel among the leading Pentecostal pastors. After spells with Deeper Life and the RCCG, he set up his own Latter Rain Assembly. In the 1990s he made a name for his daring prophecies of the annulment of the 1993 election and of the death of Abacha in 1998, but his prediction in 1999 that the axe would soon fall on Obasanjo as it had on King Agag (1 Sam. 15) misfired badly. In 2011 many Christians were unsettled by his decision to serve as the vice-presidential running mate to ex-General Muhammadu Buhari, presidential candidate of the Council for Progressive Change. His anticorruption rhetoric draws on age-old Christian motifs: "an alternative society and counter-culture to the kingdom of Babylon" (quoted by Abodunde, *Heritage of Faith* [above, n. 9], 603–5).

36. See Ukah, *New Paradigm of Pentecostal Power* (above, n. 9), 112–18

37. For an illustration, see the notional four-generation genealogy of Pastor Sunday Adelaja above in chapter 5. For the complexity of Pentecostalism's West African roots, see Adam Mohr, "'Out of Zion into Philadelphia and West Africa': Faith Tabernacle Congregations, 1897–1927," *Pneuma* 26 (2010), 56–79.

38. On the resemblances to Tijaniyya and NASFAT, see above, chapter 9. On Tablighi Jama'at in Nigeria see L. F. Oladimeji, "*Da'wah* Trend in Islam: A Case Study of the *Jama't ut-Tabligh* in Nigeria" (unpublished Ph.D. thesis, University of Ilorin, 2004); and for parallels between Tablighi and Pentecostal spirituality, see Marloes Janson, *Islam, Youth and Modernity in the Gambia: The Tablighi Jama'at* (Cambridge: Cambridge University Press for the International African Institute, 2013), 260–65.

39. See his biography: Sheikh Abubakar Gumi (with Ismaila Tsiga), *Where I Stand* (Ibadan: Spectrum, 2001 [1992]).

40. See Loimeier, *Islamic Reform and Political Change;* and Kane, *Muslim Modernity* (both above, n. 15).

41. The classic study is Murray Last, *The Sokoto Caliphate* (London: Longman, 1967), which takes a perspective close to the Sokoto establishment (his key informant was the *Waziri* Junaidu). A broader perspective informs his magisterial "Reform in West Africa: The Jihad Movements of the Nineteenth Century," in J. F. A. Ajayi and M. Crowder, eds., *History of West Africa,* 2nd ed., vol. 2 (London: Longman, 1987), 1–47. See too R. A. Adeleye, *Power and Diplomacy in Northern Nigeria, 1804–1906* (London: Longman, 1971). Later edited works include Y. B. Usman, ed., *Studies in the History of the Sokoto Caliphate* (Zaria: Department of History, Ahmadu Bello University for the Sokoto State History Bureau, 1979), and (to mark the bicentenary of the caliphate) H. Bobboyi and A. M. Yakubu, eds., *The Sokoto Caliphate: History and Legacies 1804–2004,* 2 vols. (Kaduna: Arewa House, 2006).

42. For the impact of colonialism on the Caliphate, see M. Last, "The 'Colonial Caliphate' of Northern Nigeria," in D. Robinson and J.-L. Triaud, eds., *Le temps des*

marabouts: Itinéraires et stratégies islamiques en Afrique occidentale française v. 1880–1960 (Paris: Karthala, 1997). The religious dimension is explored in M.S. Umar, *Islam and Colonialism: Intellectual Responses of Muslims of Northern Nigeria to British Colonial Rule* (Leiden: Brill, 2006). For the view from the other side, Andrew E. Barnes, *Making Headway: The Introduction of Western Civilization in Colonial Northern Nigeria* (Rochester: University of Rochester Press, 2009).

43. On the changing position of Christianity in the Muslim North, see Shobana Shankar, *Who Shall Enter Paradise: Christian Origins in Muslim Northern Nigeria, ca. 1890–1975* (Athens: Ohio University Press, 1914).

44. On the shift in the Sardauna's political self-perception to being more a Muslim leader (by implication of a kind of revived Sokoto Caliphate but also reaching beyond it), see J.N. Paden, *Ahmadu Bello, Sardauna of Sokoto: Values and Leadership In Nigeria* (London: Hodder and Stoughton, 1986), esp. chapters 9 and 16. This is an official biography, which tends to put the best gloss on the Sardauna's motives. For an alternative, less pro-Sardauna view, see the unpublished Ph.D. thesis of M.P. Smith, "Northern Identity and the Politics of Culture in Northern Nigeria" (University of London, School of Oriental and African Studies, 2004).

45. Written in 1793, some years before the jihad. See I.A.B. Balogun, "A Critical Edition of the 'Ihya al-Sunna wa Ikhmad al-Bid'a' of Uthman b. Fudi, popularly known as Usuman dan Fodio" (Ph.D. thesis, University of London, School of Oriental and African Studies, 1967), and a small book based on that thesis: *The Life and Works of Uthman dan Fodio* (Lagos: Islamic Publications Bureau, 1975).

46. Written in 1806, in the midst of the jihad, in order to give guidance to newly appointed administrators. See F.H. El-Masri, ed., *Bayan Wujub al-Hijra 'ala 'l-'Ibad of Uthman b. Fudi, "The Exposition of the Obligation upon the Servants of God,"* Fontes Historiae Africanae, Series Arabica, 1 (Khartoum: Oxford University Press, 1978).

47. In fact, so important was the Qadiriyya Brotherhood to the collective identity of Sokoto people that in Gumi's boyhood the town crier in Sokoto used to address the people as *Qadirawa* (*Where I Stand* [above, n. 39], 134). Later (p. 144) Gumi maintains unconvincingly that Usman dan Fodio "wrote quite a lot expressing his opposition to Tariqa worship." El-Masri's foreword to his edition of the *Bayan Wujub* (above, n. 46) makes it plain that Sufi mystical gnosis was a fundamental source of dan Fodio's sense of religiopolitical mission.

48. Adeline Masquelier, *Women and Islamic Revival in a West African Town* (Bloomington: Indiana University Press, 2009).

49. For an overview of the first Sharia controversy, P.B. Clarke and Ian Linden, *Islam in Modern Nigeria: A Study of a Muslim Community in a Post-Independence State, 1960–1983* (Grunewald: Kaiser, 1984), esp. chapter 4. The post-2000 adoption of Sharia in twelve states of the high North has produced a large literature, from which see P. Ostien, J.M. Nasir, and F. Kogelmann, eds., *Comparative Perspectives on Shari'ah in Nigeria* (Ibadan: Spectrum Books, 2005); Rotimi T. Suberu "Sharia and the Travails of Federalism in Nigeria," Research Report (Ibadan: Institut Français de Recherche en Afrique, 2007); M. Last, "The Shari'a in Context: People's Quest for Justice and the Role of Courts in Pre- and Early-Colonial Northern Nigeria"; and, much the most trenchant, Johannes Harnischfeger, *Democratization and Islamic Law: The Sharia Conflict in Nigeria* (Frankfurt: Campus Verlag, 2008).

50. M. Last, "The Search for Security in Muslim Northern Nigeria," *Africa* 78 (2008), 41–63.

51. See Michael Cook's exhaustive survey of the classical precedents, *Commanding Right and Forbidding Wrong in Islamic Thought* (Cambridge: Cambridge University Press, 2001). For the fainthearted, a more accessible version is his *Forbidding Wrong in Islam: An Introduction* (Cambridge: Cambridge University Press, 2003).

52. S. L. Sanusi, "Politics and Sharia in Northern Nigeria," in B. F. Soares and R. Otayek, eds., *Islam and Muslim Politics in Africa* (New York: Palgrave Macmillan, 2007), 182–83. A distinguished career as a banker culminated in his appointment in 2009 as governor of the Central Bank of Nigeria, a post from which he was dismissed by President Goodluck Jonathan in 2014 for exposing government corruption in the disposal of oil revenue. A member of the royal lineage of Kano, he was shortly afterward elected its emir.

53. For the period up to the late 1990s, see Toyin Falola, *Violence in Nigeria: The Crisis of Religious Politics and Secular Ideologies* (Rochester: University of Rochester Press, 1998); and especially Mustapha, *Sects and Social Disorder* (above, n. 14), 15, which distinguishes four temporally overlapping surges of violent sectarianism, beginning from the 1940s and culminating in Boko Haram.

54. On the origins of the Northern Christian Association, see Smith, "Northern Identity" (above, n. 44), 299–301.

55. See Iheanyi M. Enwerem, *A Dangerous Awakening: The Politicization of Religion in Nigeria* (Ibadan: Institut Français de Recherche en Afrique, 1995).

56. The signal events, which each triggered major episodes of violence, were two evangelistic rallies, one at an advanced teachers' college at Kafanchan (Kaduna State) in 1987 and one at Kano racecourse in 1991, addressed, respectively, by the Rev. Abubakar Bako, a convert from Islam, and the well-known German evangelist Reinhard Bonnke.

57. Adam Higazi, "Political Histories of Conflict: Power, Authority and Collective Violence in Plateau State, Nigeria" (unpublished D.Phil. thesis, University of Oxford, 2010), esp. chapter 5 on Jos. COCIN (Church of Christ in Nigeria) is the name taken by the congregations founded by the Sudan United Mission, a holiness-evangelical society. COCIN is particularly strong in Plateau State and close to its Christian political elite.

58. The first serious academic address to this problem by a Nigerian was Yusufu Bala Usman's *The Manipulation of Religion in Nigeria* (Kaduna: Vanguard Press, 1987).

59. See David Pratten, esp. "The Politics of Protection: Perspectives on Vigilantism in Nigeria," his introduction to a special issue of *Africa* 78 (2008), 1–15; and "Agaba and the 'Rugged Life': Youth and Violence in Southern Nigeria," in R. Ginio, L. Bethlehem, and P. Ahluwahlia, eds., *Violence and Non-Violence in Africa* (London: Routledge, 2007), 84–104.

60. On the OPC, see Wale Adebanwi, "The Carpenter's Revolt: Youth, Violence and the Reinvention of Culture in Nigeria," *Journal of Modern African Studies* 43 (2005), 339–65; and Insa Nolte, "Ethnic Vigilantes and the State: The Oodua People's Congress in South-Western Nigeria," *International Relations* 21 (2007), 217–35. The OPC broke into two factions, one ("elders") under Dr. Frederick Faseun, the other ("youth"), more populist, under Gani Adams. For rival accounts, see F. Faseun, *OPC: Our History, Our Mission* (Lagos: Inspired Communications, 2005); and M. M. Ogbeidi, *Leadership Challenge: Gani Adams and the Oodua People's Congress* (Lagos: Publisher's Express, 2005).

61. Thus Insa Nolte, "'Without Women, Nothing Can Succeed': Yoruba Women in the OPC, Nigeria," *Africa* 78 (2008), 88 n. 12.

62. A. Higazi, "Social Mobilization and Collective Violence: Vigilantes and Militias in the Lowlands of Plateau State, Central Nigeria," *Africa* 78 (2008), esp. 123–26.

63. Marshall, *Political Spiritualities* (above, n. 9), 206.

64. See Murray Last, "From Dissidence to Dissent: The Genesis and Development of Reformist Islamic Groups in Northern Nigeria," in Mustapha, *Sects and Social Disorder* (above, n. 14), chapter 2, which traces the genealogy of contemporary movements like Boko Haram to the paradigm case of Usman dan Fodio's jihad and brings out the extent to which that in turn was consciously modeled on the precedent of the Prophet's own campaigns.

65. El-Masri, *Bayan Wujub* (above, n. 46), 53, "On Practices Wherewith a State Cannot Survive." Mostly quoted from a work of unknown authorship called *Diya al-khulufa* (Light of Leadership), which (in an agreeably un-Macchiavellian way) includes lying, envy, and breach of promise as among the vices a ruler must avoid.

66. Ukah, *New Paradigm of Pentecostal Power* (above, n. 9), 103.

67. Further on the Yoruba Christian concept of *Ẹmi*, see J. D. Y. Peel, *Religious Encounter and the Making of the Yoruba* (Bloomington: Indiana University Press, 2000), 264–65

68. John 10.10: "The thief cometh not, but for to steal, and to kill, and to destroy: I am come that they might have life, and that they might have it more abundantly."

69. *Afẹnifẹre* was adopted as the AG's popular name in the 1950s, when it was also known as *Ẹgbẹ Ọlọpẹ* (Party of the Palm Tree) from its party emblem, the oil palm (*Elaeis guineensis*), being a potent symbol in Yoruba culture of spiritual power, abundance, and wisdom. The name *Afẹnifẹre* was revived to refer to the Awoist movement as it reorganized itself in the bleak years after Awolowo's death in 1987—on which see further Dr. Wale Adebanwi's *Yoruba Elites and Ethnic Politics in Nigeria: Obafemi Awolowo and Corporate Agency* (Cambridge: Cambridge University Press, 2014).

70. Respective publication data: (Olayiwola) Lagos: Sakirabe Publishers, 343 pp.; (Abodunde) Ibadan: PierceWatershed, 803 pp. Both books seem to circulate mainly through private religious networks. I was introduced to Abodunde through a mutual friend, and he gave me a copy himself; while I acquired a copy of Olayiwola's on a visit to the headquarters of MUSWEN (Muslim Ummah of South-Western Nigeria), a non-Salafist organization based at Arisekola's Mosque, Ibadan, through the courtesy of Professor D. O. S. Noibi.

71. One may perhaps place Olayiwola ideologically from the genealogy he constructs for himself. He singles out among the *mujahidin* (militants) and *mujaddidin* (revolutionaries) whom he admires Jamaluddin al-Afghani, Sayyid Qutb, Hassan al-Banna, and Usman dan Fodio: Abdulfattah O. A. Olayiwola, *Islam in Nigeria* (Lagos: Sakirabe Publishers, 2007), 95.

72. For example, the African-church movement of the 1890s through the 1910s (Abodunde, *Heritage of Faith* [above, n. 9], 147–275, especially chapter 11, "Liberté, égalité, fraternité") was an indirect response to the rise of racist attitudes among Europeans closely connected to the colonial takeover of Nigeria.

73. Olayiwola, *Islam in Nigeria* (above, n. 71), 38.

74. Ibid. x.

75. Louis Brenner, "The Jihad Debate between Sokoto and Borno: An Historical Analysis of Islamic Political Discourse in Nigeria," in J. F. Ade Ajayi and J. D. Y. Peel, eds.,

People and Empires in African History: Essays in Memory of Michael Crowder (London: Longman, 1992), 21–44.

76. Olayiwola, *Islam in Nigeria* (above, n. 71), 149–51. He also castigates Ahmadiyya—the *takfir* against which by the World Muslim League in 1970 he strongly endorses—for its opposition to violence in the name of Islam.

77. B. Anderson, *Imagined Communities: Reflections on the Origin and Spread of Nationalism* (London: Verso, 1983).

78. See James P. Piscatori, *Islam in a World of Nation-States* (Cambridge: Cambridge University Press, 1986).

79. Olayiwola, *Islam in Nigeria* (above, n. 71), 185, 206.

80. Ibid. 186.

81. See above, chapter 5. For a Yoruba example of the Pentecostal adaptation of such a local cultural form see Ukah's discussion of the use of *oriki* (praise poetry traditionally addressed to *orișa*, kings, chiefs, and big men) in the RCCG: *New Paradigm of Pentecostal Power* (above, n. 9), 321–24.

82. Abodunde, *Heritage of Faith* (above, n. 9), chapter 28, "A Global Christianity."

83. See, for example Ludek Broz, "Conversion to Religion? Negotiating Continuity and Discontinuity in Contemporary Altai," in Matthijs Pelkmans, ed., *Conversion after Socialism* (New York: Berghahn, 2009), chapter 2, esp. 23.

84. On the crucial and far-reaching importance of translation for Christianity, unlike Islam, see Lamin Sanneh, *Translating the Message: The Missionary Impact on Culture* (Maryknoll: Orbis, 1989).

85. For a description of just such a setting, in Ukraine, see Catherine Wanner, "Conversion and the Mobile Self," in Pelkmans, *Conversion after Socialism* (above, n. 83), 175.

86. Christianity (as indeed Islam) has in fact related to culture in various ways, as H. Richard Niebuhr showed in *Christ and Culture* (New York: Harper and Row, 1951). The Pentecostal message here is close to his fifth option (chapter 6, "Christ the Transformer of Culture"), whose genealogy he traces back to St. John's Gospel, through St. Augustine and F. D. Maurice.

87. For concrete examples, see the remarks of Chief Olanrewaju Adepoju, or the 1978 memorandum of D.O.S. Noibi and S.T. Malik (neither of them Salafists), cited above, chapter 8.

88. Olayiwola, *Islam in Nigeria* (above, n. 71), 21.

89. Ibid. 275.

90. See Tony Hodges, *Jehovah's Witnesses in Central Africa* (London: Minority Rights Groups, 1976).

11. THE THREE CIRCLES OF YORUBA RELIGION

1. I use "Yoruba" in the conventional sense, as used by the vast majority of self-described Yoruba, namely people who have the Yoruba language as their mother tongue or who, even if they have lost it or live outside the Yoruba homeland, still have close links with those who do, like the children of Yoruba parents who have moved abroad. But I do not count as Yoruba people of some other background who have assumed Yoruba names or who refer to themselves as Yoruba in the context of their practicing *orișa* religion.

2. Pierre Fatumbi Verger, *Notes sur le culte des orisha et vodoun á Bahia, la Baie de Tous les Saints au Brésil et a l'ancienne Côte des Esclaves* (Dakar: IFAN, 1957) and *Orixás: Deuses Iorubás na Africa e no Novo Mundo* (São Paulo: Corupio, 1981).

3. Sandra T. Barnes, ed., *Africa's Ogun: Old World and New,* 2nd ed. (Bloomington: Indiana University Press, 1997); Joseph M. Murphy and Mei-Mei Sanford, eds., *Ọṣun across the Waters: A Yoruba Goddess in Africa and the Americas* (Bloomington: Indiana University Press, 2001); Joel E. Tishken, Toyin Falola, and Akintunde Akinyemi, eds., *Sàngó in Africa and the African Diaspora* (Bloomington: Indiana University Press, 2009).

4. J. Lorand Matory, *Black Atlantic Religion: Tradition, Transnationalism and Matriarchy in the Afro-Brazilian Candomblé* (Princeton: Princeton University Press, 2005).

5. For phenomena in the New World, particularly Cuba, I am especially indebted to what I have learned from my onetime Ph.D. student Amanda Villepastour (formerly Vincent). I hope that her fine thesis, "Bata Conversations: Guardianship and Entitlement Narratives about the Bata in Nigeria and Cuba" (University of London, School of Oriental and African Studies, 2007), will be published before too long.

6. J. D. Y. Peel, *Religious Encounter and the Making of the Yoruba* (Bloomington: Indiana University Press, 2000), 109–11. For some studies of the cult complexes of particular towns, see J. K. Olupona, *Kingship, Religion and Rituals in a Nigerian Community* (Stockholm: Almqvist and Wiksell, 1991) on Ondo; Andrew Apter, *Black Critics and Kings: The Hermeneutics of Power in Yoruba Society* (Chicago: University of Chicago Press, 1992) on Ayede-Ekiti; and John Pemberton and F. S. Afolayan, *Yoruba Sacred Kingship: A Power Like That of the Gods* (Washington, D.C.: Smithsonian Institution Press, 1997) on Ila-Orangun.

7. Compare the account of Oduduwa as "the chief goddess of the Yorubas" and the wife of Obatala, that is found in A. B. Ellis, *The Yoruba-Speaking Peoples of the Slave Coast of West Africa* (Chicago: Benin Press, 1964 [1894]), 41–43, or in J. Olumide Lucas, *The Religion of the Yorubas* (Lagos: CMS Bookshop, 1948), with the more conventional accounts in S. Johnson, *The History of the* Yorubas (Lagos: CMS Bookshop, 1921), 3–14, E. B. Idowu, *Olodumare: God in Yoruba Belief* (London: Longman, 1962), 22–25, or J. K. Olupona, *City of 201 Gods: Ile-Ife in Time, Space and the Imagination* (Berkeley and Los Angeles: University of California Press, 2011), chapter 8, "Oduduwa, the God-King."

8. The term *ẹsin ibilẹ* now has a limited currency to mean "traditional religion" too. Its adherents have variously been termed in Yoruba *oloriṣa* (those who have *oriṣa*), *aboriṣa* (those who worship *oriṣa*), *ibọgibọpẹ* (those who worship wooden idols and the palm tree), and *keferi* ("pagans," a Muslim designation adopted by Christians).

9. On possession, see J. L. Matory, *Sex and the Empire That Is No More* (Minneapolis: University of Minnesota Press, 1994), passim, s.v. "mounting."

10. See M. O. A. Abdul, "Yoruba Divination and Islam," *Orita* 4 (1970), 167–79; T. G. Gbadamosi, "'Odu Imale': Islam in Ifa Divination and the Case of Pre-Destined Muslims," *Journal of the Historical Society of Nigeria* 8 (1977), 77–93; and Razaq D. Abubakre, *The Interplay of Arabic and Yoruba Cultures in South-Western Nigeria* (Iwo: Daru 'l-Ilm Publishers, 2004), 210–15.

11. The best evocation of this time of exceptional interreligious amity is to be found in the novel by Wole Soyinka, *Ìsarà: A Voyage around 'Essay'* (London: Methuen, 1990), which is a quasi-fictional recreation of the world of his father in Ijebu Remo in the early 1940s.

12. *Orita* is also the name of the journal produced by the Department of Religious Studies at the University of Ibadan.

13. For example, a booklet of 159 pages by John Adejoro-Oluwa, *If the Foundations Be Destroyed* (Ikeja: Plummet Publishing, 2005), has its chapter 2 devoted to an attack on Yemoja—a "water spirit or mermaid . . . the ubiquitous principality [of darkness] . . . among the Yorubas in Nigeria and Brazil," whom he further identifies with the Igbo women's deity Idemili, with Ashtoreth, the Phoenician goddess worshipped by Jezebel, with the scarlet woman of Babylon of the Book of Revelation, and (following a well-worn theme of Protestant polemic) with the queen of heaven of Catholic Mariolatry.

14. Olupona, *City of 201 Gods* (above, n. 7), chapter 9.

15. Ibid. 293.

16. See Toyin Falola and M. D. Childs, eds., *The Yoruba Diaspora in the Atlantic World* (Bloomington: Indiana University Press, 2004), and there especially the chapters by Eltis, Lovejoy, and O'Hear.

17. For intellectual critiques of great sophistication, see Stephan Palmié, "Introduction: On Predications of Africanity," in *Africas of the Americas: Beyond the Search for Origins in the Study of Afro-Atlantic Religions* (Leiden: Brill, 2008); *Wizards and Scientists: Explorations in Afro-Cuban Modernity and Tradition* (Durham: Duke University Press, 2002), esp. chapter 3; and most systematically in *The Cooking of History: How Not to Study Afro-Cuban Religion* (Chicago: University of Chicago Press, 2013). For a broad overview of the field, with particular reference to the work and influence of Melville J. Herskovits, see Kevin A. Yelvington, "The Anthropology of Afro-Latin America and the Caribbean," *Annual Review of Anthropology* 30 (2001), 227–60.

18. David H. Brown, *Santería Enthroned: Art, Ritual, and Innovation in an Afro-Cuban Religion* (Chicago: University of Chicago Press, 2003), 19.

19. See Stephen D. Glazier, "Wither [*sic*] Sango? An Inquiry into Sango's 'Authenticity' and Prominence in the Caribbean," and Luis Nicolau Parés, "Xango in Afro-Brazilian Religion: 'Aristocracy' and 'Syncretic' Interactions," chapters 11 and 12, respectively, in Tishken, Falola, and Akinyemi, *Sango in Africa and the African Diaspora* (above, n. 3).

20. See table of Yoruba slave destinations between 1651 and 1867, as analyzed by Eltis in Falola and Childs, *Yoruba Diaspora* (above, n. 16), 30–31.

21. Two cases are Philip Jose Meffre, mentioned above, Ilesha-born possibly in the 1820s, who was in Brazil for some years before 1862, when he returned to West Africa; and Martiniano Eliseu do Bonfim, born at Bahia in 1859, taken by his father to be educated in Lagos 1875–86, and initiated there as a *babalawo* (Matory, *Black Atlantic Religion* [above, n. 4], 46 and passim). It seems to me almost certain that Bonfim would have become aware of Meffre in Lagos (though by then Meffre no longer practiced as a *babalawo*). A very small error needs to be rectified in Matory's account (reproduced in Palmié, *Cooking of History* [above, n. 17], 51): the school at Faji in Lagos that Bonfim attended was Anglican (CMS), not Presbyterian. Meffre was a member of Breadfruit CMS Church.

22. On the complexities of the cultural passage of Ifa from Nigeria to Cuba, see the fascinating case study by Michael Marcuzzi, "The Ipanodu Ceremony and the History of Orisa Worship in Nigeria and Cuba," in Toyin Falola and Ann Genova, eds., *Orișa: Yoruba Gods and Spiritual Identity in Africa and the Diaspora* (Trenton: Africa World Press, 2005), 183–208.

23. As Luis Nicolau Parés shows clearly (as cited above, n. 19).

24. Brown, *Santería Enthroned* (above, n. 18), 148–57.

25. Peel, *Religious Encounter* (above, n. 6), 114–15.

26. Nicely brought out in Karin Barber, "How Man Makes God," *Africa* 51 (1981), 724–45.

27. For examples of individual accumulations of *orișa* in nineteenth-century Yorubaland, see Peel, *Religious Encounter* (above, n. 6), 107.

28. For this and other examples of *babalawo* rationalization, see ibid. 117.

29. See Brown, *Santería Enthroned* (above, n. 18), 115. Compare for Brazil, Stefania Capone, *La quête de l'Afrique dans le Candomblé* (Paris: Karthala, 1999), 64, showing the ground plan of a *terreiro* that had Ogun, Exu, Oxossi, Xango, Nana, Oxala, Yemanja, Logunede and Oxum (sharing a room as two strongly Ijesha deities?), Oloque, Omolu and Oxumare, and Yansan.

30. On Oyotunji, see Tracey M. Hucks, *Yoruba Traditions and African American Religious Nationalism* (Albuquerque: University of New Mexico Press, 1912), and Kamari M. Clarke, *Mapping Yoruba Networks: Power and Agency in the Making of Transnational Communities* (Durham: Duke University Press, 2004); also Stefania Capone, *Les Yoruba du Nouveau Monde: Religion, ethnicité et nationalisme aux États-Unis* (Paris: Karthala, 2005). Despite their titles, these excellent books are essentially not about Yoruba people—in the sense in which I have defined them (see n. 1 above)—but about non-Yoruba people doing things with Yoruba-based culture.

31. Palmié, *Cooking of History* (above, n. 17), chapter 4.

32. See especially Capone, *Quête de l'Afrique* (above, n. 29), chapters 7 and 8.

33. On this phenomenon, see Debra L. Klein, *Yorùbá Bàtá Goes Global: Artists, Culture Brokers and Fans* (Chicago: University of Chicago Press, 2007).

34. See 'Wande Abimbola (with Ivor Miller), *Ifá Will Mend Our Broken World: Thoughts on Yoruba Religion and Culture in Africa and the Diaspora* (Roxbury: Aim Books, 1997).

35. As Abimbola astutely noted back in 1979, in a conference paper on Yoruba religion in Brazil, cited in Stephan Palmié, "The Cultural Work of Yoruba Globalization," in Toyin Falola, ed., *Christianity and Social Change in Africa: Essays in Honor of J. D. Y. Peel* (Durham: Carolina Academic Press, 2005), 70–74.

36. A classic formulation was in Bengt Sundler's *Bantu Prophets in South Africa*, 2nd ed. (London: Oxford University Press, 1961), chapter 7, "New Wine in Old Wineskins." See too Charles Stewart and Rosalind Shaw, eds., *Syncretism/Anti-Syncretism* (London: Routledge, 1994), and Stephan Palmié, "Against Syncretism: 'Africanizing' and 'Cubanizing' Discourses in North American Orisa Worship," in R. Fardon, ed., *Counterworks: Managing the Diversity of Knowledge* (London: Routledge, 1995), 73–104.

37. Hucks, *Yoruba Traditions and African American Religious Nationalism* (above, n. 30), chapters 7 and 8. *Ẹgbẹ* means "society" or "club" in Yoruba, and Sankofa is an Akan *adinkra*-cloth symbol (= go back and get it) interpreted to mean the recovery of the African past.

38. See above, chapter 8, esp. nn. 16 and 17.

39. A case in point is the use of Ifa as a historical source, purportedly giving a contemporary account of the lives of *orișa* in primordial Ife, by Akintunde Akinyemi in Tishken, Falola, and Akinyemi, *Sango in Africa and the African Diaspora* (above, n. 3), chapters 2 and 9. Another instructive instance is Wande Abimbola's awkward struggle to reconcile the idea of Ifa as a source for Yoruba history, containing evidence about such things as the

introduction of guns or early Yoruba Islam, with a "theological" view of it as unchanged since primordial times: "The Literature of the Ifa Cult," in S. O. Biobaku, ed., *Sources of Yoruba History* (Oxford: Clarendon Press, 1973), chapter 4.

40. B. Maupoil, *La géomancie à l'ancienne Côte des Esclaves* (Paris: Institut d'Ethnologie, 1943).

41. K. Noel Amherd, *Reciting Ifá: Difference, Heterogeneity and Identity* (Trenton: Africa World Press, 2010). This is quite the most important study of Ifa in Nigeria since the classic works of William Bascom and 'Wande Abimbola, and it breaks new ground in relation to the practical details of consultation in specific time/place contexts.

42. J. K. Olupona and Terry Rey, eds., *Òrìṣà Devotion as World Religion: The Globalization of Yoruba Religion* (Madison: University of Wisconsin Press, 2008).

43. For this observation I am indebted to Amanda Villepastour.

44. Palmié, *Cooking of History* (above, n. 17), 164–65. He suggests that open recruitment patterns developed only in the New World, against a presumptively kin-based recruitment in old Yorubaland. But while is true that much cult recruitment *was* kin-based, it was not exclusively so. Ifa could redirect individuals to new cult attachments, and the expansion of cults into new areas (as with Sango in the nineteenth century) clearly implies open recruitment.

45. Ibid. 169.

46. Samuel Johnson, *Rasselas, Prince of Abissinia* (London, 1759), chapter 49.

47. Samuel Johnson, preface to *A Voyage to Abysssinia, by Father Jerome Lobo: A Portuguese Missionary . . .* (London: Elliot and Kay, 1789 [1735]), 12.

48. Here see further Michael Bundock, *The Fortunes of Francis Barber: The True Story of the Jamaican Slave Who Became Samuel Johnson's Heir* (New Haven: Yale University Press, 2015).

INDEX

Note: n following a page number denotes an endnote with the relevant number.

CPSIA information can be obtained
at www.ICGtesting.com
Printed in the USA
LVOW11s1114130817
544850LV00002B/278/P